CAMBRIDGE COMMONWEALTH SERIES

General Editor: Professor E. T. Stokes

CANADA AND
THE TRANSITION TO COMMONWEALTH

CAMBRIDGE COMMONWEALTH SERIES

Toward 'Uhuru' in Tanzania: Andrew Maguire

Developing the Third World: The Experience of the Nineteen-Sixties: Ronald Robinson (ed.)

Mackinnon and East Africa 1878–1895: A Study in the 'New Imperialism': John S. Galbraith

The Durham Report and British Policy: A Critical Essay: Ged Martin

The Making of Modern Belize: Politics, Society and British Colonialism in Central America: C. H. Grant

Politics and Christianity in Malawi 1875–1940: John McCracken

These monographs are published by the Syndics of the Cambridge University Press in association with the Managers of the Cambridge University Smuts Memorial Fund for the advancement of Commonwealth Studies.

Canada and the transition to Commonwealth

BRITISH-CANADIAN RELATIONS
1917–1926

PHILIP G. WIGLEY

Department of History
University of Edinburgh

CAMBRIDGE UNIVERSITY PRESS

CAMBRIDGE

LONDON · NEW YORK · MELBOURNE

Published by the Syndics of the Cambridge University Press
The Pitt Building, Trumpington Street, Cambridge CB2 1RP
Bentley House, 200 Euston Road, London NW1 2DB
32 East 57th Street, New York, NY 10022, USA
296 Beaconsfield Parade, Middle Park, Melbourne 3206, Australia

© Cambridge University Press 1977

First published 1977

Printed in Great Britain by
Western Printing Services, Bristol

Library of Congress Cataloguing in Publication Data
Wigley, Philip G.
Canada and the transition to Commonwealth.
(Cambridge Commonwealth series)
Bibliography: p.
Includes index.
1. Great Britain – Foreign relations – Canada.
2. Canada – Foreign relations – Great Britain. 3. Great Britain – Foreign
relations – 1910-1936. 4. Commonwealth of Nations – Foreign
relations. I. Title.
DA47.9.C2W53   327.41′071   76-48989
ISBN 0 521 21157 3

For Alison

CONTENTS

ABBREVIATIONS

State papers

The various classes of British state papers referred to in the footnotes are listed in the Bibliography, section I. Canadian state papers cited are of the Department of External Affairs.

Parliamentary debates

GB, HoC   Debates of the British House of Commons, with date
Canada, HoC   Debates of the Canadian House of Commons, with date

Parliamentary papers

These are referred to in the footnotes by their Command number only. Full reference will be found in the Bibliography, section IV.

Journals and documents often cited

CHR   Canadian Historical Review
DCER   Documents on Canadian External Relations
JCPS   Journal of Commonwealth Political Studies
JICH   Journal of Commonwealth and Imperial History

PREFACE

In 1976 we are witnessing the elaborate celebrations marking the bi-centenary of the Declaration of Independence, the point at which two hundred years ago thirteen of Britain's American colonies began their revolution and broke away from the first British empire. Less acknowledged will be the fiftieth anniversary of another such declaration, one whose language was avowedly not revolutionary but which in its own way effectively proclaimed the independence of Britain's self-governing colonies from what was briefly known as the third British empire. The Balfour Declaration of 1926 was an agreed manifesto, setting out the equality of Britain and the dominions and their individual autonomy within the commonwealth association. It attempted in this way to measure and define their post-war relationship to each other, to incorporate into appropriate constitutional terms the far-reaching developments that had been taking place, piecemeal and *de facto*, over the previous decade. No revolutionary wars were needed to make good the claims advanced here for the dominions, because by 1926 (with the possible exception of the Irish Free State) they were generally satisfied that their status was both adequate and secure. The Balfour Declaration thus represented as much a retrospective analysis as a prescription for future change, and it is with these ten years or so which lead up to this moment of definition that this study will be concerned.

The work has grown out of a dissertation submitted to Cambridge University, and in its preparation I have incurred many debts of gratitude to individuals and to institutions. Professor Nicholas Mansergh of St John's College, Cambridge, gave me persistent encouragement over a number of years, and to him above all I owe thanks. Norman Hillmer of the Directorate of History in Ottawa has read many sections of the work and been most generous with his time and advice. Ian Nish at the London School of Economics was good enough, when extremely busy with other business, to offer very helpful comments on chapter 4. Brian Tennyson of St Francis Xavier University, engaged in similar research, kindly aided me with some details of the 1926 Imperial Conference. For their unfailing assistance I am much indebted to the staffs of the Public Record Office in London and the Public Archives of Canada in Ottawa.

For permission to study and to quote from private collections of papers I owe thanks to a number of people. Professor Craig Brown kindly gave me access to the diaries of Sir Robert Borden. Professor A. J. P. Taylor offered anecdotes and advice in introducing me to the Lloyd George papers, Mr John Grigg provided lunch and tea when opening to me the papers of his father. Mr Donald Simpson supplied a most helpful introduction to the letters of E. J. Harding. I must thank the Trustees of the British Museum for permission to quote from a letter in the Balfour papers, and the authorities of the Bodleian Library, Oxford, for permission to use the papers of Lord Milner.

The editors of the Commonwealth series at Cambridge University Press deserve a word of thanks for their patience, as do Susan Haggis and Ann Watt for helping to prepare the final typescript. My wife's relief at the completion of this work must not preclude a particular and final word of thanks to her.

Part of the material in chapter 6 was first published as an article, 'Whitehall and the 1923 Imperial Conference', in *Journal of Imperial and Commonwealth History*, i, no 2 (1972–3).

Introduction

During the years from 1917 to 1926, Great Britain's relations with the overseas British dominions were profoundly and extensively modified, to a degree that made this decade a transitional period of the greatest importance in the history of the British empire–commonwealth. It marks the time when the dominions moved from a status of colonial autonomy under Britain's imperial aegis to a position where they could claim the right to practical independence in their international as well as domestic affairs, within the framework of the British commonwealth. The major question, or cluster of questions, in terms of which this evolution was measured and defined, concerned the conduct of the empire's foreign relations – in particular, the dominions' role and responsibilities in what had hitherto been accepted as a united, undifferentiated imperial foreign policy. It is this general area that I am principally concerned with in this study, with an emphasis not only on matters of foreign policy as such, but also on the equally significant problems of communications and consultation between Britain and the dominion governments.

The primary relationship I wish to examine, as illuminating these various aspects of the general inquiry, is that between Britain and Canada. Canada, the senior partner in the imperial structure (until the 1907 Colonial Conference it alone carried the title 'dominion') was also the most advanced in terms of population and economic development. Its perspective on imperial relations was arguably the most complex, in part as a result of its geographic and strategic proximity to the United States, and also because of the racial and sectional divisions in the country. In addition, and of obvious importance to this work, Canada in this period was by far the most assertive of the dominions as regards imperial questions, at least until 1925. Thus we shall find that for most of the decade under consideration, Canadian attitudes and preoccupations stimulated, and to a large extent directed, the broad trend of developments in the dominions' fundamental relations with Great Britain. Even when the initiative for reform was taken up by others, the senior dominion would continue to exercise a dominant influence on events.

The association of the overseas dominions with imperial foreign policy was of direct and crucial importance to the basic legal ties that held the empire together. For at the core of the imperial nexus was the concept of a common imperial citizenship, and the diplomatic unity of the empire was in this sense a logical constitutional necessity: all the king's subjects must make peace and war together. 'If & when the doctrine of "Civis Romanus sum" is finally interred', one Colonial Office official worried in 1920, 'there will be very little left of the Br[itish] Empire.' In subsequent years, to be sure, the connection between the empire's constitutional law and its foreign policy has been fully appreciated by historians, to the point where too often studies of British–dominion relations have been construed in purely constitutional terms, with undue attention paid to legal problems and developments in dominion status. The substantive issues of policy, around which such changes took place, have elicited relatively little interest. From the constitutional point of view, nevertheless, the years from 1917 to 1926 are obviously critical ones, being the span of time between resolution ix of the 1917 Imperial War Conference and the definition of dominion status contained within the Balfour Declaration. And in covering this ground again, I have no intention of playing down the importance of constitutional change, or of suggesting that things might have been very different. An emphasis on the constitutional aspects of imperial relations, however – though to be fair the lack of confidential government records has been of great importance in this respect – has tended to burden the interpretation of the period with several unwarranted assumptions. Principally, with reference to the general subject of foreign affairs, the transition in imperial relations from empire to commonwealth has been considered to be a fairly straightforward, uncomplicated process, with developments 'broadening down from precedent to precedent' towards dominion independence. Indeed, such was the regularity and seeming consistency with which advances were made that there has been a temptation to invest the march of events with an inevitable or ineluctable quality; and by extension to think of the years from 1917 to 1922 – when considerable dominion interest was expressed in an integrated, co-operative imperial foreign policy – as merely a passing deviation from the larger movement towards complete local autonomy in external affairs. Another trait in historical writing has been to suppose that the attitudes and responses of the British government were monolithic, coherent, passive and uniformly conservative. Britain, by this token, simply responded to pressures for change coming from the dominions – from Canada in particular – with greater or lesser goodwill, trying all the while to retain what it could of a united imperial diplomacy.

It is now possible to show that these assumptions are far from correct, and, beyond that, to place the study of constitutional questions within a more comprehensive analysis of the period. Britain's relations with the dominions after 1917 developed in a complex way, in which the pattern of change was not at all easily discerned. Thus for instance, the supposed shift in the direction of this development, whereby a 'centralist' phase ended in 1922 and a 'decentralist' phase ran thereafter to 1926 and beyond, becomes in retrospect a far from straightforward change of course. On Canada's part, the emergence of national aspirations during and after the First World War had quickly imposed definite guidelines as regards the dominion's status and function within the imperial structure, and these applied to an important extent over and above the political circumstances of the day. Mackenzie King's conviction, that by late 1923 he had successfully disengaged Canada from stringent and embarrassing imperial obligations, must be judged against the awkward fact that at no point had his predecessors committed the country to imperial policies beyond the immediate sanction of the dominion government. And if we consider this discrepancy from the British angle, further reservations about King's interpretation of events become apparent. For one thing, problems of communication had already jeopardized the efforts to involve the overseas governments in a reciprocal system of consultation and commitments regarding questions of foreign policy. More importantly, the British government's own approach to policymaking in collaboration with the dominions after 1917 was itself the subject of severe and protracted internal confrontations between the Colonial and Foreign Offices. At several critical points, in fact, it was the refusal of the latter department to be shackled in its operations by what it deemed dominion interference that constituted the principal threat to the empire's diplomatic unity. By these criteria, British–dominion relations were moving along a 'decentralist' path well before the dominions themselves were aware of it.

The event that was to bring the various different parties concerned with British–dominion affairs – the Colonial Office, the Foreign Office, the Canadian and other overseas government leaders – most forcefully up against each other was the 1923 Imperial Conference, a moment that marks something of a structural climax within the period under consideration. Foreign policy, defence, the making of international treaties, economic affairs (hived off to a subsidiary conference) – in each of these areas debate turned on whether Britain and the dominions were to move forward as a more cohesive and unified partnership or proceed in greater independence of each other, associated as commonwealth partners but with few tangible common commitments. The failure in each case to establish any collective policies represented an acknowledged major step forward for the supporters of devolutionary change, change whose powerful momentum was simply confirmed by subsequent events down to the Locarno treaties of late 1925. That the 1923 Conference proved in this way to be a critical point of departure for British–dominion relations – more significant in the development of practical dominion autonomy than the Imperial Conference of 1926 – has been recognized for some years, and Canadian historians in particular have given credit to King as the principal champion in the proceedings of the devolutionary cause. Still to be understood, however, is the precise cross-play of interests at the conference, in particular the fact that the British authorities were not themselves attempting to hew to a strictly 'centralist' line. The Colonial Office, as ever, were acutely concerned to maintain the forms of imperial unity, as far as possible. But their voice was effectively silenced in a British delegation dominated by foreign secretary Lord Curzon, whose own department (as indicated above) had little patience for collective policy-making with the overseas dominions. In these circumstances it was left to Australia's premier Bruce to make the case for a united imperial approach to external and economic affairs alike. His absence of achievement, in foreign affairs especially – and by the same token King's success – must be judged in the light of the guarded British response in these matters.

By 1923, of course, it is no longer accurate nor sufficient for the purposes of this work to confine the inquiry to Britain and the 'overseas dominions'. Added to the ranks by this time was the Irish Free State, a newly-established dominion whose relationships to Britain and the British empire – geographic, historical, spiritual – were quite outside the normal pattern. Not an overseas dominion but a unique *offshore* dominion, its status not conferred by convention but wrested from Britain as a prize of war. A prize? For many in Ireland dominion status was clearly no more than a dubious consolation prize for capitulation in the Anglo-Irish struggle, an artificial device commanding only resentment or opposition. On the other hand, the Free State leaders who attended the 1923 Conference were undoubtedly disabused of their own worst illusions, watching the frank and sometimes acrimonious exchanges between Britain and their newly-acquired overseas partners. Dominion status might after all provide them with a vehicle for establishing national Irish self-determination, and it was on that premise that the Cosgrave–FitzGerald administration began to develop their own strategy for the radical devolutionary reform of British–dominion relations. To say the least, however, their attitude to the empire–commonwealth continued highly ambivalent, since it had yet to

be seen whether their commonwealth associates would accept a programme of change that for the Irish government was virtually a political
necessity. More particularly, it remained to be seen how far those overseas
governments also looking for greater dominion autonomy – Canada, and
increasingly after 1924 South Africa – would support Irish initiatives as
being relevant to broader commonwealth ends. Such was the background,
in part at least, to the Imperial Conference of 1926 and the Balfour
Declaration, with which a decade of transition was to be drawn to a close.

I

The threshold of responsibility, 1900–1916

In studying the course of British–dominion relations from 1917 it will be helpful as a preliminary exercise to look back for a moment before this period, to take note of some of the events and circumstances giving rise to the decade of developments which is our immediate concern. The most direct link in the causal chain is of course the pressures, the frustrations, the changes generated by two-and-a-half years of war. But we should go back briefly beyond the war's beginning, for even in the pre-war period Canada and the other dominions were starting to experience their coming of age: their first awareness of possible responsibilities, as dominions, to Britain and the imperial connection. This process owed little at first to any nascent feelings of national maturity within the overseas colonial communities. It was touched off, rather, by a palpable shift in the international – and by extension the imperial – balance of power, as a result of which Great Britain's place in the world rather suddenly became less secure. The Boer War and its aftermath provided an initial indication of the new order of things. Here for the first time Britain's splendid imperial isolation seemed to be a posture of weakness as much as strength. On the imperial side, it was true, there were still definite grounds for satisfaction. Prompt assistance from India had counted with telling effect for the British effort, manifesting India's role as the keystone of an imperial arch that as yet convincingly spanned Britain's territorial possessions. In addition, in an impressive show of solidarity, colonial contingents had also reinforced Britain's forces in South Africa, and revealed to the British government that the colonies were a source of great potential strength to the mother country. These positive aspects of the war, however, had to be weighed against an unpromising international situation. Where isolation had hitherto afforded Britain freedom from unwanted external obligations, it now meant a lack of allies; moreover, while the British navy was still able to guarantee the empire's standing in the world, the army in its confrontation with the Boers had proved to be a sorry instrument of imperial power.

From the experience of that war came new priorities and new attitudes.

Cordial relations were strengthened with the United States, and with France were encouraged; an alliance with Japan was constructed in 1902; army reform and reconstruction was set in train. Not least, the overseas colonies were invited to collaborate in a new imperial design by assuming some of Britain's burdens. 'The weary Titan', Joseph Chamberlain confidentially confessed to their leaders in 1902, 'staggers under the too vast orb of its fate ... We think it is time that our children should assist us.' Two years later prime minister Arthur Balfour acknowledged to the British House of Commons that these children of empire were now grown up, referring generously to 'those self-governing Colonies of the Empire over which no office in this country has any control at all'. In the light of these persistent overtures from the British government Canada and the other proto-dominions began to reconsider their position in the empire, and to formulate answers to three essential questions – about the way they should render this solicited assistance to the mother country; about the extent to which they would thereby be associated with British defence and foreign policies; and hence, about the type of consultative machinery through which they and Britain could discuss in confidence the imperial problems of the day.

The responses to this closely-related set of problems varied considerably amongst the overseas governments, as might be expected from the broad differences in their geographic and strategic outlook on the empire and the world, and the fact that only intermittently could they be exposed to each other's points of view. On the matter of defence contributions British ministers could initially take heart from a generally sympathetic reaction. Following the 1902 Colonial Conference Natal volunteered the sum of £35,000, Cape Colony £50,000 and there was even a promise of £3,000 a year from Newfoundland for a naval reserve. Australia pledged £200,000 and New Zealand £40,000 (which it soon raised to £100,000) as annual donations towards the costs of a Royal Navy squadron to be based in their part of the world. Conspicuously absent from the lists, however, was Canada, where Sir Wilfred Laurier offered no more than vague talk about building a Canadian navy – whose size, specifications and disposition in peace and war posed such theoretical dilemmas for the Admiralty as to make the very idea bristle with difficulties. Such intimations about a local dominion naval force were directly in keeping with Laurier's reticent approach to imperial commitments, an approach fully justified by the delicate racial balance of his government's political support. Yet, soon enough, this tentative Canadian thinking proved to be of wider relevance in imperial defence planning. By 1907 Australia and New Zealand were both pressing Whitehall to revise the 1902 scheme of contributions, and in the face of Admiralty stalling Australia early in 1909 unilaterally announced its intention to rechannel defence spending into the establishment of a fleet unit of its own. By 1913, this basic policy having endured several changes of government, the elements of an Australian naval force were being assembled in that dominion's ports. In this same year New Zealand, disabused of its illusions that the Admiralty would strengthen the navy in the Pacific, also withheld its pledged defence contributions and drew up plans for a locally-based naval unit.

Canada's approach to the problem of imperial naval defence, of course, followed in the end a very different line of development. At first Laurier found it possible to take no definite decisions at all, covering his avoidance of the issue – and the sustained reproaches of Canadian imperialists – with a determined optimism. In 1907 he told the House of Commons:

The condition which prevails in Europe is an armed peace, almost as intolerable as war itself. This cannot last for ever; it seems to me the date is not far distant when these nations, the wisest, the most advanced, the most civilized in the world, will recognize the folly that has been carried on for centuries and will come back to a more humane system such as we have on this continent.[1]

The notion that for Canada war would be avoided, rather than prevented through any active assisting role; the notion that Europe must one day learn from North American patterns of coexistence – here were strong Canadian themes, which were to serve again in the early 1920s. Unexpectedly, however, in March 1909 they had to give way, before the powerful repercussions of the 'dreadnought crisis'. Britain, it appeared, was falling behind in the naval race with Germany, and this apprehension compelled the Laurier government to reassess their position. Spurred on by the opposition Conservatives they agreed to lay the foundations for a Canadian navy. To give positive form to this commitment, nonetheless, turned out to be a very demanding assignment for the prime minister, involving him as it did both in sharp confrontations with the British administration and mounting political difficulties at home. The domestic side of the problem requires little further consideration here. More germane are its imperial aspects, which set important precedents as regards the dominions and naval defence, and underlined the necessity of clarifying two other critical problems inherent in dominion relations with Britain: the possible extent of any overseas involvement in strategic policymaking, and the shape of the machinery through which dominion governments might in this way advise or consent.

By the time Laurier broached the question of a Canadian naval policy

[1] Canada, HoC, 27 March 1907.

with Whitehall, his own attitude on these latter points was already fairly well developed. On several different occasions, he had felt compelled to prevent British and other overseas ministers from imposing what in his view were inhibiting structures upon British–colonial relations. It seemed at first that the Canadian premier was open to charges of bad faith in thus opposing any plans for more integrated schemes of empire co-operation. In 1897 Laurier had himself told Joseph Chamberlain, 'If you want our aid, call us to your councils', yet five years later he plainly refused to endorse the colonial secretary's design for an imperial council. But Laurier had never seriously contemplated surrendering any local autonomy to such a body (in this he was supported by a broad majority of press and public opinion in Canada) and indeed, in calling his bluff, Chamberlain must have known that his own government were hardly prepared for an innovation of this nature. In 1907, when Australia, New Zealand and the Cape Colony raised this matter again at the Colonial Conference, it was Laurier once more who pointedly opposed any alteration in the existing *ad hoc* role played by the conference. Nor would he sanction a second proposal of Australia's prime minister Alfred Deakin, that an independent imperial secretariat be set up outside the administration of the Colonial Office. In both cases Deakin took his stand on the principle of greater dominion equality with Great Britain, arguing that the overseas governments should free themselves from the restraints of control by a single British department of state. For Laurier, however, such equality threatened to impose greater responsibilities, and he refused to be drawn in this direction away from the constitutional safety of an unequal, inferior status in the empire. So the changes agreed to in 1907 were minimal: the Colonial Conference became the Imperial Conference (the colonial secretary relinquished the chairmanship to the British prime minister), the self-governing colonies became dominions, and a secretariat was created under the auspices of a new Dominions Department within the Colonial Office. None of these adjustments held unwanted implications as regards dominion commitment to imperial policies; and the conference system would continue to allow overseas ministers to discuss such matters with Britain without prejudice.

Given his insistence on these explicit safeguards, Laurier's decision to launch Canada into a programme of naval construction in 1909 might appear inconsistent, for it seemed bound to some extent to elevate the dominion to a new threshold of strategic capability, and by extension to enhance its standing in the imperial circle. And there were other ways, as well, in which Laurier had acknowledged an underlying confidence that Canada was fast becoming a nation in its own right. For example, when

Richard Seddon of New Zealand talked in the 1902 imperial discussions of his 'colony', Laurier insisted on using 'country' for Canada. Did this square entirely with his equal insistence that the dominion in no way aspired to be the imperial partner of the mother country? In the last analysis, however, both Laurier's confidence and his reticence were for the prime minister fully commensurate with Canada's basic status of colonial autonomy, which left the dominion free to develop a national consciousness, even a local naval force, while at the same time free to avoid commitments in advance to imperial defence and foreign policies. It proved difficult, nonetheless, to defend this position against imperial objections. In the first place the Admiralty, who naturally expected to be consulted over the Canadian naval building programme, had to be told in 1909 that local priorities must prevail over imperial ones, and against their own judgement must be made to accept plans for a two-coast naval force (the Admiralty thought a Canadian force in Atlantic waters pointless) which would be under full dominion control in peacetime. The moment for Laurier to defend the other side of his position, and insist on Canada's continued freedom of action in relation to imperial strategic policies, came at the 1911 Imperial Conference.

The 1911 Conference, in fact, witnessed a general reconsideration of all the important features of British–dominion relations, for it was apparent soon enough that the Canadian prime minister's defence of the *status quo* at previous imperial gatherings had done little to weaken the enthusiasm for change shown by other overseas leaders. Most prominently, Sir Joseph Ward from New Zealand was now championing a full-blown scheme of imperial federation coupled with a new department of state for imperial affairs, to be hived off from the Colonial Office. Andrew Fisher of Australia, like his predecessor Deakin, called afresh for a dominion voice in the making of the empire's foreign policy. In addition, initiatives were being taken by the administrative staff of the Committee of Imperial Defence with the aim of involving the dominions in high-level defence discussions through that body. On each of these proposals (the latter was disclosed to the premiers at the conference) Laurier was concerned to register his own reservations – though in the event he was by no means made to stand in isolated defiance against united forces of change. Indeed in the opening phase of the conference it was the premier of New Zealand who played the lone hand, discovering that there was a solid weight of opposition to his resolutions on federation and administrative regrouping. Significant here was the presence of General Louis Botha, first prime minister of a united South Africa and an ardent dominion nationalist, with whom Laurier was on the best of terms. 'He and I agree about everything', Botha wrote home. 'We have destroyed root and branch the proposal for an Imperial Council ... and we have succeeded in keeping the Conference as a round table affair.'[2] As to foreign policy, the question of a voice for the dominions was effectively answered by the British authorities themselves. In an impressive display of confidence in his overseas colleagues, the foreign secretary Sir Edward Grey provided a comprehensive account of the empire's external affairs; but it was clear at the time that this was not consultation, and the British prime minister, Herbert Asquith, had in any case made it plain that the home government could never share responsibility for foreign policy with the dominions. Similar limitations characterized the proposed development of the Committee of Imperial Defence as a medium for defence talks. The C.I.D. was purely advisory, a creature of the prime minister of the day, and though dominion attendance was to be encouraged it would be only at the British leader's discretion. There was little advance here on existing practice, visiting overseas ministers having already been occasionally invited to attend when the C.I.D. happened to be dealing with a topic relevant to them.[3] They might henceforth appear more frequently in the committee, but the British government would continue to withhold direct consultation on defence policy and avoid the risk of unmediated dominion access to their central planning authorities in this field.

Not surprisingly Laurier found himself in ready agreement with these carefully restricted developments, designed (for all Asquith's claims to the contrary) to keep the dominions at least one remove from the *arcana imperii*. The more the British government fought shy of engaging the dominions in legitimate policy consultations, the more easily would Canada be kept free of commitment to such policies. But with his government's decided policy to build a Canadian navy, Laurier had nonetheless given an important hostage to fortune as regards his dominion's imperial obligations, and during the conference British ministers were determined to draw from him the assurances they felt were due on account of this naval programme. Grey, for his part, saw fit to warn that Britain would tolerate local navies in the empire only as long as they did not compromise a united imperial foreign policy, and he emphasized that the mother country could not be expected to guarantee a dominion's security if it ever attempted to

---

[2] P. N. S. Mansergh, *The Commonwealth Experience* (London, 1969), 155. Botha and Laurier had first met at the 1907 Imperial Conference.

[3] The C.I.D.'s secretariat, itself an innovation in British administrative procedure, kept records of the committee's proceedings and working papers. The right of occasional attendance did not, of course, give dominion ministers access to these past deliberations.

pursue an independent line in foreign affairs. This polite threat, however, was somewhat wide of the mark in 1911: no dominion showed the slightest anxiety to breach the empire's diplomatic unity, Canada least of all. Far more relevant was the line of inquiry taken by the Admiralty, who demanded to know in effect just when the naval forces at Canada's disposal might reasonably be expected to assist in holding the imperial ring. Here Laurier was on less comfortable ground, trying at once to proclaim a readiness to assist Britain in any emergency while refusing to be drawn into specific promises of support in advance. He had to insist by turns that Canada's essential goodwill to the empire was unimpaired, that its freedom of action must also remain unimpaired, that a major war involving the empire was still unlikely.[4] But most telling – and here Laurier drew together his views on both foreign policy and defence planning – was his cool declaration that Canada in any event was not going to take part in wars that were not its primary concern.

There are questions which seem to me to be eminently in the domain of the United Kingdom. We may give advice if our advice is sought; but if your advice is sought or if you tender it, I do not think the United Kingdom can undertake to carry out this advice unless you are prepared to back that advice with all your strength, and take part in the war and insist upon having the rules carried out according to the manner in which you think the war should be carried out. We have taken the position in Canada that we do not think we are bound to take part in every war, and that our fleet may not be called upon in all cases, and, therefore, for my part, I think it is better under such circumstances to leave the negotiations of these regulations as to the way in which the war is to be carried on to the chief partner of the family, the one who has to bear the burden in part on some occasions, and the whole burden on perhaps other occasions.[5]

The responsibility for imperial defence and diplomacy would have to rest where it lay.

Laurier's defence of Canadian autonomy at the 1911 Conference was maintained with a singleness of purpose that left some bitterness in British circles. Yet in the end the Canadian leader's uncompromising position

---

[4] CAB 2/2/2: CID mtgs 112–14, 29–30 May 1911. When the British authorities tried to convince him that war might be much closer than he supposed, Laurier could only take refuge in moral outrage. He told the C.I.D. on 30 May, 'All the nations of Europe today, in my humble opinion, have gone, if I may say so, mad.' S. Roskill, *Hankey, Man of Secrets*, 1: *1877–1918* (London, 1970), 107.

[5] Cd 5745: 117.

stood out relatively little, given that on all major issues the conference's decisions indicated no substantial agreement about any closer imperial association, and often marked a new degree of decentralization. On naval matters, for example, while Laurier himself drew the fire of the lords of the Admiralty, Fisher of Australia was quietly warning that his dominion also proposed to take its own decisions over naval support in time of war.[6] Moreover, the Admiralty lords themselves, in their calmer moments, went a long way to accepting not only the *de facto* freedom of dominion navies but their full legal independence as well, including their right to fly flags of their own choosing.[7] On the organizational side imperial federation was demonstrably lacking support. The Committee of Imperial Defence, it is true, offered fresh incentives for inter-imperial briefings, yet its purely advisory status within the British administration seemed bound to compromise the best intentions of its secretariat and leave the empire's foreign and defence policy planning in the hands of the home government. By these criteria the Canadian prime minister could be satisfied as well as relieved about the conference, for he had been able to get his essential demands recognized while at the same time helping to further an over-all trend in British–dominion relations whose basic aims and direction he strongly endorsed.

Having succeeded so well in his naval and imperial designs, it was ironic that within months of the 1911 Conference Laurier should suffer political defeat over an issue which itself had important imperial ramifications. At the beginning of the year his government had announced the completing of a reciprocity treaty with the United States, a policy that initially received wide support across the dominion but attracted an increasing volume of criticism as the months went by. In Britain, empire enthusiasts had naturally been dismayed over the Canadian venture, committed as they were to the idea of linking the dominions and the mother country through a network of exclusively imperial trading agreements. Too late, it seemed, the urgent necessity to educate overseas opinion towards such a goal was being demonstrated. But in the event Laurier proved unable to contain the domestic opposition to North American reciprocity (in French Canada in particular he was now doubly under attack as the proponent of both a navy and reciprocity) and when in September 1911 a Canadian general election was held the Liberals were defeated by the Conservative party under Robert Borden. By the British tariff reform imperialists, Laurier's defeat was welcomed as an unexpected

6 CAB 2/2/2: CID mtg 113, 30 May 1911.
7 D. C. Gordon, *The Dominion Partnership in Imperial Defense, 1870–1914* (Baltimore, 1965), 287–8.

incentive to renew their efforts.[8] For one leading member of the British military establishment, at least, it was 'the most hopeful sign from an imperial point of view that I have seen for a long time'.[9] And indeed for Canada's imperial relations the change of government in Ottawa was to bring to the centre of the stage a new protagonist, whose ideas and initiatives were designed to provide for Canada a much more committed role in the empire's affairs than that so cautiously pursued by Sir Wilfrid Laurier.

In one limited respect Borden and Laurier took a similar position in their dealings with imperial questions: as prime minister each regarded these matters as more or less his private *ex officio* prerogative, with the result that the personal opinions and decisions of the premier normally determined the official attitude of his cabinet and government. This dominant part played by the prime minister was reflected in the structure of Canada's administrative service in these years. Until 1909, Laurier like his predecessors had found it unnecessary to have a separate office to deal with imperial or other external matters; and even when the Department of External Affairs was established in that year it was given a minimum of personnel and was placed under the charge of the secretary of state, a minor post in the Canadian cabinet. The new organization brought some badly needed order to the handling of documents and dispatches, but, that apart, it made little impact on Laurier's handling of imperial affairs. Borden was prevailed upon by the under-secretary of the fledgling department to attach it to the prime minister's portfolio (where it remained until 1946).[10] In these early years nonetheless, even under the prime minister's aegis the department continued to occupy an insignificant place in the making of Canadian external policies.[11] From 1913 Borden, and Arthur Meighen after him, depended heavily on the counsel of the department's legal adviser Loring Christie, as we shall see; but Christie's was a personal relationship with his prime ministers (Borden created the post for him) and not until 1925 would similarly thorough advice on

---

[8] R. Blake, *The Unknown Prime Minister* (London, 1955), 106.

[9] General Sir Henry Wilson, quoted in R. Preston, *Canada and 'Imperial Defense'* (Toronto, 1967), 304.

[10] A full account of the initiatives that led to the creation of the department is in J. Eayrs 'The Origins of Canada's Department of External Affairs', in H. Keenleyside, *The Growth of Canadian Policies in External Affairs* (Durham, N.C., 1960).

[11] When the Royal Commission on the Dominions reached Ottawa on its travels in 1914, E. J. Harding (seconded from the Colonial Office to be secretary) reported that he found the department's office 'over a barber's shop'. Harding papers, letter, 30 Aug 1914.

external affairs come through the permanent under-secretary, as on the British administrative model.[12]

From the start of his period of office, Borden's approach to imperial affairs – to the problem of naval defence in particular, as well as the larger questions of Canada's place in the empire – was in essence very different from his predecessor's. Laurier had been compelled, personally as much as politically, to discriminate, to limit, to oppose – most obviously, to isolate naval matters from the wider issues in order to distinguish sharply between local Canadian initiatives in defence policy and unspecified commitments to an Admiralty-directed imperial naval programme. Borden in turn was strongly inclined to look at things as a whole, to assess Canadian defence policy as part of the general imperial situation and take imperial require- ments much more into account in determining Canada's own response. With Laurier he could subscribe to Canada's status of autonomy – there was no going back on that. But an autonomy that was realized, even in part, through what seemed opposition to the dominion's imperial connec- tions he could never endorse; and an autonomy strengthened at the expense of imperial responsibilities was pernicious. If the development of a naval force was an index of Canada's power, that power only had meaning within the wider imperial framework. Indeed well before the 1911 election, Borden was beginning to doubt that the Liberal government's naval plans were adequate for the needs of the empire's defence, and once in office he became convinced that an immediate financial contribution to Britain for dreadnoughts, prior to any local construction, was called for. Two considerations were uppermost in Borden's mind. He was much more alarmed than Laurier by Germany's aggressive posture, and ready to realign Canadian defence policy in response to it. (Where Laurier refused to the last to acknowledge the deteriorating European situation, Borden was perhaps too ready to be convinced of the crises which threatened the empire's position.) He was also prepared to demand a reciprocal concession from Britain: a direct Canadian contribution to imperial defence, as he saw it, entitled the dominion government to direct consultations about imperial foreign policy. In July 1912 Borden travelled to London to open negotiations on both these subjects with the British authorities.

In raising the question of policy consultations Borden was of course breaking no new ground, as the 1911 Imperial Conference had examined this topic and accepted the British prime minister's limited offer of im-

---

12 The recently opened records of the department show that the *departmental* files, as opposed to the personal files of the under-secretary, contain little of high priority in the years 1909–26.

proved access to the Committee of Imperial defence. This would not provide consultation as such, as everyone knew; nonetheless the C.I.D. remained for the dominions the only forum for high-level discussions with British ministers, and Borden in 1912 sought to widen the basis of overseas representation upon it. His willingness to alter the Laurier naval programme to meet Admiralty priorities was in this respect a powerful card in his hand, and once in London he lost no time in displaying it. Shortly after arriving he told the Royal Colonial Institute:

I would like you to remember that those who are or become responsible for that Empire defence must in the very nature of things have some share in that policy which shapes the issues of peace and war. I would like you to understand that Canada does not propose to be an 'adjunct' even of the British Empire.[13]

There was ready encouragement for Borden's emphatic stand from one quarter, at least, of informed British opinion: the Round Table group, those indefatigable disciples of closer imperial ties who were prepared to promote or support any statesman or policy that lent itself to these ends. In 1911 they had provided Sir Joseph Ward with much of the substance of his proposals for imperial federation. Now after Laurier's defeat Borden became the man of the hour, and on this visit there were several private gatherings at which the Canadian prime minister was sounded and supported in his views.[14] Of greater relevance to Borden's purposes, however, was the fact that Maurice Hankey, secretary to the C.I.D., continued to be active amongst senior British cabinet ministers in promoting the usefulness of his committee as a point of contact for the dominions. He secured the necessary agreement to let Borden have a full account of the 1911 C.I.D. sessions with the overseas prime ministers, as well as an updated briefing on foreign affairs – gestures that helped get the discussions with Borden off to a positive start.

For his own part, Borden was careful to keep the questions of defence

---

[13] Speech, 10 July 1912, quoted in A. G. Dewey, *The Dominions and Diplomacy*, 2 vols (London, 1929), I, 290. It is interesting to compare these remarks with an editorial of J. W. Dafoe in the *Manitoba Free Press* written in late 1909 in the effort to convince both ultra-imperialists and extreme French Canadian nationalists that Canada was an equal with Britain in the empire: 'They cannot get away from the idea that Great Britain is the Empire in a sense in which Canada is not; that Canada is, in a sense, external to the Empire and owes allegiance and subjection to Great Britain. This idea is a relic surviving from the Colonial era.' R. Cook, *The Politics of J. W. Dafoe and the Free Press* (Toronto, 1963), 40.

[14] Borden diary, 20 July 1912; J. W. Kendle, *The Colonial and Imperial Conferences, 1887–1911* (London, 1967), 198 ff.

and consultation very much together in the negotiations, and thereby concluded agreements, though only for the short term, in both. As an emergency measure, he accepted the Admiralty's plea for the provision of three dreadnoughts from Canadian funds, though this contribution he sharply distinguished from a permanent policy. In turn the British government consented to 'a more continuous representation from Dominion Ministers ... upon the Committee of Imperial Defence'.[15] Asquith, obdurate in 1911 over foreign policy consultations, now admitted to the House of Commons 'the duty of making such response as we can' to the dominions' 'obviously reasonable appeal that they should be entitled to be heard in the determination of ... policy and the direction of Imperial affairs'. Ten days later at the C.I.D. Borden rather baldly put this new British cordiality into perspective. He was pleased that the home government were extending dominion representation on that committee, but adamant that it could be no more than a temporary solution. Canada, at least, would in the near future expect a control of foreign affairs far greater than anything the C.I.D. could provide, and any consultative arrangement designed to be permanent would have to make allowance for this. The desire for such control, he admitted, was only just beginning to be felt in the dominion, and so for the present he was content:

but in the meantime the spirit to which I have alluded is one that I think will demand consideration not only by our own Government but by the Imperial authorities as well.[16]

Thus Borden staked his claim to Canada's full participation in policy-making, joining the vanguard of those who sought for the overseas dominions a more active and responsible imperial partnership with Great Britain.

By December 1912 the financial and administrative details of the Borden government's new defence policy had been worked out, and could be put before the Canadian parliament. As an emergency contribution to Britain Borden asked for thirty-five million dollars, and simultaneously announced the new agreement regarding dominion representation on the C.I.D. Longer-term arrangements about both consultation and defence policies would have to wait, he explained, though he gave a clear indication of how he viewed the relationship between them:

we must find a basis of permanent co-operation in naval defence, and ... any

---

[15] Col Sec–Gov Gen, 10 Dec 1912, recapitulating the terms of the agreement, printed in Cd 6560.
[16] CAB 2/2/3: CID mtg 119, 1 Aug 1912; an extract from the minutes is printed in *DCER*, I, 267–70.

such basis must afford to the overseas Dominions an adequate voice in the moulding and control of foreign policy.[17]

As it was, however, he felt able to say that even under existing arrangements, 'No important step in foreign policy would be undertaken without consultation with ... a representative of Canada' – an interpretation of his July talks in London that was liberal to the point of dishonesty, and one that created a flurry of annoyance in the British capital. From Whitehall came a hasty reminder that the C.I.D. 'is a purely advisory body and is not and cannot under any circumstances become a body deciding on policy'.[18] In Canada, however, where the naval issues rather than the problems of consultation stayed as the main focus of attention, this slap on the wrist went largely unnoticed in the bitterness of a parliamentary debate which dragged on for twenty-three weeks. As with Laurier's naval plans, French Canada was vehemently opposed to the idea of defence expenditure and it was against very heavy opposition that the government secured the passage of their legislation through the House of Commons, deciding finally to use a motion of closure to end the debate. In the Senate, however, the Liberals decided to use their majority against the bill, which was thus defeated at the end of May 1913.

The months that followed the defeat of Borden's naval bill were unedifying ones for the prime minister. His short-term policy of financial assistance lay hostage to his opponents' control of the Senate (death and retirement were not expected to tip the balance in the Conservatives' favour until at least 1915). Any permanent policy, meanwhile, remained contingent upon constitutional questions unlikely to be solved in the near future. Indeed, until the initial financial contribution for dreadnoughts could be made to Britain, Borden was undoubtedly anxious to defer all constitutional discussions – for without some such tangible participation in the empire's defence, he could hardly insist upon a substantial dominion role in the conduct of foreign affairs. While the delay to his provisional naval plans continued, therefore, any immediate consideration of long-term defence policy was effectively forestalled. Under these circumstances, the only line of imperial development left for Borden to pursue was fuller representation on the C.I.D., as provided by the 1912 agreement. But even here, the enthusiasm he had displayed in London had a year later been dissipated. Perhaps he now realized that his own claims for the dominions under the agreement had been exaggerated; perhaps he felt that, with no naval assistance forthcoming, Canadian ministers sent across

[17] Canada, HoC, 5 Dec 1912.
[18] Col Sec–Gov Gen, 10 Dec 1912, published 3 Jan 1913 in Cd 6560.

to London were unlikely to be granted access to any privileged consultations. More to the point, by mid-1913 it was only too clear that Borden's efforts over consultation during his London talks had evoked no corresponding interest amongst the other dominions. When the British authorities reminded all the overseas governments in December 1912 that ministerial representation really would be welcomed, none showed a readiness to accept the offer.[19] So the Canadian prime minister was revealed as the sole dominion advocate of developing the C.I.D. for consultative purposes – and no doubt found in this another good reason for not pursuing his own policy too strenuously.

Canadian ministers were present, at any rate, at only two C.I.D. meetings before the war, one held in August 1913 and the other in July 1914, and on neither occasion were matters of consequence to Canada discussed. In attendance at the latter meeting was George Perley, minister without portfolio (though a close colleague of the prime minister) whom Borden had sent to London to act temporarily as high commissioner and to resume discussions about naval defence – control of the Canadian Senate now seemed in the offing. In the event, Perley's mission to London was extended for the duration of the war. But any hope that he might thus serve as a resident Canadian delegate to the C.I.D. was curtailed at the outbreak of hostilities, for at that point the committee ceased to function as an organ of British planning, and was not destined to be reconstituted in any form relevant to the dominions for many months.

All things considered, by the beginning of the war British–dominion relations remained in a highly unresolved state. The overseas communities of the empire, and the politicians who led them, could not have escaped a general sense of their own increased importance in the imperial scheme of things: ten years and more of dialogue and discussion about dominion responsibilities to Britain and the empire could hardly fail to produce this impression. But the formal expressions of the changing imperial balance, wherein British prerogatives of authority and control might be adjusted to accommodate the dominions – these still lacked principles or direction. Naval defence policy, in this regard, once the first step had been taken and the dominions' assistance sought, had not been co-ordinated in a consistent manner, the British authorities proving very reluctant to accept pragmatically the terms the overseas governments had chosen to offer. Yet defence planning, it must be said, was not intrinsically bound to produce such difficulties. While the Admiralty had argued and compromised, the War Office in contrast had been able to secure

[19] Kendle, *Colonial and Imperial Conferences*, 213–14. The correspondence was printed in Cd 7347.

far-ranging agreements about empire-wide standards of training, exchanges of officer personnel, the establishment of an Imperial General
Staff and so forth. Free from the need to make large-scale strategic capital
investments in advance – the fundamental problem, both financial and
psychological, of any imperial naval planning – the army chiefs had found
it possible to put together the essential design by which an imperial army
would be fitted together when required. Little did dominion leaders
suspect, however, that by 1911 staff talks had also been opened up in the
direction of France, with the result that organizational lines were secretly
taking shape that would carry the empire's contingents straight to the
trenches of Flanders – all arranged by negotiations that were so well kept
from the scrutiny of the politicians that the overseas governments had no
sense whatever of having been left out of policy consultations they might
otherwise have claimed a right to attend. But policy consultations, of
course, were in any case still an unrealized goal for dominion leaders who
sought them. Under Borden the Canadian government added a strong
voice to those demanding access to imperial policymaking, yet it was
apparent by 1913 that the various voices engaged in this theme were not
in unison. Principally, while Borden believed in developing the consultative potential of the C.I.D., Andrew Fisher of Australia felt, less urgently,
that the Imperial Conference machinery held the greater potential. In
Whitehall a slowly deepening tension between the Colonial Office (as
custodians of the Conference's business between sessions) and Maurice
Hankey of the C.I.D. paralleled the division of overseas opinion on this
question, and foretold more acute inter-departmental confrontations after
1916, when consultation with the dominions was to become an issue of
the first priority. Meanwhile there was no immediate prospect of a British
initiative in this area; and Borden, so palpably unable to offer naval
assistance in cash or kind, had nothing to underwrite his own demands
for concessions.

The coming of the war might have been expected to encourage fresh
incentives about consultation, given the immediate and generous military
aid provided from the overseas dominions. In fact quite the reverse happened. In every case the initial dominion contributions to the war effort
were both given and received without conditions, as if to underline the
fact that there was nothing as sordid as a contractual obligation or a
constitutional *quid pro quo* involved. Only as the war expanded into its
full catastrophic dimensions did opinions begin to change, and doubts
about the dominions' relationship to the war begin to arise – at first only

amongst overseas leaders, but then finally, reluctantly, amongst British ministers also. We may follow the relevant details of this first phase of the war by reference to the Canadian experience. Nowhere was the spirit of willing colonial assistance more spontaneous than in the senior dominion; and nowhere the subsequent disillusion and frustration more keenly felt.

For the Canadian government the outbreak of war brought an immediate end to the spell of barren inactivity occasioned by their abortive naval policies. Overnight, an enervating political stalemate was transformed into an earnest political truce, the unconditional terms of which Laurier, for the opposition Liberals, announced to the House of Commons when they assembled in August 1914 for an emergency session:

This session has been called for the purpose of giving the authority of parliament and the sanction of law to such measures as have already been taken by the Government ... I hasten to say that to all these measures we are prepared to give immediate assent. If in what has been done or in what remains to be done there may be anything which in our judgement should not be done or should be differently done, we raise no question, we take no exception, we offer no criticisms, and we shall offer no criticisms so long as there is danger at the front ...

It will be seen by the world that Canada, a daughter of old England, intends to stand by her in this great conflict. When the call comes our answer goes at once, and it goes in the classical language of the British answer to the call of duty: 'Ready, aye, ready.'[20]

The Liberal leader's remarks epitomized the mood in which the dominion went to war. They reflected the unreserved determination with which volunteers were already flocking to the military recruiting posts; they were promised, furthermore, on the widely held belief that the war would not be a long one. Guided by this assumption, government policy needed no detailed elaboration: Canada would simply supply whatever military assistance was needed to bring the conflict to its conclusion.[21] And so in much the same way as Laurier offered his unconditional support to the government, Borden offered the dominion's support to Britain. The control, the command, the deployment of the Canadian expeditionary forces were placed without question in the hands of the War Office. (For what they were worth, two old cruisers that the Laurier government had purchased in 1910 for training purposes were put at the Admiralty's

[20] Canada, HoC, 19 Aug 1914.

[21] From London, acting high commissioner Perley wrote that the war 'cannot go on for very many months', though he reported that Kitchener's estimate was from eighteen months to two years. Perley–Borden, 15 Aug 1914; *DCER*, I, 22.

disposal.) The notion of relating Canada's commitment to the war to the larger question of a dominion voice in imperial affairs did not arise. Like the expenditure for dreadnoughts planned for 1912, wartime assistance was thought of as an emergency contribution to a short-term problem, with no immediate connection to the development of empire relations.

Such was the unqualified nature of Canada's entry into the war that her troops, in effect, were dispatched to England on terms practically identical to those governing her earlier participation in the Boer War. Certainly they were accepted in England as coming from a willing colonial assistant, for use in another such war. The outbreak of the war, in fact, had stimulated strongly regressive attitudes in the British government. The military command, in making arrangements for a single imperial army – and more spectacularly in planning a campaign dominated by the cavalry[22] – were indeed thinking of a Boer War. But the civilian administration also, particularly with regard to imperial relations, showed similar inclinations to fall back upon traditional patterns of conduct. Never mind that they had so recently tried to encourage the overseas governments to send representatives to the C.I.D., and indicated a willingness to begin, at least, to explore the difficulties of joint consultations. The war once begun, the C.I.D. was prorogued, and throughout Whitehall the accent became one of strict constitutional propriety, marked by an implacable deference to the dominions' colonial autonomy. The freedom with which the overseas governments offered Britain their support, it seemed, must not be compromised by any thought of inter-imperial discussions about the war. Collaboration of this sort might turn unsolicited aid into an obligation, and threaten thereby the free association on which the empire's internal relations were founded. For the best of reasons, therefore, consultation during the war was calmly ruled out by the British government. It was not even felt necessary to provide regular information for the dominions about the course of the fighting.

No doubt the dominions were initially grateful to know that their assistance was entirely their own affair. As the war progressed, however, and the scale of dominion support rose to a degree never envisaged, such persistent acknowledgement of their autonomy became irritating, and before long utterly perverse. In Ottawa the Canadian government were soon encountering severe financial and economic difficulties in their attempt to meet the demands of war production; they were also greatly angered when despite their protests the British government placed far more orders for equipment with the United States than with Canada.[23]

[22] See A. J. P. Taylor, *English History, 1914–45* (Oxford, 1965), 59.
[23] G. Smith, 'Canadian External Affairs during World War One', in

Of the war at the front they knew little more than that their troops were suffering appalling losses.[24] Yet as late as October 1915 the British government, far from providing information, would not even ask Borden officially to supply more troops. Such requests continued to be transmitted (through the acting high commissioner, not the Colonial Office) as an indirect suggestion. Thus Perley could only tell Borden that 'authorities here say they cannot urge on Dominions sending more men but that they are much needed and would be very welcome'.[25] It says much for the prime minister's loyalty that two days after receiving this message the authorized limit for Canadian military personnel was raised by 100,000 to a quarter of a million men.

The isolation in which Borden was obliged to conduct the dominion's war effort was by then almost intolerable, the prime minister having meanwhile discovered to his cost that even a personal visit to London could bring him no closer to information or policy. In May 1915 the formation of a Liberal–Conservative coalition government in Britain had seemed a hopeful sign, and Borden had thoroughly approved when Andrew Bonar Law, leader of the Conservative party and a Canadian besides, had accepted the post of colonial secretary under Asquith. It was shortly after this reconstruction that he decided to cross the Atlantic and deal with British ministers at first hand. He made speeches, saw the king, visited military hospitals, dined with any number of the British establishment – he even attended a cabinet meeting; but after six weeks he had uncovered no helpful official information relevant to the war effort, and only by a bald threat to Bonar Law that further Canadian assistance might be withheld did he at last secure an interview with Lloyd George, minister of munitions and a central figure in British war operations. Lloyd George impressed the Canadian prime minister with frank attacks against the military authorities and his own departmental staff (a technique of assimilating and deflecting dominion criticism he would employ again when prime minister) but though Borden was encouraged by such ministerial candour he was still unable during the visit to establish any regular flow of information from Whitehall to Ottawa, and returned home to carry on in remote frustration.

Keenleyside, *The Growth of Canadian Policies in External Affairs* (Durham, N.C., 1960), 38–40.

[24] An inquiry from Borden in March 1915 as to when British ministers thought the war might end produced the following speculations: Harcourt (Colonial Office) 18 months, Grey (Foreign Office) 8 months, Kitchener (War Office) 12 months. The betting at Lloyds showed even odds for a finish by the New Year! Perley papers: Perley–Borden, 17 March 1915.

[25] Perley–Borden, 28 Oct 1915; *DCER*, I, 92.

It was news from Perley in October 1915, to the effect that a 'small war council having special powers' was to be set up by the British government, that gave Borden good reason to make a fresh appeal to London.[26] 'The overseas Dominions', he insisted to the colonial secretary, 'have large responsibilities to their own people for the conduct of the war, and ... the Canadian Government deem themselves entitled to fuller information and to consultation respecting the general policy of war operations.' He made it plain that he wished this to be provided by the new war council. In the face of this forthright claim, Bonar Law could hardly invoke the sanctity of colonial autonomy as an excuse for not discussing the war with the dominion governments. However, he could easily retreat to a second line of defence. He would not deny, he told Perley candidly, that Canada had every right to information and consultation about the war. The problem unfortunately, was that he could think of no feasible way that either could be provided for the Canadian prime minister. (The suggestion of dominion access to the war committee was simply ignored.) And he added rather sharply that unless Borden's government had practicable suggestions of their own to make, it was 'very undesirable that the question should be raised'.[27]

Borden was bitterly annoyed with Bonar Law's curt dismissal of his appeal, which so politely recognized his rights in principle and so bluntly rejected them in practice. Confined to bed with painful lumbago over the week of the new year, the prime minister must have brooded sourly over the British government's cavalier response to Canada's war efforts, and he sent off a vehement letter to his acting high commissioner:

During the past four months since my return from Great Britain, the Canadian Government (except for an occasional telegram from you or Sir Max Aitken) have had just what information could be gleaned from the daily press and no more. As to consultation, plans of campaign have been made and unmade, measures adopted and apparently abandoned and generally speaking steps of the most important and even vital character have been taken, postponed or rejected without the slightest consultation with the authorities of this Dominion.

It can hardly be expected that we shall put 400,000 or 500,000 men in the field and willingly accept the position of having no more voice and receiving no more consideration than if we were toy automata. Any person cherishing such an expectation harbours an unfortunate and even dangerous delusion. Is this

---

[26] The British government had established a war council in November 1914, which became the Dardanelles committee in June 1915 and the war committee in November 1915. In each of its manifestations, however, it was no more than a cabinet sub-committee, responsible to that body.

[27] Bonar Law–Perley, 5 Nov, Perley–Borden, 5 Nov 1915; *DCER*, I, 96–7.

war being waged by the United Kingdom alone or is it a war waged by the whole Empire? If I am correct in supposing that the second hypothesis must be accepted then why do the statesmen of the British Isles arrogate to themselves solely the methods by which it shall be carried on . . .

. . . if we are expected to continue in the role of automata the whole situation must be reconsidered . . .[28]

The prime minister's anger quickly cooled, however, and his letter was overtaken by a cable telling Perley to 'take no further steps at present'. The 'reconsideration', as Borden obviously knew, would have to come from London.

For several reasons, the hoped-for change in imperial wartime relations did not come while the Asquith coalition government held office. In the first place the colonial secretary quite wantonly lacked any personal interest in imperial problems.[29] This in turn only served to reinforce a strong official distaste for making procedural or constitutional innovations in time of war. At first, as we have seen, the autonomous status of the dominions had provided some justification for this passive and conservative outlook, though very soon the scale of dominion support made such deference to status seem wilfully evasive. Thereafter, however, the problems of the war itself – about which the overseas governments were so anxious for enlightenment – were held up as an insuperable barrier to imperial discussions. As early as June 1915, when Bonar Law learned that Borden might persuade the premiers of Australia and New Zealand to accompany him on his trip to London, he had pleaded with the Canadian prime minister that the arrangements for any such gathering of overseas leaders would be impossible. He continued thereafter to forestall any dominion initiatives.

Yet in the last analysis the colonial secretary was not being merely obstructive. Behind his reluctance and lack of enterprise lay the unpalatable fact that the British government themselves had no more than a tenuous grip upon the direction of the war. Under Asquith's leadership, the government had been painfully slow to assess their relationship to a conflict that had become a total war of attrition. The necessary mobilization of resources, for example, required a degree of departmental

[28] Borden diary, Jan 1916; Perley papers: Borden–Perley, 4 Jan 1916. Aitken (Lord Beaverbrook, 1917) was a Canadian, owner of the *Daily Express*, and at the time a British Conservative MP. He provided an informal liaison for the Canadian government with both the overseas Canadian forces and Whitehall.

[29] A lack of interest accepted and endorsed by Bonar Law's biographer and indeed extended by him to cover the whole range of Colonial Office wartime administration. See Blake, *Unknown Prime Minister*, 261.

co-ordination that was unavailable to conventional cabinet government. More importantly, the disposition of an armed force that had grown from thousands to millions – and was suffering commensurate losses – could not be left in the hands of the military high command. After the creation of the coalition in May 1915 the government had begun to come to terms with these problems, most notably in the establishment of a Ministry of Munitions under Lloyd George. That apart, however, the structure of executive control remained rigidly focused on the traditional cabinet, which as ever was convened without secretarial assistance and took no note of its own deliberations. Small wonder that by 1916, neither the co-ordination nor the strategic control of the war effort had been effectively secured; and that when the military campaigns of that year degenerated into wholesale and seemingly futile slaughter, the coalition came under severe political pressure. But in these circumstances, imperial discussions were out of the question. The government had no intention of compounding their own problems by exposing them to the overseas prime ministers. At the same time, of course, any examination of 'the general policy of war operations', such as Borden had called for, was virtually impossible – for until a more coherent control of the war was achieved, there would be no such policy to examine.

2

New departures, 1917–1918

In the closing weeks of 1916 the Asquith coalition government was brought to an end by a struggle for political power organized from within the British cabinet. The prime minister tendered his resignation, confident that he alone could reconstruct the administration; but after two days of negotiations a combination of ministers was successfully put together under the leadership of Lloyd George. Promised mixed but adequate parliamentary support the new regime took office on 7 December, with Lloyd George as prime minister. This second change of government since the start of the war was ostensibly not unlike the first: a shuffle and reallocation of portfolios without recourse to a general election. In several distinct ways, however, it was to mark a deep transformation in the structure and style of Britain's wartime machinery of government.

In the first place more than a simple exchange of ministers was involved. Lloyd George excepted, the Liberal leaders with whom Asquith for two years and more had endeavoured to command the war effort were gone, pushed aside in what amounted to a fundamental shift in political and public opinion towards the conduct of the war. Asquith's attempt to accommodate wartime government to the principles of liberal political philosophy was at an end, any remaining justification for it having been eradicated by the disastrous military operations of the 1916 campaigns. From inside the cabinet, from parliament and beyond, a consensus emerged that was prepared to tolerate social and economic restraints in the cause of a more efficient prosecution of the war – and under Lloyd George's supervision, the chance to consolidate and reinforce this desperate sense of purpose was willingly seized by the Conservatives. The widely reconstructed administration thus in itself heralded a vitally different approach to the war and its problems. Beyond this, however, it was soon apparent that government under Lloyd George was to function in a radically novel way. More than anything else the new prime minister's bid for power had been based on the need for a strong committee of cabinet to co-ordinate all aspects of the war effort, and once in office he moved ahead in this purpose and created a war cabinet of five ministers, responsible for all government policy and supervised by a secretariat under Maurice Hankey. The traditional prerogatives of departmental control were to be held in abeyance – hostages to the critical war situation, and equally to the forceful initiatives of the new chief executive. Yet old habits of authority would die hard, and old channels of administrative power would not easily be forced into fresh patterns. The increase in executive efficiency under the new regime could not be denied; but Lloyd George's ruthless reorganization of war government was to create in its turn a good deal of friction outside the immediate confines of the war cabinet.

At a less conspicuous level, Lloyd George's accession to power and the structural innovations that accompanied it provided a means of entry into government for a number of non-ministerial personnel who in themselves added a new dimension to the administration. Accepted for their organizing abilities, it happened that several of them were also earnest supporters of British imperialism, and they thus constituted a powerful lobby in Whitehall's corridors of power with regard to imperial affairs. This was to be particularly significant for Britain's wartime relations with the dominions. Lloyd George's disposition to involve the overseas governments more closely with the war was strongly encouraged – and encouraged, what is more, precisely in the context of his efforts to free policymaking from routine departmental constraints. Greater dominion collaboration in the war effort was seen as one of the major priorities for the new executive government system. By extension the Colonial Office, already on the defensive with the other departments of state, was put under even stronger pressure by the prime minister's empire-minded aides.

It was against this background of shifting administrative balances of power and influence that the role of the dominions in the final two years of the war was played out. As quickly as could be arranged the overseas prime ministers were invited to participate in an 'Imperial War Cabinet' in London, and so for the first time in six years they assembled together with British ministers, in a series of meetings which brought them up-to-date with the course of the war and offered them an insight into the workings of the new British civilian command. The London talks were also, inevitably, a medium through which dominion leaders could assess the changes and developments of these six past years – where not only the pressures and frustrations of their wartime efforts could be brought to bear on the British authorities, but where also dominion nationalism could demand to be taken into account. The Imperial War Cabinet, and a concurrent subsidiary Imperial War Conference, were therefore obliged to serve a multiple purpose: to register the dominions' claims as regards their constitutional and functional place in the empire; to brief their representatives on current problems; and finally, with due acknowledgement of dominion rights in any future scheme of things, to give overseas ministers a voice as to the possible terms of peace.

There was also an explicit short-term obligation, accepted by the home government, to keep the dominion governments more closely in touch with the making of war policy. Given that the British authorities had confessed they would need all the assistance the overseas communities could provide, this was hardly an excessive gesture. In practice, nonetheless, it met with administrative difficulties and ambivalent responses. A machinery of government still adjusting under the war cabinet to new routines for its day-to-day affairs proved quite unready to admit the overseas leaders to any meaningful participation in war business, and in the course of the next twelve months little was done to keep them abreast of policy decisions. This manifest failure to fulfil an acknowledged commitment to the dominions seemed doubly compounded by the terrible military failures of 1917 on the western front.

It was therefore not surprising that a session of the Imperial War Cabinet held in 1918 was conducted in an atmosphere charged with recriminations and serious dominion misgivings, with overseas ministers markedly less humble and naive than in 1917. As he had been at the previous meetings, Lloyd George was again ready to portray the military shortcomings as evidence of the urgency of his own pursuit of absolute executive authority – a task with which they must all assist. But this time the pointed criticisms of his overseas colleagues, Sir Robert Borden in particular, were not so easily turned aside to this purpose. Borden and the others were adamant that changes be seen to take place in the directing of the war effort, and they obliged Lloyd George to give them the authority, however briefly, to actively scrutinize and reshape the empire's future military policy. Events soon overtook the strategies thus worked out in the summer of 1918. But before taking their leave, the overseas leaders once more affirmed their intention to translate this moment of functional engagement with policymaking into an accepted constitutional feature of British–dominion relations.

The Colonial Office and the Imperial War Cabinet

The British war cabinet settled into its duties in the second week of December 1916, a committee of five made up of Lloyd George, Lord Curzon, Lord Milner, Arthur Henderson and Bonar Law, and in support Hankey's proven secretarial machinery from the Committee of Imperial

Defence. Of the five ministers Bonar Law alone continued 'regular' duties as chancellor of the exchequer and war cabinet spokesman in the House of Commons. Apart from this one necessary concession to the lower house, the war cabinet was to work in isolation from the legislature. It was quickly realized that this new cabinet was also to work in isolation from what had hitherto been understood as the executive – that is, the twenty-odd heads of department meeting in cabinet to determine government policy. In Lloyd George's reorganization this most established of unofficial institutions of government was prorogued *sine die*. Each department of state would have its minister still, but he was permitted to attend the war cabinet only when summoned, and then only for the particular item of business for which his views were required. These moments apart, he and his colleagues, deprived of their collective responsibilities, were soon enough confined to carrying out orders from above, delivered in the form of war cabinet 'conclusions', and carefully kept track of by Hankey or one of his assistants. Exhorted to administer rather than to govern, stranded and somewhat confused by the new channels through which executive power now began to flow, Lloyd George's ministers found themselves the handmaidens – at best the ladies-in-waiting – of the self-made monarch from Wales.

One minister who felt strongly and at once the loss of his prerogatives was Walter Long, colonial secretary in the new coalition. Courteous but easily annoyed, old fashioned and uncomplex, Long was not the easiest man to reconcile to the new order. He had supported Lloyd George's bid for power, but he expressed his apprehensions to the new prime minister on the day the government took office:

I cannot conceal from myself that we are running grave risks in the abolition of the old constitutional system of governing by Cabinet. For instance, India and the Colonies may very well complain when they learn the simple fact that the Ministers who are charged with the care of their interests in the Imperial Government are no longer members of the Cabinet.[1]

It was a valid point for Long to make. He needed no intimacy with his new portfolio to know that the dominions were stretching to the limits their economies and their manpower, and even so had little knowledge of the direction or progress of the war in Europe. But if he hoped in this way to call in the new world to redress the balance of the old, he was disappointed. Two days later the war cabinet assembled without him, and continued to exclude him from their meetings.

Long was soon back with a more modest proposal for Lloyd George,

[1] Lloyd George papers: Long–Ll. G., 7 Dec 1916.

suggesting that the dominions be sent a weekly cable of information about the war. Possibly this idea sprang from self-interested motives, for the regular dispatch of confidential news would enable the colonial secretary to see a wide range of war cabinet documents, and thus be kept in touch with government policy – in the new order of things a privilege not to be lightly discounted. At any rate, whatever the motives, the suggestion promised considerable advantages for the overseas governments. Lloyd George, however, was already thinking on much broader lines than his colonial secretary. Long wanted cablegrams. In reply Lloyd George announced his intention to hold a full-scale Imperial Conference at the earliest opportunity. The dominions, he reminded Long,

have made enormous sacrifices, but we have held no conference with them as to either the objects of the war or the methods of carrying it out. They hardly feel that they have been consulted. As we must receive even more substantial support from them before we can hope to pull through, it is important that they should feel that they have a share in our councils as well as in our burdens.[2]

The colonial secretary, it seemed, was cautiously preaching to a prime minister already fully converted to the cause. Indeed, it appears that Lloyd George had determined at once on a conference with the dominions without securing the full approval of even his own war cabinet, with the result that two weeks later Maurice Hankey was still wondering about his chief's decision, noting in his diary, 'As a matter of fact the war cabinet have not a notion of what they are to discuss, and as Bonar Law said, "when [the dominion prime ministers] are here you will wish to goodness you could get rid of them".'[3]

Yet for all Hankey's nervous worries about not having an agenda, and Bonar Law's sour reluctance – an apt reminder of his unhelpful attitudes while colonial secretary – there were many men close to Lloyd George who from the outset of his regime offered enthusiastic support for any moves towards closer co-operation with the overseas governments. In the war cabinet the imperialist viewpoint was weightily represented by Lord Milner; Philip Kerr, another charter member of the Round Table group, added his influence as the prime minister's private secretary; at the Cabinet Office Leopold Amery, one of Hankey's assistants, was also well placed to inject the imperial element into relevant matters of policy. And in his calmer moments Hankey himself must count as a promoter of fuller

---

[2] Lloyd George papers: Ll. G.–Long, 12 Dec 1916, printed in D. Lloyd George, *War Memoirs*, 2 vols (London, 1938), I, 1026.
[3] Hankey diary; Roskill, *Hankey*, I, 348.

imperial ties. As an ambitious career civil servant in a new and untried post he was cautious to a fault about being identified with any interest group, and particularly in these opening months of his job was distinctly cool towards Amery, whom he considered 'foisted on me by Milner'.[4] But his own earlier hopes for the creation of consultative machinery capable of giving the dominions a voice in imperial affairs were still alive, provided only that he could remain at the administrative centre of control. To none of these men, in their enthusiasm for empire and their privileged access to Lloyd George, were the anxieties of the colonial secretary of great concern, except perhaps as an expression of the traditional patterns of organization that now needed clearing away.

Lloyd George's decision to call an Imperial Conference thus checked Long's own initiatives. Nonetheless he could assume that the Colonial Office, which had organized such affairs since their inception in 1887 (and incorporated a conference secretariat within their department in 1907), would again be given the job of running the conference and in this way have an ample opportunity to manifest their involvement with imperial policy. Yet six years on from the last Imperial Conference such credentials looked far from convincing. Long was forgetting that even in 1911, the Committee of Imperial Defence had been used as an alternative forum for British–dominion discussions, and but for the war might have revealed further potential in this role. When the war cabinet came to discuss arrangements for the forthcoming meetings, in any event, it became clear that Colonial Office claims were not at all secure. Milner strongly opposed sticking to established procedure, and the colonial secretary, called in on this occasion to be given his say, found himself the only advocate of a conference on conventional lines. After a clearly heated debate it was settled that the dominion prime ministers should discuss the problems of war directly with the war cabinet. A cable was drafted to the overseas governments informing them

that what His Majesty's Government contemplate is not a session of the ordinary Imperial Conference. They invite your Prime Minister to attend a series of special and continuous meetings of the War Cabinet.[5]

Long was not easily deterred, however. An appeal lodged two days later found the cabinet still determined 'to supersede the idea of a Conference on former lines', but an important concession was now implied when they accepted that topics other than the war might be discussed

4 Hankey diary; *ibid*, 349, 352–3. 'He is a scheming little devil', he wrote, 'and his connection with *The Times* would make it possible for him to oust me'.
5 CAB 23/1: WC 15, 21 Dec 1916.

outside the war cabinet – though 'it was preferable not to invite such discussions'. By dint of strenuous lobbying (particularly with Austen Chamberlain, secretary of state for India and keen to give Indian representatives as large a role as possible at the London talks) the colonial secretary had within a week fashioned this conciliatory gesture into a fully-fledged subsidiary conference, the war cabinet reluctantly letting him have his way. Thus after a tense confrontation of the old establishment with the new the main lines of the 1917 imperial meetings were laid down. Strategic problems of the war and possible peace terms were to be dealt with in the war cabinet, and secondary matters would be left to the Colonial Office. While dominion premiers would alone be members of the war cabinet, they would be able to bring to London whichever other colleagues they considered necessary.

The concession of a conference was a welcome fillip to the colonial secretary, although it did little to mitigate his hostility towards the proposed sessions in the war cabinet – a cabinet whose methods of government he continued privately to disparage.[6] It was clear that most of the important business with the dominions would be transacted in the war cabinet, and Long was anxious to reduce if possible the exclusiveness of those meetings. In this he was unwittingly helped by the dominion representatives themselves. By early March the delegations from Canada, New Zealand and Newfoundland had arrived in England, and in advance of the scheduled imperial meetings the government decided to open discussions by inviting the three prime ministers to the war cabinet. W. F. Massey of New Zealand, however, insisted that his colleague, Sir Joseph Ward (with whom he had formed a coalition government), must also attend – whereupon Borden, jealous of his rights, demanded a second seat for Canada. It was a problem the colonial secretary did nothing to resolve; indeed the increased size of this meeting provided justification for his own attendance. Considerations of protocol were thus allowed to jeopardize the intended format, and to set a most important precedent for the main sessions to come.[7] Three days later the war cabinet made a second attempt to secure a measure of intimate contact with a dominion prime minister, proposing that Borden alone should be invited to discuss questions

---

[6] W. Hewins, *The Apologia of an Imperialist*, 2 vols (London, 1929), II, 104. Lloyd George, hearing of Long's complaints, told Hankey 'he didn't give a d—n if Walter Long resigned or not, and would rather welcome a row in the House and a General Election'. Roskill, *Hankey*, I, 359.

[7] Hankey noted in his diary, 'Lloyd George decided the whole caboodle must be asked but was very bored.' Lord Hankey, *The Supreme Command*, 2 vols (London, 1961), II, 568.

concerning the United States. But Long was quick to complain about this to the foreign secretary, Arthur Balfour:

I am compelled to ask that the invitation you contemplate extending to Borden alone shall be given to the others ... The only sound principle seems to me to be to invite all or none.[8]

Rather than give the colonial secretary a chance to create further difficulties the war cabinet dropped the invitation altogether.

When, therefore, the Imperial War Cabinet began its regular meetings, it was attended by the dominion prime ministers and their ministerial colleagues (an impending election in Australia prevented Hughes from participating), by eight British ministers, three Indian representatives and the military and naval service chiefs[9] – these latter possibly to keep British delegates in a majority, for fear of an adverse vote. Under the weight of such numbers intimacy had to give way to formality, and it was impossible to conduct these gatherings, as originally intended, as 'special and continuous sessions of the War Cabinet'. The day-to-day running of the war had perforce to be carried out by the British war cabinet, which continued to meet at least once a day throughout the weeks that the larger body was in session.

Despite the formal nature of the proceedings in the Imperial War Cabinet, the British government were at last able to give the overseas leaders the thorough briefing about the war that they had lacked for so long. Over the course of fourteen meetings, daily summaries of the military situation were followed by more general reports on a wide range of problems, covering manpower, material resources, finance, diplomacy, and economic strategies. This comprehensive survey not only gave the dominion ministers their first over-all picture of the war effort, but also convincingly demonstrated the urgent attempts of the Lloyd George ministry to co-ordinate and control that effort. The British prime minister's strategy of candid revelation struck exactly the right balance. On the one hand the manifest difficulties facing the empire, as he made clear, required even greater efforts from the dominions; on the other, his own resolute determination inspired the prime ministers to meet these new demands with every means possible. After only three meetings, the Imperial War Cabinet resolved that the empire 'should put forth the whole of its military

8 Lloyd George papers: Long–Balfour, 5 March 1917.
9 CAB 23/40: IWC 1, 20 March 1917.

strength in 1917', and if need be 'throughout 1918'. Behind this simple affirmation lay a sense of common and dedicated purpose that had not been known since the opening months of the war.

British leaders brought the Imperial War Cabinet to terms with the increasing demands of the war through a straightforward exposition of the outstanding problems. There was little by way of forward-looking consultation on these issues, in part at least because it was obviously difficult to foresee what demands would be made as the war progressed – if indeed it was progressing at all, given the stalemate of attrition on the western front and Russia's collapse into revolution on the east. Even allowing for a future clouded with forbidding uncertainties, however, there were other more contingent restraints upon consultation in 1917. For one thing, there was still a palpable gap between war cabinet planning and the execution of fighting strategy in the field. Four months of power had not sufficed to gain Lloyd George's civilian administration the working control over military affairs necessary to bring the generals under their surveillance, a shortcoming that compromised any policy discussions in London. Yet in any case, it was plainly evident at the Imperial War Cabinet that even amongst themselves, the British authorities were far from agreed on over-all military priorities. Against Lloyd George's un-wavering commitment to total victory – a stand that was strongly endorsed by Borden – Milner and his associates argued that the empire stood to benefit far more from a limited paramountcy over Germany, based on the expropriation of her colonial possessions. The Imperial Cabinet's agree-ment to make full effort throughout 1917 and 1918 represented success for the viewpoint of the two prime ministers – but equally, the lack of specific details in that resolution was an acknowledgement that firm strategic decisions had yet to be reached. The overseas leaders had no option but to trust the British government to do the right thing. For the moment it was enough that they had been brought up to date with the general situation.[10]

A more rewarding opportunity for tangible British–dominion con-sultations came at a later stage of the Imperial War Cabinet's proceedings, when after three weeks of appraising military affairs, the discussion turned to a consideration of possible conditions for a future settlement of peace. From the British point of view, consultation about peace terms was a practical necessity. Since any final peace treaty would be the product of an international conference, at which the dominions would understandably

---

[10] A fuller treatment of the range of strategic discussion at the 1917 meetings is provided by G. Cook, 'Sir Robert Borden, Lloyd George and British Military Policy, 1917–18', *The Historical Journal*, XIV, no 2 (1971).

not be represented, it was essential to ascertain their views in advance, and in fact promises to this effect had been made to the overseas governments as early as 1915. For this purpose, therefore, two sub-committees of the Imperial Cabinet were established under Milner and Curzon to examine the empire's economic and territorial interests as they might relate to the eventual terms of peace.[11] Here, it seemed, a type of imperial executive had at last been constituted: two small groups of British and dominion ministers, meeting to derive an imperial consensus in advance on basic questions of policy.

Yet it is apparent, even so, that what passed for consultation in these two committees was little more than dominion ratification of British conclusions. Nor was this a matter of chance, however much overseas ministers might pride themselves on meeting their British colleagues on equal terms. In these or any other imperial gatherings the British delegates enjoyed one incomparable advantage, in having the administrative support of Whitehall's civil service. Whatever intramural antagonisms Lloyd George's regime might have created amongst his ministers there was no escaping the fact that the British departments of state, together with Hankey's secretarial bureau, constituted an establishment whose resources of information, planning and talent the dominion governments could never hope to match. (It might be added that however badly they argued amongst themselves, the ministers and civil servants of the mother country were nearly always prepared to present themselves as a firmly united interest *devant les enfants*.) Here was a fundamental structural inequality which weighed strongly in the balance between Britain and the dominions, and which would continue to exert an important influence over the evolving forms of their imperial association.

In the particular case of the Curzon and Milner committees, certainly, the initiative and control of the discussions rested squarely with the home ministers. Thus Curzon's group on territorial questions, far from taking up these matters as if for the first time, was conveniently provided with the report of an earlier British government inquiry into the same subject, conducted in late 1916[12] – and in the limited amount of time available the sub-committee could do little but ratify the conclusions already reached. The overseas representatives were no doubt gratified that Curzon's final report spoke of the need for further imperial consultations before any territorial bargains could be made with Britain's war allies. The sub-

---

[11] The minutes of the Milner committee are in CAB 21/71; those of the Curzon committee are in CAB 21/77.

[12] CID, sub-committee on territorial changes. Minutes and interim reports of the committee are in CAB 16/36.

committee's conclusions, for all that, were a carefully prepared *fait accompli*.[13]

Constitutional affairs, 1917

As discussions in the Imperial War Cabinet progressed from the immediate problems of the military conflict to the possible terms for peace, a variety of other issues less directly concerned with the war was examined in the Imperial War Conference, which assembled under the chairmanship of the colonial secretary on alternate days to the Imperial Cabinet. Although a good deal of time was taken up here with matters of secondary interest, there were a number of items on the conference's agenda that were of the highest priority, notably the empire's future economic objectives, post-war imperial defence policy (to which we can turn in later chapters) and constitutional relations. Like economics and defence this latter subject was also necessarily one for future planning – there was no desire to revise the constitutional basis of British–dominion relations during the war. Nonetheless, on several grounds constitutional matters demanded some attention in 1917. In the first place the overseas governments, in the light of the acknowledged importance of their war efforts, were anxious to consolidate their claims with the British authorities to a future voice in imperial policy-making, and thus were keen to examine possible methods for improving inter-imperial consultation. Closely tied up with any discussions about consultation, of course, was the Imperial War Cabinet itself, an innovation whose function and significance remained to be fully assessed. These matters in their turn inevitably encouraged wider speculations about the future course of imperial relations. On all sides of the conference table ministers were concerned to know under what auspices they were gathered together.

Of all the parties to the constitutional discussions in 1917, the man most determined to seize and hold the initiative was Lord Milner, who brought to the study of imperial relations a long-standing interest and single-minded commitment. His importance for the 1917 talks is worth a moment's consideration. For ten years and more Milner and his ex-South Africa disciples, the Kindergarten, had been at the centre of an extensive campaign for the closer organic union of the empire, endeavouring privately to create 'an immense nexus of influence and patronage for directing public policy in imperial and other matters'.[14] Before the war

---

[13] See 44 ff.

[14] C. Quigley, 'The Round Table Movement in Canada, 1909–1938', *CHR*, XLIII, no 3 (1962), 304; cf J. Eayrs, 'The Round Table Movement in Canada, 1909–1920', *CHR*, XXXVIII, no 1 (1957). The sixtieth anniversary issue of *The*

they had little enough to show for their efforts; but the onset of hostilities offered fresh possibilities for the Milnerite cause. Admittedly on the theoretical side their major project, to build a federal constitutional model for the empire through joint negotiations between British and dominion imperialists, had to be shelved (and when Lionel Curtis, the project's director, went on to complete a model, he was obliged to publish it under his own name and without the *imprimatur* of the Round Table organization).[15] In practical terms, however, the strains placed by the war on imperial co-operation were regarded as telling evidence in support of federalist arguments. At first the Round Tablers thought it best to marshal these arguments for use at a post-war imperial conference – by which time the overseas governments would be thoroughly discontented with the existing constitutional relationship. But by 1916 Milner appeared ready for a much bolder step forward – into the open arena of British politics. With an eye to the manifest weakness of the Asquith–Bonar Law coalition he wrote to a colleague (who had suggested the revival of the Imperial Federation League, defunct for over twenty years) in March of that year:

My hope rather is that out of the present political chaos, there may emerge a new party, which will make the organic unity of the Empire one of the planks of its programme. I think this would advance matters quicker than the formation of a League of a non-party character.[16]

The level of activity, he thought, could also be stepped up overseas. A month later he was telling a leading Canadian member of the Round Table movement: 'My own view is that the time has come, or is very near at hand, when definite proposals for Imperial unification ought to take the place of the somewhat vague general propaganda.'[17] Eight months later Milner was in office, if not with a new political party then at least with many of his friends around him. In Canada, Sir Wilfrid Laurier certainly overstated the case in claiming that the dominion 'is now governed by a junta sitting in London, known as the "Round Table" ';[18] but a London newspaper article was less far from the truth in seeing that a 'new

Round Table, (1970) no 240, contains useful general articles on the beginnings of the movement.

[15] L. Curtis, *The Problem of the Commonwealth* (London, 1916).

[16] Milner papers: Milner–Sidney Low, 24 March 1916.

[17] Milner papers: Milner–Sir Edmund Walker, 22 April 1916. *The Round Table* also took a more assertive tone in its promotion of imperial federation. See 'The Imperial Dilemma', *The Round Table*, no 24 (Sept 1916); 'The Growing Necessity for Constitutional Reform', *ibid*, no 25 (Dec 1916).

[18] Quoted in J. D. Miller, *Richard Jebb and the Problem of Empire* (London, 1956), 23.

bureaucracy' had come to power,'whose ideas were not those of Mr. Lloyd George ... but of Lord Milner'.[19] The new format of the 1917 imperial discussions bore witness to the influence of the group. And it was Milner's intention not merely to see that the hybrid Imperial War Cabinet survived, but to make it the point of growth of a federated structure linking Britain and the dominions.

Nonetheless, despite the impressive political advantages that Milner with his associates now enjoyed, his campaign for imperial federation still lacked the essential support of his prime minister. Lloyd George acknowledged a personal and political sympathy for Milner.[20] He also well appreciated the collective strength of the Milnerites in his government – though the influence they enjoyed through their informal chain of connections could hardly compare with the power and control available to Lloyd George through the cabinet secretariat (where Hankey, moreover, kept a careful eye on Milner's friends). The prime minister, in any event, had called these men into office for their administrative talents and their commitment to a total war effort, not for their constitutional ideas. The same priorities held true for the 1917 imperial discussions. The overseas leaders had been summoned to London because a greater contribution to the war was needed from the dominions, and though constitutional questions were on the agenda they were only tangential to Lloyd George's major preoccupations. He was certainly not prepared to jeopardize the chance of an increased imperial war effort by committing the British government to Milner's constitutional designs.

Thus in the end it was in a personal capacity only that Milner presented his case for imperial federation to the Imperial War Conference. Initially, it seems, he offered something close to an ultimatum, threatening to sabotage the conference's proceedings unless federation was agreed upon – a striking manifestation of his major premise that the empire must either federate or disintegrate![21] In a more concerted attempt, however, to

[19] *The Nation*, 24 Feb 1917. See P. A. Lockwood, 'Milner's Entry into the War Cabinet, December 1916', *The Historical Journal*, VII, no 2 (1964), an excellent study of Milner's political activities in 1916.

[20] 'He is a poor man and so am I. He does not represent the landed or capitalist classes any more than I do. He is keen on social reform and so am I.' Quoted in K. Morgan, 'Lloyd George's Premiership: A Study in "Prime Ministerial Government"', *The Historical Journal*, XIII, no 1 (1970), 132. For an interesting insight on the affinity between democratic socialism and imperialism in these years, see Enoch Powell, 'The Myth of Empire', *The Round Table*, no 240, (Nov 1970), 440.

[21] W. Hewins, *Apologia*, II, 134, 144. No record of Milner's threat appears in the minutes of the conference, a draft unedited print of which is in CO 532/97.

convince the dominion ministers of their case, Milner and his friends removed the discussions from the conference table to the more congenial atmosphere of the dining table, where at 'a series of little dinners ... overseas men have met a number of us belonging to the Home Government'.[22] Dominion reactions, even so, were not encouraging. Massey, as expected, was 'very Imperialistic and determined to force the issue',[23] but neither Borden nor Jan Smuts of South Africa would endorse imperial federation. Smuts would have made his point by simply refusing to consider constitutional revisions during the war. Borden, while supporting this argument against wartime change, was prepared to answer the federalist position more directly by putting forward counter-proposals for the approval of the Imperial War Conference. The initiative now switched from Milner to the Canadian prime minister, who proceeded to canvass opinions amongst the overseas delegations for constitutional measures of his own.

The whole weight of Borden's experience as prime minister of the senior dominion placed him firmly against the proponents of imperial federation, and impelled him to define and promote an alternative conception of imperial development. He himself, of course, was no stranger to federalist ideas by 1917. His visit to London five years earlier in 1912 had brought him up against the Round Table persuaders. A year later his newly-appointed adviser on external affairs, Loring Christie, had soon revealed that he too subscribed to the 'either–or' school of thought, and was bent on converting the prime minister. A policy review by Christie in late 1913 argued strongly that the dominion had only two feasible options for its foreign affairs: to be fully independent, or to gain sufficient control of a truly integrated imperial foreign policy so as to meet Canadian requirements.[24] There was soon established a dominion Round Table group to drive home the logic of these alternatives, and to create popular support for closer imperial union.[25] Yet the movement in Canada had never achieved a commanding influence. In the pre-war period, there was little need for any official response to the fledgling federalist organization, and Borden appears to have taken scant notice of it amidst his other preoccupations. And the stimulus of war itself failed to create any wider

22 Milner papers: Milner–A. Glazebrook (a Canadian member of the Round Table movement), 21 April 1917.
23 Lloyd George papers: Long–Ll. G. (April 1917).
24 Memorandum cited by R. C. Brown, 'Sir Robert Borden, The Great War and Anglo-Canadian Relations', in J. Moir (ed), *Character and Circumstance* (Toronto, 1970).
25 See V. Massey, *What's Past is Prologue* (London, 1963), 35 ff.

measure of support for imperial federation in Canada. For all attempts to play up the war for their own purposes (or to turn anti-French Canadian feelings into pro-empire loyalties) the local Round Tablers found that their federalist doctrines had to work across the grain of a growing Canadian nationalism. (The publication in 1916 of Curtis's *Problem of the Commonwealth* was in this respect a distinct embarrassment to the Canadian faithful, who tried to dissociate themselves from its ruthless imperial logic.) Canada's active and total commitment to war, in short, was marked by a decided deepening of national sentiment – and at the very centre of the war effort, Borden himself was no less untouched. As the fighting took its course through 1915 and 1916, his own appreciation of Canada's place in the empire – and in the war – revealed a distinctly nationalist outlook. His conviction that Canada had a right to be consulted in the making of imperial foreign or military policies was one aspect of this new perspective. But by March 1916, for instance, Borden was also thinking that the next governor general for the dominion might well be a Canadian.[26] As he was preparing to leave for London eleven months later, he was readily able to satisfy the staunchly nationalist J. W. Dafoe, editor of the *Manitoba Free Press*, that he held no brief whatever from the advocates of federalist integration of the empire. Like Dafoe, Borden with an increasing assurance had come to regard Canada not as an adjunct to the war but as a principal in her own right, not as a colonial assistant but an imperial partner. 'I should like to think', Dafoe wrote after their interview, 'that Canadians can rely upon him to stand up to his position under the pressures which will be put upon him when he reaches London'.[27]

In reaction to those pressures, but equally in response to his own nationalist impulses, it thus came about that Borden assumed the leading dominion role in constitutional affairs in the Imperial War Conference. Closest to him in spirit in the creation of an overseas consensus was Smuts, though in view of the excessive credit given to the South African in subsequent accounts of the 1917 negotiations,[28] it is worth emphasizing that even he needed persuading at first, particularly as regards the extent

---

[26] Perley papers: Borden–Perley, 14 March 1916.

[27] Dafoe–Sir Clifford Sifton (his publisher), 12 Feb 1917, quoted in Eayrs, 'Round Table Movement', 18.

[28] Leopold Amery felt that Smuts was the 'main author' of the War Conference's constitutional resolution; *My Political Life*, II: *War and Peace, 1914–1929* (London, 1953), 109. Smuts' biographer accepted this view without further evidence; W. K. Hancock, *Smuts*, I: *The Sanguine Years, 1870–1919* (Cambridge, 1962), 429.

of possible dominion participation in the making of the empire's foreign policy. A telling entry in Borden's diary for 22 March 1917 reveals:

had an hour's discussion with Smuts and Massey as to agenda and as to resolutions to be moved respecting constitutional relations. I insisted on a clause declaring our right to an adequate voice in foreign policy. Smuts fears this may involve responsibility for financial aid in defence, etc.[29]

Five days later, in any event, all the overseas leaders had come round, and with the approval and support of the colonial secretary Borden was able to put the finishing touches to a draft resolution.[30] The results finally appeared on 16 April, as conference resolution IX.

Conceding that the war precluded any immediate revision of imperial relations, resolution IX made no specific recommendations. It offered instead a statement of principles, to serve in effect as the terms of reference for a post-war constitutional conference. Even in these general terms, however, it effectively discounted imperial federation as a future possibility. Although there must be stronger connections – a voice in foreign policy, and continuous consultations – between Britain and the dominions, the keystone of the imperial structure was not to be organic unity, but the national autonomy of the dominions:

any [constitutional] readjustment, while thoroughly preserving all existing powers of self-government and complete control of domestic affairs, should be based upon a full recognition of the Dominions as autonomous nations of an Imperial Commonwealth, and of India as an important part of the same, should recognize the right of the Dominions and India to an adequate voice in foreign policy and foreign relations, and should provide effective arrangements for continuous consultations in all important matters of common Imperial concern.

In resolution IX, the overseas ministers declared their intention to pursue a constitutional course between federation and independence, a choice that Milner and his associates had tried to prove was not legitimate. In essence, the federalists argued that status and function, the two components of constitutional development, could not be held for long out of alignment: they must point either to integration or to the break-up of the empire. The supposition behind this argument was that the dominions' willing commitment to the imperial war effort would guide them towards integration.

---

[29] Borden diary, 22 March 1917.

[30] *Ibid*, 27 March 1917. A detailed examination of the various rejected drafts put up by the other prime ministers is provided by R. C. Brown and R. Bothwell, 'The Canadian Resolution', in M. Cross and R. Bothwell (eds), *Policy by other means* (Toronto, 1972).

Here in particular, however, the federalist analysis was too narrow. Far from producing any such predominant impulse the war had given rise to a wide range of feelings in the dominions, confirming imperial loyalties but at the same time encouraging local nationalism. It was precisely this complexity of response that Borden was able to translate into resolution ix, in which the federalist alternatives were transcended. It was the dominions' declared purpose now to integrate themselves functionally in imperial affairs – not simply by continuing and expanding their material contributions to the war effort, but by gaining meaningful access to the executive centre of imperial affairs. The Imperial War Cabinet was an obvious manifestation of the new order of things. Yet this new integration was to be based on a full acceptance of their status as autonomous communities of the empire.

For all the ready acceptance of resolution ix, it nonetheless remained to be seen whether this statement of intent represented a genuine way forward, or merely an unstable compromise between imperial unity and national independence. In April 1917, in any event, its effect on the scope of constitutional speculations in official circles was negligible. Smuts was happy to think that imperial federation had been 'negatived by implication'. The Colonial Office, for their part, were somewhat puzzled as to the shape of things to come.[31] Even Milner found no cause for dismay. From the constitutional conference, he forecast, the dominions would emerge with

some permanent representation in an Imperial Cabinet dealing with Defence, Foreign Affairs and Communications; and would undertake to provide in their own way for a certain definite proportion of the cost of the Navy and the Consular and Diplomatic Service. It would be a lop-sided sort of arrangement, but might carry us on for a bit. Nothing could, in fact, be more lopsided than the present temporary Imperial War Cabinet, which, nevertheless, has I think, served a useful purpose.[32]

Clearly he hoped that the practical implications of joint consultation and policymaking might be such as to undermine the strength of dominion autonomy.[33]

For the moment, however, the most important question was the future

[31] CO 532/98: minutes, May 1917.
[32] Milner papers: Milner–Glazebrook, 21 April 1917.
[33] *The Round Table* accepted resolution ix though insisting that short of full integration no constitutional organization would work satisfactorily: 'While welcoming the changes let us not suppose that they will in themselves solve the fundamental problem which lies at the root of the politics of the Empire.' *The Round Table*, no 27 (June 1917).

of the Imperial War Cabinet, whose 1917 session was drawing to a close. On the eve of its final meeting, the British war cabinet met to consider the results of various informal ministerial soundings on this subject. One suggestion was that Smuts, who was about to take up temporary membership of the British war cabinet, might act as spokesman for all the dominion governments, an idea Lloyd George had put to Borden but which had not been well received by him. A second idea was that a minister from each government might remain in London and the Imperial War Cabinet be kept in semi-permanent session; but here again the colonial secretary had to report that the overseas prime ministers were not enthusiastic. The resistance to both schemes, of course, hinged on the need to delegate responsibility in imperial affairs from the dominion premiers to nominated representatives – an essential pre-requisite of any well-integrated constitutional structure, but one that in 1917, at least, overseas leaders were not prepared to confront. The only alternative that found general support, therefore, was a plan for an annual session of the Imperial War Cabinet, and at their final session for 1917 this policy was officially endorsed.

It is worth noting that Borden, who had worked hard to secure the necessary acceptance for this policy, was clearly pleased at the prospect of yearly meetings of the Imperial Cabinet – and small wonder, given that leave of absence from Ottawa could be organized with far less administrative disruption than was possible for the other dominion leaders. Canada's relative proximity to Britain, in this respect, was a critical advantage for the senior dominion, and one that possibly had already begun to exert a subtle but powerful influence over Canadian attitudes. At the threshold of a new co-operative venture in imperial affairs, with the door to high-level consultations beginning to open, Borden would be well placed to respond to calls to London for conferences – and by extension would feel a keener sense of frustration were such calls not to be issued. His fellow prime ministers, based as they were in the southern hemisphere, could hardly fail to have a different perspective: where a minimum of twelve weeks had to be invested in any consultations in London, the temptation to leave things to Whitehall would be understandably much greater. Whitehall, it would soon enough emerge, would often feel the same.

Canadian territorial ambitions

As we have seen, the consultations in Curzon's committee about the empire's territorial interests in any future peace settlement were something of a *fait accompli*, inasmuch as the overseas representatives were invited simply to give their approval to proposals worked out in advance by the British government. It would be wrong to imagine, nonetheless, that this approval was given only with reluctance. The C.I.D. report of late 1916 circulated to the committee had carefully scrutinized every possibility for enlarging the empire's colonial possessions – both at the expense of Germany and Turkey and by means of bargaining with allied and neutral states – and its enthusiastic reception offered convincing proof that an expansionist sentiment prevailed not only in Whitehall but also through-out the dominion delegations. Only after the Curzon committee's own report was put before the Imperial War Cabinet did any note of dissension come into the discussion, when Lloyd George himself conspicuously failed to approve the proposed plans for expansion after the war. In support of Lloyd George, Borden now chose to offer some criticisms of his own, warning the Imperial Cabinet that fresh territorial claims might well not find favour with the allied powers, and that they would moreover be in cynical contradiction to any British initiatives for a post-war league of nations.[34]

Borden's reservations in 1917 about imperial territorial expansion have been accepted as added evidence of his antipathy to the imperialists of the Round Table school, and certainly his opposition seems quite con-sistent with his feelings in this respect. At the constitutional level he had convincingly rejected their efforts to promote a federated imperial system; in turn he now was taking his stand against their strategic conception of an enlarged and self-contained post-war empire.[35] It seems fair to add that Borden was also coming to fear that British territorial gains from the war would be severely frowned on by the United States, a country only just committed to the allied cause and whose firm and lasting friendship the Canadian prime minister thought should be secured for the British empire at all costs. There would be more explicit warnings from Borden on this theme as the war came to its end. These statesman-like objections notwithstanding, there appears nonetheless to have been an element of opportunism in Borden's lack of support for imperial ex-pansion. It was noticeable that he had held back his criticisms until this full session of the Imperial War Cabinet, rather than convey them through the Canadian minister sitting on the Curzon committee, J. D. Hazen; indeed Borden's doubts stand in marked contrast to Hazen's untroubled support for the committee's own investigations. This is hardly surprising, however, for it happens that Canada herself had had claims to put forward to the committee. Only when it seemed they would come to very little did

---

[34] CAB 23/40: IWC 13, 1 May 1917.
[35] Cook, 'Sir Robert Borden', 376–7.

the prime minister choose to declare his misgivings about the empire's territorial expansion in general.

Canada's territorial aspirations, it must be admitted at once, were by far the least well-founded of those under consideration in 1917, for the simple reason that she had no enemy territory to capture, occupy, and lay claim to. Nonetheless, if others could paint the map red then there were some Canadian claims to advance, even so. The first rather tentative request concerned the Alaska 'Panhandle', the strip of territory awarded to (or as many Canadians continued to think, virtually demanded by) the United States in 1903, which had cut off the Yukon and much of northern British Columbia from the Pacific coast. Hazen asked if the American government might not be persuaded to provide Canada with a narrow corridor to the sea in this area. Here the Foreign Office indicated brief interest, responding with the suggestion that the United States could be offered British Guiana or British Honduras as an inducement. But the notion of an exchange of territory on these lines was at once criticized by the colonial secretary and by Curzon himself, and the Alaska question was not taken any further.

A second Canadian proposal, not unconnected with the Alaska problem, was similarly somewhat speculative. On the dominion's eastern edge lay Greenland, the possession of Denmark and of concern to Canadian government ministers ever since the Alaska award had gone against Canada's interests. Within months of that award Laurier had been alerted to the possibility of an 'Eastern Alaska' whereby the United States (which had already secured from Denmark a first option on its West Indian islands) might try to acquire Greenland through similar tactics.[36] Official inquiries made through the Foreign Office at Laurier's request in 1904 had come to nothing, but now in 1917 the fact that the United States had recently been able to exercise its options and acquire Denmark's West Indian islands had given fresh urgency to the question of Greenland's future. And, as Borden was reminded in London by Sir George Perley, Greenland was well placed to provide such modern services as a wireless station or even a re-fuelling point for any eventual Atlantic air routes. Under the circumstances it seemed essential to try to secure Greenland against American purchase, and Hazen put the case for a Canadian bid before the territorial committee, where it was favourably received. Unfortunately renewed inquiries to Denmark revealed that Greenland was not on the market.[37]

[36] Laurier papers: T. Cleave (Vancouver)–Laurier, Oct 1903. I am grateful to Dr I. McClymont, Public Archives of Canada, for drawing my attention to this letter.

[37] In 1919 Denmark asked the major powers to acknowledge her full sovereignty

Another long-standing Canadian ambition was directed towards the two islands of St Pierre and Miquelon, the remnants of France's North American empire which lay off the coast of Newfoundland. Canada had first expressed an interest in these islands in 1903 (at a time when France's long-standing rights to dry fish on the western shore of Newfoundland were under review) and during the British government's territorial investigations of 1916 the possibility was raised of an exchange with France based on British possessions in the Cameroons. Unfortunately however, the islands had also attracted the serious attention of the Newfoundland government, and claims had also been lodged on their behalf with the Colonial Office. By the time the Curzon committee came to discuss the position in 1917, the principal concern of British officials was to put off as far as possible any decision on these two rival appeals. In the end the Colonial Office had its way in this matter. The Curzon committee was allowed to confirm an imperial interest in the two islands, but it was to be left to France to take any initiative for an exchange.

The possibilities for Canadian territorial expansion seemed exhausted. But Canada's boldest bid in 1917 was for territory already within the British empire. The dominion, Hazen proposed to a surprised committee, should take over the West Indies. This idea was by no means a new one, having since the 1870s attracted a variety of support from interest groups both in Canada and the West Indian islands, though there had been little enough to show for their efforts over the years.[38] The one area of more sustained interest had been trade. In 1909 a Royal Commission had investigated the possibilities in this field, and their report had led to an agreement of 1912 whereby Canada and several of the islands agreed to a mutual tariff reduction of 20% for each other's products. The idea of political union had meanwhile continued to enjoy little serious attention. But in 1916 the Canadian government began to take an official interest

over Greenland. All agreed, but Britain (with full Canadian support) added a reservation that she would not necessarily recognize Denmark's right to sell Greenland to a third party. CO 886/9/79: correspondence between Britain, Canada and Denmark, Nov 1919–June 1920.

[38] The 'Canada First' movement had urged closer commercial and political relations with the West Indies in their platform of 1874. Ten years later a member of the Jamaican legislative council had discussed political union with Canada with prime minister Sir John A. Macdonald. 'It cannot come to anything', thought Macdonald, but he considered it 'a high compliment to Canada to have such a desire to join her political system coming from other Colonies.' External Affairs 25/G1/1205: Macdonald–Tupper, 4 June 1884. See more generally R. W. Winks, *Canadian–West Indian Union: A Forty-Year Minuet* (London, 1968).

in this matter, in response, it seems, to a number of enthusiastic letters on the subject of union received by the prime minister from a Canadian business in Jamaica, H. J. Crowe.[39] Possibly Borden's own strong roots in the Canadian maritimes further influenced his feelings towards the West Indies. His own province of Nova Scotia conducted a substantial part of Canada's trade with the islands, and moreover his own constituency of Halifax had a considerable black population. By June 1916, at any rate, Borden had written to his high commissioner in London, outlining the advantages of West Indian union and asking Perley to pursue this possibility with the Colonial Office.[40] Commercial gains aside, Borden made two telling observations to Perley:

The responsibility of governing subject races would probably exercise a broadening influence upon our people as the Dominion thus constituted would closely resemble in its problems and its duties the Empire as a whole.

The importance of sea power would become so obvious under the new conditions as to leave little room for arguments to the contrary.

Despite such 'imperial' arguments, Perley reported that the Colonial Office were quite unwilling to discuss the matter, at least for the duration of the war. Even so, Borden was not inclined to let it drop, and the Canadian delegation left for the 1917 London talks armed with a strong memorandum from the Department of External Affairs which urged the rightness of Canada's claims to the West Indies.[41]

In the event, however, it proved impossible to raise the question in Curzon's territorial committee, because the chairman ruled – no doubt under Colonial Office pressure – that as a purely imperial issue the future of the West Indies was outside the committee's terms of reference. And indeed behind this expedient ruling Colonial Office antipathies to Borden's designs were very strong. Where it was a question of Canada expanding into *new* territory the department could be sympathetic: in the case of Greenland, for instance, the permanent under-secretary had noted that 'The other Dom[inion]s have a prospect of getting something out of Germany; Canada has not.' But growth at the expense of the dependent empire was out of the question. Jealous of their own administrative functions at the best of times, the Colonial Office had already in 1917 seen their control of dominion affairs gravely undermined by the setting

39 Borden papers: Crowe–Borden, April–May 1916.
40 Borden papers: Borden–Perley, 3 June 1916.
41 External Affairs 25/G1/1205: memorandum, 31 Jan 1917. The memorandum makes it clear that the government were contemplating something closer to annexation than partnership with the islands, though hopes were expressed that after a transition period the blacks could be allowed the vote.

up of the Imperial War Cabinet. All the more reason to withstand a further challenge – by a dominion itself – to their colonial patrimony. Assistant under-secretary Henry Lambert minuted tersely:

I hope no countenance will be given to the [Canadian] idea. The Canadian Gov[ernment] is one of the least efficient in the Empire – that is the unvarnished truth – There is not only no reason to suppose that the W[est] Indies would desire a transfer but good reason to the contrary. And if Canada is to be admitted to the Cabinet here, there is less reason than ever that she should take out of our hands what we have up till now administered.[42]

Canadian union with the West Indies was not pursued further in 1917, though it was not abandoned by Borden. Nor was it forgotten in Whitehall, for it had attracted the interest and support of Milner and Amery. In their view dominion control of dependent territories represented a promising opportunity for tangible imperial integration, offering the prospect of a system in which the overseas governments could share with Britain not only imperial defence and foreign policy, but also imperial administration. There can be little doubt, furthermore, that the idea of developments along these lines was put before Lloyd George by the Milner group, and it will be convenient here to look ahead a little – for when Borden returned to London for the 1918 Imperial War Cabinet he found the British prime minister readily agreeable to a Canada–West Indies union.[43] Amery himself by this time had even greater plans, envisaging 'a Greater Dominion of British North America, including Newfoundland, the Bermudas, the West Indies, and even, if you liked to have them thrown in, the Falkland Islands'.[44] Once more, however, no definite decisions were taken. Borden returned home, the war ended, and when he was next in London the larger problems of the peace settlement appear to have precluded further discussion of the matter. Yet the omens remained favourable. Milner and Amery were moved to the Colonial Office in January 1919, and Borden himself had a willing parliamentary disciple in Ottawa who was ready to do any necessary work behind the scenes – ready, he told Borden,

[42] CO 537/1156: minute of 17 April 1917. Compare Colonial Office logic in 1911. At that time they accepted that dominions were likely to take over dependent colonies – and indeed used this as an argument for retaining full administrative control over dominion and colonial affairs alike! See J. A. Cross, *Whitehall and the Commonwealth* (London, 1967), 33. Even so they were quite opposed to a Canada–West Indies union. Winks, *Minuet*, 24 ff.

[43] H. Borden (ed), *Robert Laird Borden: His Memoirs*, 2 vols (London, 1938), II, 844.

[44] Borden papers: Amery–Borden, 18 Aug 1918.

to begin to plan quietly and systematically, a movement, especially among those Islands who are in favour of closer union with us, and endeavour to help it along until it comes to a point in which [sic!] negotiations should be commenced.[45]

From London Borden encouraged this campaign to proceed.

Despite some discreet Canadian initiatives, however, the project of union was to have no issue. Public opinion in the West Indies was evidently less tractable than at first supposed, and there was also some resistance from the governors of the islands, and talk of a West Indian confederation before any union with Canada. Meanwhile, Borden's relations with Milner and Amery were somewhat compromised by his insistence on Canadian signature and ratification of the Versailles treaty, a problem which overshadowed the union project. Finally (and possibly decisively) the Canadian project ran up against the entrenched interests of the United Fruit Company of Boston, who added their own powerful voice to the swelling chorus of opposition.[46] In 1920 the Canadian government managed to convene another trade conference with the islands, but by then the talk of federation was over. It was all the government could do to achieve a commercial agreement.

Policymaking and consultation

The Imperial War Cabinet and War Conference concluded their 1917 sessions in early May, and with the understanding that they would be reconvening in London in a year's time the dominion delegations departed for their overseas capitals. Smuts, prevailed upon by Lloyd George to lend his administrative talents to the British government, reluctantly agreed to stay behind in London and was seconded to the British war cabinet for the duration of the war. By all accounts the 1917 imperial meetings had been a major success. The dominion leaders had received the general appreciation of the war effort they so badly lacked, they had been sounded as to the possible terms on which the empire might make peace, and they had also managed to reach agreement in principle as regards future participation with Britain in the conduct of imperial affairs. They carried home fresh determination to drive the war through to its finish. Meanwhile, their endorsement of Lloyd George's attempts to control and improve the war effort represented welcome support for the British prime minister, always conscious of the need to strengthen his own executive position. It was clearly politically important for him, given the time and

[45] Borden papers: Frank Keefer–Borden, 6 Dec 1918. Keefer was Borden's parliamentary under-secretary for external affairs.
[46] Borden papers: H. Crowe–Loring Christie (External Affairs), 26 Nov 1919.

effort that had been invested in the imperial discussions, that they should be seen as an effective instrument for stimulating yet further the war output of the overseas empire.

But Lloyd George was not the only imperial premier who was anxious to turn the London talks to his domestic political advantage. Borden, once back in Canada, was obliged to confront a political situation that had been deteriorating alarmingly for half a year or more, and which now threatened to undermine his government's control over war policy. The manifold problems of Canada's war efforts which had engaged the Borden ministry month by long month since 1914 must fall largely outside the scope of this study, but it will be enough to indicate that the government had been compelled to operate in an increasingly bitter political environment. In short, the political truce so willingly proclaimed by Laurier at the start of hostilities had long since collapsed, to the point where by early 1917 the Liberal opposition whips had even begun to refuse 'pairs' for back-bench Conservatives serving in the armed forces.[47] And all of this at a time when a 1917 general election appeared unavoidable. The Canadian Parliament elected in 1911 had already been extended by mutual consent with the Liberals for one year to October 1917, but it seemed highly doubtful that with a possible victory within reach (by-elections and provincial elections were running strongly in their favour) the opposition leadership would agree to any further extensions. There was talk amongst Conservatives of seeking a coalition with English-speaking Liberals, as the only possible way of keeping a Laurier government from office.

What added immeasurably to the already heightened political tension, however, was the prime minister's settled conviction that the 1917 session of parliament must be asked to approve a plan of conscription for the Canadian military forces. Even before the Imperial War Cabinet talks in London, and the revelations about the general military situation there disclosed, the figures about the manpower consumption rate of Canada's own army units were beginning to speak for themselves. After August 1916 the dominion had four divisions at the western front, and these were literally being decimated every month; each division of 20,000 called for 24,000 replacements a year. At the turn of the new year there were only 65,000 reserves in England – eight months' supply – and by this time recruiting in Canada had dwindled to negligible proportions.[48] Thus there

---

[47] Borden had to ask Perley to round up those officers not active at the front and send them home to the parliamentary duties, though it seems that few heeded their prime minister's call. Perley papers: Borden–Perley, 28 Nov 1916, Perley–Borden 9 Jan 1917.

[48] Figures from Perley–Borden, 10 Nov 1916; *DCER*, I, 149. The War Office,

were serious doubts whether the dominion could continue to fulfil the military obligations it had assumed for itself. By extension, the image of his country that Borden had so persistently projected in London – that Canada was no mere colonial assistant to Britain in this war, but an imperial partner in its own right – was in danger of being exposed as a facade. Conscription appeared to be the only solution; though as Borden well knew, conscription would be bitterly opposed in parliament by Laurier and would be resisted outright by French Canada. Here was the prime minister's crucial dilemma. He could maintain a Canadian national identity at the fighting front, it seemed, only by severely undermining the foundations of that identity at home.

There was, then, every need to construe the results of the 1917 imperial discussions to Borden's best advantage, so that the government and the Conservative party might regain a measure of popular political support. For if conscription was to work it would require the widest agreement, both in parliament and across the country. And the only possible justification for conscription was to demonstrate that the advance of Canada's standing in the empire, as manifested in the London meetings as well as the western front, was sufficient to warrant such a national sacrifice. The case that Borden put to the House of Commons, in a long speech on 18 May, was therefore firmly centred on this essential connection between conscription and Canada's imperial relations. In a full review of what had passed in London he gave what details he could of the Imperial Cabinet and the Conference, and dwelt in particular on the importance of the latter's constitutional resolution. He made no secret of his own initiative in promoting the conclusions about constitutional reform, and he looked forward to the next meeting of the Imperial War Cabinet and beyond that to the constitutional conference to come after the war. Through the agreements reached in London the dominions had won a vital new position alongside the British government in the making of imperial policies, and Borden could candidly announce the terms of the new relationship:

it is not proposed that the Government of the United Kingdom shall, in foreign affairs, act first and consult us afterwards. The principle had been definitely and finally laid down that in these matters the Dominions shall be consulted before the Empire is committed to any policy which might involve the issues of peace and war.[49]

oblivious of the Canadian difficulties, continued to press the dominion government to turn the reserves into a fifth division for the front.
Perley–Borden, 10 Nov 1916, WO–Gov Gen, 25 May 1917; *ibid*, 149, 163.
[49] Canada, HoC, 18 May 1917.

Meanwhile, however, Canada must meet its obligations on the battlefield, and much depended on the dominion's performance: 'I conceive that the battle for Canadian liberty *and autonomy* is being fought today on the plains of France and of Belgium'[50] – a dual responsibility that in the face of existing losses could only be met with compulsory military service. Conscription, then, was justified as a means not simply of winning the war but also of preserving Canada's imperial standing; and it was that standing, by turns, which ultimately made conscription necessary. On the prime minister's terms the case was complete, the logical circle closed.

In the event, the carrying through of conscription engaged the Canadian government's political energies for the rest of 1917, and it was not until a coalition had been formed with English–Canadian elements of the Liberal party, and a fresh mandate obtained through a general election, that the programme could at last begin to yield recruits. But our own attention at this point must be on the other side of the picture. Borden had invoked Canada's broadening imperial responsibilities in asking for conscription. To what extent could the claims made on the dominion's behalf now be substantiated?

Given that detailed changes in the relations between Britain and the dominions were to be left to the ending of the war, it would be wrong to expect that major innovations would be set in train while the fighting remained to be finished. We might look, nonetheless, for the beginnings of change in official attitudes – for attempts to accommodate within the existing imperial structures the acknowledged demands of the dominions to be brought closer to the policymaking centre of British wartime control. In a negative sense, at the least, there did appear to be some confirmation of a new dominion status in 1917. When Borden nearly five years previously had come back from London and boldly announced to the House of Commons that Canada would henceforward be consulted on all critical imperial policies by the British government, an unqualified repudiation of his statement was quickly cabled out from Whitehall.[51] This time, there were no counter-claims advanced against his assessment of how things stood now the Imperial War Cabinet had met and completed its 1917 sessions. It remained to be seen what practical results would follow.

To a large extent any initiative for change lay with the Colonial Office. The Imperial War Cabinet had itself provided only a temporary arena for policy discussions, and until it could be reconvened the Colonial Office remained the one official channel of communication and consultation

---

[50] *Ibid*, my italics.　　　　　　[51] See above, 18.

linking the British and overseas governments. Characteristically, however, the Colonial Office continued to believe that the existing system was completely adequate to the needs of the dominion governments. Indeed the Dominions Department thought that in calling for constitutional changes, resolution ix of the Imperial War Conference was not only unclear but also gratuitous, in that communication through the Colonial Office could already provide the 'continuous consultation' Borden was demanding.[52] Yet in the circumstances of 1917 this was a dangerously blinkered attitude. Even accepting a genuine concern to alert the dominions in questions that did touch their interests, the Colonial Office continued to be badly handicapped by the exclusion of Walter Long from the war cabinet. We have noted his petition for a cabinet seat immediately the Lloyd George government was formed. By February 1917, he was desperate enough to ask whether he could attend the war cabinet if he promised only to listen! – but even on these bizarre terms he was not allowed a regular seat.[53] Under these conditions it required a watching brief of considerable vigilance, if not an impervious sense of their own importance, for the Colonial Office to maintain that no major changes in the machinery of consultation were necessary.

A matter which exemplified the Office's difficulties arose in August 1917. The war cabinet had appointed a sub-committee to study the policy of 'the clean slate',[54] and in that month they presented their report, a copy of which duly reached the Colonial Office. With the report, however, came the unofficial knowledge that the government were anxious to begin negotiations on the policy with France and were not intending to consult the dominions, in spite of the fact that dominion co-operation would be essential in any agreement with the allies. Supported by his officials, Long chose to act on his own initiative. Without consulting the war cabinet (who had yet to approve it themselves) he sent the report to the dominions for their views, noting in the minutes: 'There is no subject upon wh[ich] the Representatives of dom[inion]s expressed themselves more strongly than the necessity of Consultation before action.'[55]

[52] CO 532/108: minute of Henry Lambert, 29 March 1917, on Borden's draft resolution.

[53] Lloyd George papers: Long–Ll. G., 8 Feb 1917.

[54] A policy whereby at a future peace settlement all legal claims of enemy nations or individuals against allied governments or individuals would not be allowed.

[55] CO 532/99: report of sub-committee; Long, minute of 11 Sept 1917; telegram to dominions, 21 Sept 1917. Long's action brought no reprisals from the war cabinet, though allied discussions appear to have been postponed, in any case, until 1918.

By expedient action of this kind the Colonial Office endeavoured to keep the dominions in the picture with regard to British policy, making sure that on the 'clean slate' policy, and such matters as the control of imports and exports after the war, no inter-allied agreements were reached without prior dominion consultation. It was a useful, even ambitious effort. But it brought the dominions nowhere near the crucial issues of war policy. Thus while the colonial secretary hovered unhappily in the wings, the stage was set by the war cabinet and the British high command for the major 1917 military campaign in Flanders. Never mind that Lloyd George himself had publicly enthused about the dominions' 'right to real partnership' in war policy.[56] Without a word to the overseas governments the Flanders battle began on 7 June, the main assault following on 31 July. By this time, indeed, even a seat on the war cabinet would have given Long small hope of involving the dominions in military policymaking. That subject was now solely the prerogative of Lloyd George and a new secret cabinet committee containing only Curzon, Smuts and Milner.[57]

So another terrible campaign season dragged on, with the dominions no better placed to determine the course of events than they had been since the war began. Lloyd George ignored them, and the Colonial Office could do no more than put up a bold front to cover their lack of contact with the centre of executive authority. The dominions were once again too easily taken for granted, and it was apparent that when in November 1917 the Canadian government actually made an attempt of their own to secure some direct policy consultation about the war, the British authorities were singularly unresponsive. Borden had heard unofficially that an inter-allied conference was about to be held, and always ready to cross the Atlantic if summoned, he had been bold enough to inquire if Canada was to be represented – an 'apparently harmless enquiry' behind which the Foreign Office were quick to see 'serious constitutional difficulties'.[58] The war cabinet were ready to agree: the inquiry 'raised issues of principle affecting the whole relation of the Dominions to the British Government', and decided that 'the actual attendance of Dominion representatives at such a Conference was undesirable unless they came as British representatives'. And even this type of representation, as their reply made clear, was not going to be encouraged:

In the opinion of His Majesty's Government the real value of the forthcoming Conference and of similar international Conferences has lain not in the formal

[56] *The Times*, 27 April 1917, quoted in Cook, 'Sir Robert Borden'.
[57] Roskill, *Hankey*, I, 401.
[58] FO 371/3011: Sir George Clark, minute, n.d.

meetings, at which far too many persons and interests have to be represented to enable any great value to attach to the deliberations, but in the opportunity provided by them for informal conversations outside the formal meetings between the leading statesmen of the great Powers.[59]

Thus the Canadians, and for good measure the other dominions as well, were firmly warned against meddling in such affairs. In an attempt to end on a more encouraging note, however, the war cabinet affirmed that they were always prepared to be consulted should any accredited dominion ministers find themselves in London.

As the British government were no doubt aware, this idea of ministerial consultations in London was not much favoured by the dominions, since to brief any visiting minister normally required the same laborious cable communications that were needed for orthodox consultations conducted through the Colonial Office. It so happened, however, that the Canadian government for once were well placed to take up the British offer in spite of the inherent inconveniences, for only a few weeks previously they had appointed to London Sir Edward Kemp as minister of overseas military forces. At Borden's request, therefore, Kemp was duly invited to attend the war cabinet on 3 January 1918. And as it turned out the occasion was potentially one on which a Canadian opinion might have been of influence, since the cabinet were considering the draft of an official ministerial announcement on war aims, to be delivered by Lloyd George. At three successive meetings, each of which Kemp attended, the statement was carefully prepared; and in a rare secretarial footnote to the war cabinet minutes, Hankey recorded:

It will be observed that by the presence of the Secretary of State for the Colonies, General Smuts and Sir Edward Kemp, Imperial participation in the decision was secured so far as this was possible in the urgent circumstances of the moment.[60]

There is no record, alas, of any contribution from Kemp to the discussion. He did not ask Ottawa for instructions, nor did he cable home an appreciation of British intentions. Instead he wrote Borden a letter, which reached him long after Lloyd George had made his policy speech – a speech that proved to be the most complete statement of British war aims to be made during the war.[61] After such unpromising results, Borden did not employ Kemp in any further consultations with the British war cabinet.

[59] CAB 23/4: WC 281, 22 Nov 1917; CO 532/107: Col Sec–Govs Gen, 27 Nov 1917.
[60] CAB 23/5: WC 314, 4 Jan 1918.
[61] The text of the statement is in Lloyd George, *War Memoirs*, II, 1510.

In the search for a fresh avenue of contact to link Canada in some meaning-ful way with British policymaking, Borden might well have turned to the other Canadian representative in London, Sir George Perley. Certainly Perley himself was anxious enough, in late 1917, to be of service in this regard. After three and a half years in London as acting high commissioner (he had retained the post of minister without portfolio in Borden's government) Perley had chosen to give up his cabinet position and become full high commissioner. But when he heard about the British government's willingness to allow visiting dominion ministers to be used for inter-government consultations, he saw a possible opportunity to regain his dual status. As soon as the Canadian election of December 1917 was over and Borden safely returned to power, Perley put his case to the prime minister:

> my experience has shown me that it would strengthen the position of the Dominions in this country if each of them always had a member of the Government over here. The best way to bring this about would be to change the status of the High Commissioner for this purpose ... I think the plan suggested would help us to carry on Canada's business more satisfactorily and it would be a great pleasure to me if this forward step took place during my term of office.[62]

The high commissioner's proposal, however, was not taken up. Borden, it appeared, was not prepared to allow even such a close and trusted colleague to combine cabinet and high commissioner status.

It is worth noting that the Colonial Office were themselves most concerned to prevent Perley from becoming a medium for official consul-tations between the British and Canadian governments. In the cabinet discussion that had followed Canada's inquiry about the inter-allied con-ference, the colonial secretary, supported by a departmental memorandum, had emphasized strongly that if any scheme of ministerial consultations were to be accepted by the war cabinet it must not be extended to include the dominion high commissioners. In the Colonial Office view, the high commissioners were not members of their governments but 'officials who, like Civil Servants in this country, have no authority beyond the scope of their instructions' and who were thus unable to speak for their govern-ments on policy questions without extensive cable communications. More-over, as they were appointed for fixed terms, they did not always enjoy the confidence of their governments. Visiting dominion ministers, on the other hand, stood 'in an entirely different position', although the colonial secretary would feel obliged in any case to confirm with a dominion government before entering upon confidential discussions. In short, 'the

---

[62] Borden papers: Perley–Borden, 12 Dec 1917.

established practice of the Empire is to conduct all important business with the Governor General, who is in immediate touch with Ministers'.[63]

For the Colonial Office, here lay the touchstone of all arguments concerning relations between Great Britain and the dominions. However those relations might evolve, at no point should the constitutional position of the governor general – as both the head of the executive government of his dominion, and the channel through which affairs with Great Britain were directed – be compromised by changing methods of communication or consultation. The question of official consultation through the high commissioners began and ended at this point. If such channels of communication were allowed to develop, the governor general, and *a fortiori* the Colonial Office, would find themselves superfluous to the conduct of relations with the dominions. For all their honest efforts in attempting to provide consultation for the dominions under the existing system, the Colonial Office remained firmly opposed to any modifications in the system's essential design. Their stubborn conviction, noted above, that Borden's 1917 constitutional resolution IX was unnecessary sprang in the last analysis from the fundamental instinct of bureaucratic self-preservation.

With regard to the Canadian high commissioner, it appeared that in December 1917 the Colonial Office and the Canadian government were in unspoken agreement, neither wanting to encourage Perley's ambitions. A few months later, however, a second question concerning Perley showed that the agreement had been largely fortuitous; and showed also that Borden was not prepared to let Colonial Office tradition stand in the way of closer communications between the British and Canadian governments. The dispute arose over whether Perley should receive copies of the correspondence which passed between the Colonial Office and the Canadian governor general, a privilege he had had as an overseas member of the Canadian cabinet but one which had been removed by the Colonial Office after he left the Borden ministry. Possibly because he was not immediately aware of the ending of the arrangement (he continued to receive a selection of dispatches from the Colonial Office) but probably because he was unsure of his government's support, the high commissioner did not petition the Colonial Office for the full correspondence until he was prompted by an inquiry from Borden himself in April 1918. Once aware of Borden's interest, however, Perley immediately pressed the colonial secretary on the matter, and when Long proved obstinate complained loudly to the Canadian prime minister:

[63] CO 532/99: Henry Lambert, memorandum on status of high commissioners, 25 Nov 1917.

This means decision which despatches will be sent to me rests with some clerk in Colonial Office and experience has shown result unsatisfactory and must necessarily reduce efficiency this office and power of being helpful.[64]

To Perley's request, and to one from Borden which followed it, the Colonial Office continued to give short shrift. The proposed change 'would have a most damaging effect on the position of the Gov[ernor] Gen[eral]' and 'very likely has had in Canada'. Moreover, Perley's argument from reduced efficiency was 'a wholly unmerited reflection on his predecessor & his colleagues'.[65] A strongly worded refusal was sent to Canada on 8 May 1918:

I must really claim the right [Walter Long informed the governor general] to conduct my correspondence with Governors General in accordance with my own views of what is proper and I entertain insuperable objection to the course proposed. I hope you will convey this to Borden tactfully but clearly.[66]

Tact and clarity did not win the day, however, and in the face of continuing Canadian pressure, the Colonial Office were driven back upon a truly desperate constitutional defence. To arguments about the position of the governor general and the dislike of special privileges for Perley, the permanent under-secretary added:

Sir Robert Borden is asking for something which he could not demand if Canada were an independent state. No Foreign Power would dream of demanding that the Secretary of State for Foreign Affairs should communicate to its Ambassador in London the despatches which he wrote to the British Ambassador abroad.[67]

The analogy was grotesque. Canada was not an independent state, and the measure of her lack of independence was exactly the difference between the Canadian high commissioner and a foreign ambassador in London – or equally, the difference between the Canadian governor general and a British ambassador abroad. It was precisely because of these differences that the Canadian request could be made. The Colonial Office, it seemed, wished to have it both ways: to insist upon the paramountcy of the governor general, but also in this case to recognize Canada as an autonomous nation within the empire–commonwealth – if only to depreciate the status of her high commissioner.

In the end the Colonial Office had to concede, after Borden, returning to London for the 1918 Imperial War Cabinet, raised the matter directly

---

[64] Borden papers: Perley–Borden, 2 May 1918.
[65] CO 42/1010: Lambert, minute of 25 April 1918.
[66] CO 42/1007: Col Sec–Gov Gen, 8 May 1918.
[67] CO 42/1010: Sir G. Fiddes, minutes of 18 June 1918.

with Lloyd George. Forced to accept other important changes in communications (as will be seen) the Colonial Office had to accept this one as well. On 14 August the colonial secretary's full correspondence with the governor general was at last made available to the Canadian high commissioner.

For the Colonial Office this clash with the Canadian government was a profitless exercise in constitutional propriety. In the face of Borden's not unreasonable demand, their self-righteous truculence made nonsense of their conviction that they were providing for the dominions a perfectly adequate amount of information and an adequate opportunity for consultation. Even more alarming, the Dominions Department still seemed convinced that the overseas governments would remain content to leave all further questions of imperial relations until the end of the war. Shortly before the 1918 Imperial War Cabinet, Henry Lambert could minute dismissively:

So far extraordinary little interest – I should say extraordinary perhaps only on the assumption that the Empire is pining for a change – has been taken in [the subject] of the Empire's constitution.[68]

It was an illusory calm before the storm. In spite of the supposed moratorium imposed by resolution ix in 1917, the subject of imperial relations was raised by both Borden and the Australian prime minister William Hughes soon after they arrived in London. And there can be little doubt that Borden's own determination to discuss these issues had been stiffened appreciably by the uncompromising attitude of the Colonial Office over the matter of correspondence for Perley.

The Imperial War Cabinet, 1918

The Imperial War Cabinet reconvened in London in June 1918, and alongside it the Imperial War Conference met again at the Colonial Office. Leaving the Conference once more to deal with topics of secondary importance, the Imperial Cabinet immediately turned to an assessment of the war effort over the preceding twelve months. From the dominions' point of view, the British government had a good deal to account for. The 1917 offensive in Flanders had been a total failure, relentlessly pursued to a stalemate at terrible human cost; the campaign of 1918 seemed even less promising, with German forces themselves on the attack in several sectors along the western front. Moreover, at no point in this deteriorating situation had the overseas governments been called into consultation by the British administration, or offered any insight into the strategic policy

[68] CO 532/115: minute, 17 May 1918.

behind the military operations. Lloyd George in his opening review could do little more than report these unpalatable facts, though in mitigation he did remind dominion ministers that the collapse of Russia, and the slowness of the Americans to organize their forces effectively, had combined to count heavily against the allied efforts at the western front.[69] The British prime minister had no doubt that unconditional victory must remain the empire's goal – though on the evidence he was obliged to present that goal seemed no nearer in 1918 than it had a year before.

In 1917 an unvarnished account of the military situation to the Imperial War Cabinet had brought a positive determined response from overseas leaders, who were generally ready to accept past mistakes on the promise of a more flexible and coherent military policy for the future. But with so little improvement – either military or administrative – after a further twelve months of fighting, they were not prepared to show such forbearance a second time, and the atmosphere in the opening sessions of the Imperial Cabinet was distinctly more critical than in 1917. Once again a strong lead was taken by Borden, speaking this time from an altogether more assured position. Seniority aside (with Smuts representing as much the British as the South African point of view and Hughes in the Imperial Cabinet for the first time, the Canadian prime minister was bound to be the most prominent dominion voice) Borden now had dominant political control at home as a result of the December 1917 election, a valuable asset to bring to London (an asset that Hughes, after less fortunate political developments in Australia, lacked at these meetings). He also had in General Arthur Currie, field commander of a newly-consolidated Canadian Army Corps, a direct and high-level source of military information, and in putting together his opening speech to the Imperial Cabinet Borden drew heavily on Currie's personal criticisms of the British high command as reinforcement for his own profound misgivings about the conduct of the war. Thus while accepting Lloyd George's explanations as far as they went, Borden wasted no words in presenting a forceful indictment of the British military authorities, and concluded with feeling:

We came over to fight in earnest; and Canada will see it through to the end. But earnestness must be expressed in organization, foresight and preparation. Let the past bury the dead, but for God's sake let us get down to earnest endeavour and hold this line until the Americans can come and help us to sustain it to the end. The Americans are in earnest and they and Canada will unite to win the war unless some of the rest of you mend your ways.[70]

[69] CAB 23/43: IWC 15, 11 June 1918.
[70] CAB 23/43: IWC 16, 13 June 1918. Lloyd George told Hankey 'he had ascertained that Smuts had prompted Borden', Roskill, *Hankey*, 1, 563.

Borden's vehement indictment had not been anticipated by the British government. Lloyd George, even so, managed to turn it to his own advantage. Since the end of the 1917 Imperial War Cabinet he had paid scant attention to the overseas governments, neither consulting them over military policy nor appealing to them for support in his political struggles against the British high command, and it was clearly his own neglect as much as the lack of military success that accounted for their hostility. He responded at once, however, to Borden's criticisms about the conduct of military operations, because he saw in these a means of avoiding censure himself and possibly of improving his own control over the military authorities. Promptly he allowed the Imperial War Cabinet's review of the war effort to turn into a full-scale inquest into the conduct of military strategy, and to facilitate this he not only circulated to overseas ministers the minutes from June 1917 of his war policy committee (which at least indicated his own misgivings about the campaigns then about to begin) but on Hankey's suggestion brought the prime ministers together into a small and powerful committee. With them Lloyd George not only went over the 1917 campaigns (he remained as critical of the military command as any) but also set out to determine an over-all strategy for the successful conclusion of the war.[71] The prime ministers' committee, in fact, became a general inner executive of the Imperial Cabinet, attending not only to long-term policies but also to day-to-day problems, which it then referred to the larger body for approval.[72] It was in the committee, for example, that a firm decision was first taken in favour of allied military intervention in Siberia to reconstruct the Russian war effort, with the Canadian prime minister agreeing to provide nearly three-quarters of the empire's forces on this new front. In early July this proposal was officially endorsed by the allied powers at a meeting of the Supreme War Council in Paris.

Thus within a fortnight of their arrival in London the overseas premiers found themselves right at the centre of imperial policymaking, dealing with a wide variety of critical and current problems. This activity contrasted absolutely with the isolation they had endured – and would have to face again – when the Imperial War Cabinet was not in session. It is hardly surprising, therefore, that even as they began their study of war policy the dominion prime ministers had already decided amongst

[71] CAB 23/44: committee of prime ministers, 1918. At its first meeting the committee noted that the dominions 'should have a direct voice in the conduct of the war, and in the plans of campaign, so far as the War Cabinet had power to determine them'.

[72] See Hankey, *Supreme Command*, II, 816. As usual, Hankey provided the essential administrative co-ordination.

themselves that this time they must press for changes in the channels of empire communication; and at the end of June Borden duly informed Lloyd George that, in their view, Colonial Office control over communications between the British and dominion governments should cease, not only for the sake of improved consultation but also for clear reasons of status:

The idea of nation-hood [he told Lloyd George] has developed wonderfully of late in my own Dominion; I believe the same is true of all the Dominions. Their Prime Ministers meet with British Ministers on terms of equality around the Council Board. That important advance seems utterly inconsistent with the continuance of a system under which they are, in effect, attached to a Department of the Home Government.[73]

Despite the opposition of the colonial secretary, alarmed at this challenge to his authority, an examination of the machinery of British–dominion relations was held in the Imperial War Cabinet on 23 July.

In the event, the scope of the debate quickly broadened beyond the limited subject of imperial communications, becoming in effect a continuation of the more general 1917 talks on imperial constitutional change. Borden himself emphasized at the outset that improved cable communications between governments was only a first step towards the full participation of the dominions in imperial foreign policy. For that, he admitted, further constitutional changes would be necessary, but as a reminder that he expected such changes to come soon he was prepared to warn that

unless [Canada] could have that voice in the foreign relations of the Empire as a whole, she would before long have an independent voice in her own foreign affairs outside the Empire.[74]

This emphatic declaration was itself enough to add wide new dimensions to the discussion, and thus once again the Imperial Cabinet found themselves exploring the manifold problems pertaining to consultation and joint policymaking, and wondering afresh about resident dominion ministers in London, and, by extension, about the possibility of a permanent Imperial Cabinet.

The British ministerial delegation, generally reticent in 1917 apart from Lord Milner, this time showed altogether more enthusiasm for the inquiry into administrative and constitutional reforms, and they were inclined to think (with the exception of the colonial secretary) that any reforms that could be agreed on should be carried through at once without waiting

[73] Lloyd George papers: Borden–Ll. G., 28 June 1918.
[74] CAB 23/43: IWC 26, 23 July 1918.

for the post-war constitutional conference. As Winston Churchill dramatically expressed it, in the heat of the war 'the metal was now molten and could be moulded'.[75] Lloyd George was ready to establish an informal committee that could start work at once on constitutional changes. But the pace, and possibly the direction, of these proposed developments proved in the end to be unacceptable to the overseas leaders, W. M. Hughes in particular displaying extreme caution where constitutional matters were concerned. Had he been present in 1917 to support Borden and Smuts in their opposition to federationist plans he might perhaps have been less apprehensive at this point. As it was, fearing that even informal discussions might inadvertently commit the dominions to imperial federation of one sort or another, he refused to sanction any further explorations – with the result that constitutional changes were firmly postponed to the end of the war. The Imperial War Cabinet contented themselves with more modest reforms. On communications, there was ready agreement that for matters 'of Cabinet importance' there should be direct access between prime ministers – a vital breach of Colonial Office privileges. With regard to improved consultation between governments, the only feasible administrative advance lay in extending the practice of visiting or resident overseas ministers, through whom the Imperial War Cabinet might be able to meet from time to time between its annual plenary sessions. A resolution to this effect was duly passed, although Hughes at least was honest enough to admit that policy consultations without the dominion prime ministers themselves could hardly prove effective.

The use of resident ministers, it is clear, was accepted as no more than an expedient, designed to keep overseas prime ministers in touch with decisions taken in London rather than to give them an effective voice in policymaking. This was particularly true as regards foreign policy. Indeed, throughout the discussions over consultation, the major problem of sharing the responsibility for a single foreign policy had barely been acknowledged. There had been no attempt to determine which questions of policy the dominions might have a voice in, and, except for the peace settlement no promises that they would be consulted on any specific issues. The control of imperial foreign policy remained firmly in the hands of the British government.

As it happened, the control of military policy also remained in British hands. In the middle of August the committee of prime ministers at last completed their assessment of this subject, only to find that even after six

---

[75] *Ibid*: IWC 27, 25 July 1918. Churchill, rebuilding his political career after the repercussions of the disastrous Dardanelles expedition of 1915, had returned to ministerial office under Lloyd George as minister of munitions in July 1917.

weeks they had not managed to produce a very incisive report. They met to consider their efforts for a last time on 16 August, Borden noting guardedly in his diary:

We went over draft report and I gave my views on each of the recommendations some of which I criticized. On the whole a useful and instructive report, necessarily not very definite as conclusions respecting operations next year cannot be absolutely certain at this stage.[76]

Tentative as it was, the report still failed to receive a unanimous endorsement from the committee, Lloyd George in particular finding it too biased in favour of military operations on the western front.[77] Had the committee been able to stay in session possibly further modifications would have brought them all into line, but the Imperial War Cabinet's other work was over, and it was time to finish. Under the circumstances, it was perhaps just as well that even as the prime ministers' committee broke up, the march of events on the western front began to supersede the strategic arguments in their report. Within a few short weeks it had become happily irrelevant.

The unexpected break in the military stalemate, coming just as the Imperial Cabinet and Conference were concluding their discussions, rather overshadowed the results of their work. To some extent it also confused the intended purpose of their conclusions, obviously upsetting military calculations but also leaving administrative policies without clear guidelines. In establishing direct communications, and the right to use resident ministers, the Imperial Cabinet were trying to reduce the power of the Colonial Office and to place some of the responsibility for dominion affairs in the hands of the Cabinet Office. Throughout the autumn of 1918, however, Hughes and Massey (and for a time premier Lloyd of Newfoundland) stayed in England, and because the channels of official communication were thus confused it was difficult to tell how the new system would work.

In the Colonial Office, certainly, there was little cause for celebration. Their first attempt at co-operation with the Cabinet Office came in late August 1918, in connection with the dispatch of war cabinet documents

[76] Diary, 16 Aug 1918.

[77] Hankey, *Supreme Command*, II, 830–2. The report was based to a large extent on a memorandum of General Sir Henry Wilson, C.I.G.S., which had emphasized the western front to the exclusion of other theatres of operation. Hughes of Australia also refused to sign the report, though according to Borden he did not take a full interest in it: 'Then to Prime Ministers' Com[mittee] to take up draft report but as usual Hughes had not read it.' Diary, 14 Aug 1918.

to the overseas governments. In response to a request from Borden just before his departure from London, the British war cabinet decided that relevant cabinet papers could be circulated to the dominion prime ministers – a concession of the first importance, in that it would keep the prime ministers up-to-date with a wide range of cabinet policies.[78] Hankey, however, did not want the job of selecting the papers; and although Walter at the Colonial Office was eager to accept it, he did not have access to the full series of cabinet papers from which the selection had to be made. Only at the end of October did the two departments reach a working agreement on this matter, which gave the colonial secretary the right to choose and transmit the papers on his own authority.[79] And no sooner had the agreement been reached than the overseas prime ministers were back in London for the peace settlement, and for six months they were to receive cabinet documents of this sort directly through the Imperial Cabinet organization. It was not until the summer of 1919 that the Colonial Office could begin to reassess its function in Britain's relations with the dominions.

[78] Borden–Ll. G., 16 Aug 1918, printed in *DCER*, I, 358.
[79] CO 537/1006: Hankey–Long, 16 Oct, CO–Hankey, 22 Oct 1918.

3
The settlement of peace, 1919

On 8 October 1918 President Wilson received from the German government a note which agreed to his Fourteen Points as a basis for peace
negotiations with the allies. After some clarification he accepted the
German proposal, and on 23 October formally presented this bilateral
understanding to the European allied governments, who were then invited to draw up the terms of an armistice. Thus began the long and
complicated process of putting together a German peace settlement, an
endeavour which from the start was marked by Wilson's assumption of
two discrepant roles: the head of the most powerful allied state, but also
the disinterested mediator between the belligerent European powers. In
the months to come, the shaping of the peace treaties was to be strongly
influenced by the president's ambivalent frame of mind. Yet Wilson was
not to be the only allied statesman with an ambiguous relationship to the
peacemaking. To a comparable degree the British prime minister was also
subject to conflicting priorities, a reflection in particular of the empire's
unsettled constitutional affairs. Lloyd George was about to represent the
interests of Great Britain, whose security and economic welfare were
intimately connected with a stable Europe; but he had also to make
allowances for the views of the British dominions, whose governments had
been given every assurance that they would be fully consulted in the
making of peace. As the terms of the allied peace settlement were affected
by President Wilson's attempt to combine his two functions, so, at one
remove, the formulation of a united imperial policy at the peace conference was made all the more difficult by the synthesis which Lloyd
George was obliged to create from British and dominion interests.

A second major problem, intimately associated with imperial policymaking, was that of the form of dominion participation at the peace
conference. Four years of imperial wartime co-operation had brought the
overseas governments a greatly enhanced status in their imperial relations
and as well a degree of practical consultation with Britain about imperial
affairs. But on neither count had dominion leaders been fully satisfied, and

from their point of view the experiences of the war could only serve as guides to further development in the future. Resolution ix of 1917, with its promise of a major constitutional reappraisal now in the offing, provided its own stimulus for change. In these circumstances, the international settlement of a conflict that the dominions had helped so much to win represented a natural opportunity for consolidating their new position. By this time, moreover, a maturing dominion nationalism added an important stimulus to the aspirations of overseas ministers. It was soon evident, as they reassembled in London, that representation at the conference would of itself be as important an aspect of the peace settlement for them as an adequate voice in the empire's peacemaking policies.

Dominion representation at the conference

In late October 1918 few of the difficulties that were to arise over dominion participation in the peace settlement had been anticipated by the British prime minister. With every intention of consulting his dominion colleagues about peace terms he warned them in late October that if Germany agreed to an armistice, they should be prepared to come at once to London. But it is clear that Lloyd George expected peace talks with the prime ministers to form no more than a preliminary round of discussions before international negotiations began. There would, he intimated, be three separate levels of talks: the settlement of peace between the allies and the enemy powers; inter-allied conferences 'of at least equal importance' to be held before this; and prior to anything else, 'the deliberations which will determine the line the British delegates are to take in these Conferences'. It was these latter deliberations that the dominion prime ministers were invited to attend.[1]

A telegram from Borden two days later suggested that the Canadian government, at least, might have a very different notion of the forthcoming consultations. Borden did not question Lloyd George's invitation (it may have crossed with his own message) but it seemed that he had more than inter-imperial conversations in mind:

Press and people of this country take it for granted Canada will be represented at Peace Conference. I appreciate possible difficulties as to representation of Dominions but I hope you will keep in mind that certainly a very unfortunate impression would be created and possible a dangerous feeling might be aroused if these difficulties are not overcome by some solution which will meet national spirit of Canadian people.[2]

---

[1] CO 532/133: Ll. G.–Borden, 27 Oct 1918.
[2] *Ibid*: Borden–Ll. G., 29 Oct 1918.

Borden and his contingent were coming to England not only to discuss the settlement of peace but also to negotiate the basis upon which the dominions would participate in that settlement.[3]

The Canadians arrived in London on 17 November, and by that time the relation of the dominions to the peace settlement had already become a subject of controversy between Lloyd George and the Australian premier Hughes. The latter was acutely concerned about Japan's claims to Germany's Pacific colonies,[4] and was determined that Australia's territorial counter-claims in this area must be acknowledged. He was also generally unsympathetic to Wilson's Fourteen Points, and feared that in arranging the German armistice on the basis of these points the British government had in effect reached an understanding with the allied powers about the actual terms of peace, behind the dominions' backs. On 7 November he spoke out publicly against 'the terms of peace being decided without the Dominions first being consulted', and despite an official denial of this charge continued to speak of the armistice terms as 'conditions of peace' which had been settled in a way 'quite incompatible with the relations which ought to exist between the self-governing Dominions and Britain'.[5]

Hughes was afraid that the British government was reaching a private accommodation with the United States. Borden brought to London a very different fear: that on several crucial issues the Americans would refuse absolutely to accept the British point of view, and would in consequence withdraw from the peacemaking altogether. The Canadian prime minister had few particular claims to make of the peace settlement on his country's behalf; as he admitted to the governor general, Canada's interests 'related chiefly to trade conditions'.[6] But the future harmony of

---

[3] Borden brought with him as principal delegates C. J. Doherty, minister of justice, A. L. Sifton, minister of customs, and Sir George Foster, minister of trade and commerce. Loring Christie was in attendance, along with J. W. Dafoe of the *Manitoba Free Press* (acting as press officer), O. M. Biggar the judge-advocate-general, and several other officials brought over to handle questions of post-war trade. Dafoe wrote later that Borden had chosen Doherty and Sifton, both able lawyers, to strengthen his hand on matters of status. J. W. Dafoe, 'Canada and the Peace Conference of 1919', *CHR*, xxiv, no 3 (1943), 241.

[4] During the war Australia had occupied the German islands to the south of the equator, Japan those to the north.

[5] *The Times*, 8 Nov, 9 Nov 1918, quoted in L. F. Fitzhardinge, 'Hughes, Borden and Dominion Representation at the Paris Peace Conference', *CHR*, xlix, no 2 (1968).

[6] Borden–Gov Gen, 2 Dec 1918, printed in *DCER*, ii, 5; see Borden, *Memoirs*, ii, 876. The minutes of the private meetings of the full Canadian delegation,

British–American relations held an importance for Canada that in Borden's eyes overrode all other concerns, and it became a major preoccupation with him to get goodwill with the United States accepted as a top imperial priority. Throughout these weeks of discussions he stressed time and again that a peace settlement in opposition to American views would be intolerable to Canada, and the Canadian delegation did their best to modify and broaden what they considered narrowly imperial attitudes and ambitions. The most serious problems in this respect centred on the disposition of Germany's overseas empire. The American government, Borden had every reason to believe, would not tolerate wholesale British or dominion annexations, no matter what the military or strategic realities. Yet, as he knew equally well, the territorial claims of the other dominions constituted the most tangible evidence of their new status in the empire. Could he now oppose aspirations he had helped so strongly to foster?

The avoidance of a rift with the United States over these colonial possessions had been on Borden's mind, as we have seen, since the 1917 Imperial War Cabinet, and when he returned to London the following summer he had braved the hostility of the other dominion prime ministers and argued that these territories could best be used as a means of drawing the United States into a wider international role of her own, through which long-term collaboration with the empire might follow. By November and his return to London, however, it was more apparent than ever to Borden that imperial claims on the captured German colonies were unlikely to be dropped. Hughes, Massey, Smuts as well, were equally adamant on this score. Even Smuts, in so many respects the true statesman among the dominion leaders at the peace conference, could not allow his wider post-war hopes to obscure his country's own interests: although he subscribed to the notion of trusteeship, and was working towards the idea of mandated territories under a world league of nations, he had no thought of applying this principle to Germany's occupied colonies in southern Africa.[7]

Realizing the full strength of feeling here, Borden now sought to lessen its impact in the best way possible, by urging the British government to see that the dominions were given some form of separate representation when the allies themselves got down to peace talks. If the others would not offer the United States the control of the colonies they had occupied, then at least they could make their claims on their own behalf and the British and American heads of state possibly avoid a direct confrontation

five of which were held in these weeks, bear out the fact that economic affairs occupied most of their time. Christie papers: Canadian delegation minutes.
[7] Hancock, *Smuts*, I, 489.

over imperial expansion. On 20 November a proposal to this effect from
the Canadian prime minister was accepted by the Imperial War Cabinet.[8]
Three days later, however, in a letter to Lloyd George, the Canadian
prime minister returned to his larger preoccupation:

You know my conviction that there is at least possible a League of the two
great English-speaking commonwealths who share common ancestry, language
and literature, who are inspired by like democratic ideals, who enjoy similar
political institutions and whose united force is sufficient to ensure the peace of
the world. It is with a view to the consummation of so great a purpose that I
should be content, and indeed desire, to invite and even urge the American
Republic to undertake world-wide responsibilities in respect of underdeveloped
territories and backward races similar to, if not commensurate with, those
which have been assumed by or imposed upon by our own Empire.[9]

This theme Borden recapitulated to the Imperial War Cabinet on 26
November, where it was received politely enough – with, of course, the
unspoken assumption that the 'underdeveloped territories' in question
would not include the colonies occupied by the dominions! Until such
time as American official policy could be known and tested, no one was
going to modify his views.

Borden's concern for America's post-war attitudes and for international
stability in the post-war world had led him to the idea of a new American
empire. By the same token, if the United States was in any event going to
be asked to sanction further extensions of the British empire, then he was
sure the dominions must speak for themselves on territorial matters when
the allies began to settle the terms of peace. But there was in addition an
equally compelling reason why his awareness of the United States should
make Borden an advocate of a separate dominion voice in these talks.
Canada, after all, had suffered as many losses as the United States at the
front, and had been in the war from the beginning. Such comparisons of
her war effort with that of the United States had inevitably strengthened
the feelings of national identity which the war itself had fostered in the
dominion, and they led to the simple conclusion that, like the United
States, Canada should be fully represented at the peace talks in her own
right. All things considered, as Borden weighed up his own position at
these London discussions, and the role in external affairs that Canada

[8] CAB 23/42: IWC 37, 20 Nov 1918. For the purpose of preliminary imperial
discussions about peace terms – whatever else was to follow – the British
government reconstituted the Imperial War Cabinet, which held a series of
meetings in November–December 1918.
[9] Lloyd George papers: Borden–Ll. G., 23 Nov 1918.

should be ready to play, he found himself concluding that the time for a fundamental change was fast approaching:

I am beginning to feel more and more that in the end, and perhaps sooner than later, Canada must assume full sovereignty. She can give better service to G[reat] B[ritain] and [the] U[nited] S[tates] and to the world in that way.[10]

The negotiations of the next six months, as we shall see, would powerfully stimulate the prime minister's inclination to move Canada in this direction.

Borden was to argue his case for dominion representation in the peace talks in due course, because for the moment, apart from agreement that the overseas leaders should make their own territorial claims, the Imperial War Cabinet did not pursue the question of representation any further. Their attention turned to a variety of other problems of the peace: the treatment of the ex-Kaiser, the proposals for a League of Nations, German reparations and so forth.

There were also the distractions of a British general election to be endured, with Lloyd George campaigning hard for a fresh mandate for his coalition government. Indeed it should be noted that this election was not without influence on the Imperial War Cabinet's deliberations. Just as the public attitudes of British ministers towards German peace terms became ever harsher during the campaign (culminating in the remark of Eric Geddes, first lord of the Admiralty, that he would squeeze Germany 'until you can hear the pips squeak') so the Imperial Cabinet became themselves more vindictive in their policies. Looking afresh at the reparations question, for instance, once the election was over, they reversed an earlier position and recommended now that Britain should press for the largest amount that Germany could be made to pay, short of an allied occupation. It remained to be seen, of course, exactly what weight the Imperial Cabinet's views would carry, both with the British government and beyond that with the other allied powers.

Discussion of the peace terms in the Imperial War Cabinet terminated towards the end of December, with Lloyd George inviting his colleagues to summarize their general position for him in preparation for private talks of his own with President Woodrow Wilson. The British prime minister was careful to point out, nonetheless, that he sought only guidance, not 'rigid instructions', from the Imperial Cabinet, and as they duly recapitulated their ideas the advisory capacity of the overseas ministers was all too clear.[11] But the full realization of their effective lack of in-

---

[10] Diary, 1 Dec 1918.
[11] CAB 23/42: IWC, 43, 18 Dec 1918.

fluence only became clear when Lloyd George reported back to them on his meeting with the president. Few indeed of the policies advocated by the dominion leaders had proved acceptable to Wilson. On the one hand, Borden's hopes that the United States would accept a territorial interest in various parts of the world now appeared empty, for Wilson had rejected the idea of any such American expansion until a League of Nations could be fully established, and even so had held out little promise. Hughes, on the other hand, had his worst fears confirmed. Wilson was not only opposed to a large German indemnity, but also refused to accept Australian claims (as well as Japanese) to the German islands in the Pacific. And while Smuts and Botha might agree with Wilson's opposition to the indemnity, they too could only oppose the president's policy regarding the German empire, having anticipated the addition of German West Africa to their own dominion. The single issue on which there had been definite understanding was allied intervention in Russia: everyone was agreed that it should end as soon as possible.

This meeting of the Imperial War Cabinet was not a pleasant one. Hughes in particular, fearing the dominance of American ideas in the peace settlement, loudly reiterated his country's claim to the German islands and warned strongly against being forced to follow the president's lead when the peace conference opened in Paris.[12] For Borden, this acrimonious diatribe only confirmed that the empire's territorial interests, if not Britain's own complex commitments in Europe, stood as almost impossible barriers between the empire and the United States. And where he had earlier pleaded with his colleagues, he now had recourse to a threat:

if the future policy of the British Empire meant working in co-operation with some European nation as against the United States, that policy could not reckon on the approval or the support of Canada. Canada's view was that as an Empire we should keep clear, as far as possible, of European complications and alliances. This feeling had been immensely strengthened by the experience of the war, into which we had been drawn by old-standing pledges and more recent understandings, of which the Dominions had not even been aware.[13]

His final point served two purposes. It was a last rebuke to the British government for failing to consult the dominions fully during the war; but it was a reminder also that he expected the dominions to be given an adequate voice in the peace conference. For as yet the overseas prime ministers did not know what their position was to be at the conference.

[12] Borden, *Memoirs*, II, 889.
[13] CAB 23/43: IWC, 47, 30 Dec 1918.

It was this final item of business that they met to arrange the following day.[14]

One thing at least seemed clear. The question to be decided concerned participation in a full peace conference rather than in any preliminary inter-allied discussions. Wilson, as Lloyd George had indicated, was firmly opposed to formal inter-allied talks in Paris. The president intended to call the Germans to the peace settlement from the very beginning.

The Imperial Cabinet had before them two sets of proposals as regards the structure of the Paris conference. The first had been drawn up at a meeting in London of British, French and Italian ministers on 2 December, and envisaged five representatives for each of the five major allies, with invitations to the smaller powers to speak only on matters which concerned them directly. The dominions would be treated as smaller powers in association with Britain: they could send representatives to attend as extra members of the British delegation when questions of direct concern to them arose.[15] Informally, the British government had also accepted the idea that one of the five full-time British delegates would be a dominion minister, chosen in rotation from a panel. The second formula came from the French government, and was more specific: five representatives for the five major allies; three for the smaller allies (and two for new states deemed to be allies) to be invited where matters concerned them; and one for neutrals and states in formation, to be invited at the conference's discretion. There was no mention of the dominions. The proposal now put to the Imperial Cabinet was to accept the French formula on two conditions – that the allied agreement with regard to dominion representation should hold good; and that the number of representatives allowed the smaller powers should be left for further inter-allied discussions to settle.

This British formulation was a curious and unsatisfactory compromise. It promised to keep the dominions on a par with the smaller powers, but at the same time it put in doubt what their representation would finally be; it also failed to incorporate the understanding that the permanent British delegation would include a dominion member. It is hardly

---

[14] The question of how the empire was to be represented at the peace conference may have been postponed to 31 December 1918 because the votes in the British general election were not counted until 28 December. Until that point it was not finally known whether Lloyd George's government would be continuing in office.

[15] CAB 28/5: inter-allied conference, 2 Dec 1918.

surprising, therefore, that neither Borden nor Hughes would accept it as it stood. Both argued persuasively for its amendment, and from their criticisms emerged a much clearer definition of separate dominion representation at the conference, together with a firm commitment to at least one dominion seat on the permanent delegation. A recent assessment of their efforts by Hughes' biographer suggests that the credit for separate representation must go to the Australian, and that Borden would have settled in the end merely for the panel system.[16] This, however, does less than justice to the Canadian prime minister. As we shall see, by the time the Imperial War Cabinet met on 31 December, Borden was as adamant as Hughes that a panel system notwithstanding, the dominions must have a degree of representation in their own right. He differed from Hughes only in that he recognized the importance of both forms of representation.

The inter-allied meeting of 2 December had been for Borden a salutary lesson in imperial *realpolitik*. It was not that, in Canada's absence, unfavourable conclusions had been reached regarding dominion representation at the peace conference. Indeed, Borden later pointed to this meeting as the moment when 'distinctive representation for each Dominion' was first accepted.[17] This was not full separate representation, but it was a definite step in that direction. In the absence of the dominions, however, the allies had reached important conclusions about the peace settlement. In particular, they decided that the Kaiser should be brought to trial – an idea Borden found abhorrent. It was at this level of policymaking that he felt acutely the lack of Canadian representation, and he told the Imperial Cabinet meeting the next day that he strongly resented the British government reaching such agreements without consulting the dominion prime ministers.[18] To drive home his complaint he also saw both Hankey ('had serious talk with him as to irregular procedure and oversight. He agreed. I said I had not come to take part in light comedy'[19]) and Lloyd George. Borden, quite clearly, had come to realize that 'distinctive representation' on the basis only of their special interests would give the dominions no guarantee at all of a place at high-level negotiations amongst the major allied powers. That could only come with representation on the British delegation itself through a panel system of some sort.

In passing, it is worth noticing that similar conclusions about representation at the peace conference had been reached in another quarter,

---

[16] Fitzhardinge, 'Hughes, Borden ... ', *CHR*, XLIX (1968).
[17] Borden, *Memoirs*, II, 892.
[18] CAB 23/42: IWC, 41, 3 Dec 1918.
[19] Diary, 4 Dec 1918; Roskill, *Hankey*, II, 29.

by Leopold Amery. For Amery, it was not just a matter of allowing dominion leaders to play an active and satisfying part at the conference. The important thing was to see the conference itself in a wider context – not as a peace settlement, but as the first major piece of post-war imperial diplomacy. Britain owed it to the dominions to give them as wide a role as possible, to acknowledge that she was now pursuing an imperial foreign policy in full consultation with the overseas members of the empire. In a remarkably prescient memorandum Amery sought to demonstrate the essential relevance of the peace conference, and hinted darkly at the shape of things to come:

The extent to which the Dominions are given a really effective voice in the Peace settlement will determine their whole outlook on Imperial questions in future. If they consider that they have been treated in the full sense of the word as partners and have had an equal voice in the decision not merely of such questions as affect them locally but in the whole Peace settlement, they will be prepared to accept the idea of a single foreign policy for the British Commonwealth directed by the machinery of an Imperial Cabinet. If they feel that they have only been brought in as ornamental accessories . . . a serious, possibly an irremediable blow will have been struck at the idea of Imperial Unity. There will be no breaking off. But there will be no attempt to treat the Imperial Cabinet as a serious instrument of Imperial policy; each Dominion will begin developing its own independent foreign policy; the centrifugal tendencies will, in fact, definitely get the upper hand. . .

The only really effective [policy] is to insist upon the direct representation of the Dominions and India in the British delegation at the Peace Conference.[20]

While Amery tried to convince the British cabinet of the importance of supporting the dominions, Borden, meanwhile, had to think of his own cabinet in Ottawa, and of the wider political responsibilities that attached to the work of the Canadian delegation in London. It is never easy, as regards Borden's approach to imperial affairs, to decide how much he felt accountable to public opinion, or to the narrower political pressures exerted by his party or his ministerial colleagues. On the one hand, if Sir George Foster is to be believed, the prime minister took all too little guidance from his cabinet and tended to make policy decisions by himself.[21] On the other, while not forgetting the formidable anti-imperial bitterness of French Canada in these years, there is little evidence of a distinctively Canadian critique of the war or the peace to which Borden could have responded. Although it would 'be doing less than justice to

20 'Representation of the Dominions at the Peace Negotiations', 14 Nov 1918. Copy in Lothian papers.
21 Foster papers: Foster diary, 27 July 1917, 18 Feb 1918, 10 May 1918.

Canadians to deduce that they showed no appreciation of the great issues that were under discussion',[22] it appears that the prime minister could consider himself a fairly free agent in speaking for Canada at the settlement of peace. Yet, if Borden was not in this way constrained as to the policies he might endorse or oppose, it was true that the over-all performance of the Canadian delegation at the peace talks had an undoubted political dimension to it – it would be measured back home in political terms, and should therefore be capable of producing political benefits. And in these terms the pressure on Borden was not inconsiderable, for his political position was not as strong as it might be. A year after his dominant election victory his coalition government was badly in need of reconstruction (he had failed to do this before leaving for London) and its political support was rapidly declining. With the next session of parliament planned for February 1919, Borden's colleagues in Ottawa were already reminding their prime minister that 'your presence at opening of Parliament or very shortly thereafter is absolutely necessary'.[23] It was clear enough to Borden that he stayed in Europe at grave risk to his government's position. The only *political* justification for staying, considerations of statesmanship aside, would be to ensure that Canada obtained a conspicuous place at the settlement of peace, a place that would reflect and enhance her status – in short, some acknowledged form of separate representation.

Thus by degrees Borden had come to appreciate the necessity of dual representation for the dominions. Hughes, by contrast, was more single-minded. Weeks of intensive campaigning, in particular for the retention of the Australian-occupied German islands, had brought him to the conclusion that the dominions must be able to speak independently of Britain at the peace conference if they were to achieve their own ends. By 31 December the two overseas prime ministers were not close associates, and Hughes' tirade against Wilson on the previous day had done nothing to improve the relationship. From their different points of view, even so, they were able to complement each other's arguments when the Imperial Cabinet at last discussed the question of representation. It is to that discussion that we can now return.

The two vital principles to be first established at this meeting concerned dominion equality with the smaller allied powers. As mentioned, the British government had already accepted the idea of parity, but were now trying to evade the question of numbers. Hughes, whose lead Borden followed, shrewdly did not argue for a definite number of dominion

22 G. P. Glazebrook, *Canada at the Paris Peace Conference* (Toronto, 1942), 29.
23 Borden, *Memoirs*, ii, 884.

delegates. Both ministers instead held out for parity with a *specific* small allied power – Belgium. In the course of the discussion, however, the emphasis shifted from the size of Belgium's representation to its status as an *independent* delegation – and by the end of the day the dominions were promised equality on both counts. Only at this point were the overseas delegates fully divorced from the British delegation and given the right to sit independently of Britain at the conference. And to judge by the minutes of the meeting, it was Borden's advocacy rather than Hughes' that gained this essential recognition of dominion status.

But Borden had a second theme. The overseas ministers had been unofficially assured of a seat, in rotation, on the British delegation; and Lloyd George was careful to confirm that assurance when he spoke. But the Canadian prime minister wished to change the function of the permanent delegation, not merely to broaden its membership. It should be thought of as a British delegation no longer, but as an imperial delegation:

That delegation had authority to represent not only the British Isles, but the whole Empire. He therefore strongly urged that the delegation *representing the British Empire* should be in part selected from a panel, upon which each Prime Minister from the Dominions should have a place, and that one or more of those Prime Ministers should be called from time to time ... to sit in the delegation representing the whole Empire at the Conference.[24]

From this speech came the concept of the British Empire Delegation, by which the British and overseas delegates to the peace conference were collectively known. From it also came the understanding that the permanent delegation to the conference's plenary sessions represented not Britain but the British empire. Thus with Hughes' valuable co-operation, Borden had successfully carried through the two parts of his policy for dominion representation at the peace settlement, gaining the means to both the influence and the status that he considered so vital.

Not that the last hurdle was yet cleared. For as with the terms of peace themselves, it remained to be seen whether these British–dominion plans for representation could be successfully imposed upon the other allied leaders. By early January, in fact, uncertainty threatened everything as the allies came to see that they must after all hold a prior conference without delegations from the enemy powers. Even with that problem settled, President Wilson still took great exception to the proposed dual representation of the dominions, no matter that the proceedings would be only preliminary. It was only after further determined pressure from Lloyd George, spurred on by his dominion colleagues, that the Americans withdrew their opposition, and agreed to accept dual representation for the dominions on more or less the B.E.D.'s own terms.[25] Although one last-minute alteration – the awarding of an extra seat to Belgium and Serbia – badly stung the pride of the overseas delegates, all things considered their ambitious efforts over the preceding few weeks had carried extremely well.[26]

The negotiation of peace

With the status and authority of dual representation, the dominions entered upon the settlement of peace in Paris well placed to render a good account of themselves. Nor was this strategic position to suffer from lack of manpower: of the two hundred and seven ministers, civil servants and secretaries who composed the full British empire contingent, dominion personnel accounted for no fewer than seventy-five.[27] On 13 January the B.E.D. began its Paris meetings. On 18 January the first plenary session of the conference assembled, with the dominions duly seated in their own right. A week later, when the second plenary session began the organization of working parties, the dominions placed representatives on four of the five major commissions and on several more specialized committees concerned with territorial questions. These appointments illustrated well the advantages of dual representation. Rather than seek election as small powers, the dominions gained their seats on the committees from the allotment given to the British Empire Delegation.

As January moved into February, however, it became increasingly apparent that the dominions, despite the difficulties they had overcome, had succeeded only in arming themselves for the wrong battle. The external trappings – separate representation, the degree of international recognition which this entailed, membership on the B.E.D. – were

25 At the first meeting of the British Empire Delegation in Paris, J. W. Dafoe remembered Borden being ready for a 'fight to the finish' on this question of representation. Dafoe, 'Canada and the Peace Conference', 239. The B.E.D. meetings held in Paris during the peace conference were a direct continuation of the London I.W.C. meetings, with representation from the British and dominion ministerial delegations to the conference.

26 The final arrangement gave Canada, Australia and South Africa two representatives, New Zealand, British India and the Indian States one each. Newfoundland (whose loss of manpower during the war was proportionately the highest in the empire) was given no separate place. The dominions had no independent votes at the conference; the British empire had five votes as a unit.

27 H. Nicolson, *Peacemaking 1919* (London, 1964), 45. The Canadian contingent included 14 ministers and officials and 8 secretaries.

impressive, but they served only to mask the fact that the significant confrontations of the peace settlement were taking place on ground hardly accessible to the dominion ministers. The 'peace conference', of course, had yet to begin, and although President Wilson imagined that on the basis of the Fourteen Points the allies would negotiate directly with the Germans soon enough, as January came and went it was clear that there were still substantial allied disagreements over fundamental principles. While these disagreements remained, the Paris talks could be no more than an inter-allied conference. And the conference, unwieldy in size, inevitably produced an informal executive to direct its deliberations: the 'Council of Ten', made up of the two principal delegates of the five main allies. As early as 21 January Borden was complaining to Lloyd George that their meetings were effectively shutting out the smaller powers from decisions they had a right to be consulted about: without immediate changes 'there would seem little occasion for the Canadian representatives to remain longer in attendance'.[28] Repeating his complaint to the B.E.D. brought Borden no assurances; and when he therefore decided to speak out before the full session of the conference he was firmly put in his place by the French president, Clemenceau:

Sir Robert Borden has reproached us, though in a very friendly way ... With your permission I will remind you that it was we [the major Powers] who decided there should be a conference in Paris, and that the representatives of the countries interested should be summoned to attend it. I make no mystery of it – there is a Conference of the Great Powers going on in the next room.[29]

The Council of Ten continued to meet until the end of March. Thereafter it became the Council of Four.

If the dominion delegates were unable to prevent a concentration of diplomatic power at the peace talks, they could still consider themselves more favourably placed than the other small powers, in having at least an indirect access to the restricted allied discussions through the British Empire Delegation. At this level there remained a genuine opportunity to establish a collaborative imperial forum for the settlement of the peace, and in the opening weeks in Paris it seemed the B.E.D. might succeed in carrying British and dominion ministers over the threshold of 'consultation' that they had never fully reached through the Imperial War Cabinet. With Hankey on hand to provide the essential secretarial co-ordination, the intention was to keep the B.E.D.'s agenda nicely in line with Lloyd George's higher-level negotiations, so as to encourage in the

28 Borden–Ll. G., 21 Jan 1919, printed in *DCER*, II, 34.
29 Quoted in Glazebrook, *Canada at the Paris Peace Conference*, 54.

British prime minister a measure of responsibility to his imperial colleagues. In this vital area of administrative integration, moreover, Hankey managed to score a notable success as the B.E.D. got under way, as he explained in a letter home to his wife:

My mind is chock full of a great scheme of Imperial development which I have actually carried out: that is to say, I have got approved that I shall have an assistant secretary from each Dominion for the work of the British Empire Delegation. As this is, for all practical purposes, the Imperial War Cabinet, it means that when I return home I shall continue the same procedure with the Imperial War Cabinet. In short – I have actually started a great Imperial Office. It is at this moment in existence. I have tried to do this for six years but circumstances have always blocked it ... The Canadians and Australians absolutely jumped at it, and at our meeting yesterday I had a Canadian assistant secretary. I am firing them with my own enthusiasm and shall just make things hum.[30]

On the Canadian side Loring Christie was thus drafted into the secretariat, and with the other dominion secretaries constituted a new functional link tying the overseas delegations to the policymaking centre.

Despite Hankey's well-directed efforts, however, the B.E.D. in operation fell sadly short of his expectations. In the first place it was often not possible to establish an agreed imperial position when faced with differing British and dominion attitudes: in this respect the B.E.D. represented a rather unsteady point of equilibrium between the acknowledged constitutional parity linking Britain and the dominions and the practical disparities of national power. For all the talk about joint responsibility for joint imperial policies, the B.E.D. had no special dispensation by which they could reconcile or harmonize the variety of national interests which confronted them. Absolutely critical for the creation of any broad imperial consensus in this respect was the fact that the most vital aspects of Britain's relations with the dominions – post-war defence, constitutional organization, and of course the formulation of foreign policy itself – were all awaiting urgent post-war consideration. In such unsettled circumstances it was perhaps inevitable that the British delegates should look primarily to their own interests and designs. Yet in the end the more important failure of the B.E.D. lay in the way British priorities were *seen* to predominate – a failure largely attributable to Lloyd George. It was not that Lloyd George ignored the B.E.D. For many of their sessions he was present, and with them discussed a broad range of policy questions. He made little effort, however, to co-operate with Hankey in relating these discussions to the

[30] Quoted in Lord Hankey, *The Supreme Control at the Paris Peace Conference* (London, 1963), 26.

private allied negotiations. Too often decisions reached by the allied leaders came down to the B.E.D., too seldom imperial policy was taken the other way. Delays between heads-of-state and B.E.D. discussions of the same topic began to occur, and by April this critical time difference could be anything up to three weeks. Lloyd George revealed his own priorities in the following letter to Borden; its bluntness seems overwhelming:

I have been anxious to hold a [British Empire] Delegation meeting for the last ten days, but I have been meeting President Wilson, M. Clemenceau and Signor Orlando morning and afternoon during this time because I have felt that the one imperative thing was to force through an agreement in regard to the peace with Germany with the least possible delay. I have thought it better to go on hammering at the points still at issue between us until they were settled. I have good hope that we are now nearing an agreement on most of the outstanding points and I therefore hope to hold a meeting of the British Empire Delegation very soon.[31]

Thus the B.E.D. found themselves a secondary chamber of debate. Their powers of initiating imperial policy were compromised by a schedule of peace negotiations beyond their control; their powers of reviewing that policy fell prey to the realities of allied diplomacy.

Nor were dominion leaders any more certain of influence when exercising their rights of separate representation, in pursuit or defence of their own more local interests. In the case of territorial questions, for example, it had been agreed that the three southern dominions would speak for themselves, and their prime ministers duly put their case to the allied leaders at the end of January. But it required every effort from Borden to conciliate President Wilson, as well as support from Lloyd George, before the new dominion possessions were confirmed – as mandates under a League of Nations, moreover, rather than straightforward annexations.[32] There were other moments when by acting together overseas ministers were able to secure significant concessions from the allied leadership, as for example the right to nominate the dominions for election to a seat on the proposed League of Nations' Council. Dominion points of view, however, were with equal facility ignored or overruled. In the case of

[31] Lloyd George papers: Ll. G.–Borden, 1 April 1919. Cf Lord Riddell, *Intimate Diary of the Peace Conference and After, 1918–1923* (London, 1933), 45.

[32] Lloyd George told Hughes that 'he had fought Australia's battles for three days but would not quarrel with the United States for [the] Solomon Islands': Borden, *Memoirs*, II, 906. But what did most to reconcile Hughes was the definition of the (class 'C') mandate assigned to the islands he wanted, which in practice gave Australia virtual sovereignty over them.

reparations, for instance, Hughes was adamant that the full costs of the war should be included in any final reckoning, and when Lloyd George indicated that the Americans would only agree to a smaller sum the Australian prime minister bluntly retorted that 'he did not care two straws what the United States said or did'.[33] Fighting words, but by this point the subject was no longer open to debate: Lloyd George that same day gave his approval to the American set of figures.

It was in the end at a level which did not relate to their own immediate policy concerns that the dominion delegates were able to make a more sustained contribution to the settlement of peace, through the positions they accepted on the conference's many committees and commissions. Here, where the allies tried to determine the geo-political future for a continent in disarray, and where the details of the final treaties were slowly established, dominion personnel offered their best services. Smuts made a telling contribution to the commission that prepared the charter of the League of Nations; in addition he travelled to Budapest to report on the new Communist government of Bela Kun. Borden was designated to go even farther afield to the Sea of Marmora, but the conference he was to attend there on the Russian civil war could not be convened. Less remarkably he stayed in Paris to guide the conference's study of Greek and Turkish territorial questions, a thankless task of notorious complexity.[34] The other dominion leaders were similarly preoccupied. Yet even this labour of the overseas delegates did not find universal acceptance. Borden might remark that, at one point, his committee was 'practically settling eastern and western Thrace, with little difference of opinion', in the space of a day.[35] Four years later, planning the last phase of the peace settlement with Turkey, Sir Eyre Crowe, who had sat with Borden on the Greek committee, looked back from the Foreign Office on a different perspective:

it would serve no purpose, and could only produce friction with the allies, as well as retard the negotiations, if Dominion Delegates were to be given seats at the conference table ... These ought to be reserved so far as possible for the actual negotiators, who must be persons qualified for their responsible task by intimate knowledge of the subjects to be discussed.

---

[33] CAB 29/28/1: BED, 19 A, 11 April 1919.

[34] Meanwhile Borden's colleagues in the Canadian delegation busied themselves with treaties of a more tangible nature in an attempt to sell Canadian foodstuffs to a hungry Europe. Signing agreements with France, Belgium, Greece, Roumania, Sir George Foster noted happily, 'Here we can get any quantity of business with credits – considerable without ... if normal conditions can be brought about Canada will get good custom from the countries she has helped by her credits.' Diary, 28 March 1919.

[35] Borden, *Memoirs*, ii, 916.

It would be deplorable to repeat at Lausanne the arrangements made at the Paris Peace Conference, whereby Dominions delegates were nominated to a number of highly technical committees as the representatives of the British Empire. In this way, Sir R. Borden became the British 'expert' on Albania, Epirus, Thrace, Smyrna, etc., and Sir T. Cook the expert on Czecho-Slovakia! The result was ludicrous and embarrassing.[36]

The disdain of the professional diplomatist for the colonial amateur, however justified, was in one sense beside the point. The dominion ministers undoubtedly had sought committee work in order to contribute to the settlement of peace; however they had also undertaken it on principle, for it provided some justification for their presence at the conference. Borden, in December, had anticipated the prestige of a position that would happily combine influence and status. Instead dual representation, when tested against the realities of international diplomacy, offered the dominion delegates two quite distinct roles. Their role as status-seekers had nothing to do with influencing policy; while the little influence they did enjoy was not based upon their separate representation. Thus it came about that, as the hopes of influencing imperial policy continued to fade, the more limited victory of separate dominion representation assumed an increasing importance in its own right. The Canadian prime minister was not long in deciding that this victory should be extended as much as possible, through a further development of dominion status. His attention turned first to the question of dominion signatures for the various peace treaties, and then to dominion ratification.

Signature of the treaties

Without probing too far into the empire's legal foundations, it will be useful here to set out briefly the position of the dominions with regard to international treaties, and to place the proposed innovations of 1919 in the context of past developments. As integral elements of the British empire, the dominions were naturally without international standing in their own right, and their external relations were conducted as a matter of routine by the Foreign Office and the machinery of Britain's diplomatic establishment. The diplomatic unity of the empire, expressed and controlled in this way through the agency of the Foreign Office, was also reinforced by the formal process of treatymaking: treaties were made by the Crown and were held to be binding on the empire as a whole, irrespective of the

---

[36] FO 371/7909: minute of 6 Nov 1923. Crowe was assistant under-secretary, Foreign Office, and the chief Foreign Office representative at Paris; in 1920 he became permanent under-secretary, until his death in 1925. For a more charitable account of dominion services, see H. Nicolson, *Peacemaking*, 280.

subject under consideration or of the particular part of the empire to which it might apply. In keeping with this undifferentiated empire foreign policy, the 'full powers' authorizing a minister or official to act as a plenipotentiary for the head of state in treaty discussions were issued without geographic limitations, and treaties were therefore concluded and signed not 'for Great Britain' or 'for' a dominion but on behalf of the monarch as head of state of the empire. As might be expected, however, with the development of local responsible government in the empire after the mid-nineteenth century, the overseas colonies had indicated a desire to be associated in some relevant way with treaties bearing specifically on their own colonial affairs, and the imperial authorities had usually been prepared to make concessions in such instances. Particularly in the case of Canada, whose relations with the United States were often regulated by treaty or convention, it became the practice to allow local ministers to conduct much of the detailed negotiation, and beginning in 1887 to sign such treaties as well – though the British ambassador in Washington would add his own signature by way of an imperial *imprimatur*. Broadly speaking, the more routine or uncontroversial the question the more responsibility was left to dominion ministers, to the point where Canada managed these secondary (usually commercial) affairs, as relating not only to the United States but to other nations as well, with little imperial supervision from Whitehall.

By the time of the First World War the dominions had thus gained a measure of control over their commercial external relations at least, insofar as these could be developed through bilateral arrangements with other powers. But where they might be involved – however exclusively – in negotiations that dealt with issues of greater importance, or on the other hand in a subject that was no longer narrowly bilateral but impinged on wider imperial interests as well, they were given far less opportunity by the British government to associate themselves as distinct elements in the making of such treaties. In the 1871 discussions that produced the treaty of Washington, for instance, where British as well as Canadian problems with the United States were settled, Canada was not permitted to appear in its own right – though the Canadian prime minister was allowed to participate as a member of the British delegation, and as such to sign the treaty. Nearly forty years later, when Canada and the United States agreed to regulate their boundary waters in a 1909 Waterways treaty, the dominion was still not an official party to the agreement: two Canadian ministers had handled the negotiations, but the resulting document was signed on the British side by the British ambassador alone, and was registered as a treaty between the United States and Great Britain. All told there were only four occasions prior to the war when Canada was involved in its own right in international negotiations, and in each case the agreement that Canadian ministers signed was a 'Convention' of relatively minor importance rather than a fully-fledged treaty.[37] The last two conventions, nonetheless, had broken important new ground in that dominion representatives were sharply differentiated from their British colleagues, in one case having independent voting rights, and in both signing specifically 'for' their dominions, rather than as members of an empire delegation.[38] Through such seemingly innocuous precedents the British government were to find they had given serious hostages to fortune.

In the light of these various dominion advances in the business of treatymaking, it was hardly surprising that the question of signing the treaties of peace in 1919 should be raised. Having already established themselves at the peace conference with an unprecedented dual status as both dominion and imperial representatives, overseas ministers were unlikely to be satisfied without attesting to their position by a treaty signature in some form or other. Nor did it seem, in the beginning, that dominion signatures were going to present a problem for the British government. When in early February the Canadian prime minister first mentioned the idea to Lloyd George it received his ready support, and without any further reservations the leaders of the other dominions all gave their own keen approval to Borden's proposal.[39] A month later – a month, as we have seen, during which Borden came to realize the dominions' relative impotence in the peace settlement, and in which the possibilities for formal advances in status began to assume greater significance – the Canadian proposals were circulated to the B.E.D. and then after approval to the Colonial Office in London. Briefly, the plan was for the treaties of peace to be 'so drafted as to enable the Dominions to become Parties and Signatories thereto', and suggested that 'under the general heading "The British Empire", the "Dominion of Canada"' and so forth could 'be used as headings to distinguish the various plenipotentiaries'.[40] 'This is generally satisfactory', minuted Charles Davis of the Dominions Department;

[37] Convention with USA on Postal Orders, 1901; Convention on Pelagic Sealing, 1911; Convention on Radiotelegraphy, 1912; Convention on Safety of Life at Sea, 1913.

[38] CO 532/136: minute of Charles Davis, 19 March 1919. In addition to three dominion representatives signing the Safety of Life at Sea convention 'for' their respective dominions, the British representative signed for the empire as a whole.

[39] Borden diary, 5 Feb 1919.

[40] CO 532/320: 'The Dominions as Parties and Signatories to the various Peace Treaties', 12 March 1919.

'I see no objection to the proposed grouping of the British Plenipotentiaries'.[41]

In view of the two minor pre-war conventions whose form of signature
we have noted above, however, he was at pains to make one point clear.
There should be no restrictions on the full powers granted to the dominion
signatories:

> To give the Dominion Plenipotentiaries less ample powers than their col-
> leagues might involve a corresponding limitation of the powers of the latter
> and similarly any proposal that Treaties should be signed specially 'for' the
> Dominions might involve Mr. Lloyd George and Mr. Balfour signing only
> for the U.K.

It is clearly desirable that all the British Plenipotentiaries should have the
same full powers and should sign on the same footing and it is very satisfactory
that it is not proposed that any of them should sign 'for' the countries from
which they come.

Had the peace conference at this point begun to show signs of reaching
any conclusions, of settling its final objectives, then it is possible that this
agreed formula for dominion treaty signatures might have gone into effect
as planned. But as the weeks of March passed slowly by the peace negotiations appeared to have stalled hopelessly, and it was not until the end
of the month that Lloyd George's Fontainebleau memorandum, and the
organization of the Council of Four, injected new enterprise into the allied
discussions. Meanwhile the dominion delegates remained frustrated out-
siders, not wanting to return home empty-handed yet bitterly resenting the
days they wasted in waiting for some tangible results. Borden wrote in
his diary, 26 March: 'At present the weather is awful and the Peace
Conference also. Both are "en panne".'[42] The broader political aspect of
his frustration he confided on the same day to one of his ministers back in
Ottawa:

> I asked Mr. Lloyd George to consent to my departure early in April, but he is
> very insistent that I shall remain ... I realize of course that I might be subject
> to criticism if I should return leaving the most important matters to be dealt
> with after my departure. Under such circumstances it could be urged with a
> good deal of force that I need not have attended the Conference in person.[43]

Small wonder, then, that as Borden faced the prospect of further weeks in
Paris, with as little chance as ever for any substantial engagement with the

---

[41] CO 532/136: C. Davies, minute of 19 March 1919.
[42] Diary, 26 March 1919.
[43] Ballantyne Papers: Borden-Ballantyne, 26 March 1919.

settlement of peace, he should have given further consideration to the question of treaty signatures. And having decided that the significance of a separate dominion signature to the treaties might be enhanced still further, the Canadian prime minister was soon moving quickly into unexplored constitutional territory. It was fortunate for him that the legal hounds trying to head him off were badly divided between the Colonial Office in London and the British delegation in Paris.

The first alarm was raised when Cecil Hurst, legal adviser to the British delegation in Paris, warned the Colonial Office that Borden seemed likely to demand that his full powers should be issued not from London but from Ottawa, on the authority of the governor general – an innovation Hurst thought 'would of necessity be the beginning of the end of any unity in the control of the foreign affairs of the Empire'.[44] 'When Borden gets his toes in', Hurst went on, 'he usually shoves hard', and he hoped it could be proved that the powers of the governor general did not extend this far.[45] The alarm, however, proved false. A few days later the Colonial Office learned that Borden had given up the idea of trying to get his full power from Canada, and would accept one drawn up in the normal way in London. To indicate symbolically that his delegation acted as Canadian rather than imperial representatives, he would simply obtain an Order in Council from the government in Ottawa 'authorizing Canadian Ministers to attend the Peace Conference and act in conformity with the full power issued by the King'.[46]

What the Colonial Office authorities in London were not in a position to know was that Borden was meanwhile working hard to obtain full powers that were limited to his dominion alone, so that the peace treaties could be signed 'for Canada'. Thinking that the experts on the British delegation in Paris agreed with them in guarding against any such departure, the officials of the Dominions Department were consequently alarmed to see that the Canadian Order in Council, which arrived ten days later, ordered Borden and his ministers to sign specifically on behalf of their own dominion. But when they warned the Foreign Office not to draw up the full powers themselves on any such exclusive terms, they found they were too late. The full powers had already been issued to the delegates in Paris, and they authorized all of the overseas ministers to sign the treaties quite definitely 'in respect of' their own dominions. A

---

[44] In practice, full powers tended to be issued to delegates at a conference only in time for the formal signing; they could be back-dated as necessary to cover the full period of any negotiations.
[45] CO 532/140: Hurst–Lambert, 28 March 1919.
[46] *Ibid*: (copy) Hurst–Hankey, 31 March 1919.

strongly worded protest to the Foreign Office expressed the department's extreme annoyance, though it was now clearly beside the point.

It turned out that the Canadian delegation had been a clear step ahead on this question, having known all along about the pre-war precedents regarding separate dominion signatures. Indeed they had pointedly asked Cecil Hurst for a copy of the 1913 full powers issued to dominion representatives, and had made it clear that they were not prepared to settle for less, despite the obvious differences between those earlier technical conferences and the proceedings in Paris.[47] Hurst had not resisted. But alas for the Colonial Office's righteous indignation, it further turned out on inquiry that the new colonial secretary, Lord Milner, when questioned about it by Hurst during one of his frequent trips to Paris, had personally given prior sanction to this capitulation to dominion status.[48] Probably confused, certainly overworked by Lloyd George, perhaps not knowing his officials' mind on this business of treaty signatures, Milner had simply agreed to follow the 1913 precedent, and thereby unwittingly permitted the dominions an advance in status of incalculable importance.

Poor communications, too little time for consideration of details, confusion on Milner's part – hardly the best conditions in which to contain Borden's efforts to enhance the significance of separate representation. The acceptance of signatures 'in respect of' the dominions, however, was won only at the cost of the original idea of placing Britain and the dominions on an equal footing in the treaties. The original Canadian memorandum of 12 March had called for the straightforward signature of the British and dominion ministers under the general title of 'the British Empire'. Now, under that same covering title, the dominion ministers were to sign specifically 'for' their respective nations – but the British ministers were definitely not limited to signing 'for' the United Kingdom, and in all the final documents they signed without qualification as imperial signatories. The formula first accepted had stressed the parity, under the aegis of the empire, of all who had participated in the peace settlement. The new formula was constitutionally ambivalent; ministers signed on their own dominions' behalf, yet were already committed by the unrestricted writs of the five British signatures. It was, however, a not inaccurate reflection of dominion frustrations in the course of the settlement of the peace.

Ratification of the treaties

At the beginning of May the most important phase of the Paris peace conference came to an end, with the completion – after much hasty work

[47] Christie papers: Christie–Hurst, 3 April 1919.
[48] CO 532/140: (copy) British delegation, Paris–FO, 27 May 1919.

by the Council of Four during April – of the allied terms of peace with Germany. These were presented to the German government on 7 May, and fifteen days were allowed for an official reply. The formal signature of the treaty could not now be far away, but it was at this point that Sir Robert Borden decided he could no longer put off his return to Canada and to the neglected political leadership of his coalition government. While the other prime ministers stayed on in Paris, and would add their own signatures to the final documents, Borden felt obliged to forgo this concluding act of representation for his dominion. It is clear, nonetheless, that the question of Canadian status at the conference remained a major preoccupation with the prime minister as he prepared to leave for home. Whereas, for example, General Smuts spent these last few weeks in Paris as he had spent the previous six months – agonizing over the broad terms of the peace settlement, pleading to the end with Lloyd George that there must be modifications in Germany's favour, wondering at the last how he could possibly sign a treaty so unjust – Borden's own assessment of possible dominion influence impelled him more than ever to suppress any such misgivings and to concentrate on more practical ends. A parting memorandum for the guidance of Foster and Doherty, the two ministers who were to carry on for Canada at Paris, urged them to attend not to any substantive elements of the terms of peace, but rather to the dominion's hard-won standing at the conference:

It is most important that the status which has been secured for Canada at the present Conference should be maintained and that any proposal whether made through design, inattention or misconception, which might detract therefrom, should be resisted and rejected.

It will be recalled that the effort to win this position has been prolonged, insistent and continuous. . .

In all this insistence upon due recognition of the nation-hood of the Dominions, Canada has led the way; and in most cases her representatives have made the fight without the active assistance from, although with the passive support of, the other Dominions.

The decisions thus reached should make the course comparatively simple for the future; but it is necessary to bear in mind an inevitable tendency on the part of officials and sometimes Ministers, to forget that the United Kingdom is not the only nation in the British Empire.[49]

In Borden's memorandum there was no reference to any eventual procedure for ratifying the peace treaties; for the moment, the prime minister was content to urge his ministers to look after more immediate Canadian

---

[49] Foster papers: 'Memorandum with respect to further work of the Peace Conference', 12 May 1919.

interests in the various peace treaties themselves. In an unpublicized way, however, moves to associate Canada in this final stage of the treatymaking process were already in hand. On the day the terms of peace were handed to the German government a summary of them was read to the Canadian House of Commons and on the following day Sir Thomas White, acting prime minister in Borden's absence, spoke of Canada's signature to the German treaty. It would be an 'executive act', he said, but he promised to submit the treaty for parliamentary 'consideration' and 'legislative sanction'. Under questioning his terminology changed: it would be submitted for 'consideration and ratification of the executive act of signing', and he added later that 'ratification by this Parliament will be in the same manner as the ratification by the Imperial Parliament of the signature of its plenipotentiaries'.[50]

The analogy was not an altogether fortunate one, for in British practice ratification of treaties remained the prerogative of the Crown, and except in special cases did not depend upon parliamentary approval. Even so, there were precedents to suggest that if a particular Canadian interest could be discerned – and in this case the separate dominion treaty signatures could be taken to indicate that – then the Canadian parliament might well expect a final say in the treaties. As far back as 1854, for example, the pre-Confederation colonies had been allowed to approve the terms of the Reciprocity Treaty with the United States in their local assemblies before it was officially ratified in London.[51] In 1887 the federal House of Commons had discussed a recently completed fishing treaty with the United States (rejected in the end by the U.S. Senate) and if thereafter there had been few other occasions for debate, this was largely because Canada's external interests had on the whole been adequately regulated by conventions, with little recourse to formal treaties. In this respect, the 1909 Waterways treaty mentioned above had proved to be important: when the Laurier government did not submit it for ratification – it had after all, not been signed by a Canadian, or styled as a Canadian treaty – they ran into considerable criticism from the Conservative opposition.[52] Taken together, British and Canadian past practice might not point conclusively to a right of dominion ratification, but it seems fair to say that in the spring of 1919 the Canadian House of Commons would have been

---

[50] Canada, HoC, 8 May 1919.
[51] More conclusively, the Newfoundland assembly three years later was allowed to pass judgement on a treaty negotiated by the British government with France to regulate fishing rights on the island. When they rejected it, the treaty was scrapped. W. MacNutt, *The Atlantic Provinces* (Toronto, 1965), 257.
[52] Canada, HoC, 14 May 1909, 16 May 1911.

disappointed to have learned otherwise. In any event, here was White's definite promise – the first declaration, some seven weeks before it was signed, of his government's claim to ratify the Treaty of Versailles in the Canadian parliament.

White's statement had been made on Borden's instructions, received from Paris on 17 April.[53] And Borden himself had decided upon ratification on his own, without reference to Lloyd George, the B.E.D. or the Colonial Office. Did he simply assume the dominion parliaments would be given the right – and the time – to review the German treaty? Or had his experiences in securing a satisfactory form of signature convinced him that the only safe procedure was to steal a long march on the British government? Whatever the case, Borden kept his own counsel, and because no notice was taken in Whitehall of the ministerial announcement in Ottawa, nothing more was heard about ratification until the end of June, when the Canadian prime minister boldly informed the Colonial Office that he intended to submit the Versailles treaty to parliament.

As in the case of dominion treaty signatures, Borden was the first overseas minister to raise the subject of ratification, and once again it was he who became the chief protagonist in the ensuing controversy about the status and privileges of the dominions. What he was not to know was that this time there was a marked change in the attitude of the Colonial Office. Having strongly opposed the form of treaty signature permitted to the dominions, they now proved equally ready, when faced with insistent demands from the Foreign Office that the peace settlement must be finalized at once, to support Borden's appeals, and prevent a pre-emptive British ratification of the German treaty.

There seemed at first little chance that ratification could wait upon the pleasure of the Canadian government, especially when Borden revealed that consideration of the German treaty was planned for an autumn session of the Canadian parliament. Two days after his message the treaty was signed, and by 2 July an 'enabling' bill to give effect to the provisions of the treaty (and designed to be operative throughout the empire) was ready to be put before the British parliament. 'For the sake of the Peace of the world & for political reasons', the Colonial Office were informed, 'the matter was regarded as urgent'. The department were nonetheless apprehensive: 'I fear that Sir R. Borden... is already irritated', minuted Henry Lambert, 'and will see in the Bill a direct challenge – I wonder whether P.M. realizes this side of the question'.[54] At the last moment they were able to change the draft bill in order to leave out all reference to the

53 Borden–White, 17 April 1919, printed in *DCER*, II, 118.
54 CO 532/136: copy of draft bill; Lambert, minute of 2 July 1919.

dominions, but within a few days they were obliged to tell the overseas governments that ratification for the empire would be occurring before the end of July.

Borden now became aggressive. His reply to this cable (which Lord Milner's secretary later termed 'somewhat of a bombshell') asked only one question. As no certified copy of the treaty had reached Ottawa, and as his government had promised parliament, now prorogued, a review of the treaty before Canada agreed to ratification, Borden wanted only to know 'how you expect to accomplish ratification on behalf of the whole Empire before the end of July'.[55] Legally, as he must have known, the letter if not the spirit of British constitutional law provided a short answer to his question. Nevertheless, the force of his implied contention – that ratification without their consent would be a grave offence to the dominions – was not lost upon the Colonial Office, and Milner endeavoured to postpone ratification as long as he possibly could.

It was fortunate for Milner that the foreign secretary, Arthur Balfour, was in Paris at this moment, for in his absence the colonial secretary managed to secure from the war cabinet a temporary postponement of ratification (a decision he promptly relayed to Borden). Balfour, who had unaccountably not been kept in touch with events by his departmental officials, could only remonstrate privately with Milner, and urge him to see that further delay to ratification was impossible:

For various reasons the only three powers who are in a position to ratify quickly are France, Italy and Great Britain . . . It would be disastrous if whole of Peace of the world were to be hung up for months because Canadian Parliament had adjourned and in order to give time for Treaty to reach Australia.[56]

The only possible solution was partial ratification, at which point the dominions would 'be in exactly the same position as all other signatories including United States and Japan'. It was a position, Milner pointed out in reply, that the dominions had no wish to occupy:

I don't quite understand your view . . . that we might ratify and at the same time leave it open to the Dominions to deposit further ratifications. I can hardly suppose that it would be any particular satisfaction to them to go through what in that case would be a meaningless formality. Either our ratification binds the whole Empire or it does not. If it does not, then it does not fulfill the condition that three of the principal . . . Powers must ratify before the Treaty becomes effective . . . If, on the other hand, our ratification

[55] CO 532/132: Gov Gen–Col Sec, 10 July 1919.
[56] *Ibid*: Balfour–Milner, 23 July 1919.

does bind the whole Empire, as I believe it would, then the subsequent ratifications of the Dominions are mere impotent exhibitions of the desire for an
independence which, in this case, they have not really got.[57]

Milner agreed that a delay of months would be intolerable. A delay of a
few weeks, on the other hand, was a very different matter, for it might
prove sufficient for the dominions. At least, he thought, 'it seems to me
right to give them the chance'.

The principle upon which the resolution of the crisis turned was provided in the end by Lloyd George. The prime minister had himself
sounded opinion in the British delegation in Paris, and was now a convert
to their view that ratification must proceed at once. He would not tolerate
'waiting for seven governments represented in the Peace Conference to
ratify before we will consent to append our signature', and he wanted the
colonial secretary to tell the dominions 'that it will be impossible for the
British Government to hold up the coming into force of the peace after
ratification by two of the principal powers'.[58] Milner, construing these
instructions to mean that as long as two other major powers had not
ratified the dominions should be allowed the opportunity to do so themselves, continued to play for time. Italian plans remained obscure, but it
appeared that France would ratify in early September. 'I presume',
minuted Lambert, 'that if France ratifies 3 Sep[tember] we shall try to
put off till at least Canada has ratified'.[59]

In the event the Colonial Office did not have to withstand any further
pressure, for as August passed into September the dominion parliaments
one by one debated and approved the Versailles treaty, with no word from
either France or Italy. Australian assent, the last, came on 2 October. Italy
ratified on 7 October, France not until 11 October. On the day the
Australian cable arrived, Milner wrote a relieved note to his prime
minister:

All the Dominions have now signified their assent to our ratification, & the
whole Empire can come in by a single act.

This is rather a triumph, as by waiting we have avoided any friction or
soreness with the Dominions, while the British Empire is after all ready to
ratify as soon as any of the Allies.[60]

It was a triumph Milner deserved to celebrate. His defence of dominion
interests, coupled admittedly with good fortune, had enabled the empire

[57] CO 532/137: Milner–Balfour, 26 July 1919.
[58] Lloyd George papers: Ll. G.–Milner, 31 July 1919, enclosing a memorandum
     from Hurst on British delegation opinions.
[59] CO 532/133: minute, 6 Aug 1919.
[60] Lloyd George papers: Milner–Ll. G., 2 Oct 1919.

to function as a diplomatic unit against considerable odds. His attitude reflected a sympathetic understanding that for some if not all of the dominion governments, ratification was as much a concern of national politics as of international diplomacy. More importantly, perhaps, he also understood that if Great Britain were through expediency to put the empire's formal constitutional structure to the test, her relations with the dominions might be severely jeopardized.

Borden as well could take satisfaction from the final outcome of the ratification problem. It was the successful climax to ten months of wearing negotiations, throughout which he had represented Canadian interests with remarkable determination. These interests had remained constant: a stable peace settlement, which in particular would strengthen British–American friendship; an adequate voice for Canada in the making of the empire's foreign affairs; and an adequate recognition that within the empire Canada and the other dominions stood now as partners to Great Britain. His experiences of the peace conference had been a bitter dis-appointment to him with respect to the first two of these aims. Yet he showed clearly that he intended to pursue them still. In August 1919, for instance, he was ready to seek parliamentary approval for the new and vital Anglo–French guarantee treaty that had been negotiated in May in conjunction with a parallel American–French treaty. He would welcome the chance to make Canada a co-ordinate imperial element in this critical security pact, he told General Botha, because the combined agreements would bring 'closer co-operation and indeed a virtual alliance between the British Empire and the United States'.[61] To Borden this was worth a great deal.

But his energies during the peace negotiations had perforce been turned towards the question of status. A clear sense of direction in regard to the evolution of imperial relations led him to advocate separate dominion representation, signature and ratification to the settlement of peace, and with surprisingly little assistance from other dominion ministers, all three demands had been achieved. A substantial definition of the dominions' relations to Great Britain had still to be determined by a full-scale con-stitutional conference. In advance of this, the Canadian prime minister had made a most important contribution to the development of their status.

---

[61] Borden–Botha, 24 Aug 1919; *DCER*, II, 173. In the end Borden waited for the American part of the security pact to be completed before proceeding himself. As this was not ratified no further action on his part was possible.

4

Unity and equality, 1919–1921

In the period that began with the departure of the overseas delegations from the Paris peace conference, British–dominion relations were marked by uncertainty and ambiguity – uncertainty because in spite of the striking record of co-operative endeavours of the previous few years, the pace and general direction of imperial affairs now lacked the clarifying stimulus of war; ambiguity because the dominions' rapidly advancing position within the imperial association, which was only just beginning to make its impact at the organizational level, had been overshadowed and possibly eclipsed by their new access to international affairs gained through the peace settlement. On the surface little was changed. At a time when dominion administrations were free again to return to their domestic concerns they were happy enough to leave wider imperial problems to the management of the British authorities, retaining a commitment in principle to an active role in the conduct of foreign affairs but in practice paying very selective and sporadic attention to these matters. With the Foreign Office therefore continuing to look after foreign policy on everyone's behalf the empire's diplomatic unity seemed unstrained. Yet while Britain and the dominions in this way maintained at least a passive form of imperial co-operation and mutual responsibilities, overseas governments were interested (if not actually under pressure) to consolidate and extend the status achieved at the Paris conference. The full implications of the new departure had still to be worked out, but soon enough the dominions were being spoken of as having attained a status of virtual equality with Britain – and there were few constraints upon them to prevent that equality being manifested at the expense of the empire's essential unity.

At the Colonial Office in 1919 Milner was prepared to acknowledge the dominions as legitimate partners of the mother country, and anxious to demonstrate that they could be treated as such. He endeavoured to secure administrative changes through the machinery of the Cabinet Office that would reflect their new status, and meet their own expectations in this regard. But although Hankey responded to Milner's promptings no major reforms were achieved, and the colonial secretary's initiative did not last. There seems, critically, to have been no support for imperial reorganization from Lloyd George at this stage. The prime minister, far from realigning his administrative structures to take account of the altered balance of imperial relations, turned instead to an increasing involvement with foreign affairs, with the result that while the Cabinet Office was given no freedom to develop any new imperial sub-department, Lloyd George's own Garden Suburb in Downing Street went on to become a serious rival to the Foreign Office. Reluctantly Milner saw that responsibility for British–Dominion relations would have to remain with the Colonial Office.

The dominions, with Canada in the vanguard of developments, were meanwhile beginning to come to terms with their post-war status. Within the imperial framework in which they continued without question to locate themselves, the Canadian Government sought to exercise broader national functions, to fill out and develop the competence of a dominion–partner of the mother country. There was no intention to weaken or fragment the empire's international position. But the changes, particularly Canadian diplomatic representation at Washington, were resented by the British administration; and in any case they did prove hard to reconcile with the concept of the empire as a diplomatic entity. The problem of giving adequate external expression to British–dominion equality of status, while preserving an undivided imperial foreign policy, appeared to have no easy solutions. In this respect it was of great significance that a constitutional conference, which everyone had been anticipating since the war, and which might have reconciled some of the growing difficulties, proved impossible to convene. There was thus no opportunity for Britain and the dominions to adjust to a more flexible, devolutionary post-war relationship, with the result that manifest alterations in the balance of power, both within the empire and in the empire's external position were left unresolved to exert their influence on imperial affairs.

It was hardly surprising, with future imperial responsibilities and commitments unsettled, that there should be a very sceptical approach to imperial defence. Without any principles established to govern consultation and collaboration over policies in this area, it became extremely difficult to achieve any balanced dominion commitment to a shared naval programme. The Canadian government, assessing their own position on defence spending, found that in political terms the imperial factor counted for less and less when measured against a growing isolationist reaction. From an imperial point of view their record in this period was dismal, even irresponsible – but absolutely in keeping with the political limits imposed by the Canadian House of Commons.

For those who hoped to secure a defined constitutional readjustment, or to end the post-war drift in naval defence planning, the Imperial Conference of 1921 was a singular disappointment. Although the dominion leaders had some difficulty deciding on the terms under which they themselves should meet – did they constitute a revived Imperial War Cabinet, or an Imperial Conference on pre-war lines? – they were able readily enough to discover that there was no consensus for change in either the empire's constitutional or defence arrangements. Overshadowing these matters, however, was an even more critical issue in imperial relations, which could not simply be met by indecision or disagreement. The Anglo-Japanese alliance was up for reconsideration in 1921, the ten-year span of its term finishing during the conference itself, and it fell to the assembled premiers to decide on its future. With Canada alone but unshakeable in its opposition to renewal, the empire's united and single voice in foreign affairs appeared to be dangerously close to fragmenting, and the Canadian prime minister offered little scope for mediation. A combination of events permitted Meighen to draw back from his advanced position, and a final verdict to be left for a new conference in Washington. But by the end of the conference in any event, the Canadian point of view on the alliance had largely been accepted as the agreed imperial policy.

Milner and the reform of dominion affairs

In early June 1919, with the final settlement of the German peace terms, the B.E.D. at Paris met for the last time as a high-level committee of imperial ministers. After signing the Treaty of Versailles later that month, the overseas delegates returned to their dominions, leaving the other treaties and conventions of the peace conference to be signed by high commissioners or other dominion representatives. At their departure the Colonial Office became once more the principal channel of communications between the British and dominion governments. More significantly, the Office found that it continued to be generally responsible for the practical administration of Britain's relations with the overseas governments. In theory, certainly, this should not have been the case. At the 1918 Imperial War Cabinet the dominion premiers had been given the right of direct telegraphic contact with the British prime minister, a right they had demanded as an explicit means of restricting Colonial Office authority over their dealings with the British government. In practice, did they but know it, the cables they so deliberately sent to Lloyd George were with few exceptions passed – or rather, returned, since the Colonial Office provided the necessary de-cyphering in any case[1] – directly to the Colonial

---

[1] In August 1918 Long had strongly opposed a suggestion from Lloyd George.

Office. The reason was quite simply that the prime minister's own staff, when dealing with these cables, were invariably reluctant to take action without advice from the department best suited to give it.

Had Walter Long been secretary of state, he would no doubt have been pleased that the Colonial Office had retained so much of its former responsibility for the dominions. Nor is there any evidence to suggest that the Dominions Department of the Office were anxious to curtail the influence over policy that remained to them. They were not relishing a constitutional conference, at which their authority would undoubtedly be called into question. The attitude of Long's successor, however, was altogether different. Milner, who had come to the Colonial Office in January 1919, was primarily interested in imperial unity, and the role played by the Imperial War Cabinet and the B.E.D. in promoting such unity. 'Something is needed to take their place', he told an Oxford audience in August 1919, 'if the Empire is to preserve in peace that capacity for unity of action which they gave to it in war and during the Peace negotiations.'[2] At some point the post-war constitutional conference would come to terms with the problem of imperial reorganization. Meanwhile, as colonial secretary he was determined to provide the closest possible contact and co-operation with the dominion governments. Yet, this was an enterprise in which Milner felt the Colonial Office had little relevance, for in his view the equality of status between Britain and the dominions entailed that their mutual affairs should now be the responsibility of the cabinet and its secretariat. Three months after becoming colonial secretary, he publicly apologized for the 'antiquated forms' under which his department continued to have dealings with dominion affairs. He looked forward to the day when 'this and many other anachronisms would disappear'.[3]

Not unnaturally, Milner could not accept the position of the Colonial Office with regard to direct cable communications between prime ministers. As his secretary pointed out, because the cables were decoded and usually answered by the Office, 'the net result . . . has been that the use of the new channel of communications has merely led to delay in sending a

that a code independent of the Colonial Office be established for these cables. He threatened to resign unless 'kept informed at all times of all that passes'. Lloyd George papers: Long–Ll. G., 21 Aug 1918.

[2] Speech of 1 Aug 1919, printed as *The British Commonwealth* (London, 1919).

[3] Speech to the Manchester branch of the Royal Colonial Institute, 10 April 1919, printed in *United Empire*, x, no 5 (1919), 223–5. Cf speech of 10 July 1919: 'The only possibility of a continuance of the British Empire is on a basis of absolute out-and-out equal partnership between the United Kingdom and the Dominions. I say this without any kind of reservation whatever'; quoted in R. Borden, *Canadian Constitutional Studies* (London, 1921), 114.

reply'.[4] Two weeks later Milner raised the matter with Hankey. The existing arrangement, he argued, was 'pure camouflage, – the old system circumlocution and eyewash'. It did not concern him if Lloyd George took no interest in the cables; that was 'probably inevitable'. The cardinal point was that

> the present semi-responsibility or 1/4 responsibility of this Office in the matter is all wrong. This Office might or might not be consulted, but it ought not to be the Office *in charge*, seeing that the essence and object of the whole arrangement was to remove certain matters from the C.O. (Departmental) plane to the War Cabinet plane.[5]

The colonial secretary was unable to pursue this question much further with Hankey because in November 1919 he took leave to conduct an extensive mission in Egypt, and at his departure nothing had been settled. However, a solution of sorts was reached in January 1920 when Hughes, the Australian prime minister, himself requested a cypher exclusive of the Colonial Office system. He was by far the most frequent dispatcher of direct cables to Lloyd George, and his use of a private cypher gave Milner much of what he wanted.

There was a second administrative matter which the colonial secretary was at pains to remove 'to the War Cabinet plane'. In October 1918 the Colonial Office had secured the authority to select and transmit whatever British war cabinet papers they felt should be seen by the dominion governments. At the time this concession had been regarded as an important victory in the Office's fight to retain a partial control of dominion affairs, but reviewing the practice in July 1919 Milner could see no possible justification for its continuation. In his view, the dominion prime ministers received cabinet papers because they were members of the Imperial War Cabinet, a body which had been prorogued rather than dissolved. The Colonial Office should therefore 'merely ... act the part of postman'.[6] When pressed, Hankey was prepared to admit that the responsibility for the cabinet papers was his. Milner in turn agreed to let his department advise Hankey upon the choice of documents, and so little was changed in practice. The colonial secretary, nonetheless, had successfully defended the principle that dominion affairs were primarily a charge upon the Cabinet Office.

In 1919, notwithstanding these attempts to provide closer contact between the British and dominion governments, Milner had few grounds

[4] CO 532/138/56476: Major H. Thornton, minute of 26 Sept 1919.
[5] CO 537/1024: Milner–Hankey, 10 Oct 1919.
[6] CO 537/1025: Thornton–Wilson (Cabinet Office), 17 July 1919.

for optimism as regards the maintenance of the active imperial co-operation generated by the war. He himself could not deny that there was a post-war 'ebb-tide from the high moral and spiritual level ... of the past four years'.[7] More specifically, it was not encouraging that imperial problems held so little interest for Lloyd George. The most alarming threat, however, had come from premier Botha of South Africa, in connection with the Anglo-French guarantee treaty of May 1919. Dominion misgivings about this treaty had led to their being excluded from it unless and until any of them chose to adhere, though as we have seen, Borden at least was ready to commit Canada to the agreement. Botha, for his part, seized on the constitutional significance of this optional exclusion clause, seeing in it the final proof that the dominions had now achieved a 'status of independent nationhood'. It meant, he went on to argue, that 'in some future continental war, Great Britain may be at war, and one or more of the Dominions may stand out and maintain their neutrality'.[8] Milner at once protested to Lloyd George that Botha's view of the treaty was 'incompatible with the existence of the British Empire as a political unit', and the British prime minister duly pointed out to Botha that by 'neutrality' the latter presumably meant the right to withhold active support in wartime.[9] The South African prime minister did not choose to refute this interpretation. For Milner, nonetheless, the incident was hardly an assurance that the growth of dominion independence would strengthen imperial unity.

In submitting his protest against Botha's claims to neutrality, the colonial secretary had acted with the full support of his permanent officials. The Dominion Department had given Botha's arguments short shrift, if only because the legal unity of the empire meant that neutrality, as he understood it, was impossible. But they could see that behind this legal framework the dominions' post-war status presented an egregious problem for the empire's diplomatic unity, particularly as regards a future declaration of war. The 'new constitutional arrangements', they assumed, would have to give the dominions some definite control over such vital imperial policy decisions – though there was no indication how this could be done. The department, in short, were as concerned as Lord Milner about the empire's post-war unity. They differed with him only in thinking that the

[7] Milner, *British Commonwealth*, 5–6.
[8] CO 532/147: Botha–Lloyd George, 15 May 1919.
[9] CO 532/147: Milner–Lloyd George, 28 May 1919; Ll. G.–Botha, 26 June 1919. Hancock is wrong to say that Botha and Smuts 'exacted from Lloyd George an acknowledgement of the Union's right to remain neutral in a British war'. *Smuts*, I, 550.

Colonial Office were not yet superfluous to the conduct of British–dominion relations.[10]

By the end of 1919, the department were probably little bothered by Milner's views about administrative procedure, because in practice they faced no immediate threat of redundancy. Direct communications with the British prime minister had to some extent been instituted, and the selection of cabinet papers for the dominions had been undertaken by the Cabinet Office. Yet any fuller rationalization in the conduct of imperial affairs depended absolutely on the government's creating an effective successor for the Imperial War Cabinet, and in late 1919 there were still no plans for a change in this direction. In fact a critical opportunity for an initiative on these lines was passed over by Lloyd George at this point, when he decided that the British war cabinet should be replaced by a full cabinet of twenty. Although there was some idea of developing 'imperial' and 'home' sections, in effect there was a simple reversion to the pre-war style of cabinet government, and a consequent weakening of the executive and administrative relationships with the dominion governments that the British war cabinet had been capable of.[11] It meant, in practice, that the Colonial Office found themselves still intimately involved with dominion affairs. As ever, they looked after routine administrative matters and continued also to deal with the high commissioners. Their most important function, however, was to maintain their surveillance of foreign policy, for the Foreign Office had yet to understand the need to consult the dominions. Early in 1920, for example, five minor treaties deriving from the peace settlement were all but signed before the department were able to delay proceedings in order to seek dominion approval. Consultation in such cases was purely formal, yet in part the post-war diplomatic unity of the empire was going to consist of just such formalities. 'F.O. will have to learn', warned Henry Lambert,

that the new Constitution of the Empire necessarily acts as a clog on the conclusion of agreements such as this. We formerly spoke without hesitation for the Empire & all British subjects, provided that the territorial jurisdiction of the Dom[inion]s was secured inviolately by an accession clause. Now we

[10] It might be noted that Leo Amery, under-secretary to Milner at the Colonial Office, fully shared his chief's views about restricting the department's administrative role. Indeed in 1918 he had described Sir George Fiddes, the permanent under-secretary, as 'arid, pedantic, narrow and excruciating to any Dominion public man who comes in contact with him, even across the cables. I imagine it must have been some ancestor of his that finally decided Benjamin Franklin that America's best chance lay in revolution.' Lloyd George papers: Amery–Ll. G., 14 April 1918.

[11] Roskill, *Hankey*, II, 127.

must wait to get agreement all round. If we do not get it, we shall be driven to the old accession clause (if [the dominions] will permit that) or to split up British Nationality. This will be a very difficult and painful process, and if & when the doctrine of "Civis Romanus sum" is finally interred, there will be very little left of the Br[itish] Empire.[12]

In cases of greater importance, where a dominion interest was more obvious, the Colonial Office usually had less to worry about. For example, knowing that reparations would be discussed between allied and German ministers at the Boulogne and Spa conferences in 1920, Hankey was careful to hold talks in London with dominion representatives prior to both meetings. By the same token, when the Foreign Office came to consider the question of renewing the Anglo-Japanese alliance in early 1920, they needed no reminding that the views of the dominion governments would have to be taken fully into account.

But however broadly 'the new Constitution of the Empire' was to be interpreted in the post-war context, it was not for one moment supposed by either the Colonial or the Foreign Offices that imperial foreign policy in its entirety was now subject to the prior approval of the dominion governments. Between the formal but essentially unimportant matters now requiring dominion assent and those which demanded comprehensive consultation there lay the broad range of foreign affairs administered by the Foreign Office, the responsibility for which was borne by the British government alone. The dominions were not without knowledge of the march of these events, having since early 1917 received a steady flow of diplomatic briefings from Whitehall. However, a more active association with the general manifold of foreign policy was precluded by their unwillingness to undertake tangible external commitments. The limits of any substantial overseas interest in this respect was recognized and accepted by the British government even while the peace conference was still in session – as indicated by the optional exclusion clause for the dominions in the draft Anglo-French guarantee treaty of May 1919.

A more striking instance of dominion hostility to external obligations in 1919 was Canada's persistent opposition to any continued military activity in Russia. While the fighting on the western front had remained unfinished Borden had been prepared to send troops to the Russian theatre as part of an allied initiative; but immediately the armistice was declared his government came under strong pressure at home to get the Canadians out – so much so that until they were finally withdrawn in June 1919, nearly all the dominion's forces were deliberately prohibited by orders

[12] CO 532/160: minute of 23 Jan 1920.

from Ottawa from any active engagements against the Russian Communist forces.[13] Such was the momentum with which the external interests of the dominions were shrinking to their pre-war horizons. And a second Canadian case in point would indicate that even where dominion public opinion might actively focus on a problem beyond its borders, it was hardly to be considered a basis for positive government action. In early 1920 there was widespread concern in Canada over the fate of Armenia, and with a growing number of reports about massacres in that area the dominion government was induced to send the Colonial Office several strongly-worded representations demanding Armenian independence. In spite of their adamant tone, however, the Canadian authorities knew very well that they were based only on moral indignation: when asked in return if they would consider a mandate for a liberated Armenia, Borden's ministers showed no enthusiasm whatever. Indeed the newly-elected leader of the Liberal party, Mackenzie King, insisted that the idea of Canada having a mandated territory 'would provoke general protest from one end of the Dominion to the other'.[14] Under such circumstances, then, small wonder that consultation with the overseas dominions remained the exception rather than the rule. Philip Kerr, his Round Table idealism tempered by over three years' experience as secretary to the British prime minister, assessed the situation in April 1920:

The only method upon which the Empire can be run at present is that Great Britain should be responsible for foreign policy, keeping the Dominions informed mostly after the events, and consulting them about matters directly affecting their interests. Directly the Dominions begin to have strong feelings about general foreign policy we are up against the fundamental issue because no Government which is responsible for foreign affairs can possibly undertake to subordinate its views to those of other people unless those people are willing to share the responsibility for and the consequence of policy.[15]

Canada and the pursuit of national status

Amongst the governments and parliaments of the dominions in 1920 there were few people who would have challenged Kerr's analysis of the imperial relationship as regards foreign affairs, and few also who would have been prepared to contribute the material support necessary for any

---

13 See J. Eayrs, *In Defence of Canada*, 1: *From the Great War to the Great Depression* (Toronto, 1964), ch 1.

14 Quoted in Eayrs, *In Defence of Canada*, 1, 6.

15 Kerr–Edward Grigg, 15 April 1920, quoted in J. R. Butler, *Lord Lothian* (London, 1960), 79. Grigg was to succeed Kerr as Lloyd George's private secretary, May 1921–October 1922.

closer involvement in policymaking. A glance at the debates held in each of the overseas legislatures in the autumn of 1919, when the German peace treaty and by extension the dominions' new role in foreign affairs were under consideration, is sufficient to indicate where priorities lay. In seeking to account for themselves at the Paris peace conference, and to clarify the dominions' new standing in the empire, none of the prime ministers chose to dwell on the possibilities for further collaboration with Britain in the conduct of imperial diplomacy. Hughes and Massey were content to emphasize the territorial prizes they had won, and beyond that neither wished to assert any fresh prerogatives at all in relation to Britain. Smuts and Borden, on the other hand, drew very different inferences from the results of the peace settlement, and both clearly felt that through their independent participation at Paris the dominions were now virtually equal partners with Britain. But if the dominions were advancing in this way from a status of simple autonomy in the empire to one approaching parity with the mother country, it was certainly not in order to assume fresh responsibilities for the empire's foreign affairs: freedom of action in this respect remained unchanged. Indeed, such were the terms of the debate in South Africa, Smuts found General Hertzog's opposition Nationalists excited less by fears of collective responsibilities, as stemming from the dominions' maturing status, than by hopes of the constitutional freedom to secede from the empire altogether.

For the South African prime minister, harried by Hertzog's persistent questioning about status, here was the beginning of a campaign to bring Britain and the dominions to agree on a comprehensive definition of their constitutional relations – no easy task, yet one that Smuts considered essential in order to satisfy political and public opinion in his dominion. In Canada, one or two influential voices were beginning to reach similar conclusions about status. John Dafoe, back at his editorial desk after his term in Paris as Borden's press officer, wrote to his publisher in late August 1919:

With respect to the Peace Conference and Canada there is one comment which is quite obvious and that is, that the developments at Paris have made more apparent than ever the anomalous situation of the Dominion and has reinforced powerfully the necessity for a new definition of our status.[16]

But in parliament Borden and his ministers found they were under very little political pressure in this respect to produce definitions and distinctions about Canada's post-war status. For the debate on the Versailles treaty revealed only to clearly that the Liberal opposition had no united position

---

[16] Sifton papers: Dafoe–Sir C. Sifton, 26 Aug 1919.

from which to challenge the government's achievements at Paris. Badly divided in 1917 over the war effort, when the majority had broken rank to support conscription, they seemed even further divided over the dominion's association with the settlement of peace: while some feared that Canada had been pushed too far and too fast beyond her old colonial associations with the empire, others were equally afraid that imperial federation would soon be established; and if some were apprehensive about the external obligations imposed by the League of Nations, others felt that Canada had no rightful place in that organization in the first place. It was hardly surprising if King, (who had yet to take a seat in the House of Commons) was principally worried that the government might seize on these divided opinions to call a general election.[17]

Under the circumstances, then, it was the government speakers who easily enough held the initiative in the treaty debate, and as a result the ambivalences of Canada's imperial relationship did not have to be pursued to any conclusive lengths. Borden in his opening remarks had alluded to both imperial unity and dominion independence, pointing out that 'Each nation must preserve unimpaired its absolute autonomy, but it must likewise have its voice as to those external relations which involve the issue of peace and war',[18] and in the course of the debate both aspects of Canada's place in the empire were acknowledged. Yet it is clear, even so, that the government were less concerned with any possible collective control of imperial foreign policy than with the new degree of independence the dominions had won for themselves at Paris. Separate dominion signatures and ratification were duly emphasized, and Canada's membership of the League of Nations was displayed as further convincing proof of her international standing. And for those who were anxious that the government had gained a new freedom in external affairs only to lose it immediately in commitments to the League, there was a further reassurance from C. J. Doherty, speaking now as minister of justice: 'Between the people of Canada and the operation of the Council under article x', he promised, 'there will always be standing the undisturbed power of the Parliament of Canada.'[19] Doherty, as we shall see, was compelled here to offer assurances that he himself in Paris had sought in vain from the drafters of the League Covenant. For the moment, however, his words

[17] King Diary, 2 Sept 1919.
[18] Canada, HoC, 2 Sept 1919.
[19] *Ibid*, 11 Sept 1919. Article x of the Covenant committed members to 'respect and preserve as against external aggression the territorial integrity and existing political independence of all states members of the League'. See 115 ff, and ch 7.

came as one more indication that the government looked confidently forward to the further development of Canada's national independence under the auspices of the empire.

Within a month of the debate on the Versailles treaty, as an earnest of their attitude towards post-war imperial relations, Borden's government presented the Colonial Office with a formal request for Canadian diplomatic representation at Washington. It was not, in this case, a completely new claim that was being put forward from Ottawa, for the question of some form of permanent Canadian representation in the American capital had been discussed intermittently for many years at various political and administrative levels. As early as 1892 there had been a debate in the Canadian House of Commons on the subject, though it was not until the creation of the Department of External Affairs, during Laurier's last ministry, that the idea of a Canadian attaché to the British embassy was more fully considered, though again nothing came of it.[20] A more positive step forward was taken by Borden in 1917 while in London for the Imperial War Cabinet. In discussion with the colonial secretary it was agreed in principle that 'we can have a Canadian on Embassy at Washington',[21] and when several months later the prime minister appeared to have found the man for the job – Douglas Hazen, his minister of marine, who could not be usefully fitted into Borden's new coalition government – negotiations went forward about the terms of Canadian representation at Washington. In 1917, however, no final conclusions had to be reached. Hazen backed away from such a financially demanding position (he would not be the last to do so) and Borden lacking a ready replacement decided in the end to settle for a War Mission, which was appointed in early 1918 to look after Canadian interests in Washington at a non-diplomatic level for the duration of the war. The Mission was attached without difficulty to the British embassy, and its chairman was Lloyd Harris, a director of the Massey–Harris manufacturing concern.

The Canadian War Mission appears to have worked well within its terms of reference, and Borden had no hesitation in allowing it to run on after the armistice of November 1918. It is equally clear that he continued to regard it, both in function and status, as no more than a prelude to a fully-fledged diplomatic appointment in Washington. When

20 Fuller details of this subject will be found in R. Bothwell, 'Canadian Representation at Washington: a study in colonial responsibility', *CHR*, LIII, no 2 (1972), on which the following paragraphs are partly based.
21 Borden diary, 12 April 1917.

voting $50,000 to cover running expenses for 1919, the Canadian parliament was told that the Mission would soon be up-graded. With such clear statements of intent, it therefore says very little for the understanding of the Colonial Office that when at last the dominion government distilled their proposals into a formal request of October 1919, they should have exhibited such unremitting opposition to the idea of Canadian representation at the American capital. Yet they continued to think of it as 'clearly a separatist move', which would spell the end of the empire's diplomatic unity. In a decidedly less co-operative mood than when considering Borden's proposals of 1917, the department now questioned whether the Canadian proposals were 'desired by "Canada" as distinct from the Borden Gov[ernmen]t', and under-secretary Sir George Fiddes went so far as to suggest that representation at Washington should not be granted 'on anything less formal than an Address from both Houses of the Canadian Parliament'.[22]

In 1917 Walter Long might have been convinced by this advice to take a firmer stand against the proposed innovations. Two years later Lord Milner and Leopold Amery were not at all impressed by the desperate reflections of their civil servants, and calmly accepted the Canadian request as the basis for negotiations. In essence, the dominion government had asked for a separate minister in Washington, but one who would maintain such close liaison with the British ambassador as to avoid any possible rupture in the diplomatic unity of the empire. Amery, in turn, produced a scheme that would bifurcate the British embassy into a 'general' and a specifically 'Canadian' section, into which a minister appointed from Ottawa would fit under the over-all control of the ambassador. With this plan discussions were opened with the Foreign Office, Amery throwing out the added suggestions that the next British ambassador to Washington should be selected only after consultation with Ottawa, and that the appointment might in any event well be filled by a Canadian.[23] And although it required a good deal of detailed negotiation, both inter-departmentally and with the Borden government, an agreed scheme of Canadian representation took shape over the winter of 1919–20. The

22 CO 42/1012: minutes, 6 Oct 1919.

23 The Foreign Office, Amery later recalled, 'were livid', about these ideas (CO 532/309: minute of 12 July 1925). But they were not as far-fetched as the Foreign Office officials might have thought. In early 1919 Lloyd George had made a tentative proposal to Borden that he succeed the British ambassador, Lord Reading, at Washington, although public rumours forced Borden to disclaim any knowledge of the offer, and the idea was not pursued further. Lloyd George papers: Borden–Ll. G., 13 Feb 1919. Borden papers: Borden–White (acting prime minister), 26 March 1919.

dominion administration, it became clear, held no particular brief for representation at the cost of diplomatic unity. They were quite willing to modify their proposals, and in the end they accepted a far more unified scheme than that originally suggested. There was to be a Canadian minister plenipotentiary acting on Canadian instructions, who would be the channel of communication between the American and Canadian governments. He would be an integral part of the British mission, and when the ambassador was absent from Washington would take charge of the embassy. This arrangement was announced in both parliaments on 10 May 1920.

Yet in the end it was not all plain sailing for the dominion government. For one thing the Canadian House of Commons proved far from totally convinced about the soundness of the idea when they came to discuss it a week later. It was just as well that Borden himself, having been away from Ottawa for much of the winter and spring trying to recover his health, had returned in time to participate in this debate and to reassert his own personal commitment to the proposal. For in a poorly attended House and against a strongly reunited Liberal party, he was able to secure a majority of only five for the new agreement – an inauspicious beginning.[24] Moreover, even at this seemingly final stage of the business, there was still one essential aspect of Canadian representation that had yet to be settled with the British authorities. This was the question of diplomatic precedence, not a matter of critical importance to the day-to-day conduct of imperial foreign policy, yet one that threatened to jeopardize the entire negotiations.

Whitehall, it is fair to say, had in any event hardly reconciled themselves to the idea of a Canadian in Washington. Even as the general details were being worked out in March 1920, a Foreign Office official had minuted candidly, 'As far as [we are] concerned, we should certainly be pleased to see the appointment abandoned', and he noted as well that Lord Milner himself had admitted 'he would . . . not be sorry if . . . deadlock did arise and the request was abandoned.'[25] It was over diplomatic precedence, however, that the Foreign Office became seriously hostile to Canada. Borden's government showed extra-ordinary sensitivity on this subject. With all other difficulties cleared away, they were still insisting that within the Washington diplomatic corps, a Canadian representative should be on an equal footing with ministers from other countries despite his subordinate position within the British embassy itself. From Ottawa N. R. Rowell, the president of the Privy Council, offered the Foreign Office various historical examples, however bizarre, to support the

[24] Canada, HoC, 17 May 1920.
[25] FO 371/4566: R. Sperling, American Department, minute of 27 March 1920.

Canadian position, and Loring Christie, who was in London on other
business, did his best to press his government's case. But this special pleading succeeded only in arousing the anger of the Foreign Office officials.
Sir Eyre Crowe, the permanent under-secretary, minuted testily:

Why should all the rules of the world be thrown overboard at the desire of a
Canadian gov[ernmen]t? It is surely enough to create the anomalous position
already approved. But that the second official of an Embassy should, when the
Ambassador himself is present, be treated as if he were the head of an independent mission, is too absurd, and should, I think, not be countenanced by us.
Rather than have such an arrangement, I should prefer to let the Canadians
have an altogether separate representation – in which case they would soon
find out that they have weakened and not strengthened their position.[26]

A month later, when Canadian representation was announced, the problem
of precedence remained unsolved. Against the day when the appointment
was made, Borden's government would concede nothing, and formally
stated as much to the Foreign Office. 'The Canadian Gov[ernmen]t seem
to be trying to see how much they can make us swallow while giving
nothing in return', noted Lord Hardinge. 'Personally', minuted Lord
Curzon with disdain, 'I think the attitude of the Canadian gov[ernmen]t
intolerable.'[27]

The dominion's reluctance to compromise over precedence may appear
at odds with their acceptance of representation within the framework of
imperial diplomatic unity. As Crowe had pointed out, that unity logically
precluded the special diplomatic status they sought at Washington. Behind
this logical contradiction, nonetheless, one can discern an understandable
disquiet. Borden's government were satisfied that Canada's post-war position in the empire–commonwealth justified dominion representation at
Washington. At the same time, it was equally clear that in asking for
permission to make an appointment to the American capital they had
no intention of trying to gain complete diplomatic independence from
Great Britain, and that in their view a united imperial foreign policy was
in no way incompatible with a dominion status of equality with Britain. It
was simply a matter of understanding that the empire's diplomatic unity
was now to prevail as between associated partners, rather than between a
mother country and her colonial dependencies. Unfortunately, established
diplomatic protocol provided no means of giving adequate external expression to this new internal relationship. On the contrary, if the public

26 FO 371/4566: minute of 5 April 1920.
27 FO 371/4567: minutes, n.d. Curzon had replaced Arthur Balfour as foreign
   secretary in October 1919.

status of a Canadian representative at Washington was to be inferior to that of all foreign ministers, it would imply that the dominions remained subordinate to Great Britain. And this was as intolerable to the Canadian government as their recalcitrance was to Lord Curzon.

As it happened, the vexed question of precedence did not have to be put to the final test of experience, because the Conservative coalition government in Canada failed to carry diplomatic representation at Washington forward from principle into practice. Two factors prevented an appointment being made during their term of office. It was apparent, in the first place, that the major stimulus to complete the agreement with Britain had come very much from the prime minister, and that although Borden had the near unanimous approval of his cabinet for the new venture it was his own enthusiasm and sense of purpose that had carried the negotiations forward.[28] The inevitable result was that when the prime minister withdrew from affairs of state after May 1920, owing to his continued ill health, the incentive to fill the Washington post declined sharply. Borden's successor, Arthur Meighen, showed none of the interest of his old leader in the project, and went so far as to tell the British ambassador in Washington a few months later that he had no wish to make an appointment and would prefer to ignore the matter for the immediate future.[29] That was perhaps an over-statement; but when the new prime minister did come to take a few soundings in 1921, it became clear in any case that there was not a suitable man available for the job.[30] Under the circumstances, the Canadian government continued to be represented in Washington by its old War Mission, which in April 1921 was at last placed officially on a peacetime footing. It would be for King's administration to decide how to proceed.

Canada's association with the League of Nations in the immediate post-war period presented the dominion government with a somewhat similar problem to that of diplomatic representation at Washington. While not seeking to repudiate or undermine the empire as a single entity in foreign affairs, they saw in the League a legitimate opportunity to assert a specifically Canadian personality at the international level. To some extent, of

[28] Loring Christie's application to the detailed drafting of the Canadian argument provided its own essential continuity. See Bothwell, 'Canadian Representation'.
[29] FO 371/4567: Sir Auckland Geddes–FO, 7 Sept 1920.
[30] Sir Robert Falconer, president of the University of Toronto, was approached and so was C. A. Magrath, the head of the Canadian delegation on the International Joint Commission, but in the end neither was offered the post. R. Graham, *Arthur Meighen*, ii: *And Fortune Fled* (Toronto, 1963), 59–60.

course, the rubric under which the various elements of the British empire
had joined the League reflected and seemingly condoned the ambivalence
of the dominion position. Following the precedent of representation at the
peace conference itself, the League of Nations Assembly had as founding
members both the British empire (as an undifferentiated unit) and the
individual dominions. Membership of the International Labour Organization, itself a sibling of the League, repeated the same pattern; and by way
of confusion worse confounded, Borden in Paris obtained from Wilson,
Clemenceau and Lloyd George an explicit promise that the dominions
would also be eligible for elected membership of the League Council,
where 'the British empire' had already a permanent seat. The dominions,
in short, appeared to have all the leeway they would want for developing
their individuality in the League as partners with Great Britain. But the
ability to strike a happy balance between imperial and national priorities
in this way soon proved to be practically impossible.

It became necessary for the overseas governments to assess League and
empire relations as early as November 1919. American critics of the
League were arguing that Britain was provided with an unfair advantage
in the organization, given that in any international dispute in which she
might be involved, the dominions were bound to vote in her favour when
the League Assembly ruled on the matter. The British government
strongly contested this interpretation, on the grounds that the dominions
would *ipso facto* be parties to any such dispute as elements within the
empire, and would therefore not be able to vote at all, under the League
rule that automatically prevented disputants from sitting in judgement on
their own quarrels. They very much wanted the dominions to approve a
joint public declaration to this effect. From the latter's point of view,
however, this was not an easily answered request. Although a statement
might materially weaken American criticisms, and therefore improve the
chances of the Versailles treaty in the American Senate, it would at the
same time constitute a clear acknowledgement of the empire's unrestricted
diplomatic unity – which in post-war terms amounted to a distinct qualification of dominion autonomy. In Canada the government was split on the
question, Borden's cabinet (in his absence) agreeing to reject the British
request for a statement, the prime minister then overruling them. But this
show of Canadian support on the side of imperial unity went for nothing,
because Australia and South Africa refused outright to endorse the British
proposal, and their opposition precluded any possibility of a joint statement
being made. It should not be thought that a public British disclaimer
would have brought the United States into the League; but it is worth
noting that even as they voted to reject the Covenant in March 1920, the

Senate were still refusing to accept the empire's six votes in the League Assembly.

There was an important sequel to this difference of opinion about the dominions and their voting rights. In April 1920 the first session of the League Council was convened in Geneva, and the British foreign secretary, Lord Curzon, duly attended as the 'British empire' representative. But so little had the Foreign Office come to appreciate their new responsibilities to the dominions in external questions of this kind that the overseas governments were informed of the meeting only after it had taken place; they were neither asked to ratify Curzon's appointment, nor told what business was to be on the agenda. Yet it so happened that in Canada, at least, in advance of this first Council meeting, the government had given serious thought to the question of League Council affairs, and had found their own dominion's proper relationship to the 'imperial' representative on the Council to be an extremely difficult one to define. Should they actively press the British government for consultation in advance of each Council meeting – and thus accept a share of any tangible responsibilities that might be incurred through Council decisions? Or should they, on the other hand, leave League Council business safely to Britain – and thus waive the right to consultation on foreign policy, a right that had been established at such cost during the war?[31] With Borden recuperating away from Ottawa neither the 'collaborators' nor the 'independents' in his cabinet could draft the prime minister to their side, yet in this case it is clear that the 'collaborators' won: in mid-May the British authorities were pointedly reminded that in Canada's view, the permanent seat on the League Council was held by the empire, not the United Kingdom, and that under these conditions, no representative should attend a Council meeting without prior consultation with the dominions.[32]

Here was a splendid opportunity for the British government to accept the Canadian complaint, reassure the senior dominion that her interpretation was correct, and promise to consult the dominions about future League Council meetings. But none of this could the government do, because in November 1919 both Australia and South Africa, in support of their claims about independent voting rights, had taken the position that the British seat on the Council belonged not to the empire but only to the United Kingdom. In the face of these contrary opinions, which had not been challenged from Whitehall at the time, the Colonial Office now decided they could do nothing at all to encourage the Canadian point of view, despite their own sympathy with it, and so they sent no reply at all

---

31 See cabinet memoranda, 9, 17 Feb 1920, printed in *DCER* III, 395, 398.

32 CO 886/9/76: Acting Gov Gen–Col Sec, 15 May 1920.

to the Canadian dispatch.[33] The Canadian government did not press the matter any further in 1920, but they did not fail to draw their own conclusions. In March 1921, prime minister Arthur Meighen, answering an inquiry from N. W. Rowell, admitted that 'As I understand it, in actual practice, the British Member of the Council does not profess to speak for the Dominions.'[34] Two weeks later, in the Canadian House of Commons, the minister of justice indicated that 'The description of the British Empire as a distinct member of the League has always been interpreted as meaning the United Kingdom with the Crown colonies and dependencies.'[35]

Over voting rights, and at least until 1921 over the nature of League Council representation, the Canadian government thus manifested a definite interest in maintaining a united imperial policy in League affairs. They were determined, nonetheless, that their support of imperial unity should not compromise Canada's prerogatives as a League member. This became only too clear in late 1920, as the League Assembly prepared to meet for the first time. The Canadian government had indicated in September that they would welcome a discussion among the empire's League delegates before the Assembly opened, and partly on the strength of this initiative a conference was duly convened in London, taking the form of a session of the British Empire Delegation.[36] It was soon clear, however, that the principal objective of the Canadian delegation, led by N. W. Rowell, was not to establish a coherent imperial policy on League matters but rather to ensure that there would be a measure of diversity among the empire's six delegations. While Rowell hoped that the dominions would see 'eye to eye' with Britain on important issues, he was adamant that the independence of their membership in the League could only be demonstrated by the independence of their votes. Rowell's remarks constitute a significant point of reference in British–Canadian relations. A situation had arisen in which the development of Canada's national identity in accordance with her new international standing was at odds with the diplomatic unity of the empire, and a definite choice between the two would have to be made. For some months, to be sure, this incompatibility had lain very close to the surface: the disputed status of a Canadian representative at Washington reflected exactly the same problem of how to express Canada's *independent* adherence to a united foreign policy. The matter was now resolved, in this instance, in favour of independence. In

[33] CO 532/302: C. Dixon, minute of 1 Jan 1925.
[34] Meighen papers: Meighen–Rowell, 8 March 1921.
[35] Canada, HoC, 22 March 1921.
[36] CAB 29/28/2: BED mtgs 38–40, 5–9 Nov 1920.

the League Assembly Rowell quite deliberately cast Canada's vote in opposition to Britain, in favour of a motion to allow Albania to join the league.

In the event, Rowell was not the only dominion delegate to take this stand against the foreign policy of the British government. Representing South Africa in this first Assembly was Lord Robert Cecil, who as a member of the British delegation in Paris had been responsible with Smuts for much of the original drafting of the League Covenant. Appointed at a time when imperial relations – including the possibility of secession – was very much to the fore in South African politics, Cecil was given, one assumes, a fairly free hand in looking after the dominion's interests at Geneva, and he was in any case anxious to show the rest of the League that the British empire was more than a monolithic bloc of six votes in the Assembly.[37] The idea of acting independently of Britain in some modest way therefore suited both his own and Smuts' interests, and so he cooperated closely with Rowell over the Albania motion. They had the added satisfaction of seeing the motion carried, in the face not only of British but also of French opposition.

In supporting Albanian entry to the League Canada and South Africa were able to indicate to the other members of the organization, to American public opinion, to the British government, that in principle they were their own masters as far as the affairs of the Assembly were concerned. It was a formal gesture – a breach of the empire's diplomatic unity, but not in itself a cause for immediate alarm in Whitehall. But the Canadians had come to Geneva to act independently not only in form but also in substance. While Rowell made arrangements for the vote on Albania, his colleague C. J. Doherty gave notice that Canada proposed the abolition of article x of the Covenant – a proposal that in effect would strip the League of its intended function as the agent of collective international security.

Here Doherty was returning publicly to an issue that in early 1919 had caused considerable private disquiet to the Canadian delegation to the Paris peace conference, and to himself most of all. At the time Doherty had produced a lengthy memorandum for Borden which argued strongly that a mutual guarantee of territorial integrity amongst the members of the League was inflexible, unworkable and particularly unsuited to an emergent nation such as Canada,[38] and many of his criticisms had been echoed by the Canadian prime minister in his own final submission on the draft terms of the League Covenant. Bluntly stated, Borden's position

[37] Roskill, *Hankey*, ii, 195.
[38] Memorandum, 22 Feb 1919, printed in *DCER*, ii, 58.

was that article x, the key to collective League action, should be either scrapped or drastically watered down.[39] Canadian opposition in Paris produced no tangible modification of the Covenant – on Wilson's insistence its authority to commit member states to intervention in international disputes was retained, and it was in this form that it was presented for debate, and defended, by the Borden government before their dominion parliament. But for all the official gloss of unanimity about the League, Canadian hostility to article x had not been dissipated. In part it was sustained by the widespread antipathy expressed in the United States on this aspect of the League; but in part also because the Canadian ministers who had been in Paris were convinced that their attempt to secure the desired changes, far from having been the ineffectual protest of a minor delegation, had all but succeeded. There is little evidence to substantiate this impression, but the impression itself is clear enough.[40] The next twelve months, in any event, indicated that collective security would not be endorsed by American public or political opinion, and there was little in Canada's own public responses to the League to offset these negative North American sentiments. Had Borden retained the leadership of the Canadian government during 1920 it is possible that the delegation to Geneva might have been more restrained in their criticisms – at the very least they might have disclosed them in the first instance to the British government. But with his old leader gone, Doherty evidently found Meighen prepared to endorse his hard line, and was thus free to establish the intransigent Canadian position over article x.[41] With a fine display of bureaucratic defensive reflexes the League administrators were able to put the Canadian proposal forward without debate to the 1921 session, but there was no reason to suppose that the dominion would not return to the issue when the time came.

Constitutional principles and practice

In 1917, when British and dominion leaders at the Imperial War Conference had been confronted with proposals for constitutional changes, it was agreed that an adequate consideration of such questions warranted a formal constitutional conference, which would have to be left to the end of the war. Only at such a conference could the dominions' advances from their pre-war colonial status be fully assessed, and their position con-

---

[39] Memorandum, 13 March 1919; copy in CAB 29/9.

[40] See G. Carter, 'Some Aspects of Canadian Foreign Policy after Versailles', *Canadian Historical Association Report* (1943), 100. Doherty indicated his own feeling to the House of Commons in April 1921. HoC, 20 April 1921.

[41] See Eayrs, *In Defence of Canada*, 1, 4.

firmed (in the words of the resolution passed in 1917) as 'autonomous nations of an Imperial Commonwealth'. By the same token, and equally important to many, only then could any lingering apprehensions that imperial federation might still be a possible goal for British–dominion relations be finally removed. These problems of status once settled, it was anticipated that the conference would then be able to establish a functional system of consultation through which the overseas governments could collaborate with Britain in the conduct of their common imperial foreign affairs. Such were the expectations of 1917. Two and a half years later, by the time further attention could be given to constitutional matters, the future course of British–dominion relations could no longer be projected along such straightforward lines. The participation of the dominions in their own right at the Paris peace conference had added an entirely new dimension to their status, providing them with an embryonic international personality – and thus with an external frame of reference to set against their hitherto purely 'internal' development within the empire. During the war overseas leaders had been content to think in terms of dominion autonomy *vis-à-vis* Great Britain; now, at least insofar as the dominions might seek to operate on the international plane, they were spoken of as having gained a status of virtual equality with the mother country. And as seen above, the determination of Canada and South Africa to assert an independent and recognizable voice in their international activities was proving extremely hard to reconcile with an undifferentiated imperial unity in foreign affairs.

It could be argued by 1920 that the major advances made by the overseas delegations at Paris had rendered a constitutional conference practically unnecessary, on the grounds that international recognition by the peace conference was of greater significance for the dominions than any further imperial pronouncements about their place in the empire and the world. The appointment of a Canadian diplomatic representative to Washington, for example, was justified to the dominion House of Commons as being a natural consequence of the status won at the peace conference.[42] On a more general level, the increasing use of the word 'Commonwealth' by this time also appeared to confirm that constitutional conference or not, the dominions stood in an undeniably more mature relationship to Britain than they had in 1917. The word had attained no legal validity, and was liable to crop up in any number of hybrid formulations – Borden once spoke of 'an Imperial Commonwealth of United Nations', for instance – but its essential connotation, a departure from

---

[42] Canada, HoC, 17 May 1920: speech of C. J. Doherty, minister of justice.

an empire of subordinate colonies, was clear enough.[43] Indeed to the professional observers in the Colonial Office there were moments when the shifting balance of forces in the imperial structure seemed barely capable of controlled change. In June 1920 Sir George Fiddes minutes anxiously:

Either the Empire will crack up under the strain of readjusting our constitutional relations, or, if the centripetal prevail against the centrifugal forces, we shall in the usual British way muddle through to a solution after much trouble & friction, which is logically absurd but workable in practice.[44]

On one constitutional matter, at least, overseas leaders seemed determined to secure more orderly modifications. The role of the governors general in the administration of the dominions was a subject that Borden, Hughes, Botha and Smuts all raised with the British authorities during their time in London in early 1919. Broadly speaking they shared the conviction that if the dominions now had genuine claims to an autonomous nationhood within the empire, then the position of the governor general should correspond precisely to that of the sovereign in Britain; that is, he should simply represent the sovereign, as head of the executive, but no longer be an agent of the British government, nor the channel of communications for the Colonial Office. There was also strong feeling that future appointments should be made only with advice from the government concerned, and that dominion as well as British candidates should be considered.[45] The leaders of the three dominions, it seems fair to say, approached the question of the governor general's powers from somewhat different angles. For Hughes, who above all was known to resent the Colonial Office's continuing responsibility for British–dominion affairs, the major purpose of the proposed reforms would be to establish a direct channel of communication between himself and the British prime minister, thus by-passing governor general and Colonial Office alike. And it is worth noticing that when in 1920 the use of a private cypher gave Hughes the direct prime ministerial line he had been after, his interest in curbing the governor general's prerogatives cooled remarkably – to the point

[43] D. Hall, *Commonwealth* (London, 1971), 190 ff. The Canadian Department of External Affairs was careful to keep a file on 'Commonwealth' terminology in these years.

[44] CO 532/162: minute of 23 June 1920.

[45] Memorandum of Smuts, 'The Status of Dominion Governors General', Jan 1919, endorsed by Borden. Copy in Bonar Law papers (extracts, Public Archives, Canada): Borden–Law, 10 Jan 1923. See also Hall, *Commonwealth*, 310 ff.

where by 1921 he had become very much a constitutional 'conservative'. Borden had broader concerns. His own most relevant direct experience had come in 1916, when Canada's governor general, the Duke of Connaught, had been determined to involve himself in government policy (particularly military matters) to an extent that Borden found intolerable; and although Connaught's successor, the Duke of Devonshire, had been a model of propriety in this respect, it is clear that Borden felt the time had come to see the governor general confined explicitly to his kingly duties. Beyond this, as a champion in any case of greater dominion freedom, the Canadian prime minister was very keen to end the subordination entailed by the governor general's role as agent of a British department of state. It was the South African leaders, however, who were the most single-minded about this aspect of the matter, extremely anxious to counter the charge of their Nationalist opponents at home that under existing practice the dominion government was closely controlled by the governor general. For them most of all the suggested reforms were a political necessity, and it was not surprising that Smuts and Botha took much of the initiative in formulating the 1919 proposals and pressing them upon the British authorities.

In the event these combined representations came to nothing. With so many other problems to be settled during the months of the peace negotiations it is understandable that there should have been hesitation about such a major constitutional step being taken, though inertia apart, it appears that the proposals also ran up against the strong personal reservations of the British prime minister. Never entirely predictable in his approach to dominion matters, Lloyd George showed peculiar reluctance to see the authority of the governors general modified, and was also particularly convinced that they should continue to be British rather than dominion nationals.[46] His opposition was alone enough to forestall any further consideration of the subject, and so by the time the dominion delegations returned home it had simply been consigned to the agenda of the as yet unplanned constitutional conference.

And the conference itself? Certainly there were strong public expectations in late 1919 that such a meeting was soon to be held, and in Canada at least, this was not necessarily a cause for rejoicing. The opposition Liberals were convinced Borden was preparing to make great political capital out of this venture, and began to look to their own defences. J. W. Dafoe at the *Winnipeg Free Press* was instructed by his publisher to warn Borden editorially

[46] Borden–Bonar Law, 10 Jan 1923. *Loc cit.*

that for whatever he may be speaking he is certainly not speaking for the Canadian people and that no man living has any authority . . . to suggest what the views of the Canadian people are upon their constitutional relations.[47]

More graphically, a party stalwart bluntly informed his new leader Mackenzie King:

The Liberal Party has been Unionized into fragments, and I do not propose to stand idly by, and see it Imperialized to death.[48]

But the alarm and despondency of Borden's political opponents proved to be premature, for in the event the conference was found impossible to convene. Behind the scenes, although there was a general willingness amongst the governments of the empire to set up a conference for 1920 or 1921, and even some serious consideration given to its being held in Ottawa, the months of 1920 went by without any firm arrangements being made. In his farewell address to his parliamentary party at the beginning of July 1920, Borden bravely anticipated that the conference would still take place in 1921, though there was little enough foundation for his hopes.[49]

The change of Canadian prime ministers at this point significantly altered the situation. Where Borden had pursued every reasonable suggestion for a conference, Arthur Meighen proved to have little of his old leader's enthusiasm for such a set-piece constitutional gathering, and when the Colonial Office made fresh inquiries on the subject to the new premier in August 1920, he told them quite plainly that he saw no particular advantage in holding constitutional discussions before 1922. 'The telegram', noted the Dominions Department, 'indeed reads like an indefinite putting off of the Conference.'[50] Some months later Meighen put his views to Leopold Amery at greater length:

I am strongly impressed with the importance of letting constitutional developments proceed as a matter of growth and without prearrangement and as far as possible without concrete emphatic alteration. In a word, while things must grow and change for the better it would be just so much for the better if they did not appear to change at all . . . These words are of importance in connection with any projected constitutional conference.[51]

The conservative temper of Meighen's thinking is clear, although it depended on a peculiarly abstract notion of the empire's constitution. It

[47] Sifton papers: Sifton–Dafoe, 20 Nov 1919.
[48] Murphy papers: Charles Murphy–King, 24 Nov 1919.
[49] Borden, *Memoirs*, II, 1036.
[50] CO 42/1020: Lambert, minute of 13 Sept 1920.
[51] Meighen papers: Meighen–Amery, 26 Nov 1920.

was as if there existed a gradually modulating facade of formal constitutional relations, behind which particular changes and developments, bearing no immediate relation to it, took place. The only injunction, it seemed, was to alter the facade as little as possible. That apart, Canada remained free to pursue the various independent initiatives through which her post-war standing in the empire was being so strikingly developed. On this analysis, Meighen could calmly deprecate constitutional changes while the Canadian delegation to the League of Nations Assembly was preparing to vote independently of Great Britain and to try to scrap article x of the League Covenant.

By the autumn of 1920 the Colonial Office had more or less given up the idea of a constitutional conference within the next twelve months, and were beginning to think in more mundane terms of a straightforward meeting of prime ministers to clear up particular problems. The broader questions of constitutional principle would have to remain unrevised for the time being. As Milner explained to Meighen in a letter of early October, there were several practical problems hindering imperial co-operation, and it was essential to settle them without waiting for a formal constitutional conference. He suggested reviving the machinery of the Imperial War Cabinet for this purpose:

The meeting of such a body, which I certainly hope may take place next year, would not be beset by the difficulties which attend the early convocation of a Constitutional Conference ... It would simply meet to discuss the practical difficulties which have already arisen and which, until we can so discuss them, will continue to bother us all.[52]

He put the same case to Lloyd George, arguing that a constitutional conference

may have to come some day, but it is too soon; nobody has the leisure or disposition for it and in 1921 it would end in smoke...

The only essential thing is to get the different Prime Ministers together under your Presidency. More business can be done like that in a week than in months and years of telegrams flying backwards and forwards.[53]

Milner, it is apparent, was fast coming to terms with the post-war realities of imperial relations. In 1917, although imperial federation had been given short shrift by the overseas delegates, Britain and the dominions seemed set on a course that would maintain their integrated imperial partnership in peacetime, and two years later Milner had tried very hard

[52] Meighen papers: Milner–Meighen, 4 Oct 1920, printed in *DCER*, III, 157.
[53] Milner–Lloyd George, 8 Oct 1920, quoted in A. Gollin, *Proconsul in Politics* (London, 1964), 596–7.

to see that partnership consolidated through the administrative machinery of the Cabinet Office. Now in 1920 he realized that it was a question of sustaining even a limited degree of imperial co-operation, let alone pursuing any more elaborate schemes for closer imperial unity. So it was that an intended constitutional conference was converted into an *ad hoc* imperial meeting along more conventional lines. Lloyd George quickly accepted his colonial secretary's proposals, and within a few weeks the overseas prime ministers had all agreed to meet in London in June 1921, for a brief session devoted to a few specific issues of policy. If they touched on constitutional questions at all, it would probably be only to decide if 1922 held any better prospects for a full-scale conference. Privately Milner continued to despair about 'the chaotic position into wh[ich] our Imperial relations have got', but for the moment there was nothing more that could be done.[54]

The Dominions Department of the Colonial Office, it must be said, shared Milner's reluctant conviction that constitutional matters would have to be shelved for the time being, and on the whole they were inclined to be even more pessimistic than the colonial secretary about the trend of developments. Milner thought a brief practical meeting in 1921 might just hold things together. In their view, as time continued to go by the constitutional expectations of the overseas governments shared less and less common ground, so that even by mid-1920, to judge from the public pronouncements of the dominion leaders, Smuts was envisaging 'complete separation subject only to having a common sovereign', while in New Zealand premier Massey wanted no radical changes at all. And between them, noted Henry Lambert, 'almost every variety of view is possible'.[55] The root of the trouble, without any question, had been the dominions' unprecedented involvement in international affairs at the Paris peace conference, as a consequence of which each of them had felt free to reappraise their position in the empire and their right of access to the international world at large, and to develop some, at least, of the attributes of virtually independent sovereignty. Hughes and Smuts were both choosing to emphasize dominion independence in their speeches. Borden, somewhat more discreet in public, nevertheless had determined on diplomatic representation at Washington and an independent Canadian channel of communications with the League of Nations, and seemed to give little practical thought for the empire's diplomatic or legal unity. All told, there were few indications that in pursuing a dominion status of equality with Britain, the overseas governments were at all consciously interested in the co-

[54] Grigg papers: Milner–Kerr, 25 Nov 1920.
[55] CO 532/155: memorandum, 14 June 1920.

operative aspects of the imperial relationship. The conduct of the empire's foreign policy remained *faute de mieux* in the hands of the British administration, with no machinery for practical rapid consultation and no clear guidelines as yet as to the extent of dominion responsibility for it. More concretely, as we shall see below, amongst the dominions only New Zealand had been willing in this period to make any significant contribution to imperial naval defence, whose costs continued to be carried by the British taxpayer. Under these circumstances, reviewing the situation Henry Lambert held out little hope for any legitimate reconciliation between equality of status and the empire's diplomatic unity:

The fact is that whatever we may say about Equality of Status, its logical working out is, in existing conditions, incompatible with the continuance of the Empire, because of our international relations. If the Empire is to continue to exist there must be somebody who can conduct foreign affairs and speak for British subjects abroad, and that cannot be six authorities, five of whom do not bear, and, except for the period of the war, never have borne, any appreciable share of the cost or difficulties. This will sooner or later have to be said quite distinctly (and when it is I suspect that large sections of Dominion opinion will accept it).[56]

There was little chance, in any event, that public opinion in the dominions would have to confront any problems of constitutional revision in the foreseeable future. When the overseas prime ministers assembled in London for the 1921 Imperial Conference it was soon enough apparent that Smuts alone was anxious to propose some definite constitutional principles in order to clarify the future development of the empire–commonwealth. Not that Smuts had anything in common with the Colonial Office view of affairs. Lambert's minute in effect called on the dominions to earn their right to a voice in foreign affairs through tangible contributions to the empire's defence. Smuts, on the contrary, wished to resolve the existing ambiguities by moving firmly in the other direction, and in advance he had prepared a comprehensive statement on 'The Constitution of the British Commonwealth' which set out the various measures necessary to give the dominions the full legal equality of status with Britain that, in his own view at least, they already exercised in practice. As he expressed it,

the formal settlement of [these] matters will complete the fundamental alteration in the basis of the British Empire which has taken place recently. It will no longer be an Empire but a society of free and equal sister states.[57]

---

[56] CO 42/1039: minute of 11 July 1921.
[57] Smuts' paper is printed in Hall, *Commonwealth*, 987: see also Hancock, *Smuts*, ii, 44 ff.

But though he lobbied hard Smuts could find no support at the conference for this constitutional settlement. Meighen remained temperamentally averse to defining the principles governing British–dominion relations; Massey too wanted nothing to do with what he castigated as a written constitution for the empire. And Hughes, as sensitive in his own way about Australia's national independence as Smuts was about South Africa's, proved nevertheless to be the voice of extreme reaction at the 1921 Conference, to the extent that he not only refused to consider the Smuts paper, but even found an opportunity to attack the idea of a Canadian diplomatic appointment to Washington – an idea that privately, at least, in 1919 he had been perfectly happy to endorse.[58] There was nothing Smuts could do to prevent his colleagues from deciding that constitutional questions could be postponed *sine die*. The constitutional tinkers, as Hughes rather bluntly put it, had been soldered up in their own tin can.

Imperial naval defence, 1917–1921

Although the other prime ministers at the 1921 Conference were quick to reject Smuts' proposals to define the independence of the dominions, it would be wrong to imagine that there was any contrary disposition to support the idea of a co-operative imperial partnership – far from it. At least as far as matters dealing with imperial defence were concerned, the overseas leaders proved just as unwilling to accept any positive obligations on this account as they had been to pursue the clarification of equal status: by the time they had turned down further constitutional discussion they had also decided that future spending on the empire's naval defences should be 'for the final determination of the several Parliaments involved'. Thus in both cases the consensus of opinion at the conference favoured the rather empty *via media* of passive uncommitted inactivity, which left the dominions' relationships to Britain, to the empire, to the empire's foreign policy quite unresolved – and meanwhile left Britain, in effect, to bear the financial responsibilities for the strategic defence forces on which imperial foreign policy ultimately depended. This negative decision on defence spending brought to an end four years of study and consultation about the naval defence of the empire. It was a period during which Canadian reservations had more than once upset the Admiralty's plans for sharing the burden of defence with the dominions.

Post-war defence was first considered by the British and overseas governments at the Imperial War Conference of 1917, when after a good deal of unfocused discussion they decided to postpone the matter until the end of

---

[58] CO 532/280: E. J. Harding, minute of 28 Jan 1924. Hughes' vitriolic criticisms were deliberately omitted from the minutes of the conference.

the war. The Admiralty were asked to draw up their own defence proposals in the interim, and at Borden's suggestion they agreed to submit these in general outline to the overseas prime ministers before defining them in any detail. Fourteen months later, the Imperial War Conference reconvened to find that the Admiralty had already incorporated their ideas on imperial defence into a memorandum, a document which while not a complete defence scheme was far more than a general outline.[59] In essence it proposed a single navy run by a central naval authority, with defence contributions to come from the dominions at their own discretion; 'as far as possible' each dominion would control the disposition of its own expenditure. Control indeed was the crucial problem, to which the memorandum implied a rather contentious solution, looking to future constitutional developments to resolve administrative difficulties:

The manner in which a chain of command is to be established ... must ... be determined by the form in which it may be ultimately decided to give expression to the desire for the closer union of the Empire.

In anticipating a degree of imperial integration substantial enough to maintain a central naval authority, the Admiralty were clearly sailing very close to the wind of imperial federation. It was a course which the Colonial Office, at least, did not expect the overseas prime ministers to follow. 'I do not ... see how the proposals ... can be squared with existing ideas of self-government in the Dom[inion]s', E. J. Harding minuted before the 1918 discussions began, though he thought that departmental objections would hardly be necessary: 'I feel fairly confident that full criticism will come from the Dom[inion] representatives.'[60]

Resistance to the Admiralty memorandum, led by Sir Robert Borden, was quick to develop. In 1912, Borden had endeavoured to contribute three Canadian dreadnoughts to the imperial navy, with no firm guarantee from the British government that he would have a voice as to their deployment. Six years later conditions had changed: now the Admiralty were endeavouring to give the dominions a voice in imperial defence policy and asking for no precise assurances as to contributions. The Admiralty, however, had misunderstood the constitutional resolution IX of 1917. The dominions wanted participation in imperial policies, but not if it meant surrendering their autonomy to a centralized imperial executive. There was little need to elaborate this argument. The memorandum, purporting to be a general synopsis, could be dismissed with generalities, and on behalf of his overseas colleagues Borden officially informed the first lord

[59] Cabinet Paper GT 4571, 'Naval Defence of the British Empire', 17 May 1918.
[60] CO 532/126: minute of 6 June 1918.

of the Admiralty that a single navy was 'impracticable'. The dominions would proceed with their own plans, although for the sake of over-all coherence they agreed that once the war was over an Admiralty representative might advise each government on its particular naval requirements.

However, Borden had not scotched the idea of an imperial navy in order to avoid the development of a local Canadian force. In early 1919 he showed considerable interest in laying the foundations for a small but comprehensive navy, and a gift of two submarines from the Admiralty was a welcome beginning to such plans.[61] A more ambitious project was that Canada take over a fleet unit from Britain, an idea which the Canadian prime minister put to Lord Milner in April 1919:

[It] would serve two important purposes: first, it would be a relief pro tanto to the necessary effort of Great Britain in maintaining adequate naval strength, and secondly, it would appeal to the pride of the Canadian people and increase their sense of responsibility.

Within a measurable period the ships in question would become obsolete, and then the duty would devolve upon Canada of supplying their place with up-to-date ships of like relative power.[62]

Borden's enthusiasm for pushing forward with a Canadian naval programme was welcome news from a dominion whose progress in this field had been for so long delayed. It coincided, moreover, with similar expressions of interest from Australia and New Zealand, whose peace conference delegations were also in contact with the Admiralty with a view to taking over warships from the British navy. To the Australian navy, which had already developed strongly in the course of the war, was thus added six destroyers and six submarines; to New Zealand went a cruiser and two sloops, to serve as the foundation for a locally-based naval force. Even South Africa declared an interest in matters of post-war defence. That dominion had no plans to take over surplus British vessels, but the government nonetheless thought it worthwhile to discuss general problems of defence in London before the overseas leaders dispersed at the end of the peace conference.

It turned out that no defence talks could be arranged in London in 1919, though even if they had taken place, it is to be doubted whether much of the dominion leaders' enthusiasm would have been sustained after their return to their home capitals. Borden, in proposing the fleet unit for

61 CO 532/134: Milner–Borden, 24 Jan 1919. The director of the Canadian naval service doubted that crews could be found for them, but his objections were overruled by the cabinet.
62 CO 532/152: Borden–Milner, 18 April 1919, printed in Eayrs, *In Defence*, 1, 151.

Canada, had admitted to Milner that the idea was a tentative one, and it was not less tentative four months later when the Admiralty were ready to offer the Canadian prime minister the necessary ships. Ministerial discussions of the plan had yet to begin, Borden now confessed to Whitehall, and he therefore preferred to postpone a decision until the end of the year, by which time Lord Jellicoe, delegated by the Admiralty to tour the dominions (in accordance with their wishes of 1918) to study their naval requirements, was expected to be in Canada to lend his own professional weight to the discussions. But no more was heard of a Canadian fleet unit. For by the time Jellicoe reached Ottawa, Borden's cabinet were almost as dubious about a Canadian navy as earlier their prime minister had been about an imperial one, and Borden accepted Jellicoe's mission as his last chance to obtain even a modest expansion of Canada's naval forces.[63] It seemed at first that he would succeed, for after Jellicoe had completed his study the Canadian cabinet did agree to ask the Admiralty for a small contingent of vessels, including destroyers and submarines. At this point, however, Borden left Ottawa for a long rest from office – and no sooner was he gone than a cabinet rebellion occurred. The government's parliamentary coalition, to whom the divided cabinet appealed, declared themselves firmly opposed to any increase in defence expenditure: the only ships they would accept were (free) replacements for Canada's two antiquated cruisers.[64] Thus by mid-1920, as Meighen assumed the leadership, the controversy over naval defence was over. Politically the issue was moribund, neither government nor opposition wishing to put money into naval expenditure; and over the course of the next twelve months, a deepening economic recession only reinforced this antipathy. Meighen accepted that the subject of naval defence would be raised at the 1921 Imperial Conference, but plainly without enthusiasm. In the House of Commons, with Borden's full support, he promised the opposition Liberal party that no new defence commitments would be entertained by Canada.[65]

[63] 'There is great danger', the Canadian governor general reported to Milner, 'of nothing being done for several years if action is not taken now.' CO 42/1012: Gov Gen–Col Sec, 2 Dec 1919. Ballantyne, the navy minister, told Jellicoe that unless expanded, Canada's forces would not be worth maintaining: Jellicoe–Admiralty, 3 Dec 1919, quoted in S. Roskill, *Naval Policy Between the Wars*, 1: *The Period of Anglo-American Antagonism, 1919–1929* (London, 1968), 285.

[64] The details of this *volte face* (and of naval developments in general in 1919–20) are in Eayrs, *In Defence of Canada*, 1, 163, and ch 4.

[65] Canada, HoC, 27 April 1921. See Graham, *Meighen*, ii, 63 ff. Whereas the British government had put naval defence second on the agenda, Meighen now relegated it to seventh place, amongst the incidental subjects.

Developments in the other dominions were scarcely more encouraging. Australia, with a naval force already in commission, was urged by Jellicoe in 1919 to expand on a truly ambitious scale in order to contain (jointly with Britain and New Zealand) any possible threat from Japan. These comprehensive plans were never put in hand though, to be fair, the Admiralty themselves were highly sceptical about Jellicoe's warnings concerning Japan.[66] Indeed after August 1920 (apparently following the departure of the Prince of Wales, who in this year visited each of the dominions) the Australian navy began to be laid up, a process that by the end of 1922 left very few ships in operation. South Africa, with nothing ventured as yet on naval defence, and nothing planned, decided in early 1920 that a visit from Jellicoe could serve no useful purpose, and in this way simply chose not to consider naval defence at all. Only New Zealand responded positively to Jellicoe's mission, accepting not just recommendations for a start to their navy, but also the administrative schemes worked out for it. Then in early 1921 Jellicoe himself became governor general of New Zealand and so was able to extend his involvement in their naval developments for several years.

To judge from their individual reactions to the question of post-war naval defence, therefore, the dominion governments represented at the 1921 Conference were hardly likely to agree amongst themselves to any major programme of co-operative defence spending. After a secret conference session which studied the possible consequences of a war with Japan, the overseas prime ministers were certainly united in the view that the empire's naval strength should be kept on a par with any other power; but they could still find no agreed basis on which to share any of the financial responsibilities for this one-power standard with Great Britain.[67] Admittedly the circumstances of their deliberations in 1921 were in one respect inauspicious. On 10 July, with the Imperial Conference in full swing, the president of the United States invited all the major powers to attend a conference at Washington on naval disarmament, and while this proposal was strongly supported by the British and dominion leaders in London it necessarily rendered the empire's future defence requirements somewhat uncertain. If international standards of naval strength were going to be reviewed, then there was some justification for not reaching decisions about the empire's own defence spending. Nonetheless it was noticeable that the lack of agreement at the Imperial Conference owed much less to the prospects of a disarmament conference than to the

[66] Roskill, *Naval Policy*, I, 279–82.

[67] CAB 32/2: Imperial Conference mtg, 4 July 1921 (Secretary's note): Roskill, *Naval Policy*, I, 295.

intransigence of the Canadian prime minister. At all points in the discussions Meighen remained flatly opposed in principle to any new Canadian defence commitments whatever, and could not be shifted from this position by his overseas colleagues. Hughes, for one, tried to challenge the Canadian's seeming irresponsibility by demanding to know 'by what right the Dominions sat in this conference and discussed questions of foreign policy if they did not contribute towards seapower, which was the basis of Empire.'[68] Hughes spoke now as a convert, prepared to reverse Australian demobilization and accept a definite share of a comprehensive imperial defence programme. But Meighen would not be persuaded. As a last resort, Smuts put forward the suggestion that naval defence costs might be made a first charge upon the empire's receipts from German reparations. According to the inter-imperial allocation of these payments, this plan would leave Britain with fully 86% of the expense, but at least it had the merit of providing dominion contributions at no direct financial cost to themselves. The other prime ministers, in an unpublished conclusion, resolved to put the proposal to their parliaments, but again Meighen would not be drawn: it would be 'a hopeless task' to get the idea accepted in Canada, and he would not attempt it. The final published resolution was a testament to his obduracy. Contributions to a one-power standard were not only to be decided after the disarmament conference, but were in any event to be left for the final decision of each individual parliament.

Imperial foreign policy – The Anglo-Japanese alliance

The empire's naval defence requirements were investigated by the 1921 conference with Arthur Meighen very much a hostile witness, resolved from the outset to block any plans for co-operative naval spending. Constitutional relations were dealt with not at all. By contrast, when the time came to look at imperial foreign policy there were no such objections, everyone being in ready agreement that a comprehensive review of foreign affairs was essential and must claim a major part of the conference's time. Nonetheless it remained to be seen exactly how far the overseas prime ministers would have, or could expect to have, a meaningful voice in the assessment of policy. Their very unwillingness, Smuts aside, to examine and perhaps re-define the constitutional principles underlying British–dominion relations was bound to affect the proceedings in this respect, for it meant that the dominions' association with the empire's foreign affairs remained in the unregulated and essentially unstable condition that had prevailed since the end of the war. Even the terms under which the

[68] CAB 32/4: IC mtg 26 B, 20 July 1921.

conference itself had been convened, it must be noted, had had to take account of the ambiguities on this score. 'Imperial War Cabinet' (or perhaps 'Peace Cabinet'), 'Imperial Conference', 'Prime Ministers' Conference' – each held different implications or looked back to different precedents, and in the end the delegations had been obliged to assemble under the weighty but uncontentious title of 'Conference of Prime Ministers and Representatives of the United Kingdom, the Dominions and India'. Yet despite the unresolved ambiguities of the imperial relationship, it seemed as the 1921 Conference began that with regard to foreign policy British leaders might be prepared to offer the overseas prime ministers a genuinely purposeful role. In his introductory speech Lloyd George indicated that his government would welcome any suggestions from them 'for associating yourselves more closely with the conduct of foreign relations', and he went so far as to declare expansively, 'There was a time when Downing Street controlled the Empire; today the Empire is in charge of Downing Street'. At a subsequent meeting the foreign secretary brought the subject more sharply into focus with a lengthy opening summary of foreign affairs since 1919.[69]

These initial gestures from the British delegation should not be exaggerated. The prime minister had been careful to confine himself to general observations in his references to a jointly conducted foreign policy. Moreover, Lord Curzon, in reviewing the complexities of twenty-four months of empire diplomacy, was not so much rendering an account of his stewardship to his collective masters as simply allowing the overseas ministers to be kept in touch with, and sanction, policies for which (on his own reckoning at least) he and his department bore full practical responsibility. Yet in 1921, as everyone at the conference was aware, the examination of foreign affairs could not be so straightforward. For it was not just a matter of the dominion leaders ratifying past decisions or making vague gestures about the direction of future developments before they departed for home: falling between the completed past and a sketchily anticipated future was an issue of present policy, the renewal or cancellation of the 1911 Anglo-Japanese alliance, which required a definite decision from the conference.

With the privilege of first response to Curzon's policy review, Meighen left his colleagues in no doubt that he, at least, expected the fullest weight to be given to dominion views on imperial foreign affairs. The dominions, in his view, enjoyed 'full control of their own affairs, inclusive, in many essential phases, of their affairs with other countries'. But as 'nations within the British Empire' they were still dependent 'upon the soundness

[69] CAB 32/4: IC mtg 1, 20 June, mtg 6, 26 June 1921.

... of British Foreign Policy', and as such they had a clear right to a voice in that policy. Indeed whereas Hughes might wish to argue, in the context of imperial defence, that naval contributions were the price the dominions should pay for consultation, Meighen, on the contrary, was suggesting that consultation was the price Britain would have to pay for the continuation of the empire's diplomatic unity. And the Canadian prime minister was prepared to go further, arguing that each dominion should also be given special consideration whenever particular policies would touch its own interest most directly:

[that] as respects the determination of the Empire's foreign policy in spheres in which any Dominion is peculiarly concerned, the view of that Dominion must be given a weight commensurate with the importance of the decision to that Dominion. Speaking for Canada I make this observation with particular reference to our relations with the United States.[70]

This was a large demand for Meighen to make, and it was not well received by the other delegations. But with the Anglo-Japanese alliance about to be assessed the Canadian prime minister was determined to state his case, for he himself was strongly opposed to the renewal of the alliance, precisely on the grounds that it would ignore American interests. Here, on the eve of the main debate, was a claim to special Canadian privileges – and an implied warning that his government might not endorse a decision with which they did not agree.

The consideration of the Anglo-Japanese alliance by the 1921 Conference was the culmination of a prolonged examination of this matter, which had begun in Whitehall in January 1920. The alliance itself, a defensive treaty obliging Japan and Britain to assist each other against unprovoked aggression, had first been concluded in 1902 and most recently renewed in 1911.[71] It was to run for ten years (to 13 July 1921) at least, and thereafter it was to continue until on a year's notice either party denounced it. The Foreign Office had consequently originally intended to formulate a policy by July 1920, so that if the decision then turned out to be against renewal of the treaty, it need not run on any longer than its existing ten-year term. This arrangement, however, conflicted with Colonial Office plans for consulting the dominions about the alliance. At that time they still had hopes for an Imperial Conference in the autumn of 1920, and were anxious to use it for a general discussion of the alliance, rather

---

[70] *Ibid*: mtg 6, 24 June 1921.
[71] A recent outstanding study of the Anglo-Japanese alliance, to which the reader can be referred for further details, is Ian Nish, *Alliance in Decline* (London, 1972), esp 288–382.

than merely canvass dominion opinion by cable. The Foreign Office were therefore persuaded to put off any final decision until after the conference, and they also agreed to supply the dominions in advance of the conference with memoranda on the legal and diplomatic issues relating to the alliance. These were dispatched in May 1920. Apart from offering the dominion governments a general briefing, they made perfectly clear that the Foreign Office themselves were in favour of retaining the alliance, albeit modified to conform to the principles of the League of Nations.[72]

There remained one obligation to be discharged before 13 July 1920. The alliance as it stood was contrary to the principles of the League of Nations (because it was in defence of special territorial interests) and all League members had undertaken to terminate any such treaties at the first legal opportunity, or at least to modify them in the meantime. In this case, if the final British verdict (despite the Foreign Office's own arguments for renewal) were to go against the alliance, termination on a year's notice would not now be able to take place until the autumn of 1921, and thus the unrevised alliance would operate beyond its earliest date of abrogation – a violation of the Covenant. To cover themselves against this eventuality (however unlikely it seemed) the Foreign Office with Japan's approval sent a note to the League which promised that after July 1921 the alliance could continue only 'in a form which is not inconsistent with [the] Covenant'. Because the note was sent principally out of courtesy to the League, it was only as an afterthought that the Foreign Office stopped to consider its legal implications – and there was therefore genuine surprise when the department's assistant legal adviser declared the note to be nothing less than a formal denunciation of the alliance.[73] This unexpected turn of legal events was of cardinal importance, for it meant that the alliance, which hitherto was to have continued until terminated, would now lapse in July 1921 unless renewed or replaced. Yet with remarkable lack of concern for the other interested parties – the rest of Whitehall, the dominions, Japan herself – the Foreign Office officials kept their legal opinion to themselves. Moreover the foreign

---

[72] CO 532/161: (copies) FO memoranda by H. W. Malkin (assistant legal adviser) and C. H. Bentinck (Russian Department). Bentinck, in the first draft of the 'diplomatic' memorandum, was open-minded about whether to renew the alliance, but Lord Curzon, one of the alliance's strongest supporters, sent the memorandum back to be rewritten with a suitably pro-renewal conclusion. FO 371/5358: Curzon, minute of 8 March 1920.

[73] FO 371/5360: H. W. Malkin, minute of 15 July 1920. 'The Agreement cannot be continued after July 13, 1921, in its present form; consequently it must either be modified (i.e. a new agreement will be entered into) or it will come to an end on that date.'

secretary, it appears, did not take note of the legal ruling at the time, and remained unaware of its implications.[74]

No doubt the Foreign Office were untroubled by the unexpected legal outcome of their actions because they were confident that well before the date of expiry of the existing alliance a new one would in any event have replaced it, and all would be well. Yet their own efforts to define the terms of any such new agreement, let alone bring the dominion governments into consultation about them, proved in the event to be an extremely laborious process, and it was not until January 1921 that a special departmental committee, set up to review the matter, produced an agreed set of proposals. What they finally recommended was that the existing alliance should not be continued, but replaced instead by a common agreement about the Pacific with both the United States and Japan.[75] Only if the former would not participate in such a venture should a bilateral treaty with Japan be negotiated; and in any event it should be in such a form that the United States could later be associated with it without difficulty.[76]

The Foreign Office had at last made up their mind – but what of the dominions? By this time the long delay over imperial consultation made it possible, once again, to plan for round-table discussions at the Imperial Conference scheduled to meet in June. Lord Curzon, even so, showed no anxiety to brief the dominion governments for this conference by giving them his department's recent conclusions: still in favour of the alliance himself, he decided that the report should have no circulation at all outside the Foreign Office.[77] Thus in preparation for the conference the dominions were left with the outdated memoranda of 1920. Neither they nor the rest of Whitehall had any indication of the current train of Foreign Office departmental thinking.

Ironically, the opinions which Curzon refrained from disclosing to the dominions were remarkably similar to those reached by the Canadian government. At the beginning of February 1921 a long memorandum on the Japanese alliance was submitted to the Canadian prime minister from the Department of External Affairs by Loring Christie (who had been willingly retained by Meighen as the government's principal adviser

[74] Nish, *Alliance*, 303.
[75] Growing departmental doubts about the wisdom of leaving the United States out of any new alliance had been reinforced when the US government had made discreet inquiries of their own about the possibility of talks about the Pacific region. FO 371/5360: C. H. Bentinck, minute of 5 Aug 1920.
[76] FO 371/6672: report of Anglo-Japanese alliance committee, 21 Jan 1921.
[77] FO 371/6672: minute of 22 Feb 1921.

on matters of foreign policy). Christie had recently had a chance (through his friendship with Philip Kerr) to sound out Lloyd George about the alliance in London, and it was with the knowledge that British official thinking generally favoured renewal that he set out to summarize his own views for Meighen.[78] Most decidedly, he was not in favour of the alliance continuing. On the one hand the principal purpose of the pact as revised in 1911 – the German naval threat – was gone; on the other, a renewal now would severely exacerbate Anglo-American relations, which since the war's end had been dangerously under strain in any case, to the point where Canada's own position between the two English-speaking powers would become intolerable. The only reasonable solution, Christie felt, was to bring the two together, with Japan and other interested parties, in a conference on the problem of the Pacific, out of which could come an *entente* that would supersede the special British relationship with Japan. If such a plan were to merit serious consideration by the Imperial Conference, however, it would clearly be necessary to know in advance something of the official attitudes of the American administration, on whose co-operation much would depend. Christie therefore proposed that once the new Republican government of President Harding had settled into office in March, Sir Robert Borden should be authorized to take soundings in Washington.[79]

Two weeks later Christie's memorandum was incorporated into a cable to Lloyd George which was soon before the British cabinet. No doubt the idea of seeking to accommodate the United States had a familiar ring to foreign secretary Curzon. But having refused to respond to similar advice from his own department, Curzon continued to take a strong stand against any overtures to the United States. In the first place, he 'hoped the Government would not place their foreign policy in the hands of a representative of the Dominions in a vital issue of this kind'; he trusted further that 'the Cabinet would not rush to the conclusion that the Alliance must be dropped because the Dominions did not want it'.[80] Concealing the views of his department, he merely indica-

---

[78] Memorandum, 1 Feb 1921. Copy in King papers, printed in A. Lower, 'Loring Christie and the genesis of the Washington Conference', *CHR*, XLVII, no 1 (1966).

[79] CO 42/1032: Gov Gen–Col Sec, 15 Feb 1921. The Canadian government were to some extent under unofficial American pressure to oppose the renewal of the alliance, but this seems to have been merely coincidental to the formulation of Canadian policy. See M. G. Fry, 'The North Atlantic Triangle and the Abrogation of the Anglo-Japanese Alliance', *Journal of Modern History*, XXXIX, no 1 (1967).

[80] CAB 23/24: Cab 8 (21) 18 Feb 1921. It was now generally understood in

ted that there was 'much to be said for continuing the Alliance though he would not now elaborate the arguments in favour'. On Curzon's initiative the British reply to Meighen took note of his views but firmly rejected the idea of a mission to Washington, on the grounds that it would 'prejudice the complete liberty of action' of the 1921 Conference.

In Ottawa, Christie was not impressed with the rationale of this thesis. 'The real question', he insisted to Meighen, 'is whether ... it is more desirable to move towards a policy of British–American co-operation or away from it', and he could only assume from the British reply that they themselves did not favour such co-operation. Under these circumstances he was adamant that the mission to Washington should proceed.[81] Christie's exigent tone derived in no small part from his assumption that the Anglo-Japanese alliance had yet to be denounced, and that its termination would require the explicit agreement of all the delegations to the Imperial Conference. He was desperate, therefore, to explore the idea of a Pacific conference in advance, in order to present the conference with a feasible replacement for the alliance, for he feared that without some such definite alternative the necessary unanimity would never be secured and the alliance, *faute de mieux*, would continue. The British insistence upon 'liberty of action' seemed calculated precisely to frustrate unanimity and thus perpetuate the *status quo*.

A further exchange of telegrams brought the British and Canadian governments no closer to an agreement. Meighen recapitulated his arguments for sending Borden to Washington, and underlined them with a warning that Canada might secede from a renewed alliance.[82] In Whitehall, an increasingly anxious Foreign Office were convinced that the only way to prevent Meighen from approaching the United States independently was to show him their committee report of January 1921, and they pleaded now with Curzon for permission to release it:

There can be little doubt, if any, that the policy of Anglo-American cooperation in the Pacific advocated by Canada is the right one, and the recommendations of the departmental committee seem to supply the answer to the problem with which we are now confronted through Canada's action, namely that of holding the Empire together and obtaining unanimity of opinion at the forthcoming meeting of Colonial Premiers in June in favour of such an Anglo-American

Whitehall – though not in the dominions – that the alliance was due to end in July 1921.

[81] Memorandum 3, March 1921, copy in King papers. Meighen did not consult his own cabinet at all about the Anglo-Japanese alliance. Foster diary, 5 June 1921; and J. Eayrs, *The Art of the Possible* (Toronto, 1961), 8.

[82] CO 42/1042: Gov Gen–Col Sec, 1 April 1921.

understanding. If copies of the Committee's report could forthwith be submitted in confidence to the Canadian Government (and other Dominion Governments) it might serve to show that the views held here dovetail with those of the Canadian Government.[83]

But the foreign secretary held sway over his department, and over the cabinet, and the British reply to Meighen merely reiterated the government's opposition to the Washington mission. One vital point, nonetheless, did emerge at last: in the cable to Canada it was made clear that the alliance was due to expire in July 1921. It is difficult to say (as will be seen) how this information affected Canadian policy; but in any event Borden was not sent to Washington.

The final British preparation for discussion of the alliance at the Imperial Conference took place in a cabinet meeting of 30 May.[84] Curzon, who spoke first, was on this occasion more forthcoming about his support for a renewed alliance. He admitted that 'the natural inclination was to ask "Why should there not be a tri-partite Agreement between Great Britain, America and Japan?"' The answer was that the American Senate would never ratify such an agreement, and therefore the best alternative – 'which he thought everyone but the Canadians would accept' – was temporary renewal of the existing alliance with Japan and a declaration of intent to negotiate a new one. He was willing, however, to discuss the terms of renewal with the American and Chinese governments, 'in order to remove the objections of these countries'. Churchill,[85] while not opposing a declaration of intent to renew, spoke up for the Canadian idea of a Pacific conference, and there was an added suggestion that such a conference could possibly be convened by the American rather than the British government.[86] The final conclusions of the cabinet, remarkably enough, managed to contain each of these somewhat disparate suggestions: temporary extension of the 1911 alliance: a Pacific conference to be summoned by the United States (but only after the relevant powers had been told 'we had no intention of dropping the alliance'); private talks with the United States and China; and out of all this a modified new

---

[83] FO 371/6673: Miles Lampson (head of Far Eastern Department), minute of 8 April 1921; see also minute of Sir W. Tyrrell, 8 April 1921.

[84] CAB 23/25: Cab 43 (21), 3 May 1921.

[85] Churchill had become colonial secretary in February 1921, when Milner retired.

[86] The American Senate, more concerned about international relations than Curzon would allow, was about to adopt a unanimous resolution calling for a conference with Japan and Great Britain on the subject of naval disarmament. In June this resolution was also passed by the House of Representatives.

alliance conforming to the League of Nations. Nonetheless, until it was known whether the American government would call a Pacific conference despite a renewal of the alliance, these proposals as a whole amounted to little more than a theoretical ideal arrangement.[87]

In the weeks before the conference, moreover, a complication arose which threatened even the basic decision to renew the alliance. In early June the Japanese government informed Whitehall that in their view the note of July 1920 to the League of Nations had *not* constituted a denunciation of the alliance, which in consequence would *not* lapse in July.[88] In haste the Foreign Office sought a fresh legal opinion from the Law Officers, and barely four days before discussions in the Imperial Conference began they confirmed that the alliance was indeed about to end.

With the legal ambiguities thus apparently resolved, detailed consideration of the alliance began in the conference with a long statement from Curzon, who reviewed the past benefits of the agreement and ended with the conclusions of the British cabinet, that renewal should follow upon talks with the United States and China, and be accompanied by a Pacific conference. A second possibility, he added, might be temporary renewal for a year pending the outcome of such a conference: in this way the empire could enter the conference without any fixed long-term commitments. This alternative was offered deliberately by Curzon as a concession to Canadian opinion. But Meighen in reply to the foreign secretary would have none of it, and went on in no uncertain terms to oppose renewal of the alliance in any form.

The Canadian prime minister, to his own surprise, had found himself to be on rather stronger ground at the Imperial Conference than he had really anticipated. For he had come to London to oppose the Anglo-Japanese alliance having inexplicably failed to realize, from his earlier exchange of cables with Lloyd George, that the alliance was about to end; thus in ignorance of the legal position he had prepared his case as the plaintiff, under the impression that unless he could secure a judgement against it the alliance would continue, and it was not until the debate had actually begun that he realized that he was in fact the defendant, with the onus upon the supporters of the alliance to justify its renewal. His

---

[87] Edward Grigg, Lloyd George's personal adviser on foreign policy, urged the prime minister to act at once on the conclusions and sound the American government, if only to improve the chances of Meighen accepting a new alliance. But no approaches were made before the start of the Imperial Conference. Grigg papers: Grigg–Ll. G., 4 June 1921.

[88] FO 371/6673: British Ambassador, Tokio–FO, 7 June 1921.

arguments, of course, lost none of their utility. He dwelt first upon Japan's unwarranted attacks on China's mainland, which the alliance had patently not curtailed. But his principal contention was that an alliance with Japan, on whatever terms, would seriously compromise the empire's relations with the United States. There were only three major powers left in the world in 1921:

Does it stand to reason that two of these can group themselves together in a special relationship in a sphere in which all three have great interests, and the third be unaffected, the third look with favour upon it?

Everything pointed to an accommodation with the United States, and in this respect the timely passage of the disarmament resolution through the American Congress gave great hope that an understanding could be reached. Under such circumstances,

What is there to be lost by letting this treaty matter stand until a Conference as suggested is held, or until some sort of arrangement can be made resulting in an understanding.[89]

Hughes, the prime minister of Australia, had a ready answer to this question. To leave the renewal of the alliance in suspense, with little more than a blind hope of an *entente* with the United States, was to risk throwing away the substance for the shadow. If nothing came of a Pacific conference, the empire would find itself badly isolated in that area, for there could be no going back as a supplicant to Japan. The risk of such isolation Hughes would absolutely refuse to take.[90]

Hughes spoke well, but the stronger impression had been registered by Meighen, and the following morning a meeting of the British cabinet bore reluctant witness to this, noting without enthusiasm that the Canadian prime minister 'had opposed the renewal of the treaty even more strongly than had been anticipated'.[91] Moreover, Curzon now reported that the British ambassador in Washington had confirmed Canadian fears that renewal would have very severe consequences for British–American relations. At the same time, however, he had indicated that the American government might possibly agree to an informal *entente* (which would not have to run the gauntlet of the Senate) with Britain and Japan, and Curzon admitted that he would like to suspend further discussion in the Imperial Conference for a short time in order to pursue the matter with the Americans, and also with the Japanese. But

[89] *Ibid*: IC mtg 9, 29 June 1921.
[90] *Ibid*: IC mtg 9, 29 June 1921.
[91] CAB 23/26: Cab 56 (21), 30 June 1921.

what of the alliance itself? Renewal might alienate the American government; on the other hand it remained 'essential not to insult Japan by
doing anything which would be tantamount to casting her aside'. In the
end it was Lloyd George who produced a devious but ingenious solution,
one which would not only overcome the diplomatic dilemma but also
suitably spike the guns of the Canadian prime minister:

although it had been assumed that the communication which had been sent to
the League of Nations was tantamount to denouncing that Alliance, he
wondered whether it would not be possible now to get out of the difficulty by
saying to Japan either that we would withdraw that notification or treat it as
not being a denunciation of the Alliance. If this were done it would modify
the situation considerably, and Mr. Meighen, instead of pleading for the non-
renewal of the Alliance, would have to plead for the issue of a notice denouncing it. His point was that if the British Government and Japan agreed that the
Treaty still held good, it would then be a question as to whether we should
give notice of its determination or not, and this would depend on the result
of the Conference which it was suggested should be held between the Powers
concerned.

So the plot was hatched; and to provide a cloak of respectibility for
this fundamental reversal of the legal assumptions that had governed
policy planning thus far, Lloyd George called upon the formidable and
pliable talents of the lord chancellor, Lord Birkenhead. That same afternoon, summoned on a pretext by Lloyd George before the overseas prime
ministers, Birkenhead spoke to his new brief with easy self-confidence,
demonstrating in a clear round over all the legal jumps that there could be
no doubts about the true significance of the 1920 joint note to the League.
With suitable emphasis and decorum he concluded disingenuously:

Prime Minister, I make no observations on the policy in the matter, but upon
the technical matter on which you have asked my opinion for the purpose of
this Conference I have no hesitation whatever in saying that we should adhere
to the view that no denunciation has taken place.[92]

Once the surprise and consternation had passed, Lloyd George was
agreeably solicitous towards the Canadian prime minister, and to enable
the latter to reconsider his position he suggested that the debate be resumed in a few days. His solicitude was unnecessary. Meighen needed no

[92] CAB 32/2: IC mtg 11, 30 June 1921. Cf Lord Beaverbrook, *The Decline and
Fall of Lloyd George* (London, 1963), 81. Nish is prepared to accept
Birkenhead's legal conclusions more at their face value. See Nish, *Alliance*,
337–8.

time to resume the role of plaintiff, if only because there was little more
he could say. The Imperial Conference, guided by the sharp navigational
practice of the British delegation and their lord chancellor, was being
steered towards a compromise, and with reluctance Meighen came round
to the new course. He had to accept that the existing alliance would now
continue until denounced, and that if a Pacific conference were convened,
the British empire had no option but to enter it as an ally to Japan.
But the Canadian prime minister was not the only one who had to make
concessions at this meeting. Hughes, after all, had come to London anxious
not merely to extend the existing alliance with Japan but to settle the
terms for a new one, and he insisted to the end that a definite decision on
these terms must be reached by the Imperial Conference. He could accept
the idea of a Pacific conference:

> but I should enter that Conference with my views perfectly clear on the one
> main point, that is, my intention to renew that Treaty... I cannot agree to
> postponing the settlement of the terms upon which the Treaty is to be re-
> newed.[93]

Three days earlier, with the exception of Meighen, the conference had
been prepared to move in this direction, but now the Australian prime
minister found himself quite alone. He was left to accept the will of the
majority.

The debate was over, and with a few agreed proposals the course of
imperial policy was set. Curzon, who had wished to explore privately the
possibilities for a Pacific *entente* with the United States and Japan, now
undertook to do so at the formal bidding of the Imperial Conference. In
the meantime the alliance would continue – though in ultimate deference
to the League of Nations Covenant[94] – and would not be denounced until
a new agreement had been reached by a Pacific conference. If no such
agreement were reached the existing alliance would remain in force. At
a subsequent meeting, however, a vital revision to these conclusions was
secured by Smuts and Meighen. To state that the alliance would continue
if a Pacific conference produced no alternative agreement, argued Smuts,
was tantamount to inviting the Japanese to preserve the alliance by
wrecking any such conference, and he thought that no veiled promise
of this kind should be held out. As a result of his intervention, which
Meighen strongly supported, the final part of the conclusion was deleted,
and the empire's policy beyond a Pacific conference was left indeterminate.

[93] CAB 32/2: IC mtg 12, 1 July 1921.
[94] A second Anglo-Japanese note to this effect was sent to the League on 7 July
1921. Copy in CO 532/198.

In the event of the conference breaking down it would have to be re-considered.[95]

After 1 July, debate gave way to diplomacy as Curzon moved to fulfil his commission from the Imperial Conference, and on 10 July, prompted into action by the British initiatives, President Harding issued his own call for a conference in Washington, to consider the problems of the Pacific together with disarmament. The announcement of the Washington Conference therefore brought an appropriate end to the imperial discussions about the Anglo-Japanese alliance. It held out the hope that the policy accepted by the Imperial Conference on 1 July might well be realized, with the alliance being incorporated into a broader Pacific *entente*.

That policy, in the event, owed a good deal to the expedient ingenuity of Lloyd George and Birkenhead. Their talents, nonetheless, had been called forth only by Meighen's formidable opposition to a renewal of the Japanese alliance. Though he had failed to get the alliance terminated, Meighen had forestalled the negotiation of a new treaty, and helped to keep imperial policy uncommitted beyond a Pacific conference. As a result, the empire would enter upon the Washington talks in a position as close to neutrality as circumstances would allow. This represented a critical change from the original intentions of the British cabinet. From a longer perspective, also, the Imperial Conference's final conclusions were shaped by the force of Canadian opinion. Meighen was not the first to suggest a conference with the United States about the Pacific: the American government made tentative overtures in mid-1920, and the Foreign Office committee made very strong recommendations in January 1921. But he was the only advocate of a Pacific conference whose access to the British cabinet could not be controlled by the foreign secretary. At the cabinet meeting of 30 May 1921 Curzon proposed renewal and said nothing of his committee's report; it was Churchill who spoke up for the Canadian idea of a conference, and won for it an all-important place in British policy. Thereafter, essentially, there remained only the problem of discovering the terms under which the Pacific conference could be convened.

[95] *Ibid*: IC mtg 13, 1 July 1921. A later plea from Hughes for a definite statement on long-term imperial policy was rejected. Fry, in 'The North Atlantic Triangle ... ', is therefore right in thinking that 'the Imperial Conference had found no substitute for the alliance', but wrong in concluding that 'if the projected [Pacific] conference could not do so, then the alliance would remain.'

5
The centre cannot hold

The 1921 Imperial Conference closed with the British and dominion delegations restored once again to a unity of view on the empire's foreign policy, in spite of the strains of their vigorous disagreements over the future of the Anglo-Japanese alliance. Legal sharp practice and tactical compromise at the conference itself, together with the timely American appeal for disarmament talks at Washington, combined to give the various parties to the debate a shared hope that the alliance might be translated into a less exclusive Pacific *entente* to include the United States, and the British foreign secretary set out at once to pursue this new imperial policy with the idea of convening a special international conference in London. However, when Curzon quickly discovered that the American government would not consider any decisions about a Pacific agreement in advance of their own Washington Conference, he was obliged to leave the pace of further negotiations in their hands. This deference to American wishes, while essential as an expression of British goodwill, was nonetheless unfortunate as far as the empire's own conduct of foreign affairs was concerned, for it meant that no definite arrangements about the dominions' association with the Washington Conference were made before the overseas ministers took their leave from London. For his part Curzon assumed that a British delegation would alone represent the empire, and it was not until Lloyd George made his own independent decision that the dominions were invited to take part in the conference. Yet in what capacity would they participate, given that there had been no separate invitations issued to them? Here the Colonial and Foreign Offices revealed fundamental differences of opinion about the place of the dominions in the empire's external affairs, differences that in the end were settled only after an unexpected but highly pertinent intervention on this problem from General Smuts in South Africa. As a result the dominions gained an essential new independence with regard to their status at international conferences, put into practice first at Washington and then a few weeks later at the Genoa Conference on European economic problems.

By this time, Meighen's government had fallen at a Canadian general election and had been replaced by a Liberal ministry under Mackenzie King, albeit with a bare numerical majority in parliament. In such political circumstances, and given that his party's divisions from the war years were still healing, the new prime minister had no desire to disturb what he took to be Canada's satisfactorily independent relationship to the empire, and as long as such matters did not engage public opinion he was content to leave well enough alone. The Washington Conference yielded no unwanted commitments, the abortive Genoa Conference proved equally harmless, and his government's freedom of action in any case seemed secure. Yet notwithstanding these new dominion advances on the international stage, in the early summer of 1922 King was given grounds for thinking that Canada's association with the empire – specifically her participation in the Imperial Conference – might already have committed his government in advance to common external responsibilities. He had asked the British authorities if he could publish some classified correspondence relating to the 1921 Conference, a request that drew from London not simply a refusal but a long brief indicating that the conference played a vital role in fostering co-operative imperial policies, and must therefore operate in strict confidence. It seemed that Canada had accepted a collaborative role to play in the empire after all.

To an important extent the new prime minister had been left so long in ignorance of Canada's position with respect to imperial external affairs because the Colonial Office in these months were failing to provide the dominions with even a minimum degree of consultation about foreign policy questions. As ever the department carried final responsibility for dominion relations, yet they hardly were allowed sufficient time to sound the overseas governments even on acknowledged matters of common concern. With Lloyd George's personal policy advisers by now a department unto themselves in Whitehall, and a powerful rival to the Foreign Office in the practical conduct of foreign policy, the lines of administrative authority in London were more than usually disturbed and only increased the problems of the Colonial Office. And where Milner would do his best for his officials and for the dominions, he stepped down in early 1921 to be replaced by Winston Churchill, whose ministerial priorities lay with the middle east rather than with the self-governing members of the empire. Churchill's marked lack of interest in this side of his portfolio meant that the overseas governments had little chance to keep abreast of foreign affairs.

From this point of view the Chanak crisis, and the subsequent problems that surrounded the organization of the Lausanne peace conference, may be seen as direct consequences of Whitehall's decreased administrative co-ordination over British–dominion relations. During these autumn weeks of 1922 major decisions affecting the dominions were reached, first by Churchill and Lloyd George and then by Curzon at the Foreign Office, without any reference to the frustrated permanent officials of the Colonial Office, and there was a degree of bad feeling created amongst the dominions that had been unknown since the gravest days of the war. King's worst fears were confirmed. Not only was Canada committed to unlimited external liabilities in support of imperial foreign policies, but she was also prey to a capricious and arbitrary administrative control from Whitehall that might bring the dominions into war at a moment's notice. On both accounts King began to take steps to dissociate his government from collective imperial responsibilities, and began also to make a critical distinction between imperial diplomacy as a whole and Canada's own particular external affairs, for which alone the dominion would be accountable.

The dominions and the Washington Conference

The Washington Conference is important to the development of British–dominion relations in two distinct ways. In the first place, it successfully translated the policy proposals of the 1921 Imperial Conference regarding the Pacific region into a tangible international settlement, replacing the Anglo-Japanese alliance with a four-power treaty that included the United States and France. This new treaty in its turn helped to establish a favourable diplomatic climate for a broader international agreement on the general limitation of naval forces. Thus the results of the conference served to confirm the diplomatic and strategic unity of the empire. On the diplomatic side the foundations of an imperial post-war policy in the Pacific region were now laid down, while strategically, Britain and the dominions accepted a joint obligation to limit their combined naval strength. At the same time, however, the Washington Conference also endorsed the international status of the dominions, who, though they were not given separate representation, signed and ratified the Pacific and naval agreements on their own behalf. The significance of this independent form of accession to the two treaties, copied directly from the 1919 peace settlement, lay in the fact that the conference was the first major post-war gathering not convened under international auspices. It suggested that the dominions' right to some separate consideration in foreign affairs, which had hitherto been established only for matters within the competence of the League of Nations, was now to be extended to international affairs generally. We may turn first to this important development in imperial relations.

It was clear from the start that the American government had no intention of extending separate invitations for the Washington Conference to the dominions. President Harding's announcement of 10 July spoke of a conference with the 'principal allied and associate powers', and it was to these powers – Britain, France, Italy and Japan – that invitations were issued on 11 August. Nonetheless, the American State Department had every expectation that dominion ministers would take part in the conference in a joint imperial delegation. Accordingly they indicated that they would accept a large British contingent, and indeed at one point they were even prepared to move the conference forward to September 1921 (Harding preferred November) to facilitate dominion attendance.[1] By contrast, the British government seemed somewhat uncertain about dominion representation. In July, Curzon had tried in the first instance to arrange a conference in London, so that questions relating more specifically to the Pacific region could be settled in advance of the Washington discussions on naval disarmament. He had certainly assumed the overseas premiers would attend these London talks, though at the same time it appears to have been agreed that Britain would represent the empire in the later disarmament negotiations.[2] But Curzon's initiatives in this direction were strongly resented by the American government, with the result that the idea of two separate conferences was abandoned and all further arrangements left to Washington. The foreign secretary, nonetheless, continued to think that British representatives alone would attend the Washington Conference, despite the fact that it would now have to deal with both Pacific and disarmament problems: the empire's delegation, he told the American ambassador, would number no more than three.[3] However, an inquiry from Ottawa at the end of August showed that Meighen at least was expecting that the dominions would now participate in the conference if only in connection with Pacific affairs.

A few weeks later a draft agenda from Washington confirmed that Pacific affairs would indeed be discussed at length by the conference, and without any further reference to either the Foreign or Colonial Offices Lloyd George decided that the overseas governments should be allowed to participate, through a British Empire Delegation.[4] 'At recent

---

[1] Harvey, American ambassador (London)–Sec of State Hughes, n.d., quoted in G. P. Glazebrook, *A History of Canadian External Relations* (London, 1950), Grigg papers: (copy) British ambassador, Washington–FO, 22 July 1921.

[2] Grigg papers: memorandum of Curzon, 24 July 1921; memorandum of E. Grigg, 14 Sept 1921.

[3] Harvey–Hughes, *loc cit*.

[4] Memorandum of Grigg, 14 Sept 1921, *loc cit*.

Imperial Conference', they were duly reminded, 'it was arranged that His Majesty's Government should represent the whole Empire at Washington', but were told that the government proposed to rescind this arrangement so that 'men with special knowledge of the Canadian, Australasian and Indian points of view' could be appointed to the delegation.[5] The Canadian prime minister was the first to reply. 'Your proposal is appreciated', he cabled Lloyd George, 'and I would nominate Sir Robert Borden.' Within a few days the appointments from Australia, New Zealand and India had also been confirmed.[6]

With the dominions' representation at the conference thus established, it remained only to draw up the 'full powers' for the individual British and overseas members of the British Empire Delegation. But on this matter the Foreign Office and the Colonial Office quickly found themselves in sharp disagreement. Their conflicting views rekindled, and in fact were a direct consequence of, the arguments that had attended the issue of full powers to the dominion delegates at the 1919 peace conference. At that time the Colonial Office, anxious that the legal unity of the empire should not be sacrificed as the dominions began to establish themselves at the international level, had argued for unrestricted full powers all round in order to prevent the overseas delegates signing the treaties 'on behalf of' their respective dominions. They had denied the relevance of two awkward pre-war precedents for 'separate' signatures. The Foreign Office, with diplomatic expedience their prime concern, had capitulated to Canadian pressure, and separate dominion signatures had been sanctioned.

In October 1921 the Paris peace conference came in turn to represent a useful precedent to the Foreign Office: as their assistant legal adviser remarked, 'in the present somewhat indeterminate state of the relations of the Dominions to foreign affairs it is good to stick to a precedent when we have got one'.[7] They assumed, therefore, that the full powers for the overseas representatives should be drafted so as to enable them to sign any

---

[5] CO 532/199: Col Sec–Govs Gen, 3 Oct 1921. Smuts had already indicated that South Africa, with no concrete interests in disarmament or the Pacific, did not wish to be represented.

[6] Meighen was later to deny that he had ever agreed to Britain representing the empire at the Washington Conference – though in none too convincing a manner (see Canada, HoC, 13 March 1922). The tone of his reply here, together with the fact that neither the Colonial Office nor the other dominions queried the form of Lloyd George's invitation to attend the conference, may be taken as reasonable evidence that such an arrangement had originally been agreed to at the time of the Imperial Conference.

[7] FO 371/5620: H. W. Malkin, minute of 8 Oct 1921.

treaties 'on behalf of' their respective dominions. But once again the Colonial Office challenged this indiscriminate subservience to precedent. The 1919 peace treaties, in their view, had established that the dominions had the right to sign on their own behalf when *separately* represented at international conferences, whereas to allow the same form of signature at Washington would indicate that dominion representation of *whatever* sort at a conference entailed this right of separate signature. Since Britain's own invitation to the dominions to participate in the conference was in no way tantamount to separate representation, and the delegates were therefore to represent the empire as a whole, their full powers should be absolutely unqualified.[8] On this issue the Colonial Office were determined to have their day in court rather than let the Foreign Office again take the expedient line of least resistance, and so on 19 October 1921 the two parties submitted their case to the arbitration of the prime minister.

In 1919, Borden's active involvement in the question of dominion signatures to the peace treaties had severely compromised the efforts of the Colonial Office. In a curious way history was now to repeat itself, with intervention coming this time not from Canada but from an equally committed champion of dominion status, General Smuts. The South African prime minister had already decided there was no need to be represented at the Washington Conference. Nonetheless he had evidently become very worried about the terms under which the other governments had agreed to attend, feeling that an undifferentiated imperial delegation would threaten the advance made by the dominions at the Paris conference. So he chose now to alert the other prime ministers to the implications of their position, and it thus happened that the day the inter-departmental dispute about signatures went before Lloyd George, the prime minister also received a copy of a Smuts cable to Meighen, Hughes and Massey which urged them to press for separate invitations from the American government:

This is the first great International Conference after Paris [Smuts had reminded them] and if the Dominions concerned are not invited and yet attend, bad precedent will be set and Dominion status will suffer. If a stand is made now and America acquiesces, battle for international recognition our equal status is finally won.[9]

Smuts' telegram had a direct bearing upon the question of the form of dominion signatures at Washington. Lloyd George had no intention of presenting the American government with any last-minute request for

---

[8] CO 532/186: H. Lambert, minute of 14 Oct 1921.
[9] CO 532/175: (copy) Smuts–Meighen, 19 Oct 1921.

separate invitations, and no reason to think that any of the participating dominions would make such a request on their own initiative.[10] Smuts, even so, by taking the dominions' status at the peace conference as the criterion for all their international affairs, had suggested very persuasively that the forthcoming conference would be detrimental to dominion autonomy and so to pre-empt any unhelpful dominion reactions Lloyd George quickly offered them the next best thing. Ignoring the Colonial Office's constitutional reservations, Lloyd George explicitly promised the overseas governments that while separate invitations could not be obtained, their representatives would be on the same footing as at the Paris peace conference, and would certainly sign all treaties on behalf of their respective governments. With suitable emphasis Lloyd George concluded:

Effect of this will be that signature of each Dominion Delegate will be necessary in addition to signature of British delegates to commit British Empire Delegation as a whole to any agreements made at Conference, and that any Dominion delegate can reserve assent on behalf of his Government if he wishes.[11]

The status of the dominions at the Washington Conference was thus clearly defined, Smuts' well-timed concern for separate invitations having decisively settled the dispute between the Foreign and Colonial Offices. There is no telling, of course, whether Lloyd George would ever have accepted the Colonial Office argument for unrestricted full powers for all the members of the British Empire Delegation. It is at least ironic that, in rejecting it, the only prime minister he really pleased was Smuts himself, who had already decided not to be represented at the conference. Massey was embarrassed by separate signatures (his delegate subsequently denied that the dominions had acquired 'any form of international status'[12]). Hughes was positively antagonistic, remonstrating with Lloyd George that in meeting Smuts' wishes a precedent might be established 'which may make impossible that unity of Empire which is the rock on which it rests'.[13] Meighen alone welcomed the offer of separate signatures and acknowledged the importance of the Paris precedent, though even he showed little sustained interest in the status of the dominion delegates to the conference. In Meighen's case, however, the lack of concern was perhaps understandable. By October 1921 the Canadian prime minister

---

[10] Meighen tersely dismissed the idea of trying to obtain separate invitations from the American government. King papers, J1/74: (copy) Meighen–Smuts, 23 Oct 1921.

[11] CO 532/175: Col Sec–Govs Gen, 21 Oct 1921.

[12] W. K. Hancock, *Survey of British Commonwealth Affairs*, 1: *Problems of Nationality 1918–1936* (London, 1937), 89.

[13] FO 371/5622: (copy) Gov Gen (Aust.)–Col Sec, 24 Oct 1921.

was deeply involved in the dominion's first post-war general election campaign, and was fighting for his political life.

Compared to the negotiations about the style and status of the dominions' participation at the Washington Conference, those which led to the winding up of the Anglo-Japanese alliance need only brief consideration here. Remarkably, in the three months between the Imperial Conference and the Washington Conference, there was virtually no discussion of the alliance at either the international or the imperial level. This diplomatic hiatus was imposed by the Japanese government. In mid-August 1921 they 'desired to remain in the closest touch with the British government' about the forthcoming conference – a desire happily reciprocated by Whitehall.[14] A month later, when a draft agenda was circulated from Washington, the Foreign Office duly sought Japan's views before replying themselves to the United States.[15] However, it was not until 15 October that a reply was received from the Japanese government, which even at that late hour disclosed only an acceptance of the American agenda 'in principle'. 'In the circumstances', minuted the head of the American Department, 'we may well leave the Delegates to get in touch with their U.S. and Japanese colleagues on arrival and hearing what they have to propose [sic].'[16]

By this time, however, the Foreign Office were aware that the American government were at least prepared to discuss the idea of a three-power agreement in the Pacific as a successor to the Anglo-Japanese alliance. And although this information was not disclosed to the dominions (nor to the Japanese) the British government made their own preparations to terminate the alliance on such a basis.[17] The foreign secretary continued to think that under any tripartite agreement 'we shall certainly be left worse off than before',[18] but to a British cabinet now given a prospect of

14 FO 371/5618: Sir E. Crowe, minute of 16 Aug 1921.
15 CO 532/186: (copy) FO–British ambassador, Tokio, 18 Sept 1921. 'Obviously we cannot commit ourselves without a previous understanding with Japan.'
16 FO 371/5620: memorandum from Japanese Embassy, London, 15 Oct 1921; R. Sperling, minute of 18 Oct 1921.
17 In a letter to Loring Christie (who was to accompany Borden to the conference) Hankey explained somewhat unconvincingly that although the Foreign Office had prepared a large number of working papers for the coming discussions, 'They cannot release them, however, until they are approved by the Secretary of State, and up to now, with the immense pressure of foreign affairs ... Lord Curzon has not been able to deal with them.' Christie papers: Hankey–Christie, 20 Oct 1921.
18 FO 371/6705: minute of 23 Oct 1921.

reducing defence expenditure, the alliance with Japan had become no more than an expendable obstacle in the way of international naval disarmament. A cabinet meeting on 1 November gave Arthur Balfour, who was to head the British delegation, a clear understanding of British priorities.[19] Although he received no precise instructions about the alliance, he was left with no doubts than its demise must serve, if possible, as a means to the greater end. He had completed the draft terms of a three-power agreement even while crossing the Atlantic.[20]

The negotiation of a Pacific *entente* was conducted amongst the heads of the British, American and Japanese delegations, without the publicity given to the discussion of naval disarmament and without the direct participation of the dominion representatives. From his colleagues on the B.E.D. Balfour enjoyed absolute discretion, to the point where he did not officially report progress to them until an agreement (expanded to include France) was all but completed. The concurrence of the dominions to the new treaty was invited, and received, simultaneously with that of the other governments involved.

The four-power treaty, as many have pointed out, was a far cry from the alliance which it replaced. Gone were the commitments to mutual military aid and to the defence of special interests, in lieu of which were unsecured promises to respect territorial rights in the Pacific and to confer in the event of disputes or threats to any of the signatories. A renewed Anglo-Japanese alliance, however, if it had been drafted in conformity with the League Covenant, would probably have said little more; even Curzon had come to see that any mutual pledges of military support – the heart of the old alliance – would no longer be possible.[21] Seen in this light, the only essential change was in the extension of the old agreement from two to four powers. Moreover, when it was considered in conjunction with the new naval agreements, and the solution of many of the problems concerning China, the four-power treaty was well received by all parties, even Japan. The alliance, remarked one of their delegation, had at least been given a splendid funeral![22]

The negotiation of the four-power treaty resolved a problem of imperial foreign policy which had engaged Whitehall and the dominions for almost twenty-four months. The alliance was to end, while the empire's foreign policy, despite the heated debates of the 1921 Imperial Conference,

---

[19] CAB 23/27: Cab 83 (21), 1 Nov 1921.
[20] FO 371/6706: Balfour–FO (dispatch), 11 Nov 1921.
[21] FO 371/6705: minute of 23 Oct 1921.
[22] F. S. Northedge, *The Troubled Giant: Britain among the Great Powers, 1916–1939* (London, 1966), 286.

remained united. Although the dominion representatives had played no part in the ultimate discussions, the treaty was willingly endorsed by their governments. The Canadian government were naturally pleased to learn that the alliance was to be replaced by a Pacific *entente*. And the measure of the approval of Australia and New Zealand may be judged from the cordial reception given to the treaty by their representatives in the British Empire Delegation.[23] On 13 December, by virtue of their status and in witness to this unanimous acceptance of the treaty, the dominion delegates added their names to Balfour's when the new agreement was signed.

Borden's signature of the treaty was his last commission on behalf of the government of Arthur Meighen. Defeated in the general election of 6 December 1921, the Canadian prime minister was about to surrender the reins of office. It was altogether fitting that he had held them long enough to be an official party to the ending of the Anglo-Japanese alliance.

The new regime in Canada

The general election of December 1921 brought to a close ten years of Conservative government in Canada, and more immediately marked the end of the Conservative–Liberal coalition alliance put together by Borden in the autumn of 1917. It consolidated the revival of Liberal Party fortunes under Mackenzie King, and it brought to the federal political stage for the first time a strong contingent of Progressives, representing the powerful voice of western agrarian protest. But the results also registered a fragmented and unbalanced political situation across the dominion as a whole. The Liberals with 116 seats were just short of a majority and clearly the leading party, but they were heavily concentrated in Quebec (a clean sweep: the province would not yet forgive the Conservative leadership for conscription) the maritimes and parts of Ontario; the 65 Progressives spoke for rural Ontario and the prairie provinces; the Conservatives, reduced to 50 seats, held only 13 outside their own Ontario stronghold. Thus if Meighen had been decisively rejected, King had a far from clear mandate in assuming the leadership of the country. Though he rather than Meighen could count on the sympathy of the Progressives, there was no telling how far they would support a Liberal regime, and their unpredictable character was emphasized when it became known that, although they would constitute the second largest element in the House of Commons, they would not act as the official parliamentary opposition, preferring the uncommitted cross-benches. From the start then, the new prime minister was constrained to be cautious and uncontentious in his policies, both domestic and external, with the reconstruction of the nation's unity

[23] CAB 29/28/3: BED 60, 10 Dec 1921.

the major criterion for judging any government action. Consensus politics became the order of the day.

Canada's external relations, it is fair to say, had played little part in the election campaign. All concerned were very much aware that the outcome would be largely determined by domestic rather than external issues, and they sensed that there was little political capital to be made in this latter area, whether by criticism or justification. Naval defence, foreign affairs, the League of Nations – the imperial factor in general: no awkward issues presented themselves for public debate (Meighen was hardly able to disclose anything of his achievements at the 1921 Imperial Conference) and the election did nothing to check the country's comfortable drift on the tide of post-war unconcern. In October, a lecture by the retired Sir Robert Borden had endeavoured to recall the dominion authorities to their duties, in one respect at least. 'I have yet to learn', he admonished a Toronto audience,

that since the conclusion of the peace [the dominions'] right to 'an adequate voice in foreign policy and in foreign relations' has been recognized in any effective or practical way. This result does not seem to justify complacency or inaction.[24]

But his complaint found no response outside the lecture hall. Meighen had no desire to promote public discussion along these lines, while King would have questioned the concept of a centralized empire foreign policy anyway.

Here was perhaps the most significant development with regard to Canadian attitudes to imperial affairs in 1921. Under King's leadership the Liberals had gone a long way to resolving their own internal differences on these matters, and spoke with a much more coherent voice: between those who had earlier feared imperial federation and those who thought the empire would break up altogether there was now a commonly accepted middle position, which supported a continued Canadian association with the empire but only on the assumption that it carried no external commitments whatever. Admittedly, during a period when the Canadian government had themselves been consistently declining to assume any tangible responsibilities in this direction, it was not surprising if the Liberal and Conservative approaches to imperial relations seemed indistinguishable. But although the election campaign did not inspire either party leader to develop his views on this subject, the pressure of events was soon enough to lead to a stark reclarification of Canada's position by the new Liberal prime minister.

[24] Speech printed in Borden, *Canadian Constitutional Studies*, 116.

For the moment, there were no immediate indications that the course of British–Canadian relations was to be markedly different under the new regime, despite the somewhat awkward circumstances of a change of government while the Washington Conference was *in medias res*. It was quickly agreed that Borden should stay at the conference and complete his work on the new government's behalf. But King was instinctively apprehensive, fearing that under Meighen Canada had already been committed in principle to an integrated imperial naval defence agreement, and it required several lengthy inquiries to Borden before the prime minister was satisfied that his government's freedom of action was not covertly being bargained away, and that in any event parliament would be able to ratify all final conclusions. Characteristically, King was then easily able to convince himself that, far from having simply corrected his own mistaken impression on this score, he had in fact made a decisive intervention in the proceedings. At the beginning of February he noted fervently in his diary:

The significant point is that we are establishing precedence [sic] while conditions are in a state of flux, and so making constitutional law as well as history. To preserve the supremacy of parliament in the treaty making power as in all else is my aim as being in accord with government of and by & for the people.[25]

Meanwhile, a few days earlier a letter from O. D. Skelton, dean of arts at Queen's University and the biographer of Sir Wilfrid Laurier, had drawn King's attention from the straightforward avoidance of commitments at Washington to the question of Canada's status at the conference. Skelton was severely critical of the lack of separate representation, deeming this to be a slur upon the dominions' post-war status, and he suggested that in protest Canada should now withhold ratification of the final treaties and thus provoke a major constitutional crisis.[26] The prime minister showed no interest in such drastic action. But he did take an opportunity to learn more of Skelton's ideas, attending on 31 January a lecture by Skelton on the empire's foreign policy, in which the historian made a severe indictment of imperial diplomatic unity. The address, King noted in his diary that evening, 'would make an excellent foundation for Canadian policy on External Affairs, and Skelton himself would make an excellent man for that department'.[27]

It happened that within a matter of weeks the new prime minister had

[25] Diary, 1 Feb 1922.
[26] King papers, J1/82: Skelton–King, 27 Jan 1922.
[27] R. M. Dawson, *William Lyon Mackenzie King*, 1: *1874–1923* (London, 1958), 454.

the chance to re-examine the question of Canada's rightful place at international conferences, for shortly after the conference ended at Washington another international gathering was convened at Genoa to study the worsening problems of European post-war economic recovery. This time, however, it appeared from the outset that the dominions' status would be secure, as they each had received separate invitations from the Italian government.[28] Indeed it appeared that King had no further claims to make of the conference's organization. In early February he asked the Colonial Office whether the overseas governments were to have their own delegations or to form part of a larger imperial delegation, an inquiry which made the Office somewhat apprehensive, but he seemed content to learn that a British Empire Delegation was to be organized in accordance with past practice. Two Canadian delegates were duly appointed, with full powers to act on behalf of the dominion.

In one significant detail Canada's representation for the Genoa Conference departed from the pattern followed by Borden and Meighen. Since the Imperial War Cabinet of 1917 Loring Christie had without fail accompanied the dominion's delegations, as an adjunct to his duties as general adviser on external affairs, to imperial meetings, to the first League Assembly and latterly to the Washington Conference, and had served as the Canadian element in the joint imperial secretariats organized on these occasions by Hankey's staff. On good terms with Hankey himself, Christie in early March anticipated the continuing of their association at Genoa, and confessed that 'As Washington recedes and the memories of hotel life with it I rather think I am becoming more receptive to the idea of a journey to Genoa. I suppose these conferences get in one's blood.'[29] As it happened, however, Genoa was to follow Washington all too quickly, and Christie found himself confined to quarters in Ottawa with the task of helping Borden draft his official report about the American conference, to be ready for parliament by early April. And although Hankey was sympathetic enough to contemplate cabling King for Christie's help, he had to admit it was 'a delicate matter', and decided in the end not to intervene.[30] It was undoubtedly a prudent judgement. For King in these weeks – as his attendance at the Skelton lecture had indicated – was already beginning to have second thoughts about the advisers he had inherited from Meighen. The little Department of External Affairs, he was convinced, constituted 'a tory hive', and he was somewhat surprised

[28] King papers, J1/75: Italian ambassador (London)–King, 21 Jan 1922. Lloyd George had asked the Italian government to invite the dominions directly.
[29] Christie papers: Christie–Hankey, 7 March 1922.
[30] Christie papers: Hankey–Christie, 22 March 1922.

when a talk with Christie in mid-February 'went off better than I had anticipated, as I feared the effect of a changed administration upon him after his close association with Sir Robert Borden and Meighen'.[31] Thereafter it did not take Christie long to understand that his influence in the new administration was going to be sharply restricted. Although his resignation did not come in the end until early 1923, his days at the centre of Canadian external relations policymaking were effectively over.

So the Canadian delegates, Sir Charles Gordon and Edouard Montpetit, left for Genoa without Christie. Indeed they left without any official secretary at all, the added implication here being that on King's reading, the B.E.D. was not to be the crucible in which a united imperial policy for the conference would be formed, but quite simply the sum of its separate parts and as such a body that did not require an integrated secretarial administration. Canada was to be represented at Genoa in her own right, by virtue of the invitation from the Italian government. That being the case, the B.E.D. would neither influence Canadian policy nor determine the extent to which her delegation took part in the conference. King's instructions to his delegates, in fact, contained no reference to the B.E.D., nor to imperial diplomatic unity. 'We feel', he wrote, 'that you should not actively intervene in questions that are of purely European concern, but that you should interest yourselves in such questions as are of economic concern to Canada. It is difficult to give any more precise definition, but this indication will serve as a guide to your action.'[32] The attitudes, and by implication the decisions, of the other contingents within the B.E.D. were of no direct interest to him.

The Canadian delegation to Genoa proved able to carry out their mandate from King without prejudice to the empire's diplomatic unity, for the simple reason that very little was transacted at the conference. The conference, and the B.E.D., held their first sessions on 10 April 1922, and in dispatches to King over the next few days Gordon spoke of the potential benefits of Canada's participation at the conference as regards future trade with Europe, and of the probability of granting recognition to Russia. He also thought that the absence of the United States made Canada's presence all the more important. The American attitude, he wrote, 'has created a good deal of resentment, and for this reason, if none other, I am glad that we are here'.[33] On 16 April, however, the Russian and German delegations concluded a pre-emptive *entente* at Rapallo, and at a stroke the hopes of settling European claims against Russia, and of re-negotiating the

---

[31] Diary, 21 Jan, 14 Feb 1922.
[32] King papers, J1/73: King–Gordon, 28 March 1922.
[33] King papers, J1/73: Gordon–King, 10–14 April 1922.

German reparations question, were both severely jeopardized. Carried forward by its own momentum the conference continued for another month, but there was little of importance that it could resolve to do, and even less over which the Canadians could have disagreed with the other imperial delegates.

Yet in the end the conference turned out to be not entirely an empty formality for the Canadians. Privately, it appears, negotiations had been continuing throughout April for an international scheme to provide credit facilities for the Russian government, and although Gordon had left for Genoa quite specifically opposed to further extensions of Canadian credit in Europe, he was now convinced enough of the prospects to propose to King a dominion stake in this venture, initially for a million dollars. From an otherwise sterile conference there had thus come an unexpected invitation to break into Russian markets, albeit only on credit – but King nonetheless proved most unwilling to reach a decision on this matter (no doubt he was anxious to know how the other possible partners in the scheme were receiving the idea) and it was only when the conference was about to break up that Gordon was at last told not to proceed any further.[34] In the event, however, King's caution was fully vindicated. By the time his own negative response reached Genoa the international consortium seemed very unlikely to take shape, and the Russians had therefore backed away from any general move towards normalized trade and diplomatic relations. The excitement was over, and King was duly reassured by Montpetit (who appears not to have shared Gordon's enthusiasm) 'The Russian susceptibilities aided in some way our own cause and finally brought to nothing the responsibilities to be shared.'[35]

From King's point of view the Genoa Conference had turned out to be a completely successful affair. Canada's international status had been fully recognized in the invitation and mode of representation, the government had not had to commit themselves to any international responsibilities, and they had therefore not been confronted with any difficult problems over following a single imperial line in foreign policy. All told, Genoa compared most favourably to the Washington Conference. Here was a subject King could not leave alone. When parliament opened in March he had chastised Meighen for failing to secure separate Canadian representation to the conference, and as if that were not enough he then attempted to explore more fully the record of the Meighen administration in imperial relations – a game in which Meighen, to defend his own policies, was obliged to follow suit. Thus in quick succession the Colonial

---

[34] See Massey, *What's Past is Prologue*, 68–70.
[35] King papers, J1/78: Montpetit–King, 24 May 1922.

Office received requests to make public not only the correspondence pertaining to Canada's invitation to the Washington Conference, but also whatever could be released on the subject of the 1921 Imperial Conference, as prime minister and ex-prime minister sought to vindicate themselves before the Canadian House of Commons.

In Whitehall, where there was a deeply ingrained reluctance to see confidential records thus brought into the light of day so hastily, these Canadian requests caused much concern, and while some Washington Conference papers were duly given clearance it was decided to explain to King at some length why the British government could not possibly release Imperial Conference documents:

The Imperial Conference has a very delicate and momentous part to play in maintaining the peace of the world, the interests of the different nations of the Commonwealth, and the unity of those nations in the world-wide system of citizenship under one sovereign . . .

. . . a decision to publish would inevitably alter character and narrow utility of future sessions . . .

. . . Other Governments entrust to the British Government and Foreign Office responsibility of conducting foreign policy of the Empire upon the lines which Imperial Conference lays down . . . we place all the arguments and documents upon vital matters at disposal of Dominion Prime Ministers . . . but if everything communicated in this manner is to become subject to requests for publication afterwards when Imperial Conference is not in session and cannot weigh arguments for and against publicity, we shall be compelled against our will to communicate nothing which, in our opinion, is unsuitable for eventual publication. To impose such restrictions on inter-Imperial consultation would be to erect new barriers between Governments of Empire in the discussion of general policy . . .

. . . our view of your proposal is the same whether we regard it in our capacity of agents of the foreign policy laid down by the Imperial Conference or in our capacity of guardians of the character and practice of the Conference when not in session.[36]

Lloyd George's telegram, the full text of which ran to over eight hundred words, was a quite remarkable response to King's request for publication. It was not so much an answer as a comprehensive *apologia* for the diplomatic unity of the empire. Six months earlier (in announcing that Ireland was to become a dominion) the prime minister had spoken in a similar vein before the British House of Commons declaring ebulliently that 'The sole control of Britain over foreign policy is now vested in the Empire as a whole'[37] – a speech that had already alarmed Canadian

[36] CO 532/208: Col Sec–Gov Gen, 21 June 1922.
[37] GB, HoC, 14 Dec 1921.

nationalists.[38] Here was convincing private proof that the ideas expressed then had not been mere imperialist rhetoric. Perhaps the British government felt that King, the newcomer to the imperial club, needed to be taught the rules of procedure of the establishment. For whatever reason, he now had an explicit confirmation of the assumptions which governed Whitehall's thinking. Imperial diplomatic unity was not the contingent by-product of six separate but similar foreign policies, but a process (and a continuing process) generated by consultation and communication with the dominions, and directed by and large from Whitehall. A vital part of this process was the Imperial Conference itself. Its sessions enabled the dominion premiers to confer upon common problems, but more importantly to confer upon the British government the legitimacy for administering the empire's foreign policy. King was soon to learn, moreover, that this conception of the imperial enterprise was by no means peculiar to Whitehall. The other dominion governments, given a copy of Lloyd George's telegram, endorsed unanimously his reasons for keeping the affairs of the Imperial Conference confidential. One by one their replies were forwarded to Ottawa.

The old regime in Whitehall

The response of the other three dominions to the Lloyd George manifesto about the Imperial Conference indicated an impressive degree of support for a co-operative imperial foreign policy. It bore witness to the confidence of the dominions that on important matters of policy Britain would continue to consult them. In Whitehall, however, there were disturbing signs that the machinery of consultation was not being adequately maintained. As ever, the initiative for looking after the interests of the overseas governments in advance of policy decisions lay with the Colonial Office, presided over since February 1921 by Winston Churchill. We have seen how, despite the best convictions of his predecessor, Lord Milner, the Office had retained their practical control over British–dominion relations. Henry Lambert summed up the situation in April 1921:

whatever may be the altered status of the Dominions and whatever the ideal channel of communications, the fact remains that as long as things are as they are, no other Minister than the Colonial Secretary watches over, or can watch over, the relations of the various parts of the Empire to each other, and the Colonial Office is in fact the only office which does, or can do, the work involved in this task ... (I may here remark that whatever blunders other

---

[38] See, eg, J. W. Dafoe–Sir Clifford Sifton, 19 Dec 1921, in R. Cook (ed), *The Sifton–Dafoe Correspondence, 1919–27* (Winnipeg, 1966), 104.

Departments make in dealing with the Dominions, it is always left to us to put things straight).[39]

In practice, the dominions should have been very well provided for under Churchill's administration. The colonial secretary was one of Lloyd George's closest colleagues in the coalition government, and intimately associated with British policymaking. At a time when the prime minister's personal staff constituted virtually a separate department of state, whose influence in foreign affairs continued to challenge that of the Foreign Office, Churchill enjoyed a privileged access to his prime minister from which the dominions might have greatly benefited. Unfortunately his attention was elsewhere (for the most part with Britain's interests in the middle east) and the work of the Dominions Department received from him only the most cursory acknowledgement.

In the first fifteen months of Churchill's tenure of office, the 1921 Imperial Conference, followed by those at Washington and Genoa, had provided the dominions with some measure of participation in imperial foreign affairs. By the summer of 1922, however, the colonial secretary's lack of support was seriously hindering efforts to secure consultation for the overseas governments. When, for example, the British cabinet decided at the end of June to promote Germany's admission to the League of Nations, the Dominions Department felt strongly that the full approval of the overseas governments should be secured before any diplomatic activity began. They put their case before the prime minister's office, but without any intercession from Churchill himself they were simply overruled: the dominions were informed of British policy, and not invited to pass comment.

Similar circumstances attended the implementation of a second policy decision taken at the same cabinet meeting, concerning the settlement of inter-allied war debts. In response to American pressure for the repayment of war loans the government had decided to send a strong note to their European allies – the Balfour Note, as it became known – regarding the settlement of their own war debts to Britain, though in this instance the cabinet were prepared to allow the dominions to be consulted in advance of the note's dispatch. Despite the cabinet's conclusion, however, and several reminders from its secretary, Churchill made no effort at all to ensure that the dominions were consulted;[40] and left to fend for themselves, there was nothing the Dominions Department could do when the prime

[39] CO 532/179: minute of 29 April 1921.
[40] CAB 23/30: mtg 36 (22), 30 June; CO 532/266: Cabinet Office–CO, 30 June 1922 etc.

minister decided after all to abandon the idea of consultation. To confer with the dominions upon the general policy of debt settlement, Lloyd George indicated, might involve the government in 'difficult discussions and misunderstandings with them'. Rather than negotiate such difficulties he was prepared instead to let the dominions dissociate themselves entirely from the Balfour Note if they did not approve.[41]

Here from Lloyd George, barely a month after his homily to King, was a blunt reappraisal of the importance of the empire's diplomatic unity, one that Churchill accepted without protest, and one indeed that his indifference to the dominions increasingly encouraged. As it happened, there were no complaints from the overseas governments over the Balfour Note. But the incident did bring Whitehall a critical private inquiry from Borden's former cabinet colleague, N. W. Rowell. Knowing that the American government were not at all sympathetic to the Balfour Note, he could only suppose that the dominions had not been consulted about it – for he could 'hardly imagine any Canadian Government which was in touch at all with American sentiment approving [its dispatch]'.[42]

I confess I cannot understand it [Rowell went on]. I suppose there must be some explanation which does not appear on the surface. If the Canadian Government was not consulted then it appears to me it was a serious departure from the understanding that the Dominions should be consulted on matters of foreign policy directly affecting their interests.

Rowell's letter pointed, once again, to consultation as the only valid basis for imperial co-operation. Yet it is doubtful whether Lloyd George or Churchill gave it much attention, for by August 1922 they were more deeply involved than ever in the problems of the near and middle east. Within a matter of weeks, it was a crisis produced from these same problems that revealed how much both of them had come to take the dominions for granted.

The Chanak crisis

British difficulties in the near east centred upon the inability of the allies to make peace with Turkey after the war. In the first instance serious misunderstandings between Britain and France delayed the negotiation of a peace treaty until April 1920. Thereafter, though the treaty was signed in August 1920, and the old Turkish empire was broken up into its various parts, a Turkish nationalist uprising under Mustapha Kemal

[41] *Ibid*: (copy) Hankey–Vansittart (FO), 29 July 1922. The dominion governments were informed of the note on 1 Aug 1922.
[42] Grigg papers: Rowell–Grigg, 9 Aug 1922.

made its implementation practically impossible. A mandates system under the League of Nations (itself a cause of further friction between Britain and France) was slowly imposed on the successor states. As for the truncated Turkish homeland in Asia Minor, the allies agreed in 1920 that the Greek army could usefully be employed to bring the nationalists to heel. Over the following eighteen months, however, the Greeks proved unable to fulfil their commission, and allied unity, precarious at the best of times, weakened almost beyond recovery as France and Italy sought their own terms of peace with the Turkish insurgents. Friction within the British cabinet was equally severe, with Lloyd George persisting against all advice in supporting the efforts of the Greeks.[43] In the summer of 1922 the Greek campaign came to a disastrous end. At a moment when their forces were dangerously divided between the two sides of the Dardanelles straits, Kemal attacked in strength against the southern contingent, driving it to the coast at Smyrna and from there literally into the sea. In triumph he then swung north, and very quickly the allied forces garrisoned at the straits – of whom neither the French nor the Italians were anxious to use arms against Kemal – were threatened by the return of Turkish troops to Constantinople and the European provinces of the former Turkish empire.

On 7 September 1922, as the retreating Greek army poured into Smyrna, the British cabinet decided that the best policy would be to negotiate an armistice while preventing either side from crossing the straits to threaten Constantinople. Eight days later, however, as Curzon euphemistically reported, 'The Greek retreat was now complete', and the question of how to deal with the victorious Turks had to be faced.[44] The foreign secretary spoke up for continued diplomatic efforts, but the mood of the cabinet was far more belligerent than it had been on 7 September. Primarily this change had come about through a reconciliation between Churchill and Lloyd George. Churchill, whose interests in middle eastern policy lay principally with the new British mandates of Iraq and Palestine, had been a persistent critic of Lloyd George's indiscriminate encouragement of the Greeks. As recently as the beginning of September he had had an acrimonious exchange of letters with Lloyd George on this subject.[45] From their different points of view, however, the two ministers had both

---

[43] For a detailed account of the diplomacy of the near and middle east after the war see Northedge, *The Troubled Giant*, 144 ff. The Chanak crisis as a whole, with great attention to military detail, is examined in D. Walder, *The Chanak Affair* (London, 1969).

[44] CAB 23/31: mtg 48 (22), 7 Sept 1922; 49 (22), 15 Sept 1922.

[45] Lloyd George papers: Churchill–Ll. G., 1 Sept, 6 Sept 1922, Ll. G.–Churchill, 5 Sept 1922.

steadily opposed the spread of Turkish power, and the defeat of the Greek armies suddenly removed the differences between them. A meagre British garrison in the straits faced the threat of overwhelming Turkish forces, and Churchill and Lloyd George, in accord for the first time in months, cajoled the cabinet into agreeing that mere diplomacy would not suffice. In vain Curzon appealed against any precipitate action. His colleagues accepted the idea of an allied show of force, for which in addition to France and Italy, Greece, Serbia and Roumania should all be asked to send troops to the straits. Moreover, 'however fatigued it might be', Churchill thought 'the Empire would put up some force to preserve Gallipoli'. There was no time to consider whether any overseas regiments were at all ready for such duty. It would simply be a matter of appealing for whatever the dominions were able to muster.[46]

Churchill composed a telegram to the dominions about midday, while the cabinet meeting was still in progress.[47] Remarkably, despite the urgency of the matter, he did not give this message to the Colonial Office cypher clerk until the early evening, thus delaying its dispatch, after coding, until just before midnight.[48] The colonial secretary, it seems, had decided to give his Dominions Department no opportunity to pass judgement on the appeal to the overseas governments until after it had gone – a most blatant act of disregard. The department of course, had no inkling of cabinet policy, though they could hardly have been expected to give their blessing where the appeal to the dominions was concerned. In anticipation of any objections, Churchill simply held his hand until the officials had left the office for the weekend.

The telegram to the dominions conveyed precisely the mood of enthusiastic determination in which it had been drafted. Ignoring the fact that the overseas governments would know nothing of the situation in the near east – Foreign Office dispatches, though sent regularly, were a month out of date even in reaching Ottawa; there had last been a cabled appreciation of Turkish problems in November 1921 – Churchill began:

Decision taken by Cabinet today to resist aggression upon Europe by the Turks and to make exertions to prevent Mustapha Kemal driving the Allies out of

[46] An intimation of what must have been a bitter and somewhat incoherent cabinet meeting is afforded by Thomas Jones: 'Hankey described what had happened on 15 September when the Turkish policy was settled by the Cabinet. He and I sat here drafting conclusions which were of a most comprehensive character but some of which certainly had to be given a greater precision than was warranted by any explicit conclusion enunciated in the cabinet.' *Whitehall Diary, 1: 1916–1925* (London, 1969), 218–19.

[47] See Frances Lloyd George, *The Years that are Past* (London, 1967), 206.

[48] CO 532/213: note of cypher clerk, 15 Sept 1922.

Constantinople and in particular and above all to secure firmly the Gallipoli Peninsula, in order to maintain the freedom of the Straits.

Hopes for allied diplomacy were noted, but the major hope was that military co-operation would contain the Turks until a peace conference could be arranged. To that end the telegram concluded:

I should be glad to know whether the Government of the Dominion wish to associate themselves with our action and whether they desire to be represented by a contingent ... The *announcement* of an offer from all or any of the Dominions to send contingents even of moderate size would undoubtedly exercise in itself a most favourable influence on the situation and might conceivably be a potent factor in preventing major hostilities.[49]

It is the last sentence which places this appeal for troops well beyond the established forms of inter-imperial diplomacy. For it makes clear that the dominions were invited not only to send military assistance, but also to announce that they were doing so, and there can be little doubt that Churchill hoped that if the response was not immediate and complete, an announcement from one dominion would have a coercive effect upon the others. This point is worth making because an earlier appeal for military assistance in September 1920 (to put down a rising in Mesopotamia) had accorded the dominions the deference due to their post-war status. The inquiry had been made in strict confidence, and when Australia and Canada declined to help it had not been pursued further, and quite properly had placed no strain on the fabric of imperial diplomatic unity.[50] In the present case, however, mention of an 'announcement' of support was a clear indication that, whatever the consequence, the appeal would not be allowed to escape public attention in the dominions. And to remove any doubt that it was indeed to the court of public opinion to which they were appealing, Lloyd George and Churchill released a statement on Saturday afternoon which called for allied solidarity against Kemal and mentioned that the dominions had been asked for assistance.[51]

The crisis in imperial relations – specifically for present purposes in the relations between Britain and Canada – arose when reports of this press statement reached Mackenzie King before the decoded Churchill telegram. It is important to understand, however, that this statement itself was quite tangential to the imperial crisis. The seeds of that crisis lay in the telegram, which had already implied that publicity would be given to the dominions' support. Indeed, by the time of the British press release

[49] CO 532/213: Col Sec–Govs Gen, 15 Sept 1922. My italics.
[50] CAB 24/145; CO 532/158: correspondence.
[51] *Evening Standard*, Saturday 16 Sept 1922.

on Saturday it was already known in Whitehall that New Zealand was preparing to send a contingent.[52] (This news, carried in the English Sunday papers, was soon known in the other dominions.) This much said, it was hardly beneficial to the colonial secretary's appeal for Canadian assistance that it first reached King (who was in his own constituency, some two hundred and fifty miles west of Ottawa) through a group of newspaper reporters early on the Saturday evening.

King attended to Churchill's telegram the following morning. Lacking any official knowledge of the cause or gravity of the crisis (an inquiry was sent off to the Canadian League of Nations delegation in Geneva, where the Third Assembly was in session) he refused to take any immediate action on the British appeal. He needed time, in any case, to evaluate public and political opinion. Although there was nothing to suggest that the dominion's post-war isolationist mood was changing, a call to support the mother country was bound to evoke widely differing responses, not least within the Liberal party itself, where memories of the divisive conscription issue of 1917 were not far below the surface. And given that King's parliamentary position depended upon not only a united Liberal party but also the Progressives, whose reactions would need careful investigation, it was clear that a hasty decision on this question of military assistance could have very severe consequences. By Sunday evening, the prime minister was resolved that no assistance should be given to Britain without the sanction of parliament.

Ostensibly, King was deferring to the Canadian legislature in this crucial matter of external policy. In reality, of course, he was doing no such thing. Parliament not being in session, the prime minister, who was wholly opposed to Canada's involvement in the Chanak crisis, found himself in the fortunate position of being able to gain his ends simply by putting off any positive decisions. Under such circumstances he was in no hurry at all to convene parliament, and the following day the cabinet were easily persuaded of the wisdom of King's tactics. Unless it became necessary for them to propose a policy of assistance to Britain, they agreed that a special parliamentary session would be unnecessary.[53]

52 It happened that W. F. Massey and six of his ministers were at Government House in Wellington when the decoded cable was handed to the governor general. It took three minutes for an impromptu cabinet meeting to draft a reply and see it on its way. A. Ross, 'The Chanak Crisis', *New Zealand Heritage*, no 77.

53 Dawson, *King*, I, 410. From Geneva Canada's senior delegate, minister of finance W. S. Fielding, could give no information but he urged King to make a verbal gesture of support (King papers, J1/73: Fielding–King, 18 Sept 1922). Fielding was an imperialist of the old school, who believed that unity of

If any further justification for delay were needed, it was fully provided by a second telegram from Churchill, received on the evening of 18 September. The relevant passage speaks for itself:

It was in view of the special association which they have with Gallipoli that we have communicated with Australia and New Zealand, and we felt bound to make the message common to all the dominions . . . There is no probability of a serious war, but . . . anything that your Government can contribute towards the sense of Empire solidarity would be of the utmost value. At this juncture a statement to the effect that the Dominion of Canada associates itself with the general position of the Allied Powers . . . and would be represented by a contingent if the need arose, would be quite sufficient.[54]

It was a frank admission that Canadian support had been publicly solicited not for strategic purposes but rather because the British government had to profess the importance of imperial unity. British priorities, however, were radically different from Canadian ones. The more that Churchill tried to make light of the military situation, in an effort to induce King at least to make a public statement of support, the more convinced was King that a serious political crisis might have been brought upon him by nothing more than a spurious and out-dated imperial sentiment, which he would do nothing to endorse. His attitude stiffened, supported by an uncompromising logic. He recognized as yet no necessity to summon parliament, and without that body would do nothing to give definition to the government's position. His reasoning precluded the mildest statement of support, and on Wednesday, 20 September, in dismissing a further plea from Churchill, he said bluntly, 'We have not thought it necessary to reassert the loyalty of Canada to the British Empire.' The British government made no further requests.[55]

For critics in Canada of King's indecisiveness, there was a somewhat different line of argument. An opposition member of the Canadian Senate had suggested, in terms very similar to Churchill's, that the only requirement was a public statement of sympathy, with no commitment to send troops. To this King replied: 'Britain would hardly thank us for an assurance of that character, and in my opinion the Government that would be prepared to thus lightly consider the most serious and far-reaching of national obligations would be wholly unworthy of the trust

foreign policy was the keystone of the empire. Knowing this, Churchill himself had contacted Fielding through the British delegation at Geneva, in the hope that he could be induced to advise King along these very lines. (See CO 532/213: Arthur Balfour (Geneva)–Churchill, 20 Sept 1922.)

54 CO 532/210: Col Sec–Gov Gen, 18 Sept 1922.
55 CO 532/210: Gov Gen–Col Sec, 20 Sept 1922.

that might be imposed in it.'[56] But the truth, of course, lay elsewhere. Amongst both the Liberal cabinet and the leaders of the Progressive party (with whom King held discussions on Friday 22 September) there was ready agreement that *any* public statement amounted to a commitment – and that such a commitment must have parliamentary approval. The Progressives were no more convinced than King that matters warranted a special session.

King's political control was fully confirmed, and in private correspondence he commented on the events of the past week in tones of confident indignation. 'Surely', he wrote to a friend in England,

all that has been said about equality of status and sovereign nations within the Empire is of no account if, at any particular moment the self-governing Dominions are to be expected, without consideration of any kind, to assume the gravest responsibility which a nation can assume, solely and wholly upon an inspired despatch from Downing Street. . . . If the British Empire is to endure, it must be upon the fullest appreciation of all that self-government by its several Dominions implies, and this means not less the rights of the peoples than of the Governments concerned to have their voices heard and wishes determined.[57]

It is idle to speculate at what point King might have allowed the people of the dominion 'to have their voices heard and their wishes determined'. When King wrote those lines, the crisis in the Dardanelles had yet to reach its climax, but from the information which now poured in from London – as Downing Street sought absolution for its own sins of omission – he learned nothing which changed his mind. Expressions of pro-British sympathy across the country, though admittedly difficult to measure, were similarly of no avail. The prime minister watched unmoved as the French withdrew their forces from Chanak, leaving the British contingent to face the Turks alone, and probably never realized how close the situation came to war. On 3 October, as the British and Turkish forces faced each other across the barricades at Chanak, King wrote to a Liberal friend that

As a *consequence* of the Near Eastern crisis . . . I believe we have found the basis on which the Progressives of Western Canada may be brought into real accord with Liberals of . . . Quebec and other parts of the Dominion.[58]

It was not until 11 October that a Turkish armistice was signed.

[56] King papers, J1/80: King–G. D. Robertson, 30 Sept 1922.
[57] King papers, J1/82: King–Campbell Stuart (managing director of *The Times*), 22 Sept 1922.
[58] King papers, J1/70: King–J. Boyle, 3 Oct 1922. My italics.

The making of peace with Turkey: I

In its final phase the Chanak crisis was a crisis in British politics. On the weekend of 16 September Lloyd George decided to call an election, only to find in the weeks that followed that the rank and file of the Conservative party had no wish to keep their colours pinned to the prime minister's mast. On 19 October, in defiance of nearly all the party's cabinet ministers, a meeting of Conservative parliamentary members resolved to fight the election as an independent party. The coalition put together in December 1916 was at an end, and Lloyd George resigned that afternoon.

For the Colonial Office, the fall of Lloyd George's government came at a particularly crucial moment. In September they had been powerless to prevent or modify Churchill's appeal to the dominions for military assistance, but negotiation of an armistice enabled them to catch up with events, and on 11 October the permanent under-secretary attempted to remind the prime minister's office about dominion susceptibilities:

No doubt you have the point already in your mind, but in the arrangements that are being, or will have to be, made for the Near East Peace Conference the question of Dominion (and incidentally Indian) representation must be settled ... and it is obvious that before any decision is taken here the Dominion Governments must be consulted with as much notice as possible, otherwise the fat will be in the fire as it was three weeks ago.[59]

By this time, however, the British cabinet were wholly preoccupied with their political survival, and the days passed with no decisions taken about dominion participation at the conference. In the steady stream of 'information' telegrams prepared for the dominions in the Foreign Office, an anxious Colonial Office saw the planning of a peace conference, to be held at Lausanne, slowly taking shape. Churchill retired into hospital with appendicitis, the government falling while he was in convalescence, and it was not until 24 October that the Duke of Devonshire was named as his successor.[60] When at last he could give his consideration to the Lausanne Conference, its form had already been settled by the Foreign Office. There were to be two British representatives – and none from the dominions.

The Colonial Office were given to understand that the French

---

[59] CO 532/214: Masterson-Smith–Grigg, 11 Oct 1922.
[60] Devonshire (who had been Canadian governor general from 1916 to 1921) was to have gone to the Admiralty, and Leopold Amery to the Colonial Office. They were switched at the last moment in accordance with a convention that the Admiralty and the War Office (Lord Derby) should not both have their ministers in the House of Lords. Milner papers: Amery–Milner, 30 Oct 1922.

government had placed insuperable difficulties in the way of dominion representation.[61] There can be little doubt, however, that the Foreign Office had never seriously pressed for such representation. Sir Eyre Crowe, as noted earlier, had found 'deplorable' the participation of the dominions in the 1919 Paris peace conference, and their presence at Lausanne, he confided to the foreign secretary, 'would serve no purpose, and could only produce friction with the Allies, as well as retard the negotiations'. Curzon (who had kept his portfolio in the new government) was in complete agreement with these views. As prospective head of the British delegation to Lausanne, he was, moreover, quite certain that he would 'have no time for daily or frequent conferences with a British Empire Delegation'.[62] Thus the overseas governments were excluded from Lausanne, and the hopes for conferring with them about the empire's representation to the conference were ignored. The Colonial Office, far from being able to make amends for Churchill's impulsive request for military assistance at Chanak, were forced to add insult to injury by informing the dominions that they would be unable to attend at Lausanne.

Overseas reactions to the news about Lausanne strongly underlined the conspicuous differences in attitude to imperial foreign affairs that could now be found amongst the dominion governments. New Zealand accepted the dictated arrangements without complaint, content to trust Whitehall's stewardship of her imperial responsibilities. Australia on the other hand was deeply annoyed. Having already complained bitterly to Churchill about the Chanak crisis itself, Hughes wasted no words in reiterating his feelings:

This habit of asking Australia to agree to things when they are done, and cannot be undone, and when there is only one course open to us in practice – and that is to support Britain – is one which will wreck the Empire if persisted in ... In foreign affairs the Empire must speak with one voice, but whose voice is that to be? Surely not that of a British political party![63]

South Africa and Canada, in turn, with their own perspectives on British–dominion relations, found no such cause for dissatisfaction over Lausanne. Smuts, who had conveniently managed to avoid the Chanak crisis altogether by being in an inaccessible corner of South Africa during the critical fortnight, was not at all displeased with this added opportunity to leave the peace negotiations in British hands. To further dissociate his dominion from this piece of imperial policymaking he requested that

---

[61] CO 532/219: FO–CO, 26 Oct 1922.
[62] See above, 83-4. FO 371/7909: minutes of 6 Nov 1922.
[63] CO 532/211: Gov Gen (Aus)–Col Sec, 2 Nov 1922.

South Africa should not be asked to sign any ensuing treaties. Yet although Smuts felt constrained by the pressure of nationalism in his country to avoid such foreign policy questions wherever possible, he did at least appreciate and sympathize with Britain's own difficulties over Chanak. Privately he had already acknowledged to Churchill that he would be 'prepared so far as Union is concerned to defend action of Imperial government in approaching Dominions when crisis became imminent'.[64]

Like Smuts, Mackenzie King could accept the decision to exclude the dominions from Lausanne without protest – and indeed with great relief, for he had already made up his mind that Canada should not be associated with the peace conference, and had been 'dreading the refusal it might be necessary to send'.[65] But beyond that King was not inclined to take such a charitable view of events, or to be so accommodating. On the contrary, it was now possible simultaneously to avoid any awkward questions about not attending at Lausanne, while at the same time focusing attention on the British decision as entirely consistent with Whitehall's alarming and arbitrary behaviour over the Chanak crisis itself. The two episodes could in this way be turned to the same good account, the Lausanne Conference arrangements affording King an unexpected opportunity to demonstrate again to his own party, and to the Progressives, the dangerous implications for Canada's autonomy that the Chanak appeal had exposed. Given the degree to which the two parties had been drawn together over the crisis, a confident and politically reassured King was soon passing off the Chanak affair as positively providential:

> I thought at the time and I feel more convinced now than ever, that it was anything but a misfortune that the 'Call to Arms' was sent out at the time it was and in the manner it was. Had one ventured to present as a hypothetical case what has actually transpired, he would have been laughed out of court. We are now in a position to make our appeal to actual happenings as illustrative of the kind of possibilities of which too careful account cannot be taken in determining relations with the Empire.[66]

So it was in the closing weeks of 1922 that King began to feel he had both the political support and the moral justification for working out his own conception of Canada's imperial relations. His main proposition was that the dominion should have exactly the same independence in the conduct of her external policy as she had in her domestic policy – a thesis

---

[64] CO 532/210: Gov Gen (SA)–Col Sec, 13 Oct 1922.

[65] King diary, 28 Oct 1922.

[66] King papers, J1/74: King–W. Griffiths (secretary, Canadian High Commission, London), 13 Dec 1922.

which Borden and Meighen would have found unexceptionable. King, however, added a vital corollary: that Canadian external affairs were neither contained within nor derived from a united imperial foreign policy. The latter was no more than the coincidental common ground shared by the British and Canadian governments. Appearances were deceptive. Until the Chanak crisis (though King may not have appreciated that Meighen had been ready to dissociate the dominion from a renewed Anglo-Japanese alliance) Canadian foreign policy had indeed been co-incident with that of Great Britain, and even in these last few months Canada had not actively opposed Britain's policy. Yet this could not be taken to indicate that the two foreign policies were causally related. It was not that King wished or expected they would ever be markedly divergent from each other. He insisted only that they were distinct and that for its external affairs each government should bear its own res-ponsibilities – to which it could be added that as a secure North American community Canada was not expected to have a very extensive range of such responsibilities.

In an exchange of cables with Whitehall about the Lausanne Conference King went some way towards an exposition of these views, claiming for Canada – specifically, for the Canadian parliament – the right to decide how much of any new Turkish peace treaty the dominion would accept.[67] He had no objection to not being represented at the conference, he said, but the British government must understand that in her absence Canada could not be committed to new responsibilities. The accepted procedure for assuming such responsibilities, after all, had been established by the Paris and Washington conferences, whose format Lausanne was not going to follow. Through this correspondence King might suppose that he was lucidly setting forth the new terms of Canada's association with imperial foreign affairs, and could note in his diary at one point, for instance, 'This will prove an historic despatch. It is making history, breaking new ground in inter-imperial and international relations.'[68] Even so, he never once enlarged upon his reservations by making any direct criticisms of the empire's diplomatic unity, and after twice seeking clarification of his views the Colonial Office remained somewhat confused as to where exactly Canada now stood. They were grateful when the governor general, Lord Byng, who on his own initiative had tried to ascertain from the prime minister what was in his mind, volunteered his own interpretation of Canadian thinking. King, he intimated wanted only to avoid signing a new Turkish peace treaty; he would not object, when the time came,

[67] See *DCER*, III, 85 ff.
[68] King diary, 29 Oct 1922.

to submitting the treaty to parliament for ratification. There for the moment the matter rested.[69]

To many people, King's responses to Chanak and to the Lausanne Conference seemed to indicate that he had reverted to the position adopted at the turn of the century by Sir Wilfrid Laurier. Canada's military aid (and her willingness to accept treaty obligations) was being withheld, he implied, because she had not been called to the empire's councils. This conclusion was certainly drawn in Whitehall, where a major cause of the difficulty was thought to have been the dominions' lack of information prior to the crisis, and to prevent further such incidents an expanded service of foreign affairs telegrams for the overseas governments was promptly inaugurated by the Foreign Office news department.[70] Corresponding improvements in the machinery for prior inter-imperial consultation were less easy to provide, as ever. It was hopefully a step in the right direction when the incoming British government of Bonar Law dismissed Lloyd George's 'Garden Suburb', for this at least meant that foreign policy matters were to be confined within the established departmental structure in Whitehall. In Canada, where he had seen King's reactions to the near eastern crisis at close quarters, a former member of Lloyd George's entourage was all for encouraging the overseas governments to take further steps of their own to improve their handling of external affairs:

The essential thing is that the Dominions should equip themselves with the best possible information about foreign affairs, either by having ambassadors or High Commissioners of their own, or by having a better system of consultation & information in London, or both, so that they have an intelligent policy *on its merits* about international questions as they arise ... Mackenzie King's policy, which was Laurier's of pleading ignorance, i.e., the ostrich policy, is the most fatal of all.[71]

The Canadian prime minister, of course, had no intention of availing himself of any such facilities for policymaking, and whatever appearances might suggest he was in no way anxious to be called to imperial councils. In his first cable to Whitehall about the Lausanne arrangements, indeed, King had expressly stated that the receipt of information about the forthcoming peace conference would in no way commit Canada to any of its conclusions. And if he thus felt obliged to be so careful about mere information, he was even more on the alert against implicit or uncalled-for

[69] CO 532/211: Gov Gen–Col Sec, 31 Dec 1922.

[70] CO 532/287: memorandum (Jan 1925) of A. Willert, FO News Department.

[71] Philip Kerr–V. Massey, 17 Nov 1922, quoted in Eayrs, *In Defence of Canada*, I, 21.

consultation, from which imperial commitments might be inferred. He was surprised, therefore, to learn from the press in November that the British government, seemingly in connection with the peace settlement, had called in dominion representatives to discuss trade policy with Turkey. At once the Canadian high commissioner was asked for details, and warned by King:

The situation at the moment is a crucial one involving whole question of relations between Dominions and Great Britain in determination of matters of foreign policy ... Under circumstances would suggest that any request made to you as High Commissioner on part of British government which may be construed as amounting to consultation or representation of Canada in matters of foreign policy be immediately referred to our Government for consideration before action taken.[72]

Larkin understood well his chief's point of view. He reassured him that nothing of importance had been transacted, adding, 'Am always very careful [to] refrain from committing Canadian government either directly or by implication to foreign policy.'[73]

King's attitude to imperial relations in these months after Chanak thus held out very little promise for any return to the idea of joint imperial policymaking. The near eastern crisis, succeeded so rapidly by the unilateral British settlement of the Lausanne proceedings, had severely exposed the deficiencies of that idea and of the bureaucratic machinery that was supposed to make prior consultation a reality – even an intermittent reality. In consequence it had greatly encouraged King to repudiate the very notion of an integrated imperial diplomacy. It is possible, in the final analysis, to discern in the prime minister's reaction a definite recapitulation of Laurier's policies – not, certainly, with reference to the dictum about 'call us to your councils', but to Laurier's later stipulation to the 1911 Imperial Conference that Canada wished to be consulted only on questions of direct interest to her. With this declaration of Canada's limited imperial liabilities King was completely in accord. It became his task, after Chanak, to work out its implications in the light of the dominion's post-war imperial relations.

[72] King papers, J1/76: King–Philip Larkin, 24 Nov 1922. Larkin replaced Sir George Perley shortly after the fall of the Meighen government. He was a wealthy tea merchant, an unimpeachable Liberal, and a substantial patron of Mackenzie King.

[73] *Ibid*: Larkin–King, 27 Nov 1922.

6
Canadian diplomacy and Imperial diplomacy: 1923

For Mackenzie King to establish a satisfactory degree of Canadian independence in foreign affairs there were two separate lines of action to be pursued. First and foremost it was necessary to disengage the dominion from any commitments to a united imperial foreign policy, and to secure its freedom of response to the international effects of that policy. But then in addition there should also be the possibility, as circumstances required, to undertake external commitments solely on Canada's own behalf. Before the dominion could lay claim to a functional autonomy in the empire–commonwealth, as a practical complement to its status, its authority in both these respects had to be demonstrated. The Chanak crisis, and the ignoring of overseas representation at the Lausanne Conference, had already precipitated a considered Canadian withdrawal from imperial responsibilities and imperial policymaking. In turn the opportunity to manifest the more individual side of Canadian diplomatic independence came in early 1923 with the completion of a halibut fishing treaty with the United States. Despite the opposition of the Foreign Office the treaty was signed by a Canadian minister and did not carry a British countersignature, the first international agreement (albeit of a purely commercial nature) to be concluded in this manner. Yet although it has been remembered ever since for its unaccompanied Canadian signature, the Halibut treaty had repercussions in 1923 that went well beyond the question of diplomatic form, and contributed directly to a fundamental reappraisal of British policy towards the dominions.

The Foreign Office had been coerced into accepting Canada's wishes over the treaty because they were warned that a refusal would risk the greater disruption of an independent Canadian diplomatic appointment to the American capital. And however little they might normally take the dominions into consideration, they could still understand that, in this case, it was worth making concessions to keep Canada within the imperial ring as far as possible. Their indulgence, even so, did not stretch far – and after a further six months of trouble with the Halibut treaty,

173

over first an unauthorized Canadian release of secret correspondence and then an awkward American attempt to amend the treaty's terms, the Foreign Office had come to doubt whether it was at all worth their while trying to hold the imperial diplomatic ring together. If Canada – and, after her, other dominions – were now going to be taking diplomatic initiatives of this sort, then rather than accept an overriding responsibility for a cluster of policies they could not control the Office preferred to see the overseas governments go their own way in these matters, on their own responsibility. In preparation for the 1923 Imperial Conference they therefore insisted that Britain give the dominions the right to negotiate and sign external treaties on their own behalf, and they held fast to this radical new line against all the objections of the Colonial Office. The devolutionary tone of the conference was therefore set in Whitehall in advance. Only by letting the dominions have this new freedom of action could the Foreign Office be sure of retaining their own.

By his own reckoning, and that of his chosen adviser on imperial affairs, O. D. Skelton, King anticipated a thoroughly unpleasant Imperial Conference. He assumed that the British government would attempt to repair the breach caused by the Chanak crisis, and through the medium of the conference recall her imperial partners to their shared responsibilities for the empire's foreign affairs. The Imperial Conference, in fact, King understood as little short of an imperial executive, with which Borden and Meighen the more so had associated Canada, and whose decisions his own government might therefore be expected to accept. How else explain the peremptory call to arms that had come at the time of Chanak? His primary duty – in a way not unlike Laurier's at the Colonial Conferences before the war – thus became to identify and to withdraw from any commitments to joint imperial policies, as regards diplomacy, naval and air defence or other more mundane affairs. At a conference which did not have any urgent and dominating question of policy to consider, unlike the 1921 meeting, this was not a particularly difficult line to follow.

Thus in the event the true protagonists at the 1923 Conference were not Britain and Canada, as King was expecting, but rather Britain and Australia. Prime minister Bruce's undisguised efforts to adapt the machinery of imperial consultation in order to bring the dominions into fuller contact with the policymaking process in Whitehall placed him squarely against the devolutionary drift of Foreign Office policy. Not that there were not sharp disagreements in the end between Lord Curzon and the Canadians – these, however, were essentially misunderstandings rather than opposing points of view. And on a different level the same play of forces was true for economic affairs, which were considered in some detail by a separate Economic Conference. Canada simply insisted on standing aside, and would not be associated with imperial ventures controlled through London, while Australia led the others in appealing unsuccessfully to Britain for more co-operative policies. On balance King could leave the two conferences with a real, if negative, sense of achievement; the deeper frustration and disappointment were felt by Bruce.

The Halibut treaty

The conservation of the ocean fisheries off the Pacific northwest coast of North America had first been discussed between the Canadian and American governments in 1917, and had led two years later to the negotiation of two separate treaties designed to regulate the catching of both salmon and halibut in these waters. Even at this stage, it seems, the realization that the treaties would in practical terms not involve the rest of the empire had given rise to Canadian ambitions to break new ground at the formal concluding of the treaties: when the Salmon treaty came to be signed (in Washington) the dominion negotiator Sir Douglas Hazen had tried, without success, to keep the British ambassador from adding his customary endorsement to the document, though it is not clear that Hazen was acting directly on instructions from the Borden government.[1] His initiative in any event was quickly forgotten, as the Salmon treaty proved to be unenforceable in the United States (it had failed to distinguish adequately between state and federal responsibilities) and the Halibut treaty was also left uncompleted. But in 1922, after a change of administration in both countries, negotiations about offshore fishing were resumed, and by early 1923 a new treaty, dealing with halibut alone but with better prospects of enforcement, was ready for signing in the American capital.

Once again the exclusively North American character of the fishing agreement was not lost on the Canadian authorities, and as the negotiations reached their conclusion King made up his mind that there should be no British counter-signature to mar this piece of Canadian treaty-making.[2] King, it is fair to say, was far more committed to the gesture of an unsupported treaty signature than the Borden administration had been, and he was also in the position of having seen two opportunities for action along these lines recently slip by. In Paris in December 1922 a commercial agreement with France had been concluded, and then in London at the beginning of January a similar convention with Italy, each of them clearly bilateral in their purpose and scope but each of them completed in

[1] CO 42/1014: FO–CO, 7 Oct 1919 and minutes.
[2] King diary, 11 Jan 1923.

accordance with standard empire practice by a British counter-signature. In both cases the Canadian negotiator was King's doughty old minister of finance W. S. Fielding, old-fashioned enough in his views about empire that he would never have agreed to be the agent of any radical departures from established procedure. But the Halibut treaty was the responsibility of Ernest Lapointe, minister of marine and a man quite prepared to carry out his prime minister's designs in this matter of treaty signatures. Indeed so well was the political ground prepared that, by the time Fielding had returned from Europe to Ottawa to discover King's intentions, he found he was alone in the cabinet in wanting to retain the double imperial signature for the new treaty. Even governor general Byng had come round to agreeing with King that Lapointe should be permitted to complete the Halibut treaty by himself.[3]

King's formal request to the British government for a single Canadian signature on the treaty touched off a flurry of departmental activity, and telegrams were soon flying between Whitehall, Ottawa and the British embassy in Washington. Generally speaking the Colonial Office did not see any reason to contend the point, taking the view that in attending to this specific local issue Canada would not be acting in breach of the empire's diplomatic unity. But the Foreign Office were not at all happy with the Canadian proposal, seeing in it a very different implication. The permanent officials of the American Department were quick to warn the foreign secretary:

The Canadian objections to His Majesty's Ambassador signing together with the Dominion Minister arises from the fact that they regard [him] as representing the United Kingdom and *not* Canada. This is precisely the conception of the status of His Majesty's Representatives abroad which we cannot afford to accept.[4]

The British ambassador himself, needless to say, fully endorsed this argument. Yet in spite of this strong official resistance from Whitehall and the Washington embassy King refused to reconsider his position and remained adamant that Canada should sign alone. And in the end, with the date for the signing of the treaty fast approaching, the prime minister decided to play an unexpected winning card. He made it known that if he could not have his own way he might well respond by appointing a fully independent Canadian diplomatic representative to Washington.[5]

This ultimatum is worth a moment's consideration. The question of a

[3] King diary, 17 Feb 1923.
[4] FO 371/8489: M. Peterson, minute of 30 Jan 1923.
[5] King diary, 20 Feb; CO 532/235: Gov Gen–Col Sec, 20 Feb 1923.

Canadian appointment to the American capital had lain dormant since
the agreement of May 1920, the enthusiasm to find a suitable man for
the job having dissipated once Borden retired that summer. For their
part the King administration were not prepared in any case to fulfil the
terms of the 1920 agreement, because they could not accept the arrangement whereby a Canadian minister at Washington would automatically
take charge of the British embassy in the ambassador's absence. There
matters stood, with no move as yet to reopen negotiations with the
British government, and the small semi-diplomatic Canadian mission in
the American capital left more or less to its own devices. As a consequence
of the Chanak crisis, however, an increasing number of public demands
were heard in Canada for some form of independent representation at
Washington, demands which thoroughly alarmed the British ambassador
and the Foreign Office, and which were found to have considerable
support in the Canadian cabinet. The prime minister, it transpired, was
himself largely concerned to have an independent mission for commercial
purposes. But Fielding was sounded by the Colonial Office while in
London in December 1922, and warned that 'an agitation in the Canadian
Parliament might ... lead some, if not the majority, of his colleagues in
the Dominion Cabinet' to support an autonomous diplomatic appointment.[6] As recently as 19 January 1923 the Canadian governor general
corroborated Fielding's evidence, reporting that 'the Cabinet is composed
of every variety of opinion from the man who wants an Ambassador with
full powers to the man who wants to leave things exactly as they are'.[7]

All the available evidence thus pointed to the same unfavourable conclusion: never mind that the issue might still be one of relatively minor
national importance, in the absence of convincing arguments to the
contrary an indecisive Canadian cabinet might easily authorize an appointment that would be highly embarrassing for the British government. In
these circumstances King's warning sounded dangerously plausible, and
the Foreign Office decided they had no choice but to accept the lesser of
the two evils. At the last possible moment the British ambassador was
told not to sign the Halibut treaty, in order that this might 'assist in
overcoming the grave difficulties' of Canadian representation at Washington – difficulties, he was reminded, that 'you agree with us in desiring to
escape'.[8] Ernest Lapointe signed alone for Canada on 2 March 1923.

In Whitehall feelings about the separate Canadian signature continued
to be mixed. The Colonial Office, with legal and constitutional

---

[6] CO 42/1043: J. Masterton–Smith, minute of 20 Dec 1922.
[7] CO 42/1043: Gov Gen–Col Sec, 19 Jan 1923.
[8] FO 371/8490: FO–British Ambassador, 1 March 1923.

considerations uppermost in their mind, persisted in thinking that no immediate harm had been done. From their point of view the most important aspect of the affair was the fact that Lapointe had operated with a 'full power' that had not been geographically restricted in its scope, with the result that in strictly legal terms the Canadian minister had not signed 'on behalf of' Canada but for the empire as a whole.[9] But the Foreign Office, still smarting from their capitulation to the Canadian prime minister's threats, took little comfort from this narrow legal interpretation. On the contrary, the unaccompanied treaty signature had given rise to wider questioning, the head of the American Department, for example, wondering whether in the circumstances Britain should be prepared to accept any responsibility at all for such independently concluded agreements:

Rather ... it would seem preferable at once to offer any Dominion, which may so desire, full liberty to conduct its own foreign affairs, H[is] M[ajesty's] G[overnment] disclaiming all further responsibility. When the Dominion realizes that it is being offered the choice of becoming an independent second or third class Power with the privilege of paying for its own independence, or of remaining part of a first class Power, it will probably become more tractable.[10]

And if it didn't? At the time the implied threat could be excused as an angry outburst and the precedent created by the Halibut treaty might well have been allowed to find its place in the canon of British constitutional development without further immediate consideration. However, barely two weeks after the treaty had been signed an incident occurred which contrived to keep the treaty sharply in focus, and which also alienated a good deal of the tacit support King had enjoyed in both Whitehall and Government House. In Ottawa the new 1923 session of parliament had not opened well for the prime minister – in particular he had made a very poor show of explaining his government's refusal to be involved in the Chanak crisis – and being more than usually anxious to make political capital out of his diplomatic success with the Halibut treaty, he therefore sought permission from Whitehall to publish the correspondence (much of it classified 'secret'[11]) which had led up to the signature of the treaty. Surprisingly, without waiting for a reply from London, he then proceeded to present the relevant telegrams to the House of Commons – and brazenly met the legitimate inquiries of the

9 CO 532/246: CO–FO, 21 Feb 1923.
10 FO 371/8490: R. Sperling, minute of 6 March 1923.
11 British government dispatches and telegrams were of three categories: non-confidential, confidential and secret. The last two categories required the permission of the sender before publication.

governor general with the explanation that he felt obliged to counter charges from Meighen about conducting 'secret diplomacy'. Privately King could easily satisfy himself about this flouting of diplomatic convention

I am determined to smash this secret diplomacy between diff[eren]t parts of Empire, if it is not smashed Empire will be smashed. Who wants it except the Bureaucracy?[12]

– a somewhat altered position, we might note, from his earlier disparaging criticism of the *open* diplomacy that had attended the Chanak crisis! But whatever air of injured innocence he chose to wear it was clearly unacceptable to all others concerned for King to think he might release confidential information at his own discretion, and the governor general continued to press him for a personal apology and an assurance that he would not again act in this way. Even then Byng found himself

still at a loss to give . . . any logical reason for his action and can only say that I believe he entirely lost his head when [Meighen] pressed him again for the papers, – this, coupled with the fact (which I find in conversation with him) that he is extremely ignorant of the amenities that are always observed between Governments, as well as individuals, in connection with secret and confidential correspondence.[13]

For Byng the matter ended there and he thought it best forgotten, advice the Colonial Office were ready to accept. Not so the Foreign Office, who insisted that Canada also apologize to the American government, and who were prepared 'in the last instance to offer an independent expression of regret' if none were forthcoming from Ottawa.[14] Pressure from this quarter obliged the governor general to reopen the subject with King in early June and to draw from him the required apology.

However distasteful these repercussions were to King, they could hardly be reckoned an unreasonable price for his action, especially as his apologies to Byng and to Washington were accepted in strict confidence. Thus it was with surprise that the Colonial Office were told that the Canadian prime minister would be raising the whole question of publication of correspondence at the forthcoming 1923 Imperial Conference. It seemed an unprofitable topic for debate. Neither the Colonial nor the Foreign Office had any intention of relinquishing the discretion by which they classified telegrams and dispatches secret or confidential, and the latter

[12] King diary, 17 March 1923.
[13] CO 532/235: Gov Gen–Col Sec, 22 March 1923.
[14] CO 532/235: Vansittart (Curzon's private secretary)–Marsh (Devonshire's private secretary), 24 April 1923.

department warned that to prevent further unwarranted publication they might well mark 'secret' *all* their communications to Canada, however trivial.

In the event, to look forward for a moment, King raised a quite different issue at the Imperial Conference, one not anticipated by Whitehall inasmuch as it was purely of his own devising. Side-stepping any question of 'secret diplomacy' he chose instead to challenge the custom whereby a governor general was asked formally to give permission for the release of any *non*-confidential correspondence. Although such permission was never refused in practice, King nonetheless tried to demonstrate that this custom was a heavy constraint on dominion self-government, arguing that it implied control by the Crown of a prerogative which properly lay at cabinet level. He insisted the custom be abolished – and as no one else at the conference construed it in his terms, no one could object. But none of the other parties to the original incidents of March 1923 were the least impressed. As Lord Byng noted dryly to the Duke of Devonshire:

> Mr. Mackenzie King, who, presumably, was unwilling at the Conference to draw attention to the circumstances under which he had first raised the whole question, appears to have diverted the discussion to a question of principles of self-government with a view to obscuring the main issue.[15]

The dominions and international treaties: the parting of the ways

Beyond the somewhat inflated difficulties of the publication of correspondence the Halibut treaty continued to have repercussions into the autumn of 1923, and became such a source of irritation to the Foreign Office that they decided the whole question of the empire's treatymaking procedures must be raised at the Imperial Conference. In August the Colonial Office were officially instructed to add this matter to the conference agenda, and made to understand that it was intended specifically 'to avoid the recurrence of incidents such as those which attended the signature of the Halibut Treaty'.[16] The Foreign Office were going to take the initiative back into their own hands.

It was bad enough that the department, from the start a hostile witness to the unaccompanied signature of the treaty, had then been obliged to

15 CO 532/274: Byng–Devonshire, 16 Jan 1924. See Dawson, *King*, 468. King's biographer regards the change brought about by the Canadian premier as an important victory over the reactionary forces at Government House, Ottawa. Yet he neglects to mention King's initial serious breach of protocol in releasing the Halibut treaty correspondence, despite ample reference to the incident in the King papers.

16 CO 532/251: FO–CO, 15 Aug 1923.

wring an apology from the Canadian government for the unauthorized release of the correspondence. Insult began to be added to mere injury, however, when the treaty came to be ratified by the American Senate. In accepting the treaty (immediately prior to their own adjournment) the Senate amended it to apply to 'any other part of Great Britain', and however grotesquely phrased, this corollary placed the Canadian government in an awkward dilemma as it effectively repudiated King's claim that the Halibut treaty was an exclusively North American contract. To accept the amendment would thus be to accept defeat on this paramount issue, while to reject it and lose the treaty would be to leave the halibut fisheries open to year-round exploitation. The Canadian government were not long in deciding, however, that they would sooner sacrifice the fisheries rather than the principle of an exclusively Canadian treaty. In the circumstances, the only way they could see of saving the Halibut treaty was to obtain from the American administration an assurance that when the Senate reconvened they would be presented once more with the treaty in its original form, and encouraged to rescind their amendment. But as the Canadian authorities quickly discovered on inquiry to the British embassy in Washington, a diplomatic overture of this kind conducted through the embassy could only be carried out with the express consent of the Foreign Office.

Needless to say there was little enthusiasm in the department for such an approach to Washington. Why, after all, should the British ambassador be asked to use his good offices to rescue the Canadian government from 'the difficulty which it had created for itself' by dispensing with his signature? There was in any event no urgency, 'except from the point of view of saving the face of Canada', since Congress would not meet again until December 1923. Indeed, as the forthcoming Imperial Conference would in any event want to discuss the general subject of treaty-making, the American Department thought 'it might be better to await the conference so that the case may not be prejudiced by any action taken in regard to this particular treaty'.[17]

Understandably the Foreign Office anticipated the not unpleasant prospect of displaying Canada's problems before the Imperial Conference, the just rewards of the dominion's diplomatic precocity. If so, it was a pleasure they had to forgo, for their reluctance to meet the Canadian government's wishes brought immediate and sharp criticism from the Colonial Office, who insisted in an acrimonious exchange of inter-departmental correspondence that such tactics would only encourage King to

[17] FO 371/8491: R. Sperling, minute of 6 July 1923.

make good his earlier threat to establish an independent diplomatic mission at Washington. This line was pressed so strongly on the Foreign Office that in early September the department finally capitulated, and allowed Canadian objections to the treaty amendment to be put officially before the American government.[18] They were hardly grateful, we may assume, to learn that the State Department were only too willing to accept the Canadian case, promising to resubmit the treaty and expressing optimism as to the result.[19] Against their own inclinations the Foreign Office thus allowed the Canadian government to approach the 1923 Imperial Conference reasonably confident that the Halibut treaty would be concluded in the form originally intended.[20]

All told the Foreign Office took little comfort from the successful resolution of Canada's difficulties over the Halibut treaty. Once again the threat of a Canadian independent diplomatic appointment, and its consequences for a united imperial foreign policy, had elicited their protesting compliance with a course of action they deplored. On this occasion, however, the relevance of the argument had reached its logical limits: for the sake of the empire's diplomatic unity the Foreign Office had helped Canada to conclude a treaty which, as they understood it, was explicitly intended to subvert that unity. This realization must have struck the department, for after reluctantly agreeing to pull Canada's diplomatic chestnuts from the fire their attitude towards imperial foreign affairs underwent a very significant change.

Hitherto, while they had regarded the dominions as in principle entitled to a voice in the empire's foreign policy, the Foreign Office had reserved to themselves when possible the right to decide how and when that voice might be heard. This very guarded response to the idea of collective imperial policymaking derived largely from a deeply ingrained desire to carry on the empire's diplomatic business with a maximum of efficiency and flexibility, and in these post-war years it was reinforced by the assumption, undoubtedly correct, that in general the dominions had little interest in foreign affairs. Thus in practice the department were inclined to operate with the least possible reference to the dominions. Beyond the routine

[18] FO 371/8491: FO–British Embassy, 4 Sept 1923.
[19] CO 886/10/88: (copy) British Embassy–FO, 28 Sept 1923. Though the Canadian government had been unable to approach the American administration officially, they had made a strong unofficial plea in June which may have predisposed the State Department to meet the later request. See G. P. Glazebrook, 'Permanent Factors in Canadian External Relations', in R. Flenley (ed), *Essays in Canadian History* (Toronto, 1939), 223.
[20] The US Senate ratified the treaty without reservations on 31 May 1924.

circulation of printed telegrams and dispatches, and the occasional cabled appreciation of a specific problem, they were reluctant in their day-to-day business to anticipate which questions the overseas governments would be concerned to know about in advance, and it therefore remained to the Colonial Office to keep their watching brief over foreign affairs on the dominions' behalf. In this respect the Chanak crisis had not been without benefit, having led directly to an expanded regular flow of diplomatic information out to the dominion capitals from Whitehall. But the Chanak crisis, it must be noted, had also created a new balance of responsibility within Whitehall that in the event was not to the dominions' advantage. When Bonar Law became prime minister in the aftermath of the crisis he had hastily dismantled his predecessor's 'Garden Suburb' of personal advisers, and in similar fashion had radically curtailed the prerogatives of Maurice Hankey's Cabinet Office, in an attempt to return the full control of foreign affairs to the Foreign Office – an understandable change from Lloyd George's idiosyncratic interference in policy matters, and yet one that placed dominion interests more exclusively than ever at Lord Curzon's unsympathetic discretion. The foreign secretary's adamant refusal in November 1922 to suffer any dominion delegates at the Lausanne Conference – and this despite the severely strained feelings created by Chanak – was a pointed reminder of his lack of concern, and all too compatible with his department's belief that the overseas governments were in practice only a hindrance to diplomacy, and should not be encouraged to participate in conferences of this kind. In fact there was a marked reluctance, even now, to concede that the dominions had any substantial international credentials at all. They were members of the League of Nations; they had added their signatures to a few international treaties on their own behalf – to the Foreign Office these were relatively insignificant advances in status, and were certainly not to be understood as giving the dominions unrestrained access to the international world at large, or vice versa.

The compromises to which the Foreign Office were obliged to submit over the Halibut treaty, although calling their general attitude into question, did not initially modify it: as we have seen, the department were quite prepared to let Canada's difficulties with the treaty serve as an exemplary warning to the other dominions against overreaching themselves in their external affairs. Yet by the time they began in September 1923 to prepare for the coming Imperial Conference, and in particular to establish their over-all position on the general question of treatymaking procedures, a profound change of mind was readily apparent. In striking contrast to their previous pronouncements on this subject the department now indicated to the Colonial Office:

The Dominions have been encouraged by the events of the last few years to regard themselves as members of a community of free nations and they are not likely therefore to be content with a system under which important agreements made by them with foreign states should be thrown into a form different from that adopted for similar agreements concluded by the United Kingdom.

They therefore proposed that each dominion should be allowed to negotiate its own bilateral treaties with foreign governments, sign them without a British counter-signature, and be given exclusive full powers for this purpose. 'Both the rights and the liabilities of such treaties', the Foreign Office memorandum added bluntly, 'will be confined to that Dominion and the Government of the Dominion concerned will be responsible for seeing that the treaty is observed.'[21]

The Colonial Office were surprised and somewhat alarmed at the new era of *laissez faire* diplomacy adumbrated in the memorandum, judging its arguments both to be 'a misconception of the true position and to have a "separatist" tendency which needs to be countered'.[22] With treaties negotiated independently by the dominions they had no particular quarrel, but as ever they rejected out of hand the notion that these should also be formally concluded 'on behalf of' an individual dominion. Beginning with the Treaty of Versailles, of course, the dominions had been allowed to sign various international treaties on their own behalf, whatever the misgivings of the Colonial Office. Yet, in each case thus far both the subject under discussion and the combined signatures of British and dominion representatives had made it perfectly clear that the treaty applied to the empire as a whole. Again, any treaties involving a dominion that were narrower in scope – commercial agreements, for instance – had until the Halibut treaty always carried a British as well as a dominion signature to provide them with an imperial character; and in any event, even in the case of the Halibut treaty, the formal full powers issued for signing purposes had never been restricted in scope to the individual dominion in question. Now, however, if the dominions were to be given leave both to negotiate and to sign bilateral treaties on their own behalf, with full powers restricted to themselves alone, it would be absurd to pretend that such treaties were imperial in principle. The empire's diplomatic and legal unity, the fundamental basis of its constitutional definition, would be impossible to maintain.

Thus for the third time in under five years, the seemingly technical question of the style of full powers became the focal point of dissension in another critical debate between the Foreign and Colonial Offices about

---

21 CO 532/251: FO memorandum, n.d. (Aug–Sept 1923).
22 CO 532/251: CO memorandum, E. J. Harding, minute of 7 Sept 1923.

the principles and the evolution of imperial foreign policymaking. And for the third time the Colonial Office had to concede defeat. Their constitutional analysis was unexceptionable: it was indeed a 'true position', and at a time when the ambiguities of a decentralized commonwealth association were already placing strains upon the conduct of British–dominion relations they felt more justified than ever in setting their face against this further major change. But to a Foreign Office bent on shedding diplomatic responsibilities that they considered were beyond their control the department's narrow legal defence of the *status quo* seemed only pedantic, and in the intervening weeks before the Imperial Conference they refused to give any ground at all. As a result the official British position on treatymaking, prepared for the conference in the form of a draft resolution, fully embodied Foreign Office views. Each part of the self-governing empire, the resolution formally proposed, should be allowed to negotiate and sign exclusive treaties with foreign governments on its own behalf, and in each case the full power issued from the British authorities would be restricted quite specifically to the dominion in question.

Imperial foreign policy: the 1923 Imperial Conference

In Ottawa during the summer of 1923 Mackenzie King began his own preparations for the Imperial Conference, his first overseas assignment as prime minister and one whose physical demands alone were already weighing heavily on his mind. 'I am filled with terror', he confessed to his diary, 'at the thought of having to speak many times & my inability to work out themes.'[23] These contingent difficulties of nervousness and unfamiliarity were all the more to be feared since King anticipated that the conference was going to be a thoroughly unpleasant one, at which he would have to stand out alone against any number of co-operative imperial proposals, particularly with reference to the conduct and future course of the empire's foreign affairs. Knowing nothing of the repercussions of the Halibut treaty in Whitehall, and the Foreign Office's mounting determination to let the dominions assume responsibility for their own foreign relations, King could be guided only by the confidential records of the 1921 Imperial Conference and his own experiences since coming into office – all of which led him to believe that Britain and the other dominion governments wished to maintain an undifferentiated imperial foreign policy, that Britain by and large determined that policy, and (recalling here Lloyd George's comprehensive *apologia* of June 1922

[23] Diary, 12 Sept 1923.

on this theme[24]) that it was through the Imperial Conference itself that the overseas governments reconfirmed their support for a collective empire diplomacy. On this analysis the 1923 Conference could be expected to repair the breaches created by the Chanak crisis and the Halibut treaty signature, in order to present once more a united front to the world. And although King's resistance to this style of collaborative partnership had so far been extremely successful, to withstand the challenge of an Imperial Conference on these matters would certainly not be easy.

In the weeks after the completing of the Halibut treaty there had been signs of encouragement for the prime minister. The Canadian Parliament had generally approved the independent treaty signature (the gaffe over the hasty release of correspondence had not been exposed) and privately King had been urged to press home his advantage and move Canada on to a fully isolationist position: 'Let us serve notice on the world', suggested one enthusiastic Liberal supporter, 'that the future of Canada lies on this continent and not in Europe.'[25] But as the Imperial Conference approached, more cautious steps seemed wise. In the first place the Canadian government made a deliberate attempt to meet the British authorities on more neutral ground, as it were, at the conference by asking if they could pay the full expenses of their delegation rather than come as Britain's guests – an unprecedented and awkward request for the Colonial Office, and one they firmly refused to accept.[26] More importantly, King also decided that for assistance with the conference he would go beyond his immediate circle of official advisers and enlist the support of O. D. Skelton, who he quickly persuaded to leave his post at Queen's University in order to accompany the Canadian delegation to London. Thus it came about that Skelton, as nationalist and anti-imperialist as when King had encountered him in early 1922, assumed control of the Canadian preparations for the Imperial Conference, prodigiously mastering the details of the subjects under review and turning out a wide variety of comprehensive memoranda wherever required. His influence on the Canadian approach to the conference was extensive, and nowhere stronger than on the prime minister's understanding of the problems of imperial foreign policy.

Skelton reinforced King's own apprehensions about foreign policy with a long brief on this subject,[27] which declared at the outset that 'The fundamental question before the Imperial Conference of 1923 will be the control of foreign policy' and went on at length to warn the prime

24 See above, 157.
25 Murphy papers: Charles Murphy–King, 12 March 1923.
26 CO 532/236: Gov Gen–Col Sec, 29 June 1923 and minutes.
27 King papers, J4/81: 'Canada and the control of foreign policy' n.d. (Aug–Sept 1923).

minister that he would be strongly pressed to accept, and underwrite on Canada's behalf, a united imperial foreign policy. This pressure would have to be met by King insisting in turn that each element of the self-governing empire must be allowed its own legitimate and distinct sphere of foreign affairs, with the added and all-important stipulation that no one part should seek to influence the policy of another. In such matters, reasoned Skelton, Great Britain as well as the dominions 'is also entitled to claim self-government', and he felt therefore that inter-imperial consultations on questions of foreign policy must be strictly confined to areas where the interests of the various governments genuinely overlapped. All told the memorandum was an effective essay in persuasion. Imperial foreign policy was understood solely in terms of the obligations that it imposed on the dominions, and by Skelton's reckoning these obligations appeared to be virtually unlimited. The overseas governments, in his telling phrase, were in the position of having signed 'blank cheques' at previous Imperial Conferences, cheques that Whitehall could fill in and present for payment whenever Britain's strategic circumstances required.[28] On this analysis each dominion had evidently lost all parliamentary control, even all executive authority, over its obligations to its imperial partners and stood committed without redress to supporting the full range of the empire's foreign affairs. With such an overstated case there was little difficulty in concluding that a united imperial foreign policy offered 'a maximum of responsibility and a minimum of control'.

Skelton's conclusions, it may be noted, stand in direct contrast to the perennial criticisms about post-war foreign policy voiced by the Colonial and Foreign Offices. From their own point of view it was undoubtedly the British government that had suffered, having acknowledged the dominions' claims to a voice in foreign affairs with no firm assurances of their willingness to undertake a tangible share of imperial responsibilities. But beyond this, the Canadian adviser's memorandum was also remarkable for its distorted historical perspective. A united imperial foreign policy, he claimed, was a 'direct reversal of the whole of Dominion development in the past half-century', an interpretation of British–Canadian relations that wilfully ignored every pertinent change since 1911, including the Canadian-sponsored constitutional resolution of 1917. The whole weight of the memorandum was placed upon events since 1921, in an effort to prove that only in this most recent period had a collective imperial foreign policy been in operation. It was thus construed by Skelton as a novel attempt, imposed upon the dominions by Great

---

[28] Skelton's first draft spoke of the Imperial Conferences as 'these international poker games', but this was deleted. Mackenzie King was not a gambling man.

Britain, to reverse the course of imperial relations. In reality, of course, it was King himself who was being encouraged to reverse a consistent pattern of imperial policy developments, endorsed and extended by the Borden and Meighen governments over the preceding ten years.[29]

Yet for all its special pleading, it must be admitted that Skelton's case against a single foreign policy for Britain and the dominions was given a certain plausibility by his interpretation of the Chanak crisis. For in the light of that crisis every facet of a united imperial foreign policy stood condemned. The notion of prior consultation with the dominions; the theory of joint control; the promise of improved channels of communication; the practice, even, of confidential diplomacy – all had proved to be of no account, while the idea of collective *responsibility*, on the other hand, had been shown to carry great weight in British calculations. Skelton, knowing that no consultation had taken place at the time of the crisis, could only infer that the British government had based their appeal for military assistance upon the general endorsement that the empire's foreign policy had received from the 1921 Imperial Conference. Hence his unshakeable conviction that this conference had marked a crucial turning point in British–dominion relations, a point at which through the medium of the conference itself the dominion governments had surrendered all control over their imperial obligations. What he could not know, and perhaps would not have believed in any event, was that in Whitehall as much as in the dominions the Chanak crisis was regarded as an aberration, a flagrant breach of the empire's own diplomatic conventions, and that the appeal for military assistance had owed nothing to the 1921 Conference and everything to the impetuous enthusiasm of Winston Churchill and Lloyd George. And lacking such knowledge Skelton was free to dilate upon the potential dangers of the approaching discussions on the empire's foreign affairs.[30]

[29] C. P. Stacey, 'From Meighen to King: The reversal of Canadian external policies, 1921–23', *Transactions of the Royal Society of Canada*, VII (1969), 239.

[30] Skelton's sinister interpretation of the 1921 Imperial Conference quickly became an accepted element of Canadian nationalist beliefs. J. W. Dafoe, for example (who accompanied the Canadian delegation to the 1923 Conference) wrote of 'the scheme put over in 1921, for a single foreign policy with the Foreign Office doing all the work'. Diary, 15 Oct 1923, quoted in R. Cook, 'J. W. Dafoe at the Imperial Conference, 1923', *CHR*, XLI, no 1 (1960), 27–8. Cf T. A. Crerar, leader of the parliamentary Progressive party: 'The secret deliberations of the 1921 conference are, of course, not public but ... there can be little doubt that a new departure was made in the matter of deciding British foreign policy ... that what Britain should do in various parts of the world was a matter of common discussion.' Rowell papers: Crerar–N. W. Rowell, 8 Feb 1923.

If any further evidence were needed to support these warnings about imperial foreign policy Skelton had only to turn to the related field of naval defence, and to the policy documents on this subject that the Admiralty were circulating in advance of the 1923 Conference. The Admiralty's position was not a happy one in 1923. At a time when none of the dominions was prepared to spend money on naval defence the department were nevertheless obliged to press them to take a greater initiative in these matters, and now under Leopold Amery's guiding hand they were taking great pains to remind the overseas governments that they no longer sought an integrated imperial navy, and that instead each dominion could build up its own forces entirely at its own pace.[31] Privately Amery tried to convince King that a new day had truly arrived:

The conception of a centralized Navy run by the Admiralty, and subscribed to by the Dominions, is now completely extinct. The one idea is to give every encouragement to the younger Navies to become really efficient and adequate to play their part in the common task.[32]

In short, the Admiralty were at last accepting that they could not dictate policy to the overseas governments and would have to take whatever they could get. Yet, however undemanding their memoranda, the keen nationalist eye of Skelton was not long in discovering in the Admiralty's proposals another centralizing plot, in which, whatever the ostensible freedom of the dominions, any defence spending on their part would be carefully allocated to a unified scheme of naval development. In this respect he took particular exception to an Admiralty suggestion that their more general ideas about defence in the empire might be published in conjunction with the Imperial Conference, judging this to be an attempted direct appeal to public opinion in the dominions in defiance of local government policies.[33] All in all it was not difficult to dismiss the Admiralty's plans out of hand, and to view this new naval defence policy with the same foreboding as a united imperial foreign policy.[34] By the

---

[31] CAB 32/11: Imperial Conference memorandum E–57, 'Empire Naval Policy and Cooperation, 1923'. The Admiralty also prepared defence proposals for each of the dominions.

[32] King papers, J1/83: Amery–King, 4 July 1923.

[33] King papers, J4/81–82: Memoranda on naval defence.

[34] To be fair to Skelton, he was not entirely opposed to a Canadian naval force. At the end of his main memorandum on the subject of naval defence he added this 'personal note': 'I am convinced that while striving for international reconciliation we must meanwhile maintain defence forces; I should like to see a decent Canadian Navy, perhaps beginning with shore defences & air development. Dafoe takes the same position: and he adds that

middle of September, at any rate, King had been well and truly prepared to face up to his British protagonists on both fronts, as his diary revealed only too well:

It is quite clear whole purpose of the Conference is a centralizing imperial policy, first re foreign policy to be made in London & next for control of Navy and distribution of cost of upkeep among outlying dominions. I was quite incensed when I read Skelton's memo on Naval policy to see Admiralty proposed to issue a plan to the several dominions. An outrageous interference with the autonomy & self government of the dominions. They will break up the Empire yet. It is no longer Downing St. It is now the Admiralty.[35]

In other quarters of the empire the approaching Imperial Conference gave rise to very different expressions of concern with regard to the conduct of foreign policy and defence. For the Australian prime minister S. M. Bruce the most alarming feature of imperial relations in 1923 was that equality of status, far from bringing Britain and the dominions into a new commonwealth partnership in their external affairs, seemed only to have increased the distances between them, and both before and after his journey to England he dwelt publicly on the serious consequences of this lack of co-ordination:

An Empire such as ours, a chain of independent nations sitting as equals in the councils of the world, is a great thing; it may easily become a dangerous thing unless we have a common foreign policy and a common policy of defence.

Or as he put it another way:

If we cannot agree upon a common policy towards other nations in peacetime and on a common policy of defence, upon what, I ask, can we agree?[36]

From his vantage point in South Africa Smuts had been equally driven to challenge what he regarded as the critical state of the empire's foreign affairs, and on several occasions during 1923 had felt compelled to cable his views at length to both prime minister Bonar Law and his successor Stanley Baldwin. Smuts' apprehensions were those of the statesman rather than the imperialist, however. He was troubled not so much by the lack of inter-imperial consultation and co-operation as by the deep conviction that in 1923 Britain's diplomacy in Europe – as regards reparations, Franco-German relations and the invasion of the Ruhr – was wrong, and

he thinks public opinion in Canada will sanction advance along these lines, *provided* it does not come as the result of imperial urging and pressure.' King papers, J4/81.
35 Diary, 11 Sept 1923.
36 *The Times*, 6 Oct 1923.

disastrously wrong. At such a time it was the duty of the commonwealth dominions, as he understood it, not to fret over the machinery of consultation but to bring the British government round to a more sensible course. For this purpose he awaited the 1923 Conference with urgent anxiety.

And the others? At the Colonial Office a last-minute survey of dominion opinions on foreign affairs was prepared for the Foreign Office, and while they were obliged to take note of Bruce's and Smuts' disquiet they found there was happily far less cause for concern with New Zealand and with the newest member of the commonwealth association, the Irish Free State. In the case of New Zealand, the department noted with obvious satisfaction,

we should not anticipate that Mr. Massey's attitude would substantially differ from that which he took up in 1921. As you know, New Zealand has in recent years shown a constant disposition to fall in with any views expressed, or proposals made, by His Majesty's Government in matters affecting Foreign Relations.[37]

The Irish Free State government were admittedly rather more of an unknown factor, although one major consideration in their case was that the British authorities had only just begun, in the summer of 1923, to provide them with the weekly summaries of foreign affairs cables that were regularly sent to the other dominions. Bearing this in mind, there was little expectation of criticism from this quarter at the Imperial Conference on any specific aspects of the empire's diplomacy. Even so the Colonial Office thought the Irish might well raise 'the question of closer participation in foreign policy', with a view to establishing some system of liaison between the Foreign Office and their own officials in Dublin.[38] As it happened, however, the Colonial Office need not have troubled themselves further about the new dominion. The Irish government had too much on their mind in 1923 to give the Imperial Conference, even its deliberations on foreign policy, their best attention. On this inaugural occasion they turned out to be content to play a watching role, to find their feet amongst their experienced overseas colleagues. For 1923 they let others be the protagonists.

By comparison with this variety of hopes and fears about the empire's foreign affairs, and underlining their own remoteness from dominion feelings on these matters, the Foreign Office themselves could find little in the forthcoming conference discussions that demanded special attention,

[37] CO 532/243: CO–FO, 10 Sept 1923.
[38] *Ibid.*

and went about their final preparations in a routine fashion. With the format of the 1921 Conference as a guide Lord Curzon once again put together a detailed survey of recent foreign office affairs for the edification of the dominion delegations. Meanwhile his permanent under-secretary Sir Eyre Crowe allowed himself a few observations of his own on the current relationship of the overseas governments to the conduct of foreign policy. 'What colonial statesmen have in their minds', he concluded somewhat unremarkably, 'is a development of existing facilities for consultation and common deliberation side by side with the largest measure of autonomous responsibilities.' Yet even this modest concession to the concept of collective policymaking was little more than an empty form of words, for as Crowe himself was forced to admit, in the practical handling of diplomatic issues 'it is ... not possible to delay all action until ... the Dominions have been consulted and have agreed upon a common decision' – while it seemed as always that there were no new ways in which a feasible system of consultation could be provided.[39]

On Crowe's reading of the situation, it appeared highly unlikely that any theoretical balance between the dominions' 'autonomous responsibilities' and a united imperial foreign policy could be maintained, the more so as the Foreign Office were ready now with their resolution on treaty-making procedures to give the dominions far wider control of their external affairs. And if Crowe's analysis did not augur well for closer imperial ties, neither can it be said that Lord Curzon had paid much attention to this side of the problem. When he delivered his formal address on foreign policy a few days later, at the third session of the Imperial Conference, it turned out to be the precise counterpart of his under-secretary's memorandum: that is, while it paid lip service to a united imperial diplomacy it took no account whatever of the practical means to achieve that end. Having thus allowed himself an opening remark about the Imperial Conference furthering a foreign policy 'which is not that of these islands alone, but that of the Empire', the foreign secretary proceeded in great detail merely to summarize British diplomatic activity since the previous conference of 1921.[40]

As leader of the senior dominion, it was Mackenzie King who was the first of the prime ministers to take up the discussion on foreign affairs from the dominion side of the conference table. Although as a public speaker he was able to call on 'only the equipment and none of the

[39] FO 371/9412: memorandum, 1 Oct 1923.
[40] CAB 32/9: Imperial Conference mtg 3, 5 Oct 1923. For all his apprehension King found the speech 'the finest intellectual treat I have ever witnessed'. Dawson, *King*, 469.

graces of oratory', as one London newspaper rather unkindly put it, the Canadian premier nonetheless carried through his appointed task with considerable firmness. Drawing heavily for his arguments on Skelton's memorandum on foreign policy, King frankly expressed his government's determination to pursue 'a foreign policy of our own', which though not 'necessarily distinct from the policy of the British Empire' would allow Canada to settle independently 'any questions which we have with our neighbours, or with others, which are matters of immediate and direct concern'. Thus far Britain had imposed no handicap on the settlement of such questions, King admitted, but this led him directly to a second proposition:

If it is not possible or desirable that Great Britain or other Dominions should control these foreign affairs which are distinctly of primary concern to one Dominion, so it is equally impossible and undesirable for the Dominions to seek to control those foreign affairs which primarily affect Great Britain.

On this reckoning imperial foreign policy would be confined to such 'matters of overwhelming and enduring common interest' as merited consultation, and these would quite definitely be the exception rather than the rule.[41]

To Curzon the Canadian attitude to foreign affairs must have sounded reasonable enough – indeed it was little more than a restatement of the Foreign Office's own position. Predictably enough, however, the tenor of King's remarks found little favour with the Australian premier, Bruce. The division of imperial problems into various national components was an egregiously false idea, he protested, since an enduring common interest continued to unite a very wide range of British and dominion affairs. Furthermore, given that he had come to the Imperial Conference to contribute to the working out of a common foreign policy for the empire, Bruce found as much to criticize in Curzon's speech. The foreign secretary's survey, he felt, had given no indication of the current train of British thinking on any international matter, it had presented the conference with no policy questions that they could debate and settle. 'If the discussion continues on the present basis', he argued, 'we are going to achieve nothing at all with regard to consultation as to foreign affairs.'[42]

The differences between King and Bruce could hardly be ignored, and after the other delegations had had their say (none of them chose to dwell on the problem of working out policies for the future, though Smuts as expected found plenty to criticize about Britain's recent responses in

41 CAB 32/9: IC mtg 4, 8 Oct 1922.
42 *Ibid*: IC mtg 4, 8 Oct 1923.

European affairs) discussion was adjourned to enable the Foreign Office, as Curzon put it, 'to consider very carefully the suggestions and views ... placed before us, and if possible to come up at a later date with certain draft resolutions'. But it soon enough became clear that the foreign secretary had no intention of settling any differences by compromise resolutions. A growing personal concern over the divergent views of the dominion delegates had prompted Lord Salisbury, one of Curzon's cabinet colleagues on the home delegation at the conference, to send round a paper to the rest of the British cabinet in which he put up a few ideas of his own about the conduct of the empire's foreign affairs.[43] In particular, he thought that some new form of dominion ministerial representation in London could bring an adequate amount of practical policy consultation, with the happy result that 'Australia will find how much common action is possible, and Canada will learn how much common action is desirable.' But Curzon would have none of it. If the price of dominion co-operation in foreign affairs had to be fuller consultation he was not prepared to pay it, and when the cabinet next met he secured a decision which forbade any British initiative 'in suggesting any alteration in the present association of the Dominions with foreign affairs'. If the overseas premiers made any definite proposals, moreover – 'such, for example, as the appointment of Dominion Ministers in London, or an alteration in the status of the High Commissioners' – these were to be referred in the first instance to a further cabinet meeting.[44] Significantly the conclusion took no account of proposals which might *weaken* relations with Britain: the problem at hand was to preserve not imperial unity but rather the Foreign Office's freedom of action. But the substance of these decisions, as it happened, did not have to be revealed to the Imperial Conference, for in the weeks that followed Curzon managed to fill his time so successfully that the discussion of the principles of policymaking was never resumed.

The question engaging much of Curzon's attention, it is worth noting, was German reparation, for the sake of which France was maintaining her defiant occupation of the Ruhr valley. The foreign secretary's preoccupation with this problem was undoubtedly merited, particularly when an unexpected initiative from President Coolidge offered a possible solution to the impasse. Curzon's diplomatic activities, however, revealed all too clearly what little store he set by inter-imperial consultation on such matters. As it happened the 1923 Imperial Conference did not have to deal with any diplomatic issue of outstanding importance analogous to

43 CAB 24/162: CP 408, 10 Oct 1923.
44 CAB 23/46: mtg 48/23, 15 Oct 1923.

the Anglo-Japanese alliance in 1921, on which they were bound to reach a collective decision. Reparations, even so, were well suited to fill this role. It was the focus of tension in Europe, and of Anglo-French discord in particular, and although Smuts alone of the overseas premiers had voiced any direct concern over the preceding months presumably all of them were ready to explore the subject further. (Even the supremely cautious Skelton had advised King that reparations might be discussed by the Imperial Conference 'with advantage'.) Yet though they were so readily available, the foreign secretary did no more than brief the dominion leaders from time to time, while continuing to play a lone diplomatic hand. Not once was the conference invited to consider a collective policy about reparations, a lack of serious debate that at last drove Smuts to act publicly on the matter. An outspoken address delivered by him on 23 October, making a timely impact on the balance of international opinion on this question, represented a sad comment on Curzon's assessment of the function and usefulness of the Imperial Conference.[45]

Curzon's view of the conference was shared fully by Mackenzie King, who like the foreign secretary felt not at all accountable to it for present or future policies. And as the conference proceeded through the full range of its discussions from foreign policy to defence and on to questions of more routine interest the Canadian prime minister was careful through-out to retain his complete freedom of action, by stating at any necessary moment that he had no authority from his parliament to undertake any definite obligations and could therefore not commit himself. With regard to a tentative resolution on naval defence, for instance, he insisted to premier Bruce that 'to attempt to commit us by resolution in any way was simply to make impossible any subsequent approval by parliament of anything the conference has done in this direction'[46] though barring the consideration of conference resolutions, quite what the Canadian parlia-ment was expected to approve he did not explain. His immediate objective was to reduce the conference's conclusions to harmless formulations, and in this he was proving most successful.

There was, of course, one unexpected surprise from the British govern-ment which lightened King's otherwise severely negative approach to the conference's business. In the fourth week of the conference came the British draft resolution on treatymaking with its explicit concession to the overseas governments of the right to conduct their own individual external affairs with foreign countries, and with scarcely more than a protest from

[45] See Hancock, *Smuts*, II: *The fields of force, 1919–1950* (Cambridge, 1968), 135–8.
[46] Quoted in Dawson, *King*, 468.

the New Zealand contingent the dominion leaders thus found themselves in a position of far greater independence in this sphere. The Canadian prime minister, who had no doubt been fearing what line the British government would take at the conference over treaties, and anticipating a sharp reproof over the Halibut treaty, for once found he could accept a proposed resolution without a single word of objection, and had to confine his observations to his diary. 'Had I drafted the [accompanying] memorandum', he confessed, 'I could not have better expressed the views which were in my own mind.'[47]

Yet King was suspicious still about the conference's unfinished deliberations about foreign affairs. Premier Bruce's hopes for improved consultative machinery, it was true, seemed almost certain to remain unfulfilled. Nonetheless, guided by Skelton's memorandum, with its disquieting interpretation of the 1921 Imperial Conference, King feared lest the mere discussion of foreign policy, and the mere receipt of confidential information, might not be enough to keep Canada a party to a united imperial diplomacy. And when towards the end of the conference Lord Curzon submitted for approval a draft statement, summarizing (for publication) the conference's general appraisal of foreign policy, it seemed that King's worst fears were justified. The foreign secretary, assuming that the dominions' basic association with the empire's foreign affairs remained unchanged, calmly referred to collective imperial policies and responsibilities.

To King, the draft report was 'really an effort to commit the conference to a common foreign policy', and he set out at once to secure amendments to it. To Curzon, however, there is no reason to think that it represented anything more than a conventional recapitulation of the conference's proceedings. It was not as if the conference had in any way settled the future course of a united imperial foreign policy. Discussion after all (on Curzon's own responsibility) had been confined to a series of unilateral statements which the British prime minister Stanley Baldwin (unlike his predecessor Lloyd George in 1921) had made no attempt to sum up and clarify. Indeed the burden of premier Bruce's complaints, and of Smuts' public speech, was precisely that there had been no legitimate policy consultation at all. But on the other hand, nor had Curzon any grounds for thinking that the collective policies and responsibilities mentioned in his summary meant anything more than they had done in the published report of the 1921 Imperial Conference. It seemed natural to assume that the Foreign Office would continue to administer the empire's day-to-day foreign affairs, and that the dominions would remain only nominally associated with

[47] Diary, 25 Oct 1923.

these matters, deciding for themselves as they always had on the extent of their tangible commitments. Indeed if the conference's attitude towards naval defence appropriations was any indication of dominion feelings in this respect, this assumption was well founded. No dominion defence contributions had been promised (King had continued to hold out against any such commitments, despite Amery's best endeavours) and the British government would thus of necessity be left to bear the full practical burden for the empire's diplomacy. On this view of events, Curzon was unlikely to think that he could no longer speak for the empire. Beyond that, of course, whatever ideas King might entertain, a British foreign secretary *did* speak for an empire, as a glance at any map would show.

That much said, however, the conflict of view between the foreign secretary and the Canadian prime minister was certainly of the former's making. Despite the wide differences of opinion expressed at the opening of the conference, Curzon had failed to leave room for a conference debate on the principles of imperial policymaking, largely because he did not wish to fetter his own freedom of action. The inevitable result was that there was no agreed understanding amongst the delegates about the critical division between 'local' and 'imperial' foreign policy. Although the conference's official resolution on treatymaking had recognized a wide legitimate area for independent dominion foreign policy, and although King had also given notice that for Canada at least, the scope for a collective empire diplomacy would be strictly limited, nonetheless without further discussion on this point it was still an open question how far each of the overseas governments would consider their external affairs to be contained within a united imperial foreign policy. Unfortunately Curzon for his own part, even taking into account these important new departures, was unlikely to infer that an imperial foreign policy was a thing of the past – that the British government, in other words, unless it had the express consent of the dominions, spoke only for itself on any particular matter of policy. It was enough for Curzon to know that the dominions, in all events, retained the last word on their individual commitments to the empire to feel that he could continue safely to speak for them all. But King could not accept that line of reasoning. Because he thought that the Imperial Conference might exercise a far greater sway over a dominion's imperial obligations, he had to be sure that the benefit of the doubt would fall on his side, and that foreign affairs would be deemed to be 'local' unless otherwise agreed. And lacking that definite assurance, his only option was to dissociate Canada from whatever might be construed as a possible obligation. Hence his immediate and strong reaction to the foreign secretary's draft report.

Curzon was at first conciliatory, willingly removing all references to collective responsibilities from his summary. It was quickly apparent, however, that the Canadian delegation were not going to be satisfied with these amendments. In addition, they now insisted on deleting any implied allusions in the report to possible future courses of action – there were two such references, regarding Egypt and Turkey – which might be taken as an indication that the Imperial Conference had committed themselves in advance to joint diplomatic undertakings. And to remove any final ambiguities King also submitted a corollary to the report, which declared that the conference had been 'primarily for the purpose of exchanging information and opinions', and stipulated that its discussions 'did not commit the Governments ... or the Parliaments to which they were responsible, without their full consideration and express consent'.[48]

These additional reservations provoked Curzon's anger. Unable to comprehend the Canadian prime minister's anxieties, he confessed to his wife that he found King 'obstinate, tiresome, and stupid', and could only conclude that he was 'nervously afraid of being turned out of his own Parliament when he gets back'.[49] Under pressure from Smuts and Hankey, he agreed to delete from his draft summary the two offending references to future policy: but the recommended additional formal declaration he thought quite unnecessary – and in any case, as he told King, 'stated too broadly and not applicable to Ireland or India'. (As noted earlier the Irish had maintained a low profile at the conference, and Curzon, an anti-Home Ruler before the First World War, had clearly yet to accustom himself to their new dominion status!) But King stood his ground still, threatening in turn that if need be he would issue a unilateral statement that would in no uncertain terms dissociate Canada from the conference's conclusions,[50] and it was to avoid any such excessive solution that negotiations were hurriedly arranged to work out a more conservatively-worded corollary. As published, therefore, the report on foreign policy concluded:

This Conference is a conference of representatives of the several Governments of the Empire; its views and conclusions on Foreign Policy, as recorded above, are necessarily subject to the action of the Governments and Parliaments of the various portions of the Empire, and it trusts that the results of its deliberations will meet with their approval.

48 King papers, J4/81: draft paragraph for Foreign Affairs summary.
49 Lady Curzon, *Reminiscences* (London, 1955), 181 (cited in Dawson, *King*, 477).
50 King papers, J4/81: 'Mr. King's proposal for reservation by Canada', 7 Nov 1923.

'Foreign Policy' – but which foreign policy, or whose? In the end that was still the question the 1923 Imperial Conference had failed to answer, and it therefore left no orthodox interpretation of the empire's diplomatic affairs to guide its departing delegations. A number of attitudes and aspirations had contended for general recognition, but ultimately they were neither judged nor reconciled, and so none was abandoned. As between Curzon and King, the differences that injected a late spark of stubborn anger into the conference stemmed largely from misunderstandings – about the meaning of the Imperial Conference, about the autonomy of the dominions in their commitment to imperial affairs, perhaps even about emotional attitudes towards imperial responsibilities. In practical terms the two men were far closer to each other than they ever realized, with neither wanting essentially to restrict his freedom of action. Clearly the greater margin of difference lay between King and prime minister Bruce. As the former proceeded to disengage his dominion from imperial obligations, so the latter was soon to appoint a liaison officer to London, as a means to closer imperial integration. A wind of change was blowing, however, now that the Foreign Office were more openly decided that the principle of a united empire foreign policy made in collaboration with Britain's overseas partners should not be allowed to compromise their own diplomatic activities. And it is safe to say that King was running with that wind, while Bruce had to reach against it.

Canada and imperial economic relations

In conjunction with the 1923 Imperial Conference the British government convened a separate and parallel Imperial Economic Conference in order to discuss a wide range of economic and technical matters – the first time since the Imperial War Conferences of 1917 and 1918 that the empire's economic relations had been looked at in any comprehensive fashion, and a conference to which the overseas governments devoted a good deal of effort. The change in the economic climate since those earlier meetings was extreme. In the brave days of wartime, goods and raw materials had been scarce, demand and price levels high, and British and dominion leaders had resolutely planned how to allocate their limited resources amongst themselves in the anticipated prosperity of the post-war world. Alas, by 1923 the full measure of their false optimism was apparent to all, as ministers reconvened in general conditions of depression to see if mutual economic co-operation might alleviate the worst of their problems. Thus their deliberations were followed with considerable attention, the more so when, even before they were finished, prime minister Baldwin unexpectedly pledged his government to a radical new policy of British

protective tariffs (and by implication to imperial preferences) and prepared to put this policy to the test of a general election. Our predominant
purpose in this study, however, has been to examine the problems that
centred round the conduct and control of the empire's foreign policy, and
it would be somewhat outside the scope of the work to turn in any sustained detail to discuss the development of imperial economic relations
in these years. For a broad assessment of British economic policy between
the wars with reference to the dominions the reader may usefully be
referred elsewhere.[51] Nonetheless it will be pertinent to look briefly at
economic matters in 1923 at least to the extent of their bearing upon
British–Canadian relations. As with foreign policy, they raised fundamental questions about the possibility and the desirability of collective
action.

It might be thought that King and his colleagues would come to
London as prejudiced against committing Canada to any positive gestures
in economic ventures as in foreign policy matters, and in the main this
turned out to be so. Yet in looking at the Canadian response to the
Imperial Economic Conference it would be wrong to leave unrecorded
an initial expression of genuine interest on King's part, however brief
its duration, in developing closer ties with Britain. Strictly speaking, the
prime minister's hopes for expanding Canadian links with the mother
country lay outside the concerns of the conference proper, being in the
realm of private finance rather than imperial economic development. It
had happened that earlier in 1923, after a decidedly dull post-war period,
British investors had shown apparent interest in stepping up the level of
their activities in the dominion. A successful issue of Canadian industrial
securities on the London market had been taken to indicate the 'renewed
interest of British capital' in the dominion,[52] and in his preparations for
the Economic Conference King had been advised that fresh investment
from Britain could be encouraged to come into Canada along with
British immigrants, and provide the means necessary to integrate the
newcomers into the dominion's economy.[53] He therefore arrived in
London keen to seek both, and in a number of private conversations
with Bank of England officials and others was soon quite convinced that
his government could float a new and substantial loan in London on very
favourable conditions:

[51] Ian Drummond, *British Economic Policy and the Empire, 1919–1939*
    (London, 1972) and *Imperial Economic Policy, 1917–1939: studies in
    expansion and protection* (London, 1974).
[52] British Trade Commissioner, Toronto, *Report . . . June 1923*, (London, 1923),
    10.
[53] King papers, J1/92 and J4/85: memoranda for Imperial Economic Conference.

I think we were all agreed that a Canadian loan taken up at this time in London on good terms would mean much for the credit of Canada in England, would offset the erroneous impression the agitation of the Grand Trunk shareholders has occasioned, and would be, at this time of the Conference, beneficial in many ways.[54]

This rare burst of enthusiasm, quite at odds with King's major gloomy preoccupations in London, was conveyed at once to W. S. Fielding, his minister of finance in Ottawa:

Spirit of conference is for greater trade development between different parts of Empire. In speeches we have asked for British capital and people be sent to Canada. Financiers anxious to comply . . . We all believe it would have splendid Empire impression if announcement could be made that London had resumed investing capital in Canada. Difficult for one not in conference atmosphere to realise psychology of situation.[55]

Unfortunately King's proposed gesture did not square at all with Fielding's own financial priorities. It was ironic that the minister of finance was by far the staunchest imperialist in the Canadian cabinet, and more often than not a hindrance to the more independent outlook of the prime minister. That said, however, Fielding was also extremely orthodox in his economic thinking, and having recently in 1923 raised a new government loan from domestic resources he had no intention of inviting any further external investment, particularly in the face of a persisting slackness in the Canadian economy. So he sent a gravely discouraging reply to the prime minister, with the result that King's little moment of excitement in London soon passed, and no new Canadian borrowing was arranged.

With the exception of King's brief overture to British investors, Canada's delegation to the Imperial Economic Conference was wholly lacking in initiative, and for the most part highly sceptical of the conference's intentions. The other dominions, who like Canada faced depressed markets for their products, looked to imperial economic co-operation – specifically to a fuller scheme of British imperial preferences – for some measure of relief. For several reasons the Canadian government in 1923 had no such inclinations. In the first place domestic political considerations left them very little room for manoeuvre in economic matters, making co-operation in reciprocal imperial schemes unlikely.

---

[54] King diary, 20 Oct 1923. The Canadian government had taken over the bankrupt Grand Trunk railway in 1922 without compensation for its shareholders, most of whom were British.

[55] King papers, J1/86: King–Fielding, 20 Oct 1923.

Significant changes (in either direction) in the tariff were ruled out: a 10% cut in April 1923 had been settled only in the face of threatened resignations from the cabinet, and King was clearly in no position to consider further reductions.[56] Even to encourage British immigration schemes, no matter how selective, was to risk offending the labour unions and also the western farmers, upon whose political support the Liberal government were heavily dependent.[57] Economic policy was in any case in the conservative hands of Fielding, who held fast to traditional notions of economic *laissez faire* for the dominions, and had little enthusiasm for any broad designs for imperial economic planning and development:

Each Dominion has its own particular conditions which require to be dealt with and the best interests of the Empire can be promoted by leaving each section of it free to do what its own conditions seem to call for ... we have no grievances to present, no demands to make. What more can we do but await the proposals that come, either from the Imperial Government or from our sister Dominions?[58]

To Fielding's reservations O. D. Skelton added his own arguments against commitments in economic affairs. Economic integration at any level, in his view, held precisely the same dangerous implications for Canadian autonomy as did a united imperial foreign policy. Hence his criticism, for example, of a British suggestion for an imperial advisory committee for economic co-operation.

The proposal is simply another variant of the endless schemes for establishing a central government in London. Parliament or council or secretariat, it matters not, so long as the machinery of control can somehow be established in London. It would be a complete reversal of our long established policy ... It would commit us to central review of every important economic activity of our government, and would for example give good ground for intervention if we proposed a reciprocity arrangement with the U.S.[59]

Not one of Skelton's criticisms was true, it may be noted. There was no intention to 'govern' economic affairs from London, and there would be no 'central review' of future Canadian policies. Canada, what is more, had since the war happily and without impeding her freedom subscribed to a good many advisory imperial bodies – dealing with statistics, forestry, shipping, to name only some. But no matter. The same threatened loss of

56 King diary, 21 April 1923.
57 Dawson, *King*, 389.
58 King papers, J4/85: memorandum for the Imperial Economic Conference, n.d. (Aug–Sept 1923).
59 King papers, J4/85: memorandum, 2 Oct 1923.

independence, the same ignoring of recent developments under Borden and Meighen as had served to brief King on foreign affairs, did adequate second duty here.

For both political and ideological reasons, therefore, the Canadian delegation to the Imperial Economic Conference maintained an attitude of wary independence. On schemes where participation held no hidden implications for Canadian autonomy, and where Britain and the dominions stood properly on an equal footing with each other in accordance with accepted notions of their status as commonwealth partners – the standardization of customs procedure, the development of forestry resources – co-operation could be accepted readily enough. But even at this routine administrative level other proposals were just as quickly rejected by the Canadians. A plan for registering patents, for instance, or another for the joint publication of trade statistics in London, came up against a Canadian veto because the practical responsibilities would rest disproportionately on the British government. Even where an imperial organization served Canada's interests directly, still the government's hostility to permanent centralized institutions proved to be implacable. In this way the Imperial Shipping Committee, set up on an *ad hoc* basis in 1920 and by 1923 of proven utility to the British and dominion authorities alike, was prevented by the Canadians from attaining a permanent status. They could endorse a resolution which praised the committee's work, and in the coming years would continue to keep it busy with Canadian problems, but they would not see it established on a full-time basis.[60]

With regard to the two main issues before the conference, the extending of mutual imperial preferences and the establishment of a co-operative economic committee, Canada stayed well clear of commitments. From the very beginning King maintained that tariff preferences were a domestic rather than an imperial question, and while he was prepared to indicate the products on which a British preferential tariff would benefit Canada, he held out no promises of any reciprocal bargaining. Even after Baldwin had pledged his government to create British protective tariffs, thereby offering the essential pre-condition for a mutual preference system, the Canadian delegation would not commit themselves to any definite extension of imperial preferences.[61] By the same token they turned down an Imperial Economic Committee, though in this case they were obliged to see the matter pressed to a vote and accepted in spite of their own

60 K. Burley, 'The Imperial Shipping Committee', *JICH*, II, no 2, has a full description of the committee's activities. Even on a temporary basis the committee lasted until the 1960s.

61 CAB 32/19: IEC mtg 21, 7 Nov 1923.

objections. To the last they preferred to stand apart while Britain and the other dominions sought to work out something of a co-operative economic future.

But if Canada persisted in this way in being such a hostile witness at the Imperial Economic Conference, what in the end was she witness to? Not, as it turned out, to any thorough-going solutions to the problems of imperial trade and development. It was all very well for Amery to be lobbying hard behind the scenes during 1923 for a broader system of British imperial preferences, and for Baldwin to remind the overseas delegations that 'The resources of our Empire are boundless and the need for rapid development is clamant.'[62] The inescapable fact was that the British government were tied by Bonar Law's election pledge of November 1922 that no new tariffs would be created without a further general election, and they were obliged to admit to themselves that 'It is very difficult ... to discover any articles which are of sufficient interest to the Dominions for a preference on them to be welcome, without being of such importance to the consumer in this country that the imposition of a duty would be considered to violate the Government's pledge.'[63] As a result the British delegation to the conference could hold out to the dominions only a few concessionary import reductions on dried fruits, sugar, tobacco and other negligible items. Even under pressure from the disappointed overseas delegates the list could be stretched no further than apples, canned fish and fruit, honey and wines.

But beyond these self-imposed restrictions there were in any case, as Professor Drummond has pointed out, more fundamental limitations to reciprocal tariff concessions amongst the empire's trading partners.[64] In the first place the dominions had very little room for manoeuvre to review their own tariffs against Britain, that is to say against British manufactures. Their own maturing economies, with an expanding but heavily protected industrial development, could simply not have withstood free British competition, and so beyond a very narrow range of movement substantial preferences for Britain were politically impossible. For somewhat similar reasons Britain would never be in a position to grant tariff preferences to essential raw materials from empire sources, since to put the necessary tariffs on these materials in the first place would (barring the hypothetical case where the empire could fully supply British demand)

---

[62] CAB 32/9: IC mtg 1, 1 Oct 1923. In this inaugural speech written otherwise by Thomas Jones, the prime minister put together his own thoughts on the empire's economic development. T. Jones, *Whitehall Diary*, I, 244.

[63] FO 371/9403: British (confidential) memorandum, imperial preference.

[64] Drummond, *British Economic Policy*, 33–4.

increase the cost of British manufactures and jeopardize her export trade. Nor were the overseas producers of other commodities – wheat, wool, tea, jute – in a position by the 1920s to benefit even if Britain did introduce imperial preferences. For in these instances the empire now produced more than it consumed, and as a result the effective price to the producer was the 'world' price rather than any 'imperial' price – no matter if Britain discriminated in favour of the empire's producers, she would no longer be able to raise price levels for them.

Thus it was for a variety of powerful reasons that the 1923 negotiations about trade and tariffs were confined to their narrow parameters: there were few straightforward prescriptions any longer for the economic complexities of a decentralized and essentially non-integrated empire. Nonetheless, when Baldwin committed himself to protection at the end of October, it did seem for a moment that Britain's economic priorities were going to be radically realigned towards the interests of the empire as a whole, and the Economic Conference broke up on a more hopeful note. But after an all too short election campaign an unconvinced British electorate voted convincingly against protection and empire preference, and brought the Labour party to power. And Ramsay MacDonald's government abandoned not only the few existing preferences that were of interest to Canada but also the tariffs on which they had been based. Alone of the overseas prime ministers Mackenzie King was not compromised by these fluctuations in British fiscal policy, with nothing ventured and therefore nothing lost. For him it was one more salutary lesson as to the importance of Canada's autonomous development in the empire.

7

From Lausanne to Locarno

Different observers of the 1923 Imperial Conference, in accordance with
their particular points of view, drew their own conclusions from its
proceedings. *The Round Table*, for instance, went to some lengths to
portray the conference as the culmination of what it regarded as a liberal,
devolutionary development of imperial relations – a moment when the

> system of Imperial cooperation, long regarded as the *summum bonum* of
> Imperial attainment, was at last put into full and untrammelled effect . . . The
> Conference was a conference of equals . . . conferring together freely and
> without reserve . . . [It] perfected the machinery of the British Commonwealth
> according to the ideas of the cooperationist school of Imperial thought.[1]

In a similar though less effusive vein Geoffrey Dawson, editor of *The
Times*, could privately assert to N. W. Rowell in Canada that 'it was one
of the best conferences of the kind that has ever been held, for the reason
that there was no longer any question at issue about Dominion Status'.
Not that the Canadian contingent could be given much credit:

> the Prime Ministers really met on an equal and unsuspicious footing, and two
> of them at all events – Smuts and Bruce – played leading parts in their very
> different ways. It is impossible to say the same of Mackenzie King, though I
> liked him personally very much. He seemed to have his exiguous majority . . .
> so constantly on his mind that he was reluctant to commit himself to anything
> which could ever be misrepresented as 'entanglement'.[2]

For King himself, of course, the results of the conference bore quite an
opposite interpretation. He was not at all prepared to accept that Britain
and the dominions had sat down in London as equals, and consequently
felt fully justified in his efforts to remove Canada from all external imperial
obligations, implicit or otherwise. On his own view of events it was his
firmly negative tactics that had perhaps allowed the dominions to *leave* the
conference on more equal terms with Britain, but he was content for the

[1] *The Round Table*, xiv, no 2 (1923–4).
[2] Rowell papers: Dawson–Rowell, 26 Dec 1923.

moment not to make any political capital out of his efforts. From Ottawa there was little attempt to interpret or expand upon the conference's published reports, or otherwise play up the Canadian contribution, and it was left to J. W. Dafoe to explain in print that the 1923 Conference had been a success 'by virtue of things it declined to do'.[3] Nonetheless the prime minister was reasonably satisfied that he had established for Canada the necessary freedom of action in foreign affairs, and that dominion autonomy was sufficiently secure. In March 1924 when the House of Commons was again in session he had an opportunity to declare categorically:

When Great Britain takes a certain position in an international matter, the Dominion government may, for the same reason, take a similar position ... [we] will exercise in these matters the same rights as the parliament of Great Britain would exercise in relation to their people.[4]

King's statement was a legitimate indication of the future course of British–Canadian relations with respect to foreign policy. It emphasized also that the dominion government considered themselves under no obligations so far as existing imperial policies were concerned – time and again King had stressed this point to the 1923 Conference. Yet for all his efforts, King could not extricate the dominion entirely from the imperial diplomatic nexus. For one thing, Canada's activities within the League of Nations continued to be mediated by her imperial associations, albeit in an ambiguous fashion. As we have seen, while a 'British Empire' representative could sit on the League Council, the symbol of an undifferentiated foreign policy uniting mother country and dominions, in the first League Assembly Canada and South Africa chose to vote independently in opposition to Britain. Thereafter Canadian operations at the League revealed a similar expedient inconsistency, the imperial factor repudiated or taken into account by Ottawa as deemed appropriate. On the one hand, a persistent campaign to remove article x from the League Covenant found the Canadian administration – particularly after the Liberals gained power – operating with little reference to their empire partners at Geneva. Yet on the other, when it came time to assess two major League proposals for procedures to settle international disputes the dominion authorities proved quite willing to consult and act in concert with the London government. More than simple pragmatism, however, this ambivalent behaviour reflected also the profound lack of public interest in Canadian policies, of whatever stripe, at the League.

[3] *Maclean's Magazine*, 15 Jan 1924, quoted in Dawson, *King*, 477.
[4] Canada, HoC, 20 March 1924.

Of more pressing concern in 1924, to King if not to his voting public, were two questions of foreign policy inherited from the years of collective imperial policymaking, namely the conclusion of a peace treaty with Turkey and the settlement of an international agreement on German reparations. With both these issues Canada was associated in the first instance as a party to the Paris peace settlements of 1919, though it is fair to say that five years later anything that bore upon the problems of the Turkish peace treaty was indelibly coloured for King by the traumatic experience of the Chanak crisis. His response, certainly, to Britain's invitation to ratify the Lausanne treaty and thus endorse a final Turkish settlement was one of unbending, truculent suspicion, the prelude to a series of acrimonious exchanges about the treaty with the home government. Once more, it seemed to him, he must prevent Canada from being saddled deliberately with unacceptable external responsibilities: if the dominion was obliged to make peace with Turkey by treaty, nevertheless he still had to dissociate her from any commitment to uphold the treaty's territorial provisions. By contrast, reparations posed the opposite difficulty of how to associate Canada directly with a policy that Britain wished to negotiate singlehanded on behalf of the empire as a whole. With the Lausanne treaty King in the end found an adequate solution; over reparations he had to compromise. In both instances, though in Whitehall his reasoning appeared obscure and inflexible, the Canadian prime minister had at least served to remind the British authorities that in foreign affairs a dominion now had a right to be heard with its own voice.

By the summer of 1924 it was apparent that Canada was no longer alone in its efforts to broaden the dominions' prerogatives in imperial and external affairs. In June a change of government in South Africa brought to power General Hertzog, leader of the Nationalist party and a man who for years had nurtured the conviction that the imperial connection must necessarily inhibit his country's standing in the world. For the moment, the constraints of a coalition government were sufficient to keep the new prime minister relatively subdued as regards South Africa's constitutional relations, but clearly here was a powerful new force for devolutionary change in the empire–commonwealth who would have to be reckoned with. Of more immediate concern to the British government was the Irish Free State, the new dominion created synthetically out of a partitioned Ireland in 1921, in the hope that Irish demands for self-determination could be contained within the framework of the empire–commonwealth. Attendance at the 1923 Imperial Conference, it appeared, had encouraged the Free State leadership to think that precisely the opposite might be possible: that with the status and prerogatives of a dominion they might radically convert the imperial framework to the point where Irish national independence could become a reality. Whether this was to be a process of conversion or more bluntly one of subversion – that is, whether the Free State's ultimate goal could in any sense be squared with the broader pattern of change pursued by her overseas commonwealth partners – remained to be seen. Meanwhile the drive for constitutional concessions for the offshore dominion began in earnest with an application, based directly on the precedent established by Canada in 1920, for Irish diplomatic representation at Washington.

The government of Ramsay MacDonald, confronted by these pressures from various quarters and having themselves acted somewhat arbitrarily towards the dominions in their economic and foreign policies, decided that British–dominion relations would best be advanced by a special conference in London. They were out of office, however, before arrangements for this meeting could be taken in hand, and the returning Conservative administration showed little inclination to pursue MacDonald's course. With Leopold Amery at the Colonial Office and Austen Chamberlain at the Foreign Office there was an altogether more pragmatic tone to the conduct of dominion relations, Amery on the one hand seeking less formal ways to keep the commonwealth governments abreast of foreign policy, Chamberlain on the other ready always to brief dominion representatives *ad hoc*, while seeing that a unified imperial diplomacy based on prior collective consultation was no longer feasible, a realization by now widely shared. That much said, it was nonetheless deeply disturbing to many British and dominion circles when in 1925 the home government, in a stark demonstration of British diplomatic *realpolitik*, proceeded to negotiate and conclude the European security treaties of Locarno.

The making of peace with Turkey: II

In the wake of the Chanak crisis the British government had entered upon negotiations for a peace settlement with Turkey with little reference to the dominions, wilfully ignoring the procedure established at the Paris peace conference by which the overseas governments were given direct access to the treatymaking process. As a result, by late 1922 there was still some uncertainty about how far the dominions were to be associated with any new Turkish treaties that might be concluded at the Lausanne Conference. The uncertainty was most marked in the case of Canada, where Mackenzie King had revealed only that his administration would not commit themselves in advance to anything whatever. Yet by the time of the 1923 Imperial Conference, ten months later, many of the difficulties appeared to be over. At Lausanne a new treaty, generally accepted as being a reasonable settlement of peace, had been completed in July and signed by the British delegate Sir Horace Rumbold, and copies had been promptly forwarded to the dominion governments. There remained now only the formal process of ratification to complete the business.

As we have seen, however, King was ready at the Imperial Conference to challenge every measure, every proposal that carried with it the slightest suggestion of shared imperial responsibilities for Canada, and for him the Lausanne treaty was clearly an object of suspicion. On several occasions at the conference the prime minister indicated that Canada might not give its 'formal concurrence' to ratification – though, as ever, in his approach to imperial affairs King chose to say as little about his position on this issue as he possibly could, and as his remarks were not dwelt upon he was more than content to let the question of ratification be resolved in due course when necessary. Quite what Canada's relationship to the treaty would be if the dominion withheld consent to ratification remained unclear. But King was already quite sure in his own mind what the formal act of ratification would mean, and convinced that there would still be room for a Canadian gesture of dissociation from the treaty. In his diary he compared his own view with that of General Smuts:

Smuts point of view is that having his Parliament approve ratification it prevents [sic] one part of the Empire from apparently binding other parts; my point of view is that as we are bound anyway without participation we cannot escape the legal consequences. I am inclined to think it is inadvisable to ask Parliament to approve this treaty and that as a Gov[ernment] we should refrain from authorizing ratification of the treaty without the approval by Parl[iament] in the first place.[5]

The logical double-bind of refusing to move without the sanction of parliament while refusing to seek any such sanction, a valuable strategy learned from the Chanak crisis, could serve King equally well in dealing with the treaty that had come from that crisis.

It was not until February 1924 that Whitehall approached the dominion governments formally about the Lausanne treaty, assuming quite simply that because it committed the whole empire to making peace with Turkey they would expect to give the act of ratification their prior consent. Taking the dominions as a whole – and the empire's constitutional relations forbade any other approach – the assumption was correct: Australia, New Zealand and South Africa acknowledged their approval of the treaty without delay. But not Canada, whose response is well known. King's warnings of late 1923 that his government might not associate Canada

[5] Diary, 2 Nov 1923.

with ratification became now a definite statement that they would not do so. In fact, they would express no opinion at all on the treaty, and would neither recommend its ratification to parliament nor object to whatever the British government chose to do. And by way of a plausible justification for this somewhat implausible position King argued that to judge from the way the treaty had been negotiated and signed single-handed by the British, it must impose obligations solely on Great Britain. Ratification should therefore be a British decision alone.[6]

Here began a lengthy correspondence between the Canadian and British governments as to the nature of the Lausanne treaty and Canada's commitment to it, a correspondence rich in confusion which led to private misunderstandings and public misrepresentations. And in this regard it is unjust of King's biographer to place so much of the blame on the British government for their mistaken impressions.[7] The Canadian prime minister's attitude and objectives were clarified by hindsight, not least his own, but if they were clear to him in March 1924 it cannot be said that they were clearly transmitted from Ottawa to Whitehall.

Indeed, the difficulties began immediately with King's highly questionable argument that the treaty pertained to Great Britain alone. The Foreign Office rightly dismissed this contention; but they went on to argue in turn that the Canadian government had 'formally agreed to the signature of the settlement on their behalf',[8] itself a highly dubious interpretation of the correspondence which had passed between the two governments in 1922. Had Curzon still been foreign secretary he might well have corrected this opinion in the Office minutes, for at the Imperial Conference he had been explicitly challenged on this very point by King.[9] But with the fall of Baldwin's government Curzon's portfolio had passed to an overworked MacDonald, who had hardly the time to acquaint himself with the details of this complicated business. MacDonald, then, was obliged to trust his advisers, and a few days later repeated their interpretation of events in the House of Commons – only to find that King at once repudiated it in his own parliament.[10] If there was any common ground between the two prime ministers they appeared to be marching away from it in opposite directions. Even so it is unfair to suggest, as Neatby does,[11] that

[6] The correspondence is printed in *DCER*, III, 94 ff.
[7] H. B. Neatby, *William Lyon Mackenzie King*, II: *1924–1932, The Lonely Heights* (London, 1963), 32 ff.
[8] FO 371/10200/2709: minute of G. Rendel (first secretary, Eastern Department), 26 March 1924.
[9] King diary, 25 Oct 1923.
[10] GB, HoC, 1 April 1924; Canada, HoC, 2 April 1924.
[11] Neatby, *King*, II, 34.

MacDonald 'insisted on misrepresenting' the Canadian leader. While King's uncooperative posture was neither understood nor sympathized with by the Foreign Office's permanent officials, MacDonald himself was prepared to insist that 'the matter has to be handled tactfully to prevent it merging into a big and troublesome issue. Mr. King will help us. He is in a difficult position.'[12] This willingness to give King the benefit of the doubt was to be severely tested in the weeks that followed.

It suited the Canadian prime minister very well to claim that the Lausanne treaty did not concern Canada, for it provided another opportunity to reiterate that the dominion was responsible to itself alone for its foreign affairs, and would not assume external obligations without explicit prior consent. But it meant also that as long as King held to this line Canada would apparently remain at war with Turkey, and this was a state of affairs no more desired by the Canadian government than intended by the British negotiators at Lausanne. A memorandum from O. D. Skelton reminded the prime minister quite plainly that 'the question of ending this war of ours' would have to be resolved. Skelton, in fact, thought in any case that it would be decidedly to Canada's advantage to subscribe to the ratification of the treaty, for there were economic and commercial concessions in it that he felt sure would be profitable to the dominion. He tried more than once to focus King's attention on these considerations.[13]

But the Canadian prime minister was not to be drawn from one extreme to the other. If peace would be established only by ratifying the treaty (assuming there would not be a separate Turkish–Canadian agreement), and if ratification would in any event involve the whole British empire, he remained convinced that any *positive* concurrence in ratification on Canada's part would somehow commit the dominion more fully to the treaty's political and strategic guarantees – in effect to the collective security of the near east. What he sought therefore, was a position from which he could simultaneously make peace with Turkey and reject all such responsibilities, and he judged that the best course, still, would be to allow ratification to take place without Canadian assent. This would bind Canada, but only 'as between other countries and Br[itish] Empire. As to extent within Empire depends on view that parliament takes in light of all circumstances.'[14]

Thus having at first declined to ratify the treaty on the grounds that it did not pertain to Canada, King admitted to the British government in May that Canadian ratification would, on the contrary, implicate the

12 FO 371/10201/3025: minute of 5 April 1924.
13 King papers, J1/109: memoranda, 8, 14 April 1924.
14 King papers, J1/109: manuscript minute, nd.

dominion all too much. And yet, far from now seeking to discover the 'view that Parliament takes in light of all circumstances' – or as he had put it to the British authorities in late 1922, allowing parliament to decide 'upon the merits of the case, what action is right and proper' – the prime minister with scant attention to his own analysis simply refused to let parliament decide anything at all. To do so, he calmly explained, would only make matters more difficult:

Our unwillingness to ask the Canadian Parliament to approve the ratification of the Treaty is based on the certain knowledge that . . . Parliament would not approve steps which would imply the undertaking of Canada of a definite and positive responsibility to render aid in case action became necessary under the Straits Convention [of the treaty].

However, on the understanding that 'it will remain open to Canada as freely as in the past to decide what steps she will take actively' if the treaty ever needed to be enforced, he accepted that British ratification bound the empire as a whole. He was reassured immediately by Ramsay MacDonald that the Canadian government would indeed be free to do as they pleased in any future contingency.

It is difficult to avoid the conclusion that after two months' negotiations Canada's position in relation to the Lausanne treaty was practically what it would have been had ratification been assented to in the first place.[15] 'As freely as in the past': King's final formulation claimed for the dominion only the freedom of action it had already enjoyed in regard to the other international treaties of peace, which had been expressly ratified by Canada. Yet one can discern here an area of disagreement between the British and Canadian governments pertaining not to the Lausanne treaty itself but rather to the meaning of ratification, and at base to the nature of inter-imperial relations.

From the British point of view ratification of the Lausanne treaty disposed of the state of war existing between Turkey and the empire. The treaty imposed obligations, to be sure, but in the customary way these would fall 'on the Empire as a whole corresponding to the advantages which the Empire as a whole will derive from [the treaty]',[16] and the treaty itself had nothing to do with how these obligations were to be shared between Britain and the dominions. Indeed it was a basic British axiom that inter-imperial relations were not dependent upon treaties but

---

[15] Canada did not pass the customary 'enabling' legislation for the treaty, but the probability of complications arising from this omission was considered negligible.

[16] FO 371/10200: G. W. Rendel, minute of 26 March 1924.

rather upon the dominions' practical freedom of association with the mother country: in a word these relations were not contractual but conventional. In refusing to negotiate at Lausanne through a British Empire Delegation, the Foreign Office had certainly flouted convention for the sake of expediency. Yet they would hardly deny that whatever the mode of representation at the conference, any practical responsibilities that might arise as a consequence of the treaty would remain to be decided by the dominion governments themselves. With particular regard to Canada, moreover, there was little reason to suppose that concurrence in ratification would represent a relaxation of the dominion's consistent hostility to European commitments.

During their term of office, Borden and Meighen had accepted this point of view without question. On the understanding always that imperial and international commitments needed parliamentary sanction, they had sought for Canada a status within the empire of equality with Britain, and had established through the League of Nations the beginnings of an international Canadian personality. Such was the position King inherited at the end of 1921. But King, it is fair to say, had never been entirely satisfied that these new claims of the Borden–Meighen regime to a Canadian voice in imperial and international councils had not compromised the dominion's essential autonomy – the autonomy that his former Liberal chief, Sir Wilfrid Laurier, had defended so persistently before the war. Witness, for example, King's thoughts on the Versailles treaty in 1919, at the time of the parliamentary debate about ratification:

The position seems to be that we are bound anyway by what has been done and the method of doing it. Parliament will have to assert its rights when concrete instances arise.[17]

The implication that Canada's active role in the treatymaking process had of itself generated unavoidable liabilities, which would not have been the same had the dominion not participated directly; the view of parliament as the last line of defence against these unwarranted commitments: here at the start of his leadership of the Liberal party, these basic misconceptions about Canada's place in the empire and the world were already present. They were strengthened immeasurably by the Chanak affair, for the Canadian prime minister a crisis which provided an illuminating and vital insight into the true nature of the empire's foreign policy. He was now convinced that imperial diplomacy, directed from Whitehall, was based upon firm pledges of support from the overseas dominions, pledges that Britain could redeem at will without prior consultation or warning. In

17 Diary, 3 Sept 1919.

effect he understood Canada's relations to Britain to be contractual, and he began to work explicitly towards a termination of the contract. We have seen how this conception, reinforced by Skelton's own analysis of the preceding few years, dominated King's approach to the discussion of foreign policy at the 1923 Imperial Conference. Precisely the same considerations held true, in his view, with regard to treaties that collectively involved the whole empire. Ratification of the Lausanne treaty, rather like an unqualified 'ratification' of Curzon's foreign policy summary at the 1923 Conference, would have left Canada open to unwanted obligations. Hence his decision to make peace with Turkey simply by acknowledging the imperial writ of British ratification.

This final resolution of the problem, designed to insure Canada against any prior commitments to enforce the treaty, King reached only in stages: a later claim of his to the House of Commons that he had *never* intended to ask parliament to ratify the treaty may be regarded as pure bluff.[18] And however much he protested to the contrary, the British government had little indication of his train of thought until the last moment. Not before the beginning of April 1924 were they clearly informed that the Canadian government 'at no time authorized any British Plenipotentiary to represent us nor did we understand that they were representing any Government other than Great Britain'.[19] Needless to say, this proposition would never have passed unchallenged had it been adequately expressed earlier. In the British House of Commons MacDonald paid wry tribute to King's tactics:

The only thing I think everyone will regret – and I am sure Mr. Mackenzie King will regret this as much as I do – is that there has been a lack of clear, definite statement. We find that, as stage after stage is reached, the opposition becomes more and more definite, but it reveals itself at points when it is impossible to go back and rectify any mistakes that may have been made.[20]

From Meighen in the Canadian House of Commons came criticism also. The Lausanne controversy, it is fair to say, had created less of a stir in the dominion parliament than either King or Meighen might have wished. In early April the prime minister had anticipated that it would soon be seen as 'a matter of inter-imperial & world interest',[21] but in the following weeks the House of Commons had chosen to pay far closer attention to the government's budgetary measures than to these constitutional

[18] Canada, HoC, 9 June 1924.
[19] CO 532/274: Gov Gen–Col Sec, 3 April 1924.
[20] GB, HoC, 6 June 1924.
[21] Diary, 8 April 1924.

wrangles. Nonetheless, when the relevant correspondence was tabled in June there was a chance for Meighen to speak out, not simply against the tactics of delay but against King's entire strategy of passive resistance in his handling of the Lausanne treaty. By his failure to take an active part at any stage in the making of this imperial treaty, Meighen argued, the prime minister had wilfully relegated the dominion to the status it had held prior to the First World War: he had abandoned 'all that we had achieved over ten rather weary and bloody years'.[22] In the light of his own experience, particularly of course his critical intercession against the renewal of the Anglo-Japanese alliance, Meighen's charge was substantially correct. In accordance with post-war practice King should have insisted strongly on a seat for Canada at the Lausanne conference, if only in order to opt out directly from any definite undertakings in the peace treaty itself. As one commentator remarked a few years later, 'If the vindication of Canadian autonomy was the Premier's object, he went about in the wrong way.'[23] But King had his own assumptions about Canada and her imperial relations, and in the wake of the Chanak crisis his only concern was to find the most effective means of releasing the dominion from whatever external commitments the imperial tie might entail. In the event he was content enough simply to dissociate the dominion from conference and treaty alike, and if Canadian rights to a partner's voice in imperial policymaking were thereby jettisoned, it seemed no great loss. But it was in any case soon enough made clear, in connection with the Dawes reparations conference, that on his own terms King was still quite willing to participate with Britain in international affairs.

Together with the problem of a Turkish peace treaty, reparations were the second major piece of unfinished business outstanding from the peace conference of 1919, since which time it had been a subject of severe international controversy. Latterly in 1923 it had brought Anglo-French relations to breaking point with the French occupation of the Ruhr valley, but in mid-1924 the report of the Dawes Commission offered the hope that a new international agreement might be at hand, and a conference in London to discuss the report was arranged, to begin in the middle of July. For Britain and the dominions, reparations were first and last a matter of joint imperial foreign policy. The empire as a whole had been awarded a percentage of the payments (at the 1921 Imperial Conference this had been divided up amongst Britain and the dominions) and by

[22] Canada, HoC, 9 June 1924.
[23] Dewey, *Dominions and Diplomacy*, ii, 165.

common consent all negotiations, receipts and disbursements had been attended to by the Foreign Office. At a number of allied conferences British spokesmen had represented collective imperial interests, and without any renewed authorization from the dominions had signed agreements on behalf of all the empire's governments. However, the dissensions of the 1923 Imperial Conference – to say nothing of the Lausanne treaty ratification – had called into question such confident moments of collective imperial diplomacy, and lest they be accused of exceeding their authority the British government duly notified the dominions in June 1924 of the intended reparations conference.

By the terms of the resolution on treatymaking agreed at the 1923 Conference, it was clear the dominions would be entitled to claim representation on a B.E.D. at the forthcoming meeting. Nonetheless it was strongly hoped in Whitehall that they would not choose to exercise their rights in this instance, for the government knew that an enlarged contingent to represent the British empire would very likely create difficulties with the other allied delegations. They therefore took pains to place the occasion well below the threshold of dominion interest, pointing out that the conference would have nothing to do with military commitments (it had no brief to examine the problem of enforcing reparations payments) nor with changes in the empire's allotted percentages. In case there were any major points any of the overseas governments did wish to raise, however, the British authorities would be quite willing to hold a preliminary imperial meeting prior to the conference itself.[24]

The British cable was a well-meant attempt to present the conference as a mere formality, and was based on the assumption that the dominions had two alternatives: to be represented by British personnel or, if absolutely necessary, to participate jointly through a British Empire Delegation. Once again, however, thinking in Ottawa was crucially different. There the alternatives were taken to be *separate* Canadian representation at the conference through a B.E.D. or else the complete dissociation of the dominion from the proceedings – and recognizing that Canada had a genuine interest in reparations, King promptly indicated that his government would take part.

The Colonial Office, with a shrewd sense of what might be the line of least resistance, were prepared to make the best of the Canadian decision in spite of any difficulties that would arise about numbers at the conference. But against their advice MacDonald's cabinet decided to make a second attempt to dissuade King from direct participation, and so this time he was told – with rather more candour – that regrettably a

[24] CO 532/287: Col Sec–Govs Gen, 28 June 1924.

British delegation of any more than three members would severely upset the overall balance of the conference, and he was encouraged again to attend a preliminary meeting of British and dominion representatives, where policy aims could be assessed. If need be, King was informed, these preliminary meetings could be extended, and a B.E.D. kept in session throughout the conference, through which the British delegates could be briefed and could report back to their dominion colleagues. As if to allay any fears about responsibilities to parliament, the Canadian prime minister was also reassured that the conference's conclusions would not require ratification to become operative, and hence they would not need to be justified before the Canadian House of Commons.[25]

This appeal, for all its frankness, was seriously wide of the mark, and the suggestions for mitigating the loss of separate representation must have appeared in Ottawa as deliberately exacerbating the problem. An exclusively British delegation was bad enough. As Skelton noted, 'This would be practically convenient, would remove the possibility of criticism from other powers, and would commit the Dominions further to the assumption of the Empire as a single unit in foreign policy.'[26] Far worse was the idea of a B.E.D. sitting outside the conference, formulating a collective imperial policy and accepting conclusions that (in the absence of any formal process of ratification) the dominion governments could not even review. Since the 1922 Genoa Conference King had assumed that a B.E.D. was no more than the sum of its parts, a vehicle for providing the dominions with direct access to international diplomatic affairs. Yet under the proposals now put forward the B.E.D. would mediate between the dominions and international diplomacy, and Canadian policy would be an indistinguishable element within the imperial consensus. This he would never accept.

The Canadian prime minister was in effect seeking to transform the British Empire Delegation into a British Commonwealth Delegation, in which unanimity of view rather than unity of policy would prevail between British and dominion delegates. The dominions' association with the reparations issue, it is true, had been established in an undifferentiated imperial context; the time had arrived, however, to revise it in the light of recent developments in British–dominion relations. There would of course have to be a B.E.D. at the Dawes Conference – only at the League of Nations did the dominions have full international standing in their right. But in order that it be seen in its true perspective, as a means of

---

[25] CO 532/274: CO–FO, 1 July; (copy) cabinet conclusions, 2 July; Col Sec–Gov Gen, 3 July 1934.

[26] King papers, J1/109: Skelton–McGregor (King's private secretary), 9 July 1924.

access to the conference proper, King was determined to claim for his delegate both separate representation and separate full powers to sign on Canada's behalf. Peter Larkin, his high commissioner in London, was duly instructed to 'maintain our position strongly and permit no departure therefrom'.[27]

In the event, King was not able to proceed as he wished. Cables went back and forth across the Atlantic with ingenious solutions for creating separate Canadian representation within a three-man British delegation, but to no avail. The Australian government, while willing themselves to be represented by a British delegate, insisted on having any special privileges that might be extended to Canada; but the British government would not in any case allow the numbers to expand, and were obliged to warn King that unless he would compromise they would have to go into the conference with no Canadian representation at all.[28] In the face of these obstacles the Canadian prime minister, on Skelton's advice, agreed to forgo separate representation and to accept a compromise *ad hoc* arrangement whereby dominion delegates filled in turn the third British seat at the conference. But MacDonald, for his part, was obliged to inform the assembled foreign delegations that this arrangement, a departure from normal practice, was 'not to be regarded or quoted as a precedent'.[29]

Problems remained nonetheless. As the price of indirect representation King demanded the right to ratify the conclusions of the conference in parliament – his last vestige of control over Canadian policy – in spite of the fact that ratification was deemed unnecessary, and perhaps without realizing that the Canadian parliament was not due to meet until early 1925 MacDonald at first agreed to the demand – only to withdraw it in alarm when he saw that it could delay the implementing of the Dawes programme for six months. Once more it was Skelton who suggested compromise. With MacDonald's open acknowledgement to the conference of the dominions' accepted rights in these matters, he felt the point had been adequately emphasized that 'each part of the Empire which is concerned [with reparations] must speak for itself'. There was at the same time, he told King, such wide public approval for the Dawes Commission that the Canadian government could confidently accept any conclusions

[27] King papers, J1/103: King–Larkin, 7 July 1924.
[28] King papers, J1/103/87248: Larkin–King, 14 July; CO 532/281/33679: minutes of meeting between colonial secretary and high commissioners, 15 July 1924.
[29] The impact of MacDonald's admission was weakened somewhat when the colonial secretary, J. H. Thomas told the British House of Commons that the empire's delegates had met every day during the conference and discussed 'the whole situation not as British delegates *versus* Dominions, but as one united delegation having a common interest'. GB, HoC, 29 July 1924.

of the conference without parliamentary confirmation.[30] All things considered the prime minister was persuaded that his conception of Canada's relationship to the empire had been successfully asserted against the British administration, and that compromise on his part could in the end be a gesture of victory rather than weakness. So the Dawes Conference proceeded with Canada's representative, Senator Belcourt, taking part as arranged; and the Dawes Commission programme, once accepted by the conference, was able to become operative without any further delays for formal ratification.

The devolutionary impulse, 1924–1925

The Lausanne treaty and the Dawes Conference had each proved to be vehicles for the expression of a distinctly Canadian point of view about British–dominion relations with regard to foreign policy, a point of view which differentiated sharply between imperial external affairs and the external affairs of an individual imperial partner. In both instances King had taken the position that it was for his government to decide how far Canada was to be associated with such international questions; and however inappropriate or misconceived his reservations might be thought in Whitehall, King believed that he had successfully defended his dominion's essential freedom of action in this sphere. He would in any case have maintained that he was simply being guided by the 1923 Imperial Conference resolution on treatymaking procedures. In accordance with the provisions of that resolution he had claimed the right to opt completely out of the Lausanne treaty, just as he claimed the right to direct, separate participation in the proceedings of the Dawes Conference.

But these two issues, important as they were in underlining Canada's increasingly independent posture in imperial affairs, must also be seen as significant points of reference in the evolution of another relationship – that between Britain and the Irish Free State. Cautious and preoccupied in 1923 with the aftermath of the civil war, the government of W. T. Cosgrave and Kevin O'Higgins had not been prepared to take an active part at the Imperial Conference of that year, and were content to accustom themselves to the Free State's new dominion status. They were evidently pleased enough that the Irish delegation had been received on an equal footing with the other dominion contingents.[31] However, this passive approach was soon at an end. With the problems that attended the ratification of the Lausanne treaty, it is true, the Irish government were only

---

[30] King papers, J4/90: memorandum, 22 July 1924.
[31] D. Harkness, *The Restless Dominion: The Irish Free State and the British Commonwealth of Nations, 1921–1931* (London, 1969), 54.

indirectly concerned, since the Free State had not been in operation when the Turkish peace negotiations had first started. They could hardly play the role of an injured party in the manner of King. Nonetheless, for what it was worth the government deliberately dissociated themselves from the British position on the treaty – if nothing else as a small step towards differentiating Irish nationality from British nationality.[32]

The Irish Free State was more directly involved with the Dawes Conference, with the British authorities choosing from the outset to extend a conference invitation to the Dublin government despite the fact that the new dominion did not have any claims of its own to reparations payments. Along with the other dominions, then, the Free State was briefed about the conference and the problems of a large empire representation, and asked to co-operate with Britain for the sake of the conference's urgent purposes. In the event, however, the Cosgrave government proved even more implacable over the question of representation than King, refusing to the last to participate in the conference with anything less than a separate Irish representative. MacDonald's personal statement to the conference on the dominions' behalf counted for nothing as far as the Irish were concerned. Indeed it is important to note that they could not be persuaded to modify their demands even by King himself. The Canadian prime minister, once satisfied in his own mind that dominion status would not after all be threatened by the conference arrangements, felt sure the Irish government need have no further hesitations themselves and instructed his London high commissioner to point the way forward:

I believe you could do a good stroke for Canada Ireland and Inter-Allied Conference were you able to persuade Irish Free State Government ... either to appoint their own representative on status on which we have agreed for Belcourt or to name Belcourt as Ireland's representative ... Ireland should not hesitate to fall in line she will strengthen her position in eyes of British Empire and rest of world by following precedent set by Canada.[33]

But this initiative produced no results. After an interview with Desmond FitzGerald, minister for external affairs for the Free State, the Canadian high commissioner was told categorically that any compromise with Britain on this issue would mean the immediate defeat of the Cosgrave administration.[34] There was nothing more King could do to prevent the Dawes Conference proceeding without them.

The summer of 1924 thus found the Irish government in a strongly

[32] *Ibid*, 68.
[33] CO 532/277: (copy) King–Larkin, 17 July 1924.
[34] *Ibid*: Belcourt–King, 21 July, Larkin–Col Sec, 23 July 1924.

aggressive frame of mind about the status of the Free State in the empire–commonwealth. By comparison with Canada, which for so long had produced the major initiatives for devolutionary change in British–dominion relations, the Free State was already giving promise of a far more impatient and radical attitude towards its imperial connections than anything contemplated by King. The pace and scope of future developments in imperial affairs, it seemed, might now be set by the junior rather than the senior dominion. Certainly in the matter of the Dawes Conference the Canadian prime minister found himself in the novel position of holding ground between Britain and another dominion protagonist, from where he could attempt to interpret the problems of the one side to the other – an attempt that foreshadowed the role he would play at the Imperial Conference of 1926. On his own terms, of course, King had not shifted his ground at all: he would remain wary of Britain's motives in her dealings with the dominions, and cautious to a fault in preserving Canada from any tangible commonwealth responsibilities, for years to come. But a more active and determined pressure for the continued loosening of ties with Britain was now beginning to be felt from the newest and most recalcitrant member of the commonwealth association.

At this point, however, it remained to be seen exactly how far the Irish commitment to the fuller development of their constitutional capacities would bear directly upon the broader evolution of the empire–commonwealth. The Free State was a dominion, it is true, with an accepted right in 1924 to the privileges and autonomy that dominion status conveyed; and as the events of the post-war years had demonstrated, that autonomy was capable of rapid and significant enlargement. The hope, of course, was that the commonwealth relationship would provide the Free State with a satisfactory *modus vivendi*, that she would be content as a self-governing dominion to retain the wider British connection, and adjust to the established pace of change. But behind the facade of nominal constitutional similarity it was already clear that Ireland was a dominion with a crucially different past from the others, and beyond that was a nation – worse, an incomplete nation – whose constitutional and political realities gave it the barest claim to dominion status at all. The Free State constitution of 1921, with its strongly republican overtones, was far removed from the aspirations and sentiments of the other dominions (to speak of any of its terms as breaking 'new Dominion ground', as D. W. Harkness does, hardly does justice to its essential departure from existing practice[35]) and yet it had been able to go into effect, even so, only after an open civil war had eventually been abandoned by its opponents. The

[35] Harkness, *Restless Dominion*, 23.

continued strength of the unappeased republican opponents of the constitution – and of dominion status in any form – was bluntly demonstrated by the deliberate absence from the first Dublin parliament of forty-four Sinn Fein members, a group large enough to have been the official opposition party to the Cosgrove government.[36] With past and present circumstances together militating against the dominion settlement to such a degree, it is hardly surprising that the Free State administration should view the question of their relations to Britain and the commonwealth with an altogether different perspective from the other dominions, and feel constrained to press for constitutional changes as rapid and profound as possible. They were interested in modifying the commonwealth design imposed on them, but only in order to secure the greatest measure of national self-determination. Not until 1927 or 1928, it appears, were Irish political leaders prepared to acknowledge the commonwealth link itself as a valuable and useful asset to the Free State, and in doing so even at this point they were all too aware of taking a dangerously unsupported political position.[37]

It can be argued, in short, that in the period under immediate consideration, from 1923 to the Imperial Conference of 1926, the Free State government were involved in an essentially private and particular struggle to change the form of their country's association with Great Britain. It was a voyage of discovery through the constitutional grounds of dominion status, to see if the Free State really had been given, as Michael Collins had promised in 1921, the freedom to achieve freedom. If Ireland in its journey shared the same road with some of its commonwealth partners, it was still not yet clear that the overseas dominions and the offshore dominion were making for the same destination.

Certainly some misgivings about the Free State's ultimate intentions were felt in Whitehall, where the Dominions Department of the Colonial Office were beginning to assume responsibility for Irish affairs. Were they dealing with a fledgling dominion that would develop in conformity with its older associates, or an Irish cuckoo in the commonwealth nest? – until the department were sure they were not at all prepared to give the Free State the benefit of the doubt. Indeed no sooner had the Cosgrave administration assumed office in mid-1923 than the Colonial Office took pains to discover just how far they were obliged to consider the new dominion as on a par with the others. On the face of it there seemed little room for manoeuvre in this respect, any plans for constitutional *apartheid* running up against the provision in the Anglo-Irish treaty of

[36] F. S. L. Lyons, *Ireland Since the Famine* (London, 1971) 485.
[37] Harkness, *Restless Dominion*, 26.

1921 that the Free State would have exactly the same status in the empire–commonwealth as the dominion of Canada. But what the Colonial Office wished to know beyond that was whether any particular constitutional concessions that might be granted to Canada individually must now automatically accrue to Ireland as well. It was by no means a purely theoretical problem. Canada, after all, had since the war demonstrated by far the strongest determination to amplify its status as a dominion, a determination that showed no signs of diminishing. In fact Colonial Office apprehensions on this constitutional point stemmed directly in 1923 from an unprecedented Canadian request, which had unsettled Whitehall a good deal and was still under consideration, for the right to legislate extra-territorially for its citizens. In Canada's case it appeared that there might be some justification for limited powers to be granted; but in Irish hands such a privilege could easily lead to all manner of mischief and embarrassment for the British authorities. Hence the Colonial Office's anxiety to clarify and contain the Free State's constitutional position from the outset – and their relief when the British Law Officers ruled that the Irish Free State would *not* be entitled to advance constitutionally *pari passu* with Canada in this way.[38] It was a useful if limited safeguard while the Free State's intentions as a dominion were undetermined.

Thus Britain and Ireland each endeavoured to adjust to the Free State's new status, both parties keen to define the prerogatives of that status as far as possible to their own benefit, neither sure how far their relationship would bear upon the wider commonwealth association. But whatever the Free State's impact on commonwealth developments in the longer term, it was clear soon enough that the Irish government were equally prepared to make use of any relevant precedents already established by dominion initiatives. We have noted their response to the Lausanne treaty, for example: a moment when they could gratuitously support Canadian criticisms of imperial diplomacy. In 1924 a far more important question on which an appeal to precedent – again Canada's – could be made by the Cosgrave government was that of diplomatic representation at Washington. Although a Canadian minister was still to be appointed to the American capital, and although it was known in Whitehall that King would wish to modify the terms negotiated by the Borden government, nonetheless the essential principles concerning dominion representation at Washington that were established in May 1920 still stood, and when an Irish request for ministerial representation at the American capital was made in March 1924 both the Colonial Office and the Foreign Office accepted that they were bound by the Canadian precedent to come to terms

38 CO 532/257: correspondence, CO–Law Officers, July–Dec 1923.

with the Free State authorities, however little it might appeal to them.[39]

The value to the Dublin government of the earlier agreement with Canada, in fact, would be hard to over-estimate. Such was the extent of inter-departmental disagreement about an Irish minister at Washington, particularly as to his possible relations with the British ambassador, that without a precedent hanging over their heads the British government would probably have never entertained the Free State's application. (The overseas dominions were at odds as well, Canada and South Africa approving, Australia and New Zealand strongly opposing, an appointment; this division of opinion was ignored in departmental calculations.) As it was the negotiations were protracted. The Foreign Office, as ever, were determined to preserve their freedom of diplomatic action, and in this case would have conceded a virtually independent embassy to the Irish rather than take any responsibility 'for action over which they would, in fact, have no control'.[40] Only at the end were they brought to think that an Irish minister, although by agreement he was to function independently on his government's behalf, should at least be encouraged to maintain good relations with the British embassy, and seek assistance there when it was needed. But in the last analysis, as the Foreign Office indicated to the ambassador himself, a diplomatic liaison of this nature would have to rely on good faith:

The extent to which [any] help and advice can be given will depend very largely on the personal relations between the two men and upon their personal characteristics. It cannot be ensured by instructions conveyed in official documents. If the Irish Free State Minister plays the game, he may be quite certain of receiving all the help the Ambassador can give.[41]

Irish representation at Washington might be made to work, as long as the Dublin authorities would appoint a gentleman who could be trusted to 'play the game' and co-operate with the British embassy. Irish matters aside however, in the summer of 1924 MacDonald's government were inclined to wonder whether they could be as hopeful about the more general problem of co-operation and consultation with the overseas dominions. Five months in office, including more immediately their difficulties over the ratification of the Lausanne treaty, had been enough to convince the Labour government that the machinery for imperial consultation on matters of common policy suffered from severe deficiencies, and needed a

[39] CO 886/10/90: correspondence, Gov Gen Free State–FO–CO, March–July 1924.
[40] *Ibid*: FO–CO, 20 March 1924.
[41] *Ibid*: FO–British ambassador, 23 June 1924.

fundamental new appraisal. On the same day that the embassy in Washington was being instructed about the terms of appointment for the new Irish minister, the British prime minister elaborated his position on this wider issue in a message to all the dominions:

We fully accept principle of necessity for effective arrangements for continuous consultation in all important matters of common imperial concern, and for such necessary concerted action, founded in consultation, as the several Governments may determine (see Resolution ix of Imperial War Conference 1917). We also realize that action to be taken as a result of consultation whether at or between Imperial Conferences must be subject to constitutional requirements of each country.

With due allowance for such requirements, however, MacDonald was clearly aiming towards some better means of common imperial action on foreign policy, and he went on to point out how 'as a result of our experience since taking office' his government had realized British–dominion relations in this vital area left much to be desired. For one thing 'immediate action [is] extremely difficult, more especially between Conferences, on occasions when such action is imperatively needed'. Secondly, even when an imperial conference had decided on a clear line of policy, there was no guarantee that when a government fell from office its successor would necessarily endorse such policies. To consider both these critical matters the prime minister felt a conference of British and dominion ministers should meet as soon as possible.[42]

There was undoubtedly a good deal of self-criticism implicit in this approach of MacDonald to the dominions, considering that the Lausanne business aside, in the few months since taking office his own government had twice acted without regard for the dominions on questions of particular imperial concern, in precisely the ways that he was now suggesting needed special attention. In the first place, within a week or so of coming to power the Labour administration had decided to extend diplomatic recognition to Soviet Russia, with a speed that simply left no time for any prior consultations with the overseas governments. In vain had the Colonial Office instructed their new political masters on the responsibilities that they owed to the dominions before moving ahead with major foreign policy initiatives of this kind: the decision was ratified at cabinet level and the dominion governments were left to accommodate themselves to the new order of things as best they could. Then in the spring of 1924 had come what for Australia and New Zealand was a far bigger blow, when MacDonald's government repudiated the tariff concessions offered by

---

[42] CO 532/291: Col Sec–Govs Gen, 23 June 1924.

Britain at the 1923 Imperial Economic Conference, and ended at a stroke the intended advance towards tariff reform and imperial preference taken by the first Baldwin administration. What value imperial co-operation, either in foreign or economic policy, when judged in the light of these unilateral British actions? Yet, however poor the Labour government's record in this respect, the prime minister did seem genuinely anxious to meet with his dominion colleagues in conference. Indeed the somewhat naive appeal of his message for action to be taken on the basis of the 1917 constitutional resolution – as if nothing had happened to modify the development of British–dominion relations envisaged by that resolution – is itself a good indication that this new expression of British concern had come very much from MacDonald's own hand, and not from the permanent Whitehall establishment. The proposal for a constitutional conference reads far more as a call from the politicians rather than the civil servants, based quite candidly on 'our experience since taking office'.

The dominion most likely to be skeptical about MacDonald's proposals, given the bad feelings created by the Lausanne treaty affair, was Canada, and to judge from the initial reactions of O. D. Skelton at the Department of External Affairs the idea of a new conference to consider British–dominion consultation and co-operation was going to receive short shrift:

> Throughout all the discussion in England there runs the assumption that there must be unity and identity in foreign policy and in economic policy. Judged by this standard, the present situation of course presents deficiencies, and will probably present more in future. The fundamental necessity, particularly in Britain, is not the creation of new machinery, but the recognition of ... the fact that the Empire is a group of states each with its own peculiar domestic and foreign relations ... It is only insofar as the several parts of the Empire have a common concern in certain questions that the necessity for common action arises. This sphere is probably much more limited that Mr. MacDonald recognizes. Much of his present difficulties would vanish if he realized that it was his task to frame the policy, not of the British Empire, but of Great Britain and Northern Ireland.[43]

This critical distinction between national and imperial foreign policy must be firmly understood, he advised King, before any new arrangements about consultations could be considered.

Up to the end of 1923, it seems fair to suggest, the Canadian prime minister would have seen how far his own and British views on this central aspect of imperial relations were different, and would have flatly declined to expose himself to a pointless confrontation with the leaders of the other dominions. It is a mark, then, of King's growing self-confidence – and

[43] King papers, J1/109: memorandum, 26 June 1924.

more importantly a sign that by mid-1924 he felt Canada's place in the empire–commonwealth might be sufficiently independent and secure on his own terms – that he did not make Skelton's views the basis for a refusal. Once the difficulties of the Dawes Conference were satisfactorily out of the way, the prime minister indicated that Canada would be quite prepared to participate in a constitutional conference as MacDonald proposed. From much the same position of secure self-confidence, it may be added here, the Canadian government was also willing in the summer of 1924 to sanction the setting-up of an Imperial Economic Committee, though admittedly only on a limited and *ad hoc* basis, in London.[44] The 'centralist bogey' that had kept Canada out of any economic planning in the 1923 imperial discussions was now giving way, it appeared, to a policy of cautious co-operation.

The Imperial Economic Committee went forward, surviving in spite of its restricted *ad hoc* terms until the 1960s and even at the end of bequeathing its administrative experience to the new Commonwealth Secretariat, where its structures are still faintly discernible.[45] But the proposed constitutional conference did not meet, even though all the dominions agreed to take part. No firm plans had been settled by the Labour government before they fell from office in October 1924, and the succeeding Conservative administration decided very quickly not to carry the arrangements forward. Leopold Amery, returning as colonial secretary to the department he had administered with Lord Milner after the war, announced the change of policy to the dominion governments in early December.

Amery, it seems clear, had soon discovered that the Colonial Office civil servants had little enthusiasm for the intended conference with the dominions, and decided to scrap MacDonald's initiatives. For a politician who had been closely and enthusiastically involved in British–dominion affairs, however, this was no merely arbitrary step. Rather his announcement marks an important moment of transition in official government thinking about the conduct of Britain's relations with the dominions. MacDonald, running up against problems with the dominions in pursuing his foreign policy, had fallen back on the assumption that some improved system of consultation would nonetheless maintain a united imperial diplomacy. By contrast, since the 1923 Imperial Conference King had been arguing that only intermittently could foreign policy be regarded as imperial in scope, and that ordinarily the dominions would attend to their own foreign affairs. Amery, declaring now in effect that the machinery of consultation

44 External Affairs 25/D1/751: Gov Gen–Col Sec, 2 July 1924 and subsequent correspondence.
45 R. Leach, 'The Secretariat', *International Journal*, XXVI, no 2 (1971).

– whose shortcomings he knew only too well – need not for the moment
be reassessed, was indicating that he had moved a good way towards
the Canadian point of view. And there was evidence as well to suggest
that in the Colonial Office the Dominions Department were also coming
to recognize that British foreign policy might have fewer imperial overtones than hitherto admitted. In January 1925, passing comment on a
newspaper article by Professor A. B. Keith, Henry Lambert minuted:

> Prof. Keith's chief error seems to me to be his assumption that there is 'urgent
> need for a more general consideration of the best method of concerting united
> action in matters of foreign policy'. General consideration means academic
> discussions of principles and that is more likely to accentuate differences than
> lead to useful results. These latter can only be reached by patience and
> common-sense in practice.[46]

Since 1917 the department had struggled against the cabinet, the prime
minister's office, and particularly the Foreign Office, in their efforts to
provide prior consultation on foreign policy for the dominions. Now they
were beginning to wonder how much use these clients of theirs were
prepared to make of the services they provided. As they realized, collectively the dominions held few ideas in common about their place and role
in the empire–commonwealth. It was enough, then, if the department
could help sustain a measure of British–dominion co-operation on foreign
affairs in the short term, leaving the differences of outlook unexamined
and unreconciled.

So the idea of a special constitutional conference was rejected, and the
Dominions Department confined themselves to their watching brief over
British foreign policy, interceding on the dominions' behalf as they thought
necessary to keep the dominions aware of at least the major developments
in the foreign policy of the empire. It was a familiar enough role though
with the essential difference by 1925 that it was governed far less by the
department's own access to high-level policymaking in Whitehall, or constraints of that kind at all, than by the dominions themselves. The few
formal diplomatic matters with which the commonwealth governments
did choose to associate themselves alongside Britain – the best example in
these months was Britain's overtures to the United States regarding a new
conference on naval disarmament – represented very much the highest
common factor of imperial co-operation in foreign affairs. Beyond that
there was little to indicate any longer how far each government would
regard themselves committed by foreign policy conducted by the British
administration alone.

[46] CO 532/302: minute of 25 Jan 1925.

Only the Irish Free State, it appeared, remained unaware or unconvinced of the general devolutionary drift of British–dominion relations, and continued in accordance with their own particular designs to press at every opportunity for a greater measure of independence and a separate identity as a dominion. Their boldest initiative in this respect, followed very shortly after the agreement which gave them diplomatic representation at Washington, was the registration of the Anglo-Irish treaty of 1921 with the League of Nations as an international treaty, in accordance with article XVIII of the Covenant. There was very likely a specific tactical objective here, which should not be overlooked: the Irish Boundary Commission was about to examine the Free State's borders with Northern Ireland and the Cosgrave administration were endeavouring to establish a right of appeal to the League in the event that the Commission produced a verdict they could not support.[47] But boundary problems aside, the move to register the treaty was calculated to challenge the very basis of British–dominion relations as private and 'domestic' and not open to international scrutiny or regulation. As a Colonial Office memorandum on the subject was obliged to conclude,

it seems not too much to say that the effect of acceptance of the doctrine put forward by the Irish Free State would be to destroy the whole conception of the British Empire as it is now understood[48]

and the British authorities were understandably careful to establish their own (and the more constitutionally sound) case against the 1921 treaty as an international instrument. But however forceful the arguments there could be no de-registering of the treaty, which duly appeared in the annual Treaty Series published by the League of Nations secretariat. It was a telling piece of propaganda for the Free State.

Yet if the Irish government were hoping their manoeuvre at the League might lead to wider complaints about the empire's constitutional inadequacies they were disappointed, inasmuch as their action had little if any effect on the temper of Britain's relations with the overseas dominions. This lack of response was particularly significant in the circumstances of early 1925, for by that time it might be thought that one dominion at least which would endorse Ireland's manifestation of independence would be South Africa, where for several months the Nationalists under General Hertzog had been the leading element of a new coalition administration. Hertzog, it is true, was for the moment not an entirely free agent as regards South Africa's external affairs. Critical for years of Smuts' 'im-

[47] CO 532/282: minutes.
[48] CO 886/11/92: memorandum, December 1924.

perialist' leanings, he had himself come to power only through a pledge
to the Labour wing of the coalition that he would not attempt to alter the
dominion's constitutional ties with Britain, and therefore would not
perhaps have felt at liberty to support the idea, implicit in the Irish act of
registration, that imperial relations should be homologated to international
relations. In fact, however, far from maintaining a frustrated silence on
this subject Hertzog disclosed to the Colonial Office a point of view quite
different from that of the Free State. Replying in January 1925 to Amery's
news that a constitutional conference would not after all be convened, the
new South African prime minister took the opportunity to spell out
something of his own attitudes to imperial affairs. He felt satisfied, certainly that

members of the Commonwealth have *inter se* acceded wholeheartedly to [the
view that every member ... by itself constitutes a distinct National entity with
equal status] and have formed it as the basis for joint consultation and
common action in relation to foreign affairs and common interests.[49]

Thus on his own analysis, and contrary to the Free State view, the
dominions were already on adequate and equal terms with Britain, and he
went on to say that his own apprehension about commonwealth relations
did not therefore concern internal freedoms, but rather external recognition. A far greater effort was needed, he insisted, to bring foreign powers
to treat the dominions as 'distinct national entities' and in this way end
their disadvantaged position in international affairs; without that acknowledgement the self-governing commonwealth countries would remain
second-class international citizens. Here was the germ of a fresh South
African demand for greater clarification of dominion status, which the
1926 Imperial Conference would have to confront. Eighteen months and
more before that conference, however, it is clear that Hertzog, far from
pulling the commonwealth towards further constitutional changes in the
same harness as the Irish Free State, was approaching that goal very much
from a direction of his own.

King would in general have supported premier Hertzog's conviction
that the dominions had achieved a reasonable degree of equality with
Britain in their imperial relationship. Writing in January 1925 to his
assistant high commissioner in London he could speak of the 'satisfactory and pleasant [Imperial] relations which at present exist'.[50]
Nonetheless for the Canadian prime minister perpetual vigilance remained very much the price of dominion freedom, and in these same

[49] CO 532/312: Gov Gen (SA)–Col Sec, 27 Jan 1925.
[50] King papers, J1/115: King–W. L. Griffiths, 24 Jan 1925.

months he found it all too necessary to discourage fresh British efforts to provide closer liaison with the overseas governments on foreign affairs. The trouble lay with colonial secretary Leopold Amery, and his good intentions and unsparing efforts to maintain whatever consultative contacts he could with the dominions. On returning to office late in 1924, Amery felt his energies would be best directed towards an informal, more pragmatic channel of communications employing the dominion high commissioners. Though the time might have passed when Britain could act in foreign affairs with the assumed support of all the dominions, nevertheless a means was still needed – and a better means than the telegraph – by which policies could be explained, by which the dominion governments could if desired raise questions. In that way the dominions would at least be *au courant* with British thinking; at best they could confer an informal approval on British policy without committing themselves to any definite obligations. Such had been Amery's motives in arranging a meeting of the high commissioners with Baldwin, himself and the new foreign secretary, Austen Chamberlain, in November 1924. The overseas representatives were provided with a thorough briefing on League of Nations affairs and British problems in Egypt.

On receiving his high commissioner's account of this meeting, King's worst suspicions were immediately aroused, particularly when the London government followed up the briefing with a request for a statement of Canadian support over Egypt (where the murder of the British high commissioner, Sir Lee Stack, had suddenly precipitated a crisis).[51] To the governor general there was a loud verbal complaint about the idea of assisting Britain with Egypt, which to judge from the prime minister's own record amounted to a classic overstated 'domino theory' of Canada's imperial involvement:

I pointed out that [even to state the importance of keeping open the Suez Canal] unless asked for an opinion was to give advice which would have to be supplemented by preparedness to serve in case of conflict & I thought it would be most unfortunate for Canada & Gr[eat] Br[itain] for this c[oun]try to be drawn into such a position. With the U.S. keeping out of the League of Nations not to be involved in European wars for Canada to be drawn in with our present taxat[io]n & huge war debt w[oul]d mean a move towards annexation in many parts which in time it might be difficult to resist.[52]

To the high commissioner in London went a more considered but equally uncompromising analysis of what the British authorities were up to: it was

[51] Neatby, *King*, 43–4.
[52] King diary, 23 Nov 1925.

'a determined effort on the part of the Home Government to have the Dominions drawn into all matters of foreign policy regardless altogether of the extent of our interest ... [and] to form in London some sort of central council, advisory or otherwise, of the British Dominions'.[53] Canada's honour was in good hands, however. Peter Larkin convinced his chief that he had volunteered no opinions at the meeting, and at a similar gathering held at short notice in March 1925, Larkin's assistant attending in his absence promptly informed the prime minister that mindful of his earlier warnings he had not spoken a single word.[54] With regard to Canada, at least, Amery sought in vain for any informal dialogue through the high commissioner.[55]

The difficulty, of course, lay in convincing King that discussion did not imply commitment. The Canadian prime minister maintained that high commissioners meeting together constituted a 'conference', nothing less, and as he explained to Larkin, it was the Canadian cabinet 'who will be held responsible for the outcome of [any such] conferences', and who should therefore have formal notice of what was to be discussed – a proviso that cut across any notion of informality. In this regard, as it happened, a pertinent idea was put forward to British ministers by Philip Kerr. To confer with the high commissioners in a group, he suggested to foreign secretary Austen Chamberlain (in anticipation of King's own reaction), 'would immediately create the impression that some new and secret imperial organization was being created', and he therefore urged Chamberlain to see them only individually, and to treat them exactly as he would the ambassadors of allied states. In this way an essential personal contact could be established without suspicion or fear.[56]

Kerr's analysis, however, offended against Chamberlain's view of the empire. High commissioners must not be thought of as ambassadors, he insisted in turn to Amery, precisely because 'the essence of our policy is that the British Empire is one and indivisible'; to make any concessions on the lines suggested by Kerr 'would be a recognition of separatist feeling, and a denial of unity'.[57] A public statement, dwelling on the responsibilities of his new office, had already confirmed Chamberlain's strong private feelings:

[53] King papers, J1/103: King–Larkin, 12 Dec 1924.
[54] King papers, J1/122: L. Pacaud–King, 24 March 1925.
[55] Amery recalls that at the suggestion of Larkin the planned policy briefings degenerated into weekly 'at home' sessions when he merely chatted to the high commissioners. No correspondence regarding such meetings is to be found in the King papers, however.
[56] Chamberlain papers: Kerr–Chamberlain, 18 Nov 1924.
[57] *Ibid*: Chamberlain–Amery, 25 Nov 1924.

The first thoughts of an Englishman on appointment to the office of Foreign Secretary must be that he speaks in the name, not of Great Britain only, but of the British Dominions beyond the seas, and that it is his imperative duty to preserve in word and act the diplomatic unity of the British Empire.[58]

Small wonder that King felt obliged to react so strongly to the high commissioners' November briefing on foreign affairs.

Yet one should not take these initial reflections of the foreign secretary too literally. Behind Chamberlain was a department that since 1923 had consistently sought their independence from the diplomatic affairs of the dominions, and were unlikely to put imperial unity before freedom of action. And after only a few weeks in office, a candid personal memorandum from Chamberlain written for Amery showed that the new foreign secretary was prepared after all to be realistic about imperial relations.[59] If the dominion governments wanted information or consultation on policy he would see their representatives, he promised, and he acknowledged that there might be problems keeping a suspicious Canadian government briefed on British policies. But the emphasis of the memorandum, in any case, was upon practicalities:

There are crises in which someone must act at once. Apart from the Dominion aspect and in so far as these can be treated by us as domestic, we recognize this . . . but it is very necessary to insist that the Empire shall not be paralysed in an emergency because conditions of time and space prevent a meeting of the seven Prime Ministers at a couple of hours' notice.

MacDonald had recognized the dilemma and called for a conference to discuss it. Chamberlain simply reasserted Foreign Office priorities: action, and if possible (or desired) consultation.

The action, it is true, might well continue to be taken in the name of the empire – for all that Chamberlain acknowledged Canadian susceptibilities, he was not willing to cease thinking in imperial terms. Lord Curzon, Skelton remarked to King, had tended to think that 'the British Empire' meant Britain's empire.[60] Chamberlain had perhaps the same cast of mind. But by the time he accepted the seals of his office the advancing independence of the dominions had given the phrase an altogether more tentative significance. Within the imperial context it was now necessary to distinguish and to make allowance for the British commonwealth of nations.

[58] Speech of 10 Nov 1924, quoted in Neatby, *King*, 40.
[59] CO 532/274: memorandum 'for the information of Mr Amery and for such use as he may think fit to make of it', 20 Dec 1924.
[60] King papers, J1/109: Skelton–King, 14 April 1924.

Imperial diplomacy and the League of Nations

In one important area of foreign policy the distinction between empire and commonwealth was more than usually shrouded in both legal and practical ambiguities. On the Council of the League of Nations sat a 'British Empire' representative, and when in December 1924 Chamberlain occupied the seat personally for a session of the council, and chose to reiterate that he spoke there not in the name of Great Britain only but of the whole British empire, the weight of his remarks was not merely rhetorical. But neither were the reactions that they provoked. For example, the *Washington Post*, recalling America's earlier refusal to take its place in the League of Nations, was quick to argue that Chamberlain's speech bore out

what was from the first maintained by critics of the League, that the six (now seven) British votes would be, at least whenever the imperial government desired it, cast as an indivisible bloc and count as six (or seven) votes in the Assembly against the one vote of any other power.[61]

In a different quarter, Chamberlain's statement also brought sharp protests to Mackenzie King by some Canadian nationalists, alarmed their country's status was being traduced by the British foreign secretary; and from inside the Canadian administration O. D. Skelton took the occasion to add his own influential voice to this chorus of Canadian complaints. In a memorandum to the prime minister he warned:

If our position in the League is not to be hopelessly prejudiced, and if the dogma 'one Empire foreign policy' is not to be accepted, it will be necessary to review the whole question [of the position of the dominions in the League] soon, and in the meantime to prevent as far as possible being committed to this attitude.[62]

King did what he could to reassure this disturbed body of nationalist opinion, pointing out that the British foreign secretary had had no authorization from Canada to speak at the League Council in these terms. But he was obliged to admit nonetheless that 'there is a certain amount of vagueness in the position of Great Britain and the Dominions in the League'.[63] As we have seen above, as early as 1920 the status of the 'British Empire' member of the Council had created difficulties and misunderstandings between the mother country and the overseas governments, and had led Canada (and Australia and South Africa as well) to assume

[61] External Affairs, 25/D1/727/80: memorandum, Jan 1925, citing *Washington Post*, 11 Dec 1924.
[62] *Ibid.*
[63] King papers, J1/125: King–Sir Clifford Sifton, 22 Jan 1925.

in practice that the Council representative did not speak on the dominions' behalf.[64] This lack of definition may be taken, nevertheless, as symptomatic of a wider ambivalence throughout the period about dominion status and imperial diplomacy at the League of Nations.

Membership in the League was from the outset claimed as the hallmark of the dominions' post-war status, a justified extension beyond the constitutional aspirations that they had laid claim to in 1917. Through the League, in fact, the dominions had added an entirely new dimension to their status in being given access to the basic privileges, at the very least, of fully international states. From this development, quite unforeseen in 1917, came an important shift in the terms used to place the dominions in the empire's constitutional framework. They had hitherto been regarded as 'autonomous nations of an Imperial Commonwealth'. After 1919, however, emphasis was increasingly placed upon their status of equality with Great Britain – an altogether more ambitious designation.

The Canadian government in particular chose quite openly to assert their equal status at the League, as witness their deliberately independent voting at the first Assembly. More dramatic however, was the sustained Canadian campaign against article x of the League Covenant, the critical guarantee clause under whose terms the members of the League were pledged to uphold each other's territorial integrity. Canada's opposition to this article had begun in Paris, as the League's regulations were being drafted, with the root-and-branch antipathy of Borden and his ministerial colleagues to any such stringent conditions of membership; and it led the dominion's delegation to the first Assembly in 1920 to table an explicit motion calling for the complete removal of article x from the Covenant. The assembly responded by appointing a committee on amendments to consider the motion further, and not until the second Assembly in 1921 was there a debate on the issue – though again no conclusions were reached, and the question was put forward once more. Bureaucratic procrastination had its limits, however and it was soon after this that the League authorities showed signs that Canada's unflinching hostility to article x was being taken seriously, to the extent that a sub-committee of the League Council were appointed to give their own consideration to the implications of the offending article. Under the scrupulous chairmanship of Arthur Balfour, they felt able to conclude semi-officially that article x would not after all impose definite and fixed military obligations upon League members.[65] It seemed that Canada could abandon its campaign for abolition with honour. But with the subject down for formal consideration

[64] See above, 113-14.
[65] CO 532/251: FO memorandum (Aug 1923).

at the 1922 third Assembly the new Canadian delegation (now representing King's Liberal government) decided to press on, no longer for
abolition but instead for an amendment that would formally limit each
member's commitments. Though as W. S. Fielding confessed to King from
Geneva, 'we were not very anxious to have anything done and only took
up the case because it had been left on the order paper'.[66]

In the wake of the Chanak crisis, however, the final stages of the
Canadian campaign against article x became somewhat more aggressive,
representing not only the dominion's continuing anxieties about League
responsibilities but also King's claims to the freedom of Canadian diplomatic action. The Assembly had managed to defer judgement on the new
idea of a formal amendment to the 1923 session. But when the British
government arranged an inter-imperial discussion of the Canadian proposals in London prior to the opening of that session, in the attempt to see
if differences with the Canadian position could be resolved, King refused
to confer on the matter and sent his delegates directly to Geneva.[67] Yet in
the end this decision to play a lone hand at the League did not bring
Canada any nearer to a conclusive result. An amendment to the Covenant,
it turned out, was in any event out of the question, because of the opposition of too many influential member states. And when as a last resort the
Canadian delegation tried to make their case by submitting an 'interpretive
resolution' to the Assembly, it was only to see this device fail as well. By
one vote it fell short of the unanimity necessary for such motions, and it
therefore remained no more than a practical guide to international opinion
about article x.[68] Nonetheless it was by no means an empty victory.
Successive Canadian administrations, convinced from the outset that man-
datory military obligations had no place in any League of Nations, had
shown sufficient determination – and quite clearly had carried the burden
of the tacit misgivings on this matter of a good many other member
nations – to produce an open reappraisal of League policy. The League
was hardly made a more effective instrument for their efforts. If nothing
else, however, the decision emphasized that the search for collective security would have to look for solutions more sophisticated than the simple
phrases of article x.

Although the King government had pursued a deliberately independent
initiative against article x, they had no desire to entrench themselves in a

---

[66] King papers, J1/73: Fielding–King, 15 Sept 1922.
[67] CO 886/10/88: Gov Gen–Col Sec, 25 Aug; CO 532/251: C. W. Dixon, minute
of 28 Aug 1923.
[68] The vote was 29–1, Persia alone opposing, with 22 abstentions. The rest of the
commonwealth members voted for the resolution.

position of calculated defiance of Great Britain in their other dealings with the League. This was shown clearly enough when the League – to an important extent as a direct response to the persistent Canadian criticism of article x – undertook a more thorough exploration of the related problems of collective security, disarmament and the arbitration of international disagreements. In 1923 their deliberations gave rise first to a draft Treaty of Mutual Guarantee, and following that to the Geneva Protocol for settling international disputes. With both these proposals the Canadian government might well have considered themselves involved at a purely international level. Yet in both instances they welcomed consultation with the British government, specifically with a view to forming an imperial consensus, and to this end a general exchange of attitudes regarding the Treaty of Mutual Guarantee took place between Britain and the dominions in the first six months of 1924. Britain's final objections were circulated to the dominion governments in May, and in a reply of 12 June the Canadian government indicated that their own reply would 'not be despatched ... until His Majesty's Government has signified concurrence therein'. After receiving British approval it was sent on 9 July 1924.

The Geneva Protocol was similarly discussed in late 1924 and early 1925, and again King agreed 'that it is highly desirable that similar attitudes should be adopted towards Protocol' by the British members of the League.[69] Amery was prepared to organize a special meeting of the Imperial Conference for this purpose, a suggestion which proved impracticable, though King noted that if consultation by cable and dispatch were found inadequate he would seriously consider the idea. As it was, a mass of British departmental papers on the Protocol gave Canada and the other dominions a fully-documented insight into the home government's reflections, and assisted each of them towards the conclusion that the objections to the scheme were ultimately insurmountable. With their consent Austen Chamberlain announced their rejection of the Protocol, and that of his own government, in the League Council in March 1925.

At least in Canada's case, however, it would be wrong to dismiss these dominion reflections on the Geneva Protocol as an empty ritual, a mere acceptance of British conclusions based on British policy documents. On the contrary, King's government went into the question of the Protocol with admirable thoroughness from their own point of view, treating the issue in effect as the first serious exercise in Canadian policymaking for the Skelton-directed Department of External Affairs. In addition to the British papers, numerous individual memoranda were commissioned from

[69] CO 886/11/94: Gov Gen–Col Sec, 29 Dec 1924.

civil servants and military personnel in Ottawa and a special inter-departmental committee was established to weigh up all the evidence and make final recommendations.[70] From their deliberations came a carefully-articulated *Canadian* position on the Protocol, which they felt bound to oppose as much for North American reasons as for any imperial or European criteria. They had to accept the impossibility, for instance, of imposing sanctions upon the United States should that country – not a party to the League or the Protocol – trade with a country deemed an 'aggressor' in an international dispute. Indeed the committee report was frank enough to provide a further insight into the Canadian 'official mind' of 1924–25 on League affairs more generally:

It is unlikely that the Covenant would have taken its present form or have been signed by Canada, had it not been expected that the United States would enter the League. It would be unwise now to reaffirm and strengthen the commitments made in that expectation.[71]

Canada's rejection of the Protocol, in short, was very much its own decision. Under the circumstances it was only to be regretted, though perhaps not to be wondered at, that so much official administrative effort in Ottawa should have been accompanied by so little public interest about the Protocol across the country. With touching concern the prime minister was himself obliged to admit, in a letter to N. W. Rowell (a keen promoter of League interests in the dominion),

the lack of any real public opinion in Canada on the question of the Protocol. It is quite true that, aside from Sir Robert Borden, Senator Dandurand, and yourself, and a few newspapers, including the *Manitoba Free Press* ... the Protocol has received very little considered attention. That may be partly a defect in the existing methods of thrashing out vital public issues and expressing the conclusions arrived at, or it may be a silent verdict, right or wrong, to the effect that the proposals of the Protocol do not concern Canada.[72]

Alas the image of the King government 'thrashing out vital public issues' displays the prime minister in one of his wilder flights of self-justifying fancy! By 1925, unfortunately, parliamentary and public attention had focused on nothing more substantial in League affairs than Canada's annual contribution to the organization's expenses.[73] More

[70] External Affairs, 25/D1/813–14: memoranda etc.

[71] *Ibid*: committee report, 5 March 1925.

[72] Rowell papers: King–Rowell, 10 May 1925. (Dandurand was a member of the 1925 Canadian delegation to the League, and elected president of the Assembly that year).

[73] H. Skilling, *Canadian Representation Abroad* (Toronto, 1945), 154.

relevant by far to King's style of political management – in this as in so many aspects of Canada's external affairs – were the 'silent verdicts' that he had learned to listen for so well.

Thus all things considered, the empire's unity of approach manifested over the Treaty of Mutual Guarantee and the Geneva Protocol, although it was the legitimate expression of collective imperial policymaking, did not necessarily reflect any comprehensive agreement within the empire about international security. Unity of view did not stem from unity of purpose. The British government rejected the two instruments because they were deemed impractical; but the Canadian government, for one, did so for its own additional reasons, which certainly included a profound antipathy to the notion of collective security. (The government of the Irish Free State, it should be added, rejected the Protocol too – but at the same time explicitly repudiated any suggestion that it was acting in unity with Britain and the other dominions.[74]) And when from the ashes of the Protocol there arose a new proposal for the maintenance of Europe's northern frontiers, the underlying differences of attitude amongst Britain and her commonwealth partners were soon apparent. On 20 March 1925, back from the League Council, Chamberlain won cabinet approval for further talks on security with France, Belgium, Germany and Poland, and three days later the dominion high commissioners were assembled to hear the foreign secretary expound upon the new possibilities. He pleaded for their help in gaining the support of their governments for his efforts. But here we have moved away from League of Nations affairs and back to the troubled course of British foreign policy. For this was the meeting attended in the absence of the Canadian high commissioner by Lucien Pacaud, his assistant – a meeting whose format and intentions Mackenzie King had condemned out of hand three months before it took place. As noted above, Pacaud therefore held his silence,[75] which in the coming months King was scrupulously to maintain. Meanwhile, the British foreign secretary moved steadily forward in his European negotiations towards the treaties of Locarno – a step which carried him past a further critical milestone away from the empire's diplomatic unity.

The Locarno treaties

When Chamberlain's new round of European talks began in late March 1925, the British government were hopeful that the issues of continental security under negotiation would prove straightforward enough to allow some measure of concurrent consultation with the dominions by cable.

[74] Harkness, *Restless Dominion*, 70.
[75] See above, 233.

However, as the discussions proceeded it was apparent soon enough that the tentative nature of their progress, indefinable from day to day, ruled out the possibility that the foreign secretary's diplomacy might be guided by an imperial dialogue. At best the Colonial Office were able to supply the overseas governments with accounts of the main points of agreement coming from Locarno, and these were not accounts on which considered dominion views were invited. Thus, apart from an initial word of encouragement from the New Zealand government, and a subsequent private expression of misgiving from Australia's prime minister Bruce, there were no clearly defined dominion attitudes about European security for Chamberlain to make reference to during the course of his negotiations.

Notwithstanding the lack of consultation with the overseas governments, the foreign secretary could hardly be unaware of the possible conflict of interest between a security pact in Europe and the diplomatic unity of the empire, and indeed he had had no easy task in persuading his ministerial colleagues that the two might be reconciled. As early as January 1925, in fact, a high-level government committee set up to consider alternatives to the Geneva Protocol had already realized that the limits of dominion support for any European security treaty were bound to be narrow, and had concluded that the best British policy would, therefore, be a simple promise to defend the integrity of the Channel ports west of the Rhine. Such a guarantee, it was noted, 'went as far as it was possible to ask the Dominions and India to assent to, in the direction of meeting French and Belgian anxieties for security'.[76] Thus when Chamberlain indicated subsequently that he might have to pursue European security a good deal further into the continental interior there were understandably some misgivings within the British cabinet. Against him in particular on this issue was Amery, who argued that the empire should remain aloof from European problems and who in early March – when Chamberlain himself was absent taking soundings on the continent – nearly won the cabinet round to his point of view. A hasty letter to his chief from Sir Eyre Crowe at the Foreign Office, summarizing the cabinet discussions with an acid pen, alerted the foreign secretary to his opponent's efforts:

Mr. Amery, as usual, dilated on the impossibility of doing anything, because the Dominions would never agree to anything being done. All that was required was to avoid the danger of any talk of entanglements . . . I confess I have never heard even Mr. Ramsay MacDonald, in his most woolly-headed pronouncements, talk such utter rubbish as Mr. Amery poured forth.[77]

[76] CAB 16/56: CID report 559 B, Jan 1925.
[77] Chamberlain papers: Crowe–Chamberlain, 12 March 1925. See also K. Middlemas and J. Barnes, *Baldwin, A Biography* (London, 1969), 352 ff.

Chamberlain returned to London in time to consolidate his position and secure the necessary mandate to continue his negotiations unhampered. But as late as mid-June 1925 Amery had to admit to the foreign secretary

that I have acquiesced as far as I have done a good deal because I have thought that in the end what we shall commit ourselves and the Empire to is something so remote and contingent that we are not likely in fact ever to be called on to intervene, and that the Pact will consequently from an inter-Imperial point of view, serve as a warning rather than create [disunity] [78]

Two months later, with the outlines of a European agreement becoming clearer, the colonial secretary was to be found still on the same theme, this time more questionably making light of his government's endeavours in a letter to King:

The whole thing is in fact an effort to use Britain's influence and guarantee to bring about real peace between France and Germany with a very contingent obligation to act against either party if they wantonly violate it, an obligation the conditions of which I can hardly imagine likely to be realized. [79]

Even as the Locarno treaties were taking shape, it might thus be noted in retrospect, considerations of empire unity were already beginning to lead statesmen of Amery's disposition towards a policy of appeasement.

Throughout the Locarno negotiations Chamberlain's vision was broader than Amery's. He too was moved by considerations of a united imperial foreign policy, but from within a very different context of diplomatic and strategic practicalities. In the first place he had harboured no illusions as to the participation of dominion ministers in the diplomatic proceedings themselves. Nor could he suit his diplomacy to the dominions' convenience. As he explained to the House of Commons after the treaties were completed:

I could not go, as the representative of His Majesty's Government, to meeting after meeting . . . to conference after conference . . . and say 'Great Britain is without a policy. We have not yet been able to meet all the governments of the Empire, and we can do nothing.' That might be possible for an Empire wholly removed from Europe . . . It was not possible for an Empire the heart of which lies in Europe. [80]

Here was Chamberlain's strongest conviction – that the empire's security was hostage to the international relations of Europe, and that without

[78] Chamberlain papers: Amery–Chamberlain, 15 June 1925.
[79] King papers, J1/111: Amery–King, 11 Aug 1925.
[80] GB, HoC, 18 Nov 1925.

British participation those relations would never be made stable. 'If we withdraw from Europe', he prophesied to Amery, 'I say without hesitation that the chance of permanent peace is gone and that the world must make up its mind that sooner or later – perhaps in a couple of generations – a new disaster will fall upon us and civilization itself may perish. The suggestion for a mutual pact offers the one way out.'[81] In such circumstances he could not withhold a British guarantee to Europe for want of prior dominion consent. He was not deterred, therefore, by a complaint from the Australian premier that without consultation he was committing the empire to make war. If the dominions would admit that Britain's defence was an imperial interest, then they must also understand that the first line of that defence was now on the Rhine.

Chamberlain was confident that he was acting in the best interests of all the governments of the empire. Others were not so sure. For instance *The Round Table*, shrewdly observing events from the imperial perspective, while initially it had admitted the validity of the 'Rhine frontier' thesis[82] was severely critical of Chamberlain once the final terms of the Locarno agreements were known. The foreign secretary, it thought, had accepted far too much responsibility for the sanctity of this new frontier:

We are now, to all intents and purposes, making the frontiers both of France *and Germany* in the Rhineland part of the frontiers of the British Empire, and to that extent putting it within the discretion of European Powers to determine when Great Britain is to go to war on the continent of Europe.[83]

Beyond this, it also remained the case that on an international issue of first-rate importance the foreign secretary had chosen deliberately to act without recourse to any machinery for collective imperial policymaking. He himself was the first to regret that an imperial conference could not have been convened in the spring of 1925, for he was convinced that he could have secured full overseas support for a European security pact. 'As it is', he admitted to Amery, 'all that we can do is to leave to the Dominions their full liberty of action', and in the final Locarno agreements that liberty was set out clearly enough. But in any event Chamberlain could not accept that the security pact would represent a radical departure from imperial diplomatic practice. The principle of 'dominion option', after all, had been recognized as early as 1919, when Britain and America had proposed a guarantee treaty with France. It was reiterated in early

81 Chamberlain papers: Chamberlain–Amery, 19 June 1925.
82 *The Round Table*, xv, no 3 (1924–5); Chamberlain papers: Chamberlain–Philip Kerr, 6 April 1925. Chamberlain had written asking for support for his ideas from the magazine.
83 *The Round Table*, xvi, no 1 (1925–6).

1922 during further bilateral talks on security between Britain and France. He agreed it was not an ideal arrangement: 'but in the present constitution of the Empire Government after Government has found that it was the only course which it was within their power to take.'[84]

Chamberlain's appeal to these earlier precedents did give his own diplomatic practice a certain plausibility. In 1925, even so, the effect upon imperial relations of an independent British undertaking of this nature, with nothing more tangible than an option clause as a means of involving the dominions in the treatymaking process, was quite different from what it would have been in 1919 or 1922. To be sure, the earlier agreements had granted the overseas governments the right to dissociate themselves from prior military commitments, and in 1919 it had been known that South Africa had intended to opt out. (The 1922 talks had been abandoned at a much more tentative stage.) Yet within the context of the empire's diplomatic unity, this new formula had signified only that in exceptional circumstances Britain herself might have to go beyond the writ of a collective imperial foreign policy. By the time of Locarno, with the dominions far freer in principle to conduct foreign affairs on their own prerogative, the substantial diplomatic unity of the empire could no longer be taken for granted in the same way. Indeed, such unity depended now to a far greater extent upon the positive sanction of the overseas governments, and had come therefore to have a much more tentative and limited application to foreign policy. In these altered circumstances Chamberlain's major new initiative in European security matters could hardly be construed as merely one more exception to the general rule. Rather, it strongly confirmed a growing trend towards independent diplomatic action amongst the self-governing partners of the empire–commonwealth.

Reactions to the Locarno treaties in the dominion capitals, ranging from unquestioned support to unqualified rejection, further underlined the fragmenting multiplicity of views about the empire's foreign policy. New Zealand and Australia both endorsed the new British commitments in Europe, and in New Zealand's case the government were ready to carry their approval through to a formal act of parliamentary ratification. Positive assent could scarcely go further. But the other dominions, by degrees, proved unwilling to offer their support. From Pretoria, Hertzog made it known that South Africa would not accept any of Locarno's responsibilities – a decision which evoked no surprise in Whitehall and little interest, it seems, in the dominion itself. 'There is a great apathy in South Africa over these great issues', a despondent General Smuts

84 Chamberlain papers: Chamberlain–Amery, 5 Aug 1925.

admitted to Sir Robert Borden in December 1925, and it was undeniably Smuts in opposition rather than Hertzog in power who was moved to dwell on the implications of the new treaties:

Locarno has done good work [he went on to Borden] by getting Germany into the League. But from the Empire point of view a very evil precedent has been set. The British Empire Delegation for which you and other Imperial statesmen were responsible seems to have disappeared and the united front broken. Will it ever be restored again? ...[A] development such as this holds the seed of future decay and dissolution for the Empire.[85]

If Smuts was dismayed, there were evidently few people in South Africa who shared his feelings. Indeed it was ironic that it should be the Irish Free State government in Dublin who were far closer to Smuts' train of thought about Locarno, fully alive themselves to the dangers – or as they would see it, the possibilities – of imperial disintegration that were inherent in the new security pact. Thus the Cosgrave administration welcomed the chance to proclaim the Free State's lack of adherence to the treaties, not because of doubts about the treaties themselves but simply in order to stress their own separateness from Great Britain.[86] For them, Locarno became a further significant step along the commonwealth route to national independence.

In Ottawa too, the Locarno treaties were regarded as being of little direct concern to Canada. In the first place, the way they had been negotiated seemed to indicate a marked lack of interest on Britain's part in collective imperial policymaking, as O. D. Skelton pointed out to King:

In any case it is the British Government, not the Dominion Governments, which has declared against diplomatic unity. It decided to go ahead with these negotiations and sign the treaties without consulting the Dominions. It decided also to insert the optional clause.[87]

But this apart, the explicit continental obligations entailed in the treaties were of dubious relevance to Canada:

If a case can be made out for a guarantee by Britain it by no means follows that Canada has a similar interest or similar duty. Britain is part of Europe, Canada separated by three thousand miles of sea and incalculable differences in culture, in problems, in outlook. We are British North America; Britain is British West Europe ... Is it not now Europe's part to look after itself?[88]

[85] Rowell papers: (copy) Smuts–Borden, 23 Dec 1925. Cf a speech of 11 November 1925, quoted in *The Round Table*, xvi, no 1 (1925–26).

[86] Harkness, *Restless Dominion*, 72.

[87] King papers, J4/92: memorandum, 1 Jan 1926.

[88] *Ibid.*

It was in any event unlikely that King and his cabinet would have looked for reasons to challenge Skelton's guidance, though as it happened there was even more of an excuse for them to endorse his opinions. At a general election held in late October 1925 the Liberal party had lost a good deal of political support, and were clinging desperately to office with a minority government. It was not a moment to let problems of external policy add to the worries of an already barely tenable position, and after considering Skelton's brief the ministry had no hesitation in steering clear of Locarno.

For Skelton, who had of course been endeavouring to pull the Canadian government away from imperial responsibilities for a number of years, the Locarno treaties simply reinforced the logic of his nationalist point of view. More significant by far in this respect were the views of Loring Christie, Skelton's predecessor as chief adviser on external affairs and hitherto a committed exponent of Canada's participation in a united imperial foreign policy. With the Locarno agreements, as Britain gave notice of a shift from a traditional position of non-alignment towards involvement in the problems of continental security, Christie was convinced that the foundations of a meaningful co-operative imperial diplomacy were being fatally undermined. Such co-operation had after all presupposed a fundamental unity of interest shared between Britain and the dominions, at least with regard to the broad outlines of foreign policy. Even when in practice co-operative policymaking had tended to be honoured more in the breach than the observance by the British authorities, nonetheless one could still assume the existence of an underlying common imperial point of view. But now Britain was giving notice of a long-term strategic commitment to Europe, one which her commonwealth partners could not be expected to share – and yet equally a commitment they had no right to keep Britain from entering into. In Christie's view it was therefore incumbent on Canada, at least, to establish her independence from the mother country's radically altered position. Writing from England to his former chief Sir Robert Borden he made clear his changed attitude:

I cannot escape the conviction that . . . in order to play our unique part in the English-speaking world we must assume a more independent and detached position than existing forms allow us; that we cannot afford to wait long in thinking it out; that we cannot expect the other Dominions from an entirely different position to see a similar need.[89]

And when Philip Kerr at *The Round Table* insisted the empire could survive the strain of Britain's new moves in Europe, Christie was determined to disabuse him of his illusions:

[89] Meighen papers: (copy) Christie–Borden, 25 Feb 1926.

To be specific it is going much too far to say today that a Locarno war would necessarily be a world war in which Canada must play precisely the part that Great Britain might have to play. Whether Canada in such a case ought to be at war at once or at all, what she ought to do and so on, are not questions that are [easily] calculable ... [But it] would be monstrous to insist that Canada must declare herself for ever bound to the orbit of the affair between the Frenchman and the German.[90]

In Christie's reappraisal, and in Skelton's cool discrimination between British and Canadian strategic security, a new element in Canada's imperial relations was emerging. Both argued the need for Canada to pursue her own course in foreign affairs – in itself nothing new. Yet in both cases the overriding concern was not merely for diplomatic freedom but for freedom from the consequences of British foreign policy, which in the Locarno treaties had taken such a decided turn towards Europe. This reaction to Locarno is perhaps best viewed in comparison with some remarks of Sir Edward Grey, made at the 1911 Imperial Conference. For the benefit of those dominions whose thoughts were turning to separate local navies, the British foreign secretary had issued a warning against straying from a commonly accepted foreign policy:

If the actions of the forces in different parts of the Empire is determined by divergent views of foreign policy, it is obvious that there cannot be union, and the Empire would not consent to share an unlimited liability, the risks of which it cannot gauge, because this liability would be imposed upon it by different parts of the Empire having different policies.[91]

Fifteen years later it was Britain herself who had deliberately moved away from an imperial foreign policy – and Canada who was making claims to her freedom of action.

[90] Christie papers, 26/106: Christie–Kerr, 15 March 1926.
[91] Quoted in Hankey, *Supreme Command*, I, 128.

8

The 1926 Imperial Conference: equality defined

The 1926 Imperial Conference was convened against the background of the Locarno treaties, and, if nothing else, was intended to provide a forum for the detailed, confidential discussion of the treaties so conspicuous by its absence during the actual course of their negotiation. The precise measure of this new British commitment to European continental security, and, notwithstanding the various initial reactions of dominion leaders, the extent to which it could conceivably be incorporated into the fabric of British–dominion relations were both matters for careful assessment at the conference. Within Whitehall there was noticeable concern that the Locarno treaties must be frankly and satisfactorily justified to the dominion delegations when they reached London. True to form, the Colonial Office tended to view the ramifications of Locarno from the legal and constitutional angle, and saw that there were a number of awkward questions that would have to be resolved, whatever the dominions ultimately chose to do. The Foreign Office, equally consistent with past responses, displayed a more practical cast of mind – though not entirely in self-interest. Admitting the seriousness of the lack of prior consultation over Locarno, they took steps during 1926 to establish a better flow of communications on foreign affairs to the dominion capitals. But for a department that had seldom been prepared to apologize to the rest of the empire for the direction and purposes of its policies such acts of contrition were strictly limited, and in general Foreign Office officials were inclined to think that the Locarno treaties would not in the end demand any special pleading from the British government before the bar of the Imperial Conference. Placed in their full diplomatic context the treaties represented not any unwarranted or radical British incursion into European affairs but a calculated defence of the empire's interests as a whole. The peace they were designed to ensure would benefit dominions and mother country alike, while in any wars resulting from them Britain would undoubtedly act only in self-defence, with a strong moral claim to the support of her self-governing commonwealth partners. It remained to be seen, however, how far the dominions could be brought to accept this expedient line of reasoning.

It had long been realized that the Imperial Conference of 1926 would be asked to consider constitutional questions of one kind or another, perhaps of a far-reaching nature, and by the beginning of the year moves were already under way in Whitehall to prepare the ground for such discussions. Shaped by the compulsive influence of Leopold Amery, British strategy became to anticipate and formulate concessions to as wide a range of specific demands as possible, so that any probing of the empire's underlying constitutional principles would be seen to be unnecessary, even undesirable. Amery's restructuring of his own department, from which came a new Dominions Office designed to elevate British–dominion relations to a more exclusive, egalitarian plane, seemed an excellent case in point. But during the summer of 1926 it became clear that administrative gestures, even on such a grand scale, would not relieve constitutional restlessness in all dominion quarters. From Pretoria, General Hertzog, appreciating at last the efforts made earlier by his old adversary Smuts, gave warning that South Africa must demand a definite, publishable statement on equality of status from the conference. The Irish Free State also appeared unlikely to be appeased by piecemeal reforms. And even though their own designs might bear less directly upon the commonwealth's broader development, the disturbing possibility of a combined Irish–South African thrust at the conference could not be ruled out.

In these calculations Canada was more of an unknown factor, in both figurative and literal terms. The Mackenzie King of 1923 – inexperienced, suspicious, truculent – had given way to a far more composed statesman, who was finding the devolutionary pace and trend of the empire–commonwealth increasingly to his satisfaction. Unexpectedly this benign outlook on events was badly shaken in June 1926 by a major constitutional dispute with the Canadian governor general Lord Byng, and in the end King found himself in a position where he only knew he was to represent Canada at the Imperial Conference two weeks before he had to sail. Nonetheless his role at the conference was an important one, for a great deal was to turn on the extent to which he would support, or oppose, the constitutional claims of the more insistent South African and Irish leaders.

The impact of Locarno

Until the British and dominion heads of government had met to consider the Locarno treaties fully amongst themselves and to reach any final collective conclusions, the authorities in London confined themselves to acknowledging without observation the various responses to the treaties that reached them from dominion quarters. Assuming meanwhile that the best opportunity for an adequate discussion of Locarno would be provided by an imperial conference, in late 1925 they set about finding a generally convenient conference date. It is an indication that the expectations of Austen Chamberlain and the Foreign Office about the outcome of any such discussions were probably not very high, however, that they displayed no great anxiety over the calling of a particularly early meeting with the dominions. Initially, plans were considered in Whitehall for an imperial conference to be held at any time up to the end of 1927, fully twenty-four months away.

Despite this apparent lack of urgency, there were nonetheless signs that the Foreign Office were beginning to realize how critically the Locarno treaties had called into question the principle of the empire's unity of policy in foreign affairs, and that they were concerned to make some amends. Even as he had placed the finished treaties before the British House of Commons in November 1925, the foreign secretary had voiced the hope that means could be found 'by which our foreign policy can become in every act and at every hour the foreign policy of the Empire and not the foreign policy of this country alone'.[1] Early in the new year an internal Foreign Office memorandum by P. A. Koppell took up this question at greater length. Koppell, a high-ranking departmental counsellor, endeavoured to draw his colleagues' attention to the variety of difficulties that persisted in inhibiting any concerted British–dominion conduct of foreign affairs, and saw fit to warn that unless a number of administrative changes could be put in hand at the British end the 'important link' of imperial diplomatic unity was in danger of breaking completely.[2] Circulated through the Office to the various section heads Koppell's memorandum was warmly received, albeit in a spirit of sympathy rather than one of thorough-going reform: it evoked no definite promises to bring the dominions more closely into consultation over foreign policy. But it did reveal a limited degree of guilt about the dominions in the department, and it was to be instrumental later in the year in the creation of a new Foreign Office unit to supervise and expand the flow of diplomatic policy papers out to the dominions. Although this was not exactly breaking new ground – in 1922 the Chanak crisis had stimulated a similar response from Whitehall – at least it showed a willingness to keep the dominions in closer touch with departmental thinking. Chamberlain for his own part continued to wish, somewhat forlornly, that the high

[1] HoC, 18 Nov 1925, quoted in Hall, *Commonwealth*, 559.
[2] FO 372/2197: memorandum on Consultation with, and Communication of Information to, the British Dominions on Foreign Policy, 16 Jan 1926.

commissioners in London could be 'authorized to meet me regularly as a body to discuss the urgent questions of the day': in this way 'they would at least know what points in our policy most affected their respective Dominions'.[3]

But it would be wrong to read too much into these declarations of personal and departmental concern regarding the dominions. Honest regrets apart, the implicit assumption behind Foreign Office thinking was that any substantial initiatives for improved consultation must come from the dominion governments themselves, and, by extension, that the conduct of British foreign policy could not in the meantime wait upon suggestions and developments from that quarter. The claims of expediency – as we have seen, a constant and powerful factor in all the department's dealings with the dominions – continued to govern their outlook. This was evident in an exchange of correspondence with the Dominions Office early in 1926, with respect to the legal scope of the Locarno treaties. The Dominions Office were anxious to clarify a number of difficult points with a view to ascertaining the dominions' precise constitutional position under the treaties. But the Foreign Office could see 'no practical purpose' in 'entering upon a dialectical incursion into the niceties entailed by adhesion or non-adhesion of the Dominions to the Pact':

Surely the position is that in theory the Empire goes to war *as a whole*: whether a Dominion takes an active part must depend on the Parliament of that Dominion. And no amount of theorising in advance is going to alter that. If a threat to peace under the treaty arises, the Dominions will *all* be as a matter of course consulted. But *our* action under the Locarno Treaty will not – indeed cannot – be dependent on the unanimous imprimatur of all the Dominions. We shall act as the British Parliament of the day decides.[4]

When later the Foreign Office did pause to examine the exact legal position this pragmatic attitude seemed fully justified. They found it virtually impossible, particularly in 'the absence of any satisfactory arrangements for the conduct of a British Imperial Foreign Policy' to determine whether a dominion's individual endorsement of Locarno would place it on a substantially different footing from the other dominions if action ever needed to be taken. Thus they could only conclude that the overseas governments had no more than a 'moral duty' to support Britain under the treaties, whether they formally adhered to them or not.[5] Yet the department were satisfied, even so, that such support would be forth-

---

[3] Chamberlain–Sir Robert Borden, 27 Feb 1926, quoted in Eayrs, *The Art of the Possible*, 133.

[4] DO 35/12: C. H. Smith (FO)–Harding, 10 March 1926.

[5] *Ibid*: (copy) FO memorandum, August 1926.

coming. After all, argued the legal adviser somewhat cynically, any war involving Britain would probably involve the League of Nations, and would almost certainly be a war of self-defence. On both grounds the dominions were bound to be drawn in. 'The difficulties', Chamberlain agreed, 'are, indeed, more theoretical than real.'[6]

Perhaps it was only to be expected that the Foreign Office, Chamberlain included, should in the last analysis seek to make light of the problems raised by the Locarno treaties by dismissing them as ultimately moral matters, and largely theoretical at that. Clearly it was a very tempting line of reasoning to fall back on, suggesting as it did that even after Britain's unilateral negotiations at Locarno the department could carry on with the conduct of imperial foreign affairs on their own initiative with an easy conscience, confident that in the last resort, if not always the immediate moment, British diplomacy would continue to command an empire-wide measure of support. Yet, however reassuring this view of the imperial association, it failed by a wide margin to grasp the full implications of the Locarno treaties for British–dominion relations. No doubt there was much truth in the basic contention that the overseas dominions would support Britain without reservation should the mother country, as a result of Locarno, ever be threatened directly by a continental power. To that extent there remained a strong moral commitment to preserve the integrity of the empire which carried great weight with dominion public opinion; and for all those who feared that Locarno only increased the risk of such European threats to Britain, it could reasonably be argued that it was the new treaties themselves which afforded the best guarantee of a lasting continental harmony. Beyond that, however, it should have been recognized that on a number of separate levels the Locarno agreements in effect stood between Britain and the dominions, a measure of their fundamentally different attitudes to the empire's security. In the first place, whatever the dominions' anticipated response to a direct challenge to the British Isles, it was equally certain that if ever Britain had to fulfil her Locarno responsibilities *on the continent* to maintain Franco-German equilibrium, she could count on little military support from her commonwealth partners. To that degree at least overseas official and public opinion alike was still inclined to regard the English Channel as the empire's immediate European boundary, no matter how much Chamberlain emphasized the idea of a new strategic frontier at the Rhine. (When British spokesmen such as Amery took the opposite course and tried to play down these continental responsibilities, it was only by casting doubts on the credibility of the Locarno treaties *per se*.)

[6] FO 372/2198: memorandum by W. E. Beckett (assistant legal adviser) Sept 1926; minutes by Sir C. Hurst, Chamberlain.

More generally, the very idea of a pledged British guarantee regarding the continent's balance of power, no matter how remote the prospect of actual involvement, had understandably raised strong suspicion in dominion circles that a major reorientation of British foreign policy was taking place, in which a new set of specifically European priorities was going to be imposed on the broader pattern of imperial diplomatic affairs. The Foreign Office's answer to any reservations at this level, of course, was simply to invoke the League of Nations, in order to demonstrate that Britain's obligations in Europe would after all be no more than those of all League members, the dominions included, and unlikely therefore to be carried out independently. But they fell very short of the mark in supposing that a League of Nations umbrella thrown over Britain's Locarno commitments would of itself guarantee the strategic support of the dominions. For one thing, it could hardly be denied that the Locarno treaties had been negotiated only after League efforts to establish some form of collective security in Europe had broken down, and thus to some extent had underlined the League's own lack of effectiveness. More to the point, it was in any case extremely unlikely that the dominions, for all that they vaunted their separate membership of the Assembly, were more ready to acknowledge a commitment to European security because of the League. If nothing else, Canada's persistent and successful efforts to emasculate article x of the Covenant were reminder enough of the deep-seated dominion resistance to any such tangible obligations.

All things considered, then, the Foreign Office's sanguine reflections about Locarno's repercussions on imperial relations were largely determined by the narrowness of their outlook, which had taken in only a limited part of the total prospect. Or perhaps more accurately, it was not their narrowness of view but rather their general willingness to apprehend these problems through the congenially obscuring mists of imperial moral sentiment, leaving the sharper details and less regular features of the landscape unexamined. What they failed to realize was that in other quarters of the empire–commonwealth the Locarno pact had had the contrary effect of thinning these same sentimental mists to the point where Great Britain, both in her relations with the dominions themselves but even more so in her new ties with Europe, lay altogether more exposed. More urgently than ever did dominion statesmen feel compelled to take a fresh, hard look – at the mother country, at their own positions, at the realities of an imperial relationship which from all sides could now be seen to be in need of more precise definition. In short, from the perspectives of the various dominions the Locarno treaties came to be regarded primarily as a point of departure, a moment of release even, after which the course of British–dominion relations could hardly proceed unaltered. And given the dominions' widely differing responses to the treaties already expressed Britain and her commonwealth partners seemed bound in the direction of greater divergence and independence.

Not that all dominion leaders accepted Locarno as inevitably a stimulus to decentralization. In Australia prime minister Stanley Bruce was inclined, on the contrary, to think that Britain's unilateral negotiation of the security pact would prove to be a positive cathartic experience for the empire generally, from which would come greater understanding and co-operation. In his view the British action, apart from manifesting the mother country's new strategic priorities in Europe, had served principally to point up the gross inadequacies in the existing machinery for inter-imperial consultation on foreign affairs – so much so that far-reaching reforms in the system must surely be put in hand. He anticipated, therefore, that 'some basis for the conduct of the Foreign Affairs policy of the Empire as a whole will be laid down at the next Imperial Conference. There is no question but that this will be the most important question dealt with.'[7] These remarks should not be dismissed as merely the expression of an idiosyncratic 'centralist' ideology on Bruce's part, nor as a simple reaction to events that had caught his government off guard. The Australian prime minister was as well-briefed on British foreign policy-making as any commonwealth leader, having in late 1924 (in the aftermath of the 1923 Imperial Conference) taken the unprecedented step of establishing in London a special political liaison officer, R. G. Casey. Casey, given high-level access to the Foreign Office as well as the blessing and assistance of Sir Maurice Hankey's cabinet secretariat, provided for his chief in Canberra a significantly improved insight into Whitehall's 'official mind', on foreign affairs in particular.[8] Thus Bruce's opinions, while not echoed in other dominion capitals in these early months of 1926, were neither dogmatic nor unconsidered.

Had the Locarno pact broken down during these months and the threat of a continental war appeared, then a discussion along the lines suggested by him might well have come to dominate the 1926 Conference. Unfortunately the very success of the new treaties militated against this possibility. By October 1926 and the assembling of the dominion delegations in London, Germany had been admitted into the League of Nations, European relations were cordial, and Chamberlain had received both a knighthood and the Nobel Prize for Peace. Under such favourable international

---

[7] DO 117/9: R. Casey–Harding, 10 March 1926, enclosing Bruce–Casey, Feb 1926.

[8] See R. (Lord) Casey, *Friends and Neighbours* (Melbourne, 1954), 30–1.

auspices, problems of foreign policy – as unresolved and important as ever, yet for the moment seemingly not of immediate critical urgency – could not effectively be brought forward to the centre of the stage. Instead these matters had to be approached indirectly, the conference being obliged in the first instance to give priority to a root-and-branch examination of constitutional affairs. Any conclusions reached on the constitutional level would bear directly, of course, on a subsequent consideration of foreign affairs. But as we shall see, they were to offer little hope for prime minister Bruce's vision of a revitalized collective imperial foreign policy.

Constitutional strategy and tactics, 1926

In working out tentative guidelines for the 1926 Imperial Conference, the British authorities in Whitehall could be reasonably certain that constitutional questions of one sort or another would come up for consideration. Even a rough glance over the period since the previous conference of 1923 showed a number of problems, from the Lausanne treaty to Locarno, whose constitutional implications were as yet far from resolved, and whose cumulative effect had been to cast a recognizable and admitted shadow of uncertainty, if not confusion, over the fabric of British–dominion relations. In retrospect the pronouncements of the 1923 Conference itself, on treaty-making and more generally on the dominions' right of limited liability for imperial foreign policy, had done very little to keep the mother country and her self-governing partners stabilized within their old imperial orbits. Nor had the Colonial Office been able to exercise any effective control over events, lacking both the means to impose the 'imperial factor' upon the consciousness (or the conscience) of the Foreign Office in their conduct of foreign policy, and the authority to restrain refractory dominion governments. It was not surprising if they felt that the balance of imperial relations had become in consequence severely disturbed, with British–dominion common interests manifestly weakened and the limits of collective policymaking more circumscribed than ever. Before any working equilibrium could be restored, constitutional matters would obviously require attention, so that the general constitutional guidelines governing Britain's relations with the dominions could be brought back into alignment with the practical conduct of affairs.

It is clear that in weighing up the anticipated constitutional problems for the 1926 Conference, the Colonial Office were far more inclined to locate and attend to specific outstanding difficulties rather than encourage any major revision of the empire's broader underlying constitutional principles. Here the department very much took their lead from colonial secretary Leopold Amery, whose restless and fertile imagination had inspired him time and again to put forward fresh practical suggestions to consolidate the links between the British and dominion governments. Indeed, by 1926, and as a direct consequence of Amery's own initiatives since joining the Baldwin cabinet, we should no longer speak of 'colonial secretary' and 'Colonial Office' in the context of this study. For in what he was pleased to think of as a significant reform of the imperial administrative machinery, Amery had hived off the relevant group of officials from the Dominions Department of the Office into a separate Dominions Office, a new department of state that he felt sure would help to place relations with the dominions on a more equitable footing. The initial separation, carried out in July 1925, had not been complete: Amery simply added the new portfolio to his existing one, and the two departments rested on the same physical and administrative foundations. Nonetheless, as he had explained to Mackenzie King beforehand,

> The main feature of the proposed reorganisation is that the essential difference between the relationship of the British Government to its partner Governments and its relationship to the dependent Governments of the Empire should be recognized and made explicit to the general public, and for that matter to the world at large.[9]

With this important structural change well in hand, and hopeful that the devolutionary drift in British–dominion relations could be checked by further such reforms of a practical nature, Amery's new department looked ahead to the Imperial Conference. Without doubt there was still much that needed to be done. In December 1925 a preliminary Dominions Office memorandum, which was to form the basis of Britain's agenda preparations for the conference, advised that 'The whole system of communications between the Governments of the Empire on matters of common interest is likely to come under review.'[10] In addition it went on to identify a number of particular legal and constitutional points – the form of British and dominion representation at international conferences, the standing of foreign consuls in the dominions, and the like – that would probably also claim the conference's attention. Although it was unlikely that any of these matters, great or small, could be adequately dealt with without reference

---

[9] King papers, J1/111: Amery–King, 19 March 1925. The separate establishment of the new Dominions Office, under Amery, consisted of a parliamentary under-secretary, Lord Clarendon, and a permanent under-secretary. Sir Charles Davis was promoted from assistant under-secretary in the Colonial Office to this post. Not until June 1930 were separate secretaries of state appointed to the Colonial and Dominions Offices.

[10] CO 537/1113: memorandum, 9 Dec 1925 and minutes; circulated as CP 532 (25).

to broader questions of principle, particularly in view of the undefined constitutional status of the dominions, the department were content to leave such questions unexamined for the moment. Even when, in March 1926, the cabinet's agenda committee took note that 'one or more of the Dominions may raise far-reaching questions regarding their international status' at the conference, the accent remained upon practicalities. Working papers were commissioned for the constitutional items already outlined by the Dominions Office, but no official policy study was called for on dominion status *per se*.[11]

These were early days, however. As the Imperial Conference drew nearer there were unequivocal warnings that the British strategy of piece-meal constitutional reforms was badly misconceived, and would be unlikely to carry the day against exigent dominion pressure, from a number of quarters, for a fundamental constitutional readjustment. By far the toughest and most explicit statement of intent in this respect came from South Africa, in a letter from General Hertzog to Amery of late July 1926. The South African prime minister, in setting about his own preparations for the Imperial Conference, had evidently been taking the trouble to brief himself more closely about the constitutional ideas of his predecessor General Smuts, and had discovered to his obvious surprise not only Smuts' unpublicized attempt to bring constitutional matters before the 1921 Imperial Conference, but also the full extent to which the former prime minister's policies corresponded to his own in 1926. Having for years taunted his opponent for supporting the concept of an imperial 'super-state', Hertzog could do no more than express a sense of retrospective and perhaps guilty frustration at the years of wasted opportunities – together with a fresh determination to lose no further time in putting constitutional affairs to rights. His trenchant remarks may speak fully for themselves:

You will perhaps remember that in January 1925, in writing to you I remarked upon the unsatisfactory manner in which the status of the Dominions was recognized internationally. [A]s we viewed the matter, the failure of proper recognition by foreign Powers was due to the fact that it was not sufficiently insisted upon over against such Powers, that 'every member of the Commonwealth by itself constituted a distinct national entity with equal status'.

Since writing the above I have not only been confirmed in my views as therein expressed, but experience during the eighteen months which have since elapsed, have taught and reflection convinced me that an authoritative statement on the subject of Dominion status to the world, is absolutely essential

[11] DO 117/10: agenda committee, minutes and report, circulated as CP 124 (26).

to the interests of the Empire, no matter whether we look at those interests from the point of view of international or inter-imperial relations, or from the point of view of the requirements of each individual Dominion separately . . .

Under these circumstances I feel it to be imperative that at the Imperial Conference in October we shall in all earnestness try to put an end to this undesirable state of affairs. I feel convinced that there is nothing else we can do at that Conference which shall have such an abiding influence for good in the Empire and so facilitate our endeavours to make imperial cooperation a success for the future. If we do not achieve that end, I say frankly, that I do not think that anything substantial will be attained.

I hope, therefore, that the necessary opportunity and time will be at our disposal for considering and concluding upon the subject. We shall have to face fundamental facts as to the independent status of the Dominions, and we shall have to publish those facts to the world. I say this because during the last eight days I have been very much occupied in perusing papers in connection with previous Conferences, and I hope you will excuse me if I say that with nothing have I been so struck as with the apparent unwillingness of representatives attending those Conferences to face essential facts as to our constitutional rights or, when faced, to have them published beyond the confines of the Council Chamber . . .

I give you the assurance that if the statements which I have come across in these papers as to our Dominion status, coming from Great Britain's most responsible leaders, had been published and authoritatively announced, as to my mind they ought to have been announced, much of the bitterness and political wrangle in South Africa at least would never have occurred, and the word 'Empire' would have had a different significance to what it unfortunately has with thousands because they are being kept in the dark.

Amongst the papers which have fallen into my hands during the last eight days is a memorandum by General Smuts, entitled: 'The Constitution of the British Commonwealth', submitted to you in 1921, with your comment of the 20th June of that year. I was, indeed, struck with the similarity of ideas between General Smuts, as expressed in that document, and my own . . . I need hardly tell you how glad I have been to find that also your convictions are running along the same lines . . .

. . . [Y]ou have no conception what irreparable harm is being done to Empire cooperation through the policy of secrecy pursued in an atmosphere of constitutional fog. As long as this continues, you will have nothing but suspicion and strife; and I really cannot be a party to such tactics, nor do I consider it right over against the people whom I represent.[12]

There could, after this, be no mistaking Hertzog's intentions at the approaching conference, and in any case the South African prime minister felt confident enough of his position to speak publicly on his home ground

---

[12] DO 117/32: Hertzog–Amery, 26 July 1926.

on the same broad themes. Under the circumstances Amery must have been understandably disconcerted to discover that on Hertzog's view of things, 'your convictions *are* running along the same lines'. It appeared Hertzog might be hoping, five years after the event, to redeem a pledge of support that Amery had offered in 1921 (as a junior minister, and by then no longer in the Colonial Office) to Smuts. Yet how could he reasonably explain to Hertzog that to define the constitutional position of the dominions in 1921, even on Smuts' terms, would have been far more acceptable to him than in the post-Locarno context of 1926? Rather than make the attempt, the dominions secretary chose instead to prepare his ground at the British end for any necessary retreat – indicating quite explicitly to Chamberlain, for instance, that in reconsidering the events of 1921, he would not now endorse Smuts' proposals 'quite in the same way'.[13] Considering that in later years Amery the elder statesman was to record benignly that the dominion delegates met only 'open doors' when their constitutional thrusts were made at the conference of 1926[14] it is as well to witness him here, a somewhat chastened dominions secretary quietly attempting to close one or two doors of his own before the conference got under way.

If South Africa were bent on obtaining constitutional satisfaction from the 1926 Imperial Conference, it was only to be expected that the Irish Free State would also be weighing in with constitutional demands of their own. In the months preceding the conference there was little to indicate the precise questions the Irish government were intending to raise, though they could be assumed to have in mind a number of issues relating to the status of the dominions. As noted earlier, however, while in practice both dominions might prove to be equally assertive with regard to constitutional demands, it did not necessarily follow that their ultimate objectives were the same, given their markedly different evaluations of the commonwealth connection. General Hertzog had been determined for some time that the dominions could have an adequate and satisfactory freedom of action within the British commonwealth – provided that full international recognition, and acceptance, of British–dominion equality could be established. But the Free State leaders, it is safe to say, together with a significant section of Irish public opinion, were as yet by no means convinced that a sufficient degree of freedom was possible while Ireland remained a dominion. In their pursuit of greater autonomy for the offshore dominion the milestones of their achievements stood out clearly enough behind them: diplomatic representation at Washington, the registration of the 1921

[13] DO 117/33: Amery–Chamberlain, 19 Oct 1926.
[14] Amery, *Political Life*, II, 381.

Treaty at the League of Nations, and other matters.[15] Even so the Cosgrave administration were in an ambivalent position, uncertain how far their strategy of pressing for greater autonomy at every turn would carry them. On the one hand, the Free State Irish would tolerate the commonwealth only as long as it served as a vehicle for national independence, and moreover a vehicle permitting movement towards that goal at an acceptable speed. But on the other hand, the pace at which the Dublin government could impose constitutional devolution upon their commonwealth partners depended very much on how far Britain and the overseas dominions were willing to tolerate such developments merely for the sake of placating the Free State – and that, in the end would be governed by their own collective judgement as to the offshore dominion's ultimate worth to their commonwealth association.

With reference to 1926, it is therefore important to gauge (borrowing a useful Irish–American term) the Free State's constitutional clout, particularly as compared to South Africa. How far would each be able to push their demands at the Imperial Conference? How seriously would Britain and the other dominions view the risk of secession, should any of these demands prove unacceptable? (Alternately, though this is a consideration more apposite for the 1970s than the 1920s, how far would a threat of expulsion from the commonwealth deter either of them?) All things considered, there seems little reason to differ from the opinion of Professor Nicholas Mansergh as to the relative weight of the two protagonists:

[W]hile South African secession from the Commonwealth would have been a serious perhaps fatal blow to its prestige and pretensions, Irish Free State secession would have had no such disastrous consequences. The Irish Free State was a Dominion in name, not in spirit, and the failure of the Dominion experiment there would not necessarily have had disruptive consequences overseas.[16]

There is another factor to be kept in mind, however. It remained to be seen how the conference itself would develop, and in particular how South Africa and Ireland would respond to *each other*'s initiatives. If the efforts of the one served to inhibit the other then perhaps few constitutional concessions would be won after all; alternately, mutual co-operation between the two delegations might generate a powerful momentum for change.

15 See Harkness, *Restless Dominion*, ch 5. For example in 1924 the Free State government secured an alteration in the wording of Irish passports which deleted any reference to 'British subject'.

16 P. N. S. Mansergh, *Survey of Commonwealth Affairs*, 1: *Problems of External Policy, 1931–1939* (London, 1952), 10–11.

While South Africa and the Free State worked out their strategies for constitutional change at the Imperial Conference, in Canada Mackenzie King was engaged during the summer of 1926 in a much more immediate constitutional struggle, which culminated in a federal general election in mid-September. Only at that point did King know that he was once again prime minister, and would be expected after all to attend the Imperial Conference in London, however unprepared. To a large extent the events of these months in the senior dominion are the stuff of Canadian political history and cannot concern us here. Yet because the central issue was a fundamental constitutional disagreement between King and the Canadian governor general Lord Byng, it will not be out of place to touch upon aspects of the affair – which soon acquired the label of 'the King–Byng dispute' – if only to see how far King's approach to the Imperial Conference was influenced by its repercussions.

From the legal point of view the King–Byng dispute is a familiar enough landmark in British empire constitutional history, and has been studied at length.[17] The dispute turned on two critical moments: King's decision to carry on as prime minister in late October 1925, despite the results of a general election which put the Liberals into a weak minority position; and his subsequent request, in June 1926, for another general election at a time when a motion of censure against his government was pending in the House of Commons. Byng refused a dissolution to the prime minister (who resigned) only to grant it a few days later to the Conservative leader Arthur Meighen after the latter's failure to sustain an administration in office. Both Eugene Forsey and King's own biographer think that the governor general acted correctly in denying King a dissolution,[18] and there seems little reason to challenge this view. Rather there would now appear to be evidence that King himself was warned, when he decided initially against resignation in October 1925, that he would not automatically be granted another dissolution. Though King denied that any such warning had been made, a memorandum to the Dominions Office written in January by Byng's secretary stated plainly enough that 'His Excellency also gave the Prime Minister to understand that he would not grant him another dissolution.'[19] Beyond that, as King himself recorded, Byng was in any case so reluctant to accept his prime minister's decision to carry on

[17] Eugene Forsey, *The Royal Power of Dissolution of Parliament in the Commonwealth* (Toronto, 1943), covers the subject most fully. See also R. Graham, *The King–Byng Affair, 1926: A Question of Responsible Government* (Toronto, 1967), a documentary account.

[18] Forsey, *Dissolution*, ch 5–6; Neatby, *King*, II, 149.

[19] Neatby, *King*, 85; DO 117/4: Gov Gen–Dom Sec, 18 Jan 1926.

after the 1925 election that he wanted his official opposition to be made public![20] An impossible desire, though it is a clear indication of his frustration and misgivings, and strongly suggests that while King did not resign, he was not given leave to carry on *carte blanche*. The governor general's own later feeling about the whole affair, as he told King, was that the major crisis had been this earlier one – that he had allowed King to carry on at all.[21] Thus for the prime minister to approach him for a second dissolution under *any* circumstances was to risk a refusal. To do so as a means of avoiding an opposition motion of censure on his government was to add egregious insult to injury.

Although Byng may safely be credited with the legal and moral honours, his confrontation with King must also be seen in the political and inter-imperial context of mid-1926, in which light the conduct of the protagonists inevitably had a different appearance. Byng, it is fair to say, was open to misrepresentation whatever he chose to do. By granting a dissolution to King he would obstruct parliament in its legitimate efforts to censure the Liberal administration. Yet how could he deny his prime minister a dissolution – whatever the circumstances – without appearing to regress to the prerogatives of a nineteenth-century colonial governor, and by extension to call into question Canada's post-war status of equality with Britain? A third option, to consult the Dominions Office and abide by their decision, was equally unprofitable: who in Canada would accept that the dominion's affairs of state, even at such a critical juncture, should be open to the arbitration of Downing Street? Byng was at least shrewd enough to avoid this pitfall, despite King's own demands that he seek London's advice[22] – though as it was, there were many in Canada and elsewhere who would not believe that the governor general had not privately asked for the opinion of Amery and his Dominions Office staff. In short Byng could not win, could not vindicate himself. And when within a week of his refusing King a dissolution of parliament he had offered one to the defeated government of Arthur Meighen, his judgement as governor general became doubly open to criticism. It was Meighen's judgement, of course, that was principally at fault. The Tory leader should have openly refused the reins of power, forced an election, and campaigned against a government brazenly trying to avoid the censure of parliament. Instead his attempt and immediate failure to govern severely compromised the governor general's own repudiation of King, and at once put the political and constitutional cards back into King's own hands.

20 King diary, 3 Nov 1925.
21 King diary: interview, 21 Sept 1926.
22 Byng papers: King–Byng, 28 June 1926.

The discredited Liberal leader could now cast off the stigma of censure and defeat and campaign for re-election as the constitutionally injured party, a prey to Byng's colonialist pretensions and the ambiguities of Canada's status in the empire–commonwealth. While he never forgot that his political opponent in the election was Meighen rather than Byng it was a role King played to perfection, and to Meighen's chagrin and ultimate political destruction he produced for the Liberals the first comfortable parliamentary majority they had enjoyed since forming a government in 1921.

Such were the circumstances of the 1926 election, therefore, that King's victory and return to power were bound to be at the governor general's expense, personally if not institutionally. At the personal level matters were effectively resolved by the curtailing of Byng's tour of duty (he was due in any event to return home before long) and his swift replacement by Lord Willingdon. Institutionally it could hardly be supposed that the governor general's prerogatives could be curtailed in quite the same simple way – though with the Imperial Conference due to convene in London the Canadian prime minister had an ideal opportunity to press a case for reform, indeed could proceed straight from the campaign trail to the conference with his constitutional struggles still a highly topical affair. Even so, it would be wrong to suggest that it was his dispute with Byng which prompted King to raise the question of the governor general's powers at London. Well before matters had reached their climax in the events of June 1926, both prime minister and governor general were agreed that the latter's dual constitutional mandate – which made him head of the executive, but also the agent and channel of communication for the British government – no longer squared with the realities of executive autonomy in a commonwealth dominion, and that while a governor must continue to represent the sovereign there was no longer any justification for his representing the British government of the day.

As we have seen above,[23] the constitutional role of the governors general had already been challenged at the end of the war, when Borden, Hughes, Smuts and Botha all expressed strong reformist feelings on the subject. Had the 1921 Imperial Conference been prepared to deal with constitutional affairs, as Smuts in particular hoped it would, then dominion governors might well have found themselves explicitly restricted to the activities of a sovereign-delegate. Instead, in the absence of any such formal change each of them had to find a practical *modus vivendi* with his political advisers, and in this regard it must be admitted that Byng had shown himself fully sympathetic to the spirit of reform, to the point where

[23] See above, 118-119.

he felt he ought not to act independently of his prime minister at all, no matter the duties his office bore to the British government. In November 1924 he therefore ceased communicating privately to the Colonial Office, admitting to King that to do so would compromise his relations with his Canadian advisers – and implying that he was no longer prepared to serve two constitutional masters.[24] King for his own part could happily inform British prime minister Stanley Baldwin in April 1926 that the governor general

has succeeded in banishing from the public mind and from the mind of his Ministers any suspicion that he regards himself as the representative of the Government of Great Britain or of any of its Departments rather than as the representative of His Majesty[25]

Yet it seemed right enough that the Canadian prime minister was intending to ask for some formal acceptance of this *de facto* constitutional situation from the 1926 Imperial Conference, and that he should assume as well that there must now be a new channel of communications, independent of the governor general, for the conduct of official relations between Britain and the dominions.[26] It was precisely in keeping with these changes that he also took steps at this time to appoint a Canadian minister to Washington, thereby filling the post that prime minister Borden had fought for and won in 1920, but which since then had remained inoperative.[27]

In the light of these developments, the King–Byng dispute can thus be seen as the final stimulus to an already well-established desire for constitutional change with regard to the office of governor general, and, by extension, to the formal system of communications between Canada and the British government. It served to highlight the case for a reform which in itself was a perfectly moderate, evolutionary step on the road to full equality between mother country and dominion. Mackenzie King the poli-

[24] King diary, 10 Nov 1924.
[25] King–Baldwin, 16 April 1926, quoted in Neatby, *King*, 146.
[26] Chamberlain papers: British ambassador, Washington–For Sec, reporting conversation with King of early May 1926.
[27] The position at Washington was offered to Vincent Massey, a Toronto Liberal and director of the Massey–Harris manufacturing company, who had been briefly minister without portfolio in 1925. The appointment was ratified by the British government during the 1926 Imperial Conference, though its terms were significantly different from the 1920 arrangement negotiated by Borden. In particular, the Canadian minister was to be the head of a fully independent mission, and was not to have charge of the British embassy in the absence of the ambassador. See CO 886/10/90: correspondence, 1926; Massey, *What's Past is Prologue*, 110–11, 121–3.

tician was willing to play up the constitutional elements of the dispute in more lurid and drastic terms for the purposes of the September 1926 election, but once returned to office and the immediate duties of representing Canada at the Imperial Conference King the statesman proved to have no further drastic plans to reconstruct the empire's constitutional relations.

What then can we say, on the eve of the 1926 conference, of the Canadian prime minister and his view of Canada's place in the empire–commonwealth? First of all surely, that he no longer felt himself to be the uninitiated and nervous defender of his dominion's freedom. Three years earlier, and with many weeks of preliminary work behind him, the approach of the 1923 Imperial Conference had found King 'filled with terror at the thought of having to speak many times & my inability to work out themes'.[28] By comparison the man who sailed for London in October 1926 was, despite his lack of preparation, reasonably self-assured. Politically vindicated, more experienced in his public and ceremonial duties, King could also be confident that the course of events in British–Canadian relations since 1923 had left very few Canadian axes to grind at the London conference. The settlement of the Lausanne treaty controversy, the terms of participation conceded by Ramsay MacDonald for the Dawes Conference, the British decision to negotiate the Locarno treaties – each occasion had afforded King the chance to dissociate Canada further from a collective imperial diplomacy and to let the dominion be seen to be autonomous in her external relations. By the beginning of 1926 there seemed little to challenge the idea – advanced by King against such opposition in 1923 – that collaborative imperial ventures in foreign policy would be the exception rather than the rule. In private correspondence the Canadian prime minister could display notable equanimity as to the future. The necessary distinctions separating 'local' from 'imperial' foreign affairs, he admitted to N. W. Rowell, might continue to present difficulties: 'but with good will and some experimenting I have no doubt that the line of demarcation will eventually be drawn with reasonable clearness'. On the subject of dominion status *per se* he was more guarded, frankly considering British–dominion constitutional equality to be 'an aspiration rather than a fact'. Even so he spoke without undue concern only of removing 'the anomalies which still remain'.[29]

Yet although much of King's aggressiveness was gone by 1926, it cannot be said that he was either complacent or fully satisfied about Canada's imperial relations; indeed to do so would be to mistake the

[28] King diary, 12 Sept 1923.
[29] King papers, J1/123: King–Rowell, 7 Dec 1925, 4 Jan 1926.

essential character of the man. For notwithstanding the welcome trend of developments since the 1923 Imperial Conference, there remained in King a powerful feeling that to maintain dominion freedom required continued watchfulness on his part, in all his dealings with the British authorities. His whole approach to Canada's empire relations, in fact, was marked by a fundamental suspicion, which by this time was virtually an element of his public personality, that the British government (more precisely the permanent British establishment ensconced in Whitehall) had not and would never give up their hopes for a centralized imperial structure, with the dominions committed to collective policies on all fronts – diplomatic, strategic, economic. Others, as we are told, might have their dream of commonwealth in these years.[30] For King there was this contrasting nightmare of empire, which he found impossible to relinquish. Assiduously reinforced by the warnings of Skelton, Clifford Sifton and other Canadian nationalists, and from London by high commissioner Peter Larkin, it would haunt him virtually to the end of his political life. That a number of his closest friends in England should themselves be convinced imperialists certainly adds a strong note of ambiguity to his suspicions about British 'centralist' intentions, yet apparently it did little to mitigate them.[31] Whitehall's policymakers were simply not to be trusted on matters relating to the dominions, and King had developed an acute sensitivity for judging all policy moves from that quarter. For example, when Amery had announced the setting up of the Dominions Office, King's initial pleasure at seeing the dominions set apart administratively from Britain's colonial empire quickly soured on second thoughts:

the more I reflect, however, the more I feel such a distinction helps to perpetuate a position of subordination on part of Dominions ... once a colony has become self-governing it should be on equality of status with no need for supervision from Gr[ea]t Br[itain] – The Sec[retar]y of State for Foreign Affairs is the one to correspond with the Secr[etar]y for External Affairs in the Dominions, normally the Prime Minister. It is along these lines I shall go.[32]

It is the note of determination, however, as much as the tone of frustration, that should be observed here. Increasingly King was coming to see himself not only as the doubting antagonist of Whitehall but, more confidently and positively, as the champion of the liberal, devolutionary tradition in imperial relations, with the task of completing the transition to common-

---

[30] M. Beloff, *Imperial Sunset*, II: *Dream of Commonwealth* (forthcoming).
[31] J. E. Esberey, 'Personality and Politics: A new look at the King–Byng dispute', *Canadian Journal of Political Science*, VI, no 1 (1973), 52.
[32] King diary, 1 April 1925.

wealth against the resistance of reactionary imperialists. A diary entry of November 1925, responding to preliminary news from London about the next Imperial Conference, reflects rather well a new balance of feelings between his ingrained suspicions and an awakening sense of purpose:

The Br[itish] Gov[ernmen]t are preparing for another Imperial Conference, in which an effort will be made to work out an Empire policy – It seems to be my fate to have to take the side that *appears* to be anti-British, but which in reality being anti-Imperial is British in the truest significance of the term.[33]

By the time the conference was due to begin, with his political difficulties resolved Mackenzie King was all the more inclined to adopt a balanced approach to imperial affairs.

Thus by October 1926 events in Canada and imperial developments more generally were combining to place King in a relatively uncontentious and moderate position for the Imperial Conference, although with South Africa and the Irish Free State yet to declare their hands it remained to be seen precisely what sort of role the Canadian prime minister would play in the proceedings. But there were signs in other quarters to suggest that, even on constitutional questions, the conference might not be the scene of irreconcilable differences after all. Some months earlier *The Round Table* had urged the dominions to realize that they need no longer countenance any fears of subordination within a centralized imperial structure. 'The real alternatives before the Dominions', it had emphasized, 'are no longer between a dependent status and independent nationhood, but between a nationalism which sees its fulfilment in isolation and a nationalism which sees it in an active participation in the world's affairs.'[34] From an unofficial source at least, here was a frank British acceptance of the dominions' full freedom of action within the imperial association, and it was an acceptance borne out more directly for King in a pre-conference interview with E. J. Harding of the Dominions Office. The British authorities, he learned from Harding, while they would challenge any attempt to make the dominions fully separate kingdoms, 'would be prepared to go to almost any length in the matter of autonomous rights of the Dominions, provided the concept of unity within the Empire was maintained'.[35] Given such promising flexibility on Britain's part, King was bold enough to think that the only major problem

---

[33] *Ibid*, 19 Nov 1925.
[34] *The Round Table*, XVI, no 2 (1925–6), 231.
[35] King diary, 17 Oct 1926.

requiring a definite solution from the conference would be the status of the dominion governors general. Once it was agreed that these officials would no longer represent the British government, he confidently informed Austen Chamberlain, then Ireland and South Africa, let alone Canada and the rest, would have a concrete and sufficient manifestation of their full equality of status with Great Britain.[36]

It is worth noting that what the Canadian prime minister reassuringly saw as Britain's open-minded, pragmatic approach to the conference had been shaped by thorough and sometimes acrimonious preparation inside Whitehall, and was anything but an unconsidered position. As mentioned above, the British government had begun briefing themselves on constitutional matters for the conference some six months in advance, with policy studies on the particular issues likely to be raised for discussion. Despite these labours, however, it was clear from the start that they were far from anxious to see all or any of these issues dealt with by the 1926 Conference. Rather the British strategy was a defensive one, to marshal the necessary material to meet constitutional points brought up by dominion leaders, while choosing to leave specific problems untouched if possible. Hence of the constitutional memoranda drafted in Whitehall during the spring and summer of 1926 none was distributed to the dominions, while at the same time a number of pertinent matters were intentionally not put on the conference agenda. The diplomatic representation of the dominions in foreign countries; the status of foreign consuls in dominion capitals; the question of dominion representation on the League of Nations Council; the status and authority of the 'British Empire' member of the Council – these and other matters were left to the initiative of the dominion delegations at the conference. To some degree at least, this deliberate British reticence was a doubly defensive strategy. In the first place some of the issues under consideration were known to involve virtually intractable legal and constitutional dilemmas, for which even the most pedantic or imaginative experts in Whitehall had little relish. (It was admitted, for instance, that the status of the 'British Empire' League Council member was ultimately beyond definition![37]) But more importantly, it was also the case that the Dominions Office and Foreign Office found themselves severely at odds with each other on nearly all the questions that were looked at prior to the conference, with the obvious if cynical corollary that the narrower the final scope of the conference's constitutional inquiries the better.

36 *Ibid*, 25 Oct 1926.
37 DO 117/21: British cabinet committee on inter-imperial relations, final report, Oct 1926.

The subject that produced the most serious disagreement between the two departments of state – and this was a matter that could not, in any event, be kept from the agenda of the conference – was the making of international treaties by Britain and the dominions, and more particularly the style of signature for such treaties. As we have seen earlier in this study, at a number of critical points treatymaking had been the focus of sharp constitutional differences between the Colonial and Foreign Offices, the former striving to preserve the outward legal signs of diplomatic unity amongst empire countries, while the latter, more concerned with their own freedom of diplomatic action, were prepared to give the dominions greater autonomy in international affairs. The recommendations of the 1923 Imperial Conference on this subject, granting the dominions the right to make treaties with foreign powers on their own behalf, represented a complete victory for the Foreign Office point of view. But the 1923 Conference, while accepting the principle of autonomous dominion initiatives in foreign affairs, had not attempted to establish any criteria for 'local' and 'imperial' diplomacy, and three years later it was this lack of definition, and its obvious importance to any broader consideration of British–dominion constitutional equality, that pointed to a reassessment of the 1923 rubric on treaties.

The main point of inter-departmental controversy related to the 'central panel', the constitutional convention whereby Great Britain continued to sign international treaties of all kinds on the authority of geographically unlimited 'full powers', in effect binding not just the British Isles but the entire British empire. Seven years after the anomalies of this convention had been criticized in connection with the Paris peace treaties, it was still the case that in any international agreements relating to both mother country and dominions, the latters' rights to sign on their own behalf were beside the legal point, given the unrestricted writ of the British signatories. Legally, of course, the 'central panel' had the cardinal value of sustaining the diplomatic integrity of the empire *vis-à-vis* foreign powers, and by extension underlining the basic distinction between inter-imperial relations and international affairs. To the Foreign Office these were such expedient benefits, saving Britain and the dominions from a variety of potential problems in international law, that they were not at all prepared to relinquish them, whatever the demands for equality of status. No matter that it had suited them to give the dominions a limited freedom of action in 1923; it now seemed even more imperative to halt the devolutionary drift in the conduct of the empire's foreign affairs. The permanent officials of the Dominions Office, however, had also changed their views in these intervening years. At the previous conference, in a last attempt to reconcile equality of status and diplomatic unity, they had appealed for a standard form of treaty signature by which Britain and the dominions alike would operate with geographically unrestricted 'full powers' for the empire as a whole. In 1926 the standard was different. Equality was now the only major consideration for them, and they felt in this case that Britain must become the equal of the dominions, conforming to their own limited diplomatic independence by giving up the 'central panel'.

In the British agenda committee dealing with this issue there was little readiness for compromise, and departmental feelings ran rather high, but in the end the Dominions Office were able to establish their case for change. Against the formidable legal opposition of the Foreign Office's Sir Cecil Hurst they secured an official British statement prior to the conference that alternative treaty forms would be established if desired. The home government, it was promised, would be prepared to sign treaties for the United Kingdom and dependent colonies alone, while trusting the dominions to maintain the empire's legal unity by making all treaties of their own in the name of the king as official contracting party.[38]

This final British formulation on treaty signatures was a significant concession to the principle of equality of status. The expected pruning of the constitutional powers of the governors general would be a further acceptance of the same principle. Yet as the Imperial Conference got under way it turned out that these concessions might count for very little even so, in the face of Irish and South African demands for altogether more radical constitutional measures. The Free State delegation, as Mackenzie King was discovering himself, were bent on virtual sovereignty if they could get it: 'FitzGerald is inclined', he noted, 'to the extreme view of having five countries each with a separate King, operating in all particulars as distinct nations.'[39] Treaty forms and the governor general's powers aside, the Irish were preparing to bring forward a variety of other specific constitutional proposals of their own in pursuit of this end. Nor was General Hertzog to be deterred from setting his own constitutional pace at the conference. The South African premier was in this regard a more known quantity than the Irish, his sight fixed on only one goal – the full international recognition of dominion autonomy, of the dominions as the complete constitutional equals of Great Britain. And Hertzog, it appeared from the first session of the conference, would not settle for less. Behind the formal politeness of his opening address lay the possibility, failing an explicit and satisfactory definition of dominion status, of South

[38] DO 117/22: British cabinet committee on inter-imperial relations, minutes, July–Oct 1926; CAB 32/47: IC, memorandum E-104.

[39] King diary, 18 Oct 1926.

Africa's seceding from the empire–commonwealth. It was a possibility that hastened the setting up of a high-level prime ministers' committee under the chairmanship of Lord Balfour, to see how far South African and Irish demands could be met.

The 1926 Imperial Conference, then, was obliged at its outset to face up to the task of constitutional definition, and to attempt to formulate equality of constitutional status in language sufficiently clear to be broadcast to the world at large. It was an undertaking that was unpalatable to many, and King was speaking not only for himself when he reiterated to the Balfour committee that he was well satisfied with the existing situation.[40] But in deference to the overriding concern for the preservation of the commonwealth association (and perhaps in consideration of nationalist feeling in Canada[41]) King was willing at least to discuss the problem – an attitude which may have helped others sit down and talk. In Balfour's committee the Canadian prime minister was at once placed in a position of some influence, holding the middle ground between Australia and New Zealand on the one hand and South Africa and Ireland on the other while constitutional drafts and counter-drafts were considered.[42] The principal result of the committee's labours, even so, was less of a compromise between the differing points of view than a combination of them, less an analytic definition than a synthetic description. Britain and the dominions were held to be

autonomous communities within the British Empire, equal in status, in no way subordinate one to another in any respect of their domestic or external affairs, though united by a common alliegance to the Crown, and freely associated as members of the British Commonwealth of Nations.[43]

Thus were the various elements of the commonwealth relationship distinguished and articulated, though of necessity their importance relative to each other was left unstated. For the immediate purposes of the Balfour committee, however, it was 'equality of status' and the implications

---

[40] CAB 32/56: IC, inter-imperial relations committee, mtg 1, 27 Oct 1926.
[41] During the conference a cable from Sir Clifford Sifton and a memorandum from J. W. Dafoe kept King well aware of the nationalist lobby in Canada. See R. Cook, 'A Canadian Account of the 1926 Imperial Conference', *JCPS*, III, no 1 (1965), 60.
[42] The deliberations of the Balfour committee can be followed in detail in Hall, *Commonwealth*, 621–35. The most authoritative primary sources for the closed sessions are private letters from Sir Maurice Hankey, to prime minister Baldwin, 29 Oct, 1 Nov 1926 (copies in DO 117/48) and to Balfour himself, 1 Nov 1926 (Balfour papers, Add 49704).
[43] Cmd 2768, 9.

entailed by equality that received the most attention. Once definition had been settled and General Hertzog assured of a tangible declaration on status – and in the event the final constitutional formula was hammered into shape after only three sessions of the committee, on 1 November – then the prime ministers turned from constitutional phrase-making to address themselves to practical changes based on the principle of equality. With Hertzog appeased, it was the Irish Free State delegation who now made the running in the committee, producing on the day after definition had been settled an extensive list of problems demanding attention.[44] For a further nine meetings the Balfour committee were thus occupied in fashioning legal and constitutional reforms, ranging in the end from a technical change in the King's title to the form of accrediting foreign consuls in the dominions. It was here that the opportunity was taken to settle the status of dominion governors general, with a firm recommendation that this should henceforward correspond to that of the sovereign in Great Britain. Solutions were also adumbrated by the committee for other problems incapable of immediate settlement, so that in this way a process of revision was set in train which was to culminate in the passing of the Statute of Westminster in 1931. At every point of change in these five years, equality was to be the pre-eminent criterion by which the commonwealth's constitutional forms were judged.[45]

Around the work of the Balfour committee some differences of opinion have arisen, with recent studies choosing to emphasize either the definition of status or the extensive programme of reforms that make up the balance of the committee's report; the comparative contributions of individual dominion leaders on the committee have been similarly weighed up.[46] This question of relative significance, however, should perhaps be looked at in two different ways. In the first place it seems quite unprofitable to try to discriminate between the two aspects of the Balfour committee's achievements. Definition was vital to the success of the conference, incorporating equality of status into a general declaration which met the demands of the South Africans and serving as a prelude to further developments. (It is surely significant that the Irish delegation's list of 'anomalies' so pertinent to the subsequent discussion, was not finalized until definition had

[44] 'Existing Anomalies in the British Commonwealth of Nations', 2 Nov 1926, reprinted in Harkness, Restless Dominion, 101.

[45] Cmd 2768: IC inter-imperial relations committee, report.

[46] For example, compare D. Hall, 'The Genesis of the Balfour Declaration', JCPS, 1, no 3 (1963), and Harkness, Restless Dominion, 96 ff. Hall stresses definition. Harkness, with an eye to the Irish contribution, suggests that once definition was out of the way the Free State delegation 'got down to the real work' of the conference.

been virtually completed.) Yet the ensuing reforms can hardly be discounted. They made equality manifest at a variety of relevant points, and what is more, they would not have been put into effect unless particularly requested by dominion ministers in the Balfour committee. As we have seen, although the British delegates were thoroughly briefed on all the issues expected to be dealt with, they were strongly inclined not to act on them until prompted. And in at least two instances when anticipated questions were not forthcoming (regarding procedure for *de jure* recognition of foreign states and the status of the 'British Empire' representative on the League Council), matters were allowed to remain unsettled.

That much said, if one wishes to assess the impact of the two leading protagonists, South Africa and the Irish Free State, then it is certainly possible to argue that South Africa carried the greater weight at the Imperial Conference. Hertzog's was a voice strong enough to demand definition of status and secure it, even when no one else at the conference – the Irish included – was especially committed to definition, and indeed when a number of British and dominion delegates were in principle opposed to it.[47] The Free State delegation could not claim a comparable victory, for the simple reason that they were not alone in pressing for the concrete constitutional reforms that Balfour's committee went on to deal with after definition. They often took the initiative – in a much-quoted letter Kevin O'Higgins was to complain with some justification that 'the onus of the "status" push – anomalies and anachronisms – has fallen very largely on ourselves'[48] – but they were able to count on the telling support of both South Africa and Canada as the prime ministers got on with their work. For Harkness to portray the Irish as having 'seized the helm of the British Empire ship' is thus to give a misleading picture.[49] There were other hands, just as strong and more experienced, on the wheel.

And on one occasion at least, in spite of the clear British policy of conceding to dominion claims of equality of status, all such hands were needed. Surprisingly the subject of concern was treaty forms, an issue hardly expected to arouse controversy given that the home authorities had already indicated their willingness to give up the 'central panel' style of signature on behalf of the British empire. In the event, however, and official attitudes notwithstanding, the small sub-committee set up to finalize the practical details became the scene of a bitter last-ditch resistance by Sir Cecil Hurst, legal adviser to the Foreign Office. In open defiance

[47] Hankey–Baldwin, 1 Nov 1926, *loc cit.*
[48] T. White, *Kevin O'Higgins* (London, 1948), 221.
[49] Harkness, *Restless Dominion*, 121.

of stated British policy Hurst took the line that with dominion status now defined and confirmed, signatures for 'the British Empire' would no longer be a threat to British–dominion equality, and indeed were all the more necessary as a vestigial symbol of the empire's legal unity. For fully ten meetings he withstood the combined pressure of Hertzog, Skelton and FitzGerald, doggedly refusing to accept the case for change.[50] This at least was not a battle the Irish would have won for themselves.

Balfour, calmly but alertly supervising the progress of his committee, was as anxious as Hurst that international opinion should not discount the unity of the commonwealth association. To this end, he couched the committee's conclusions on status within the text of a brief historical analysis of British–dominion relations. It would be wrong, he warned, to suppose that status had been defined 'rather to make mutual interference impossible than to make mutual co-operation easy'. Definition had merely confirmed that each dominion was 'the sole judge of the nature and extent of its co-operation' – and Balfour's text asserted that 'no common cause will, in our opinion, be thereby imperilled'.[51]

To the foreign observer these may have seemed optimistic words, for at a later page of the committee report he could read that the dominions had not subscribed to the Locarno treaties, and at the very least could infer that the commonwealth's common causes had not been tangibly strengthened. Indeed to judge from the conference's approach to foreign affairs generally, there were grounds for thinking that few such causes were common any longer to the interests of Britain and the dominions. Premier Bruce of Australia, it will be recalled, had felt sure that Locarno would reinforce the case for a unified imperial foreign policy when the Imperial Conference of 1926 convened. On the contrary, far from displaying any determination to consolidate the empire's diplomatic unity the conference moved still further from a collective foreign policy, openly acknowledging and discussing the local external affairs of the individual dominions as an established element of commonwealth relations.[52] The Locarno treaties, it is true, were given not unsympathetic consideration by the dominion delegates, with Australia and New Zealand (together with Newfoundland) prepared to endorse them more fully by separately approving their ratification. But because Canada, South Africa and the Irish Free State were equally decided in refusing ratification, in the end it was accepted that

[50] CAB 32/57: IC, treaty procedure sub-committee.
[51] Cmd 2768: IC, inter-imperial relations committee, report.
[52] CAB 32/46: IC mtg 8, 25 Oct 1926.

Britain alone should formally adhere to the treaties. Nonetheless all the dominion delegates, with the notable exception of the Irish, did make this discussion of Locarno the occasion to pledge their general willingness to come to Britain's defence if ever necessary,[53] and in the broader context of the Imperial Conference it was clearly encouraging to see General Hertzog as keen as any in his expressions of support. With definitions of status secured, he was already feeling confident enough about South Africa's future in the commonwealth to promise her assistance to Britain along with the others.

Such sentiments, to be sure, were more easily voiced while the prospects for a lasting peace in Europe were so bright. At such a time who was to complain if the dominions were in reality much more concerned to avoid war rather than actively to prevent it? In the Balfour committee, even so, there was no desire to disguise the fact that Britain was far more involved than the dominions in European security, and indeed in defence and diplomacy generally. The report touched on this point when it remarked that equality of status did not extend to equality of function. But though the discrepancy was thus acknowledged, it was certainly not dwelt upon – for the simple reason that functional inequalities could not be removed by discussion round a conference table. 'Here', noted Balfour, 'we require something more than immutable dogmas.' With hindsight it must be admitted that in the decade preceding the Second World War, disparities of function proved to be a major handicap to effective commonwealth co-operation. In 1926, however, they were taken to represent no more than a temporary imbalance, which the evolving partnership of the commonwealth would in time overcome. The Locarno treaties were an essential component in this analysis. Though on the one hand they epitomized Britain's predominant and particular role in the partnership, on the other they offered present peace and a future stability during which the transition to full equality could be accomplished.

In the meantime, however, the emphasis remained of necessity upon status, and it was by its achievement on this score that the 1926 Conference was judged, and declared a success. 'Equality of status has been sought and found in Dominion autonomy', affirmed *The Round Table*, and it took singular note of General Hertzog's assurances that the bonds of British–dominion unity would prevail under the new dispensation:

There is nothing to prevent the most ardent protagonist of national liberty

[53] CAB 32/56: Balfour committee mtg 7, 4 Nov 1926. The emphasis in Neatby's account of this meeting, which suggests that the Canadian delegation did nothing but refuse to adhere to the treaties, is altogether misleading. *King*, 180.

from being at the same time a warm supporter of the Empire and of co-operation with the Empire as now accepted by the Imperial Conference.[54]

In London prime minister Bruce, playing down his misgivings about definition (and his disappointment at the absence of developments in the sphere of imperial economic co-operation) added his own public word of appreciation for this new South African spirit: 'If the Conference had accomplished nothing else' he told an audience at Australia House, 'that was a great and wonderful achievement.'[55] Only in the Irish Free State, it appeared, was there no positive reaction to the 1926 Conference. Fitz-Gerald and O'Higgins returned home to argue that all their constitutional claims had been met satisfactorily, but parliamentary and public opinion alike in the offshore dominion remained unimpressed and unappeased.[56]

Mackenzie King was particularly satisfied with the constitutional results of 1926, and could subscribe to them without reservation. With reforms of his own in mind, he had arrived in London to find himself in more of a middle position than anticipated, though one that had provided him with a role none the less congenial to play in the proceedings. Against Hertzog in the Balfour committee, on the one hand, he had notably defended the conference from any 'separatist' declaration of constitutional principles when definition was under discussion.[57] But having thus spoken up for the unity of the commonwealth association, King could also fully endorse the committee's declaration on equality of status, and the constitutional re-forms which followed from it. Taken together, they constituted above all for the Canadian prime minister a final and incontrovertible judgement against a united imperial foreign policy, and a guarantee that in foreign affairs the dominion governments could be masters each in their own house. The onus was now clearly upon Britain (or indeed upon any dominion initiating foreign policy) to ascertain in advance if it could speak for its commonwealth partners, and, by extension, this meant that King could at last communicate with Whitehall on foreign affairs without any unnecessary doubts that in so doing he was prejudicing Canada's freedom of action.

There were no positive guarantees here, of course, for future British–Canadian co-operation. But it was at least to be hoped that when issues were presented for Canada's consideration they could be studied from a constitutionally neutral point of view, as befitting communications between partners of equal status. In this respect King attached great importance to

[54] *The Round Table*, xvii, no 2 (1926–7).
[55] *The Times*, 22 Dec 1926.
[56] Harkness, *Restless Dominion*, 120–1.
[57] Hankey–Baldwin, 29 Oct 1926; *loc cit.*

the fact that the Crown and the British government were no longer to be jointly represented in Canada by the governor general. While the drama of the King–Byng dispute has tended to convey the impression that the exclusive reason for this constitutional change was to circumscribe the powers of the governor general's office, it should not be forgotten that for King it was equally important in clearing the way for the establishment of a British high commission in Ottawa, as the primary Canadian channel of communications with Whitehall. This more than anything would signify equality, and would leave the conduct of commonwealth relations uncompromised by considerations of status.[58]

But the Canadian prime minister was prepared to hint at a much more important development. With equality of status and dominion autonomy finally made manifest, he thought it possible that Canadian public opinion might come to view empire–commonwealth relations in a more co-operative light, even to the point of considering shared external commitments. Thus to Chamberlain he suggested that if constitutional reforms had been dealt with earlier, and a British high commission had been in Ottawa at the time of the Locarno negotiations, it might well have been possible to consult fully on the matter and bring Canada into the security pact.[59] Brave words after the event, and perhaps nothing more; certainly they were not borne out by subsequent developments in the inter-war period. Yet at least they show how much considerations of status had counted in King's assessment of British–Canadian relations. By this token, they can only reaffirm the positive achievements of the 1926 Imperial Conference.

[58] British high commissioners were established in the dominions in 1928. See N. Hillmer, 'A British High Commissioner for Canada', *JICH*, I, no 3 (1973–4).

[59] Chamberlain papers: Chamberlain–Amery, 26 Dec 1926, reporting a conversation during the conference.

Conclusion

In the spring of 1927 two of the more elderly statesmen of empire, born within a year of each other in the late 1840s, shared their thoughts on the nature and meaning of the constitutional conclusions that had emerged from the 1926 Imperial Conference. From Canada, it appeared to Sir George Foster that there was no real cause for alarm or despondency:

We are discussing in Canada the results of the Imperial Conference, and have come, I think generally, to the conclusion that nothing new has taken place, but are confirmed in the view that special efforts must hereafter be made to link together in sentiment and co-operation the various parts of the Empire, clustering around and converging towards the greatest possible imperial unity.

In reply Arthur Balfour could do no more than add his own assurances in the same vein:

As regards the Imperial Conference, you are perfectly right; – nothing *new* has been done; and I have for many years held, and publicly expressed, the views embodied in our report. But though the facts are as they have long been, the result of the Report no doubt brings their truer character home to many on both sides of the Atlantic who did not thoroughly realize the situation.[1]

For Foster and Balfour, perhaps in the long view across the immense changes from early Victorian, pre-Confederation days the period that has been studied here genuinely did appear as one of ordered stability, with the dominions in their settled and autonomous courses all the while. Yet from our imposed, shorter perspective it is none the less difficult to discount the significance of change and development in this transitional decade that begins in 1917, and it is by looking in detail at British–Canadian relations in these years that this study has attempted to uncover the process of this change more clearly. Above all care has been taken to look at developments from the viewpoints of both Whitehall and Ottawa, in order to show how changes were encouraged by pressures and policies

[1] Balfour papers: Foster–Balfour, 8 April 1927, Balfour–Foster, 4 May 1927.

from both quarters. Too often it has been assumed that the metropolitan government had only a secondary role to play in this process, simply reacting and readjusting when necessary to initiatives put forward by the dominion. Britain's own position has been taken to be relatively constant: a belief in imperial unity (and in the dominions' belief in imperial unity), a desire to maintain, if not tighten, the bonds of the imperial association, by involving the dominions with policymaking where practicable and by close co-operation at the administrative and procedural level, and a corresponding reluctance to make concessions that would go against the unity of the imperial association. Intrinsic to this interpretation, these attitudes have been assumed to be homogeneous throughout Whitehall.

This study has sought to show that it is now possible to carry the argument a good deal further, and to think of British views as evolving, during the period from 1917 to 1926, towards a much more 'de-centralist' position. Moreover, at a number of points along this line of development there were sharp differences of opinion between departments, most obviously between the Colonial and Foreign Offices, which bore directly upon British–Canadian (and British–dominion) relations. Perhaps the best example to illustrate the significance of these inter-departmental disagreements, both for British responses to Canadian demands and also for the pressures for change in Whitehall itself, is the reform over these years of the process of treatymaking. In April 1919, in contradiction to Colonial Office policy, the Foreign Office were willing to concede signatures 'on behalf of' the dominions. A few months later, however, it was Colonial Office support which proved advantageous, if not decisive, in Borden's efforts to obtain separate dominion ratification of the Versailles treaty. Thereafter in the face of Colonial Office resistance the principle of 'restricted' signatures was extended in 1921 and again in 1923, in the latter case the Foreign Office deliberately championing the advanced point of view in order to free themselves of unwanted responsibilities for dominion affairs. Yet three years later, over the question of 'British empire' signatures, it was they who defended to the last the conservative position.

In each of these encounters, it will be noticed, the advocates of change won the day – a pattern that would hardly have emerged had either party consistently dominated the formulation of British policy. The two departments, after all, had quite different priorities with regard to the overseas dominions. The Colonial Office, with immediate responsibility for the conduct of British–dominion relations, were chiefly concerned to maintain the unity of the imperial, and latterly the commonwealth, association. The Foreign Office, while admitting the importance of legal and diplomatic unity, were interested first and foremost in the making of foreign policy, and thought little of taking the dominions into account, particularly while their material commitments to the empire's defence remained of such marginal value. Diplomatic expediency and freedom of action remained the department's guiding principles, so that when in turn Mackenzie King laid claims to a Canadian foreign policy they were happy enough to dissociate themselves from it, and to offer the dominions whatever independent diplomatic responsibilities each cared to assume.

As regards the dominions' association with the empire's foreign affairs, a great deal thus turned upon this fundamental difference of outlook between the two departments. The dominions in 1917 laid claim to an active role in policymaking by virtue of their status, and were supported in this by the Colonial Office. But it was soon apparent that if they were ever to have the 'continuous consultation' promised in resolution ix the empire's administrative machinery would have to be radically revised, for in practice the Foreign Office would simply not tolerate the delays that consultation through the ordinary channels of communication would entail. In 1917, to be sure, Borden and Smuts rejected one definite solution to the problem of integrated policymaking when they vetoed Milner's proposals for imperial federation. Nonetheless they could anticipate that a constitutional conference would not be long in meeting, specifically to work out what sort of administrative changes could be made. And in the meantime the Imperial War Cabinet itself held great promise for efficient imperial consultations. Operating above departmental level as an extension of the British cabinet, and organized by Hankey's secretariat, there seemed every chance that it could develop into a central administrative office for imperial affairs, making use between sessions of resident ministers or perhaps the dominion high commissioners.

For several reasons the Imperial Cabinet machinery did not evolve in this direction. In the first place, the overseas governments were loath to give any London-based ministers the necessary policymaking discretion. Further, under Walter Long the Colonial Office never endorsed this new departure, seeing in it a severe threat to their constitutional prerogatives. But most important was the attitude of Lloyd George, for whom imperial questions were not in the last resort of abiding interest. Thus despite a number of assistants with imperialist views (in which Hankey may be counted) the cabinet secretariat remained preoccupied with the business of the British cabinet, and meanwhile through the 'Garden Suburb', his secondary level of personal administrative machinery, the prime minister pursued control not of imperial but of foreign affairs. In 1919 Milner tried briefly to tip the administrative balance but with no lasting success. Consultation remained slow and inconvenient, and was employed as the exception rather than the rule. The conduct of the empire's foreign affairs became only intermittently a collaborative imperial exercise.

The failure to secure adequate administrative improvements in this period of transition from war to peace was critical to the future course of British–dominion relations. Without any integrated participation in policymaking, the dominions had few if any 'imperial' outlets in which their status could find development, and which could thus counterbalance the growth of an otherwise 'national' status. Here we must reckon, in Canada's case, the additional and unique absence of territorial gains made from the war. The other dominions, if they had little else, had at least their ex-German colonies to remind them of wartime co-operation and the imperial connection; Canada, alas, had not been able to take over territory from the Colonial Office, never mind from a foreign power. Lacking this tangible, powerful association with empire, Canada's status came to be measured in purely national terms: diplomatic representation at Washington, the beginnings of an international intercourse through the League of Nations, the right of extra-territorial legislation. By this time, of course, the meaning of dominion status had undergone a most important change. Because of the position attained by the dominions at the Paris peace conference in 1919, there was a tendency thereafter to think of them no longer as merely 'autonomous', but as enjoying a constitutional *equality* with Great Britain. A status of autonomy might possibly have been accommodated within a united imperial framework, indeed the 1917 constitutional resolution ix had implied nothing about direct dominion access to international relations. But a status of equality could hardly ignore such implications. In the League of Nations in particular, as the Canadian delegation to the first Assembly made clear, in the final analysis equality could be realized only in direct opposition to a united imperial diplomacy.

With the shift from autonomy to equality as the principal criterion of dominion status, and the corresponding interest in individual, national manifestations of that status, the plans for a constitutional conference at which the dominions were to secure an integrated voice in the empire's foreign affairs receded quickly into the future. In mid-1919 the conference was anticipated within a year. By mid-1920, however, Henry Lambert had noted that the differing constitutional expectations amongst the dominions were already irreconcilable, and a year later the assembled prime ministers put the conference forward indefinitely. This decision was very largely a defensive one, taken in order to place constitutional readjustment beyond the reach of dissident dominion nationalists. Yet at the same time no administrative improvements were made to the existing machinery of consultation, and the dominions' legitimate participation in policymaking thus remained confined to only the most major imperial issues. Unfortunately even at this level of importance consultation could not be taken for granted. In 1922 a preoccupied Winston Churchill caused the dominions to be ignored over both the attempted admission of Germany to the League of Nations and the Balfour Note on allied war debts.

The Chanak crisis, symptomatic of this growing administrative neglect of the overseas governments, brought thorough discredit upon the empire's consultative machinery and upon the British government in charge of it. When Canada and South Africa failed to support Britain's declared policy in the near east a breach was made in imperial diplomatic unity that need never have occurred. With regard to British–Canadian relations, however, the crisis had a far more important result, leading O. D. Skelton to mistake the very basis of the imperial association. Rather than assume the crisis was an aberration, Skelton came to decide that the overseas governments had written 'blank cheques' at the 1921 Imperial Conference in support of imperial foreign policy – that in other words through consultation, and perhaps even mere information, they had been materially committed at Britain's sole discretion to enforcing a collective policy. British–dominion relations, on this analysis, were thought to be governed not by constitutional convention but by explicit contractual agreements. Dominion autonomy, it appeared, had been mortgaged for the sake of imperial unity to a set of specific external obligations.

King's approach to Canada's imperial affairs after Chanak was heavily influenced by this reassessment. The Lausanne treaty, the Halibut treaty, and above all the 1923 Imperial Conference each offered the prime minister an opportunity to free the dominion from the contractual relations he believed it was a party to. Not until mid-1924 did he begin to show signs – accepting MacDonald's invitation to a special constitutional conference, for instance, and allowing a Canadian delegate to join an *ad hoc* Imperial Economic Committee – that he considered Canada's autonomy to be relatively secure. The terms on which King had chosen to defend his dominion's interests were very much of his own and Skelton's devising, and it is safe to say that no other prime minister understood British–dominion relations in this way. Nevertheless from these encounters with the British government King ultimately derived the assurances he sought, so that by the time of the Locarno treaties he had few axes left to grind with the mother country.

By then the Foreign Office and Dominions Office had come to make their own peace with a devolved commonwealth association. The latter, preparing for the 1926 Conference, showed themselves largely concerned with removing inequalities of status from the practical operation of British–dominion relations; and in successfully getting rid of 'British empire' signatures emphasized just how far they would go in this direction. The former department, though unhappy with the implications of this particular reform for the empire's legal unity, revealed few corresponding anxieties about a united imperial diplomacy. Chamberlain could argue at length that in the Locarno treaties British policy had retained an imperial configuration – that the new imperial frontier was on the Rhine. He allowed himself, also, a complaint to Borden about inadequate facilities for consultation. Even so, he was not unduly troubled when the dominions stayed out of the new European agreements, for he recognized their underlying commitment to come if needed to Britain's aid.

That commitment, he accepted, was ultimately no more than a moral one. Yet was it not moral force that had sustained so much of the British–dominion relationship over the years? Perhaps the most important achievement of the 1926 Conference had been to make this truth plain – in which case, thought Chamberlain, the old forms need not all be lost:

Between you and me [he wrote to Hankey] we have I hope wiped out the prejudice against the words British Empire by removing the misapprehension as to its import which existed in the minds of Hertzog and O'Higgins. Keep British Empire therefore everywhere you can and get rid of 'British Commonwealth of Nations' which is not a term of art.[2]

The foreign secretary's distaste for the avant-garde, however, would not stand in the way of constitutional developments. Not the least of the freedoms of the newly-defined association was the right to choose their own name.

[2] Chamberlain papers: Chamberlain–Hankey, 21 Nov 1926.

Bibliography

I MANUSCRIPT SOURCES

British State Papers. Public Record Office, London
Colonial Office
CO 42 Canada, correspondence
CO 532 Dominions, correspondence
CO 537 Dominions, supplementary correspondence
CO 886 Dominions, confidential print

Dominions Office
DO 35 Dominions, correspondence
DO 117 Dominions, supplementary correspondence

Foreign Office
FO 371–2 Correspondence, general

Cabinet Office
CAB 23 Cabinet minutes
Other files as listed

Canadian State Papers. Public Archives, Ottawa
Department of External Affairs

Private Papers
Beaverbrook Library, London
  Lloyd George papers
Bodleian Library, Oxford
  Milner papers
British Museum, London
  Balfour papers
Grigg, Mr J., London
  Grigg papers

Public Archives, Ottawa
  Ballantyne papers
  Borden papers
  Foster papers
  Kemp papers
  King papers
  Law papers (selections)
  Laurier papers
  Meighen papers
  Murphy papers
  Perley papers
  Rowell papers
  A. Sifton papers
  C. Sifton papers

Royal Commonwealth Society, London
  Harding papers

Scottish Record Office, Edinburgh
  Lothian papers

II UNPUBLISHED THESES

R. Bothwell, 'Loring Christie and the idea of Bureaucratic Imperialism', Ph.D.,
  Harvard University, 1974.
G. Cook, 'British–Canadian Relations, 1911–191', Ph.D., University of Oxford, 1970.
N. Hillmer, 'British–Canadian Relations, 1926–1937', Ph.D., University of
  Cambridge, 1975.

III GOVERNMENT PAPERS

Dominion of Canada, *Parliamentary Debates, House of Commons.*
Great Britain, *Parliamentary Debates, House of Commons.*

IV PARLIAMENTARY PAPERS

Cd 5745	*Imperial Conference, 1911*, proceedings
Cd 5746	*Imperial Conference, 1911*, papers
Cd 6092	*Agreement between Canada and certain West Indian Colonies*, 9 April 1912
Cd 6560	*Committee of Imperial Defence*: representation of self-governing Dominions
Cd 7347	*Correspondence relating to the representation of the self-governing Dominions on the Committee of Imperial Defence*
Cd 8566	*The Imperial War Conference, 1917*
Cd 9177	*The Imperial War Conference, 1918*
Cmd 864	*Trade Agreement between Canada and the West Indies*, 8 June 1920
Cmd 964	*Treaty of Peace with Turkey*, 10 August 1920

Cmd 1474   *Conference of the Prime Ministers and representatives of the United Kingdom, the Dominions and India, 1921*

Cmd 1627   *Conference on Limitation of Armaments, Washington*

Cmd 1987–8   *Imperial Conference, 1923*

Cmd 1990   *Imperial Economic Conference*, summary of conclusions

Cmd 2009   *Imperial Economic Conference*, proceedings

Cmd 2084   *Imperial Preference resolutions of the Imperial War Conference, 1917, and the Imperial Economic Conference*

Cmd 2146   *Correspondence with Canadian government*, settlement of peace with Turkey

Cmd 2301   *Consultation on matters of foreign policy and general Imperial interest*, correspondence with the Dominion governments

Cmd 2768   *Imperial Conference, 1926*, proceedings

V NEWSPAPERS AND PERIODICALS

The Times, 1917–1926
Evening Standard, 16 September 1922
Ottawa Citizen, 16 September 1922
Sunday Times, 17 September 1922
The Round Table, 1910–1926

VI COLLECTED DOCUMENTS

Documents on Canadian External Relations, 6 vols, *1919–1939* (Ottawa, 1967–72)

Keith, A. B., *Selected Speeches and Documents on British Colonial Policy, 1763–1917* (Oxford, 1963 ed)

Speeches and Documents on the British Dominions, 1918–1931 (Oxford, 1966 ed)

Madden, A. F., *Imperial Constitutional Documents, 1765–1965: A Supplement* (Oxford, 1966)

Riddell, W. A., *Documents on Canadian Foreign Policy, 1917–1939* (Oxford, 1962)

VII ARTICLES

Bothwell, R., 'Canadian Representation at Washington: a study in colonial responsibility', *Canadian Historical Review*, LIII no 2 (1972)

Brebner, J. B., 'Canada, the Anglo-Japanese Alliance and the Washington Conference', *Political Science Quarterly*, L no 1 (1935)

Brown, R. C., 'Sir Robert Borden, The Great War and Anglo-Canadian Relations', in J. Moir (ed) *Character and Circumstance* (Toronto, 1970)

Brown, R. C. and Bothwell, R., 'The Canadian Resolution', in M. Cross and R. Bothwell (eds), *Policy by other means* (Toronto, 1972)

Burley, K., 'The Imperial Shipping Committee', *Journal of Commonwealth and Imperial History*, II, no 2

Carter, G. M., 'Some Aspects of Canadian Foreign Policy after Versailles', *Canadian Historical Association Report* (1943)

Cook, G., 'Sir Robert Borden, Lloyd George and British Military Policy, 1917–1918', *The Historical Journal*, xiv no 2 (1971)

Cook, R., 'A Canadian Account of the 1926 Imperial Conference', *Journal of Commonwealth Political Studies*, iii no 1 (1965)

'J. W. Dafoe at the Imperial Conference, 1923', *Canadian Historical Review*, xli no 1 (1960)

Dafoe, J. W., 'Canada and the Peace Conference of 1919', *Canadian Historical Review*, xxiv no 3 (1943)

David, E., 'The Liberal Party Divided, 1916–1918', *The Historical Journal*, xiii no 3 (1970)

Dignan, D. K., 'Australia and British Relations with Japan, 1914–1921', *Australian Outlook*, xxi (1967)

Eayrs, J., 'The Origins of Canada's Department of External Affairs', in H. Keenleyside, *The Growth of Canadian Policies in External Affairs* (Durham, NC, 1960)

'The Round Table Movement in Canada, 1909–1920', *Canadian Historical Review*, xxxviii no 1 (1957)

Esberey, J. E., 'Personality and Politics: A new look at the King–Byng dispute', *Canadian Journal of Political Science*, vi no 1 (1973)

Fitzhardinge, L., 'Hughes, Borden and Dominion Representation at the Paris Peace Conference', *Canadian Historical Review*, xlix no 2 (1968)

Fry, M. G., 'The North Atlantic Triangle and the Abrogation of the Anglo-Japanese Alliance', *Journal of Modern History*, xxxix no 1 (1967)

Galbraith, J., 'The Imperial Conference of 1921 and the Washington Conference', *Canadian Historical Review*, xxix no 3 (1948)

Gibson, J., 'Mr Mackenzie King and Canadian Autonomy, 1921–1946', *Canadian Historical Association Report* (1951)

Glazebrook, G. P., 'Permanent Factors in Canadian External Relations', in R. Flenley, *Essays in Canadian History* (Toronto, 1939)

Hall, D., 'The Genesis of the Balfour Declaration of 1926', *Journal of Commonwealth Political Studies*, i no 3 (1963)

'The Government of the British Commonwealth', *United Empire*, xi no 9 (1920)

Hillmer, N., 'A British High Commissioner for Canada', *Journal of Imperial and Commonwealth History*, i no 3 (1973–4)

Jebb, R., 'Conference or Cabinet?', *United Empire*, xi no 4 (1920)

Johnson, D., 'Austen Chamberlain and the Locarno Agreements', *University of Birmingham Historical Journal*, (1961)

Leach, R., 'The Secretariat', *International Journal*, xxvi no 2 (1971)

Lockwood, P. A., 'Milner's Entry into the War Cabinet, December 1916', *The Historical Journal*, vii no 2 (1964)

Lower, A., 'Loring Christie and the genesis of the Washington Conference', *Canadian Historical Review*, xlvii no 1 (1966)

Lowry, B., 'The Canadian "Dalmatia" and the Paris Peace Conference, 1919', *B.C. Studies*, no 14 (1972)

Madden, A. F., 'Changing Attitudes and Widening Responsibilities, 1895-1914',
  Cambridge History of the British Empire, III: *The Empire-Commonwealth,
  1870-1919*

Morgan, K., 'Lloyd George's Premiership: A Study in "Prime Ministerial
  Government" ', *The Historical Journal*, XIII no 1 (1970)

Neatby, H. B., 'Laurier and Imperialism', *Canadian Historical Association Report*
  (1955)

Prang, M., 'N. W. Rowell and Canada's External Policy, 1917-1921', *Canadian
  Historical Association Report* (1960)

Powell, E., 'The Myth of Empire', *The Round Table*, no 240 (1970)

Quigley, C., 'The Round Table Movement in Canada, 1909-1938', *Canadian
  Historical Review*, XLIII no 3 (1962)

Ross, A., 'The Chanak Crisis', no 77 *New Zealand Heritage*

Smith, G., 'Canadian External Affairs During World War One', in H. Keenleyside,
  The Growth of Canadian Policies in External Affairs (Durham, NC, 1960)

  'The Alaska Panhandle at the Paris Peace Conference', *International Journal*, XVII
  (1962)

  'The Clandestine Submarines of 1914-1915', *Canadian Historical Association
  Report* (1963)

Soward, F. H., 'Sir Robert Borden and Canada's External Policy, 1911-1920',
  Canadian Historical Association Report (1941)

Stacey, C. P., 'From Meighen to King: The reversal of Canadian external policies,
  1921-23', *Transactions of the Royal Society of Canada*, VII (1969)

Tucker, G., 'The Naval Policy of Sir Robert Borden, 1912-14', *Canadian Historical
  Review*, XXVIII (1947)

Tunstall, W., 'Imperial Defence, 1897-1914', *Cambridge History of the British
  Empire*, III: *The Empire-Commonweath, 1870-1919*

Watt, D., 'Imperial Defence Policy and Imperial Foreign Policy, 1911-1939: The
  Substance and the Shadow', *Personalities and Policies* (London, 1965)

Wheare, K. C., 'The Empire and the Peace Treaties, 1918-1921', *Cambridge History
  of the British Empire*, III: *The Empire-Commonwealth, 1870-1919*

VIII BOOKS

Amery, J., *Joseph Chamberlain and the Tariff Reform Campaign*, VI: *1903-1968*
  (London, 1969)

Amery, L. S., *My Political Life*, II: *War and Peace, 1914-1929* (London, 1953)

Lord Beaverbrook, *Men and Power* (London, 1956)
  Politicians and the War (London, 1960)
  The Decline and Fall of Lloyd George (London, 1963)

Beck, J. M., *Pendulum of Power* (Toronto, 1972)

Beloff, M., *Imperial Sunset*, I: *Britain's Liberal Empire, 1897-1921* (London, 1969);
  II: *Dream of Commonwealth* (forthcoming)

Berger, C., (ed), *Imperialism and Nationalism, 1884-1914: A Conflict in Canadian
  Thought* (Toronto, 1969)

Blake, R., *The Unknown Prime Minister* (London, 1955)

Borden, H., (ed) *Robert Laird Borden: His Memoirs*, 2 vols (London, 1938)

Borden, R., *Canadian Constitutional Studies* (London, 1921)

British Trade Commissioner, Toronto, *Report on Financial, Industrial and Commercial Conditions in Canada, to June 1923* (London, 1923)

Butler, G., *A Handbook to the League of Nations* (London, 1928)

Butler, J. R., *Lord Lothian* (London, 1960)

Lord Casey, *Friends and Neighbours* (Melbourne, 1954)

Cook, R., *The Politics of J. W. Dafoe and the Free Press* (Toronto, 1963)
   (ed) *The Sifton–Dafoe Correspondence, 1919–1927* (Winnipeg, 1966)

Cross, J. A., *Whitehall and the Commonwealth* (London, 1967)

Curtis, L., *The Problem of the Commonwealth* (London, 1916)

Lady Curzon, *Reminiscences* (London, 1955)

Dawson, R. M., *Constitutional Issues in Canada, 1900–1936* (Oxford, 1937)
   The Development of Dominion Status, 1900–1936 (Oxford, 1936)
   William Lyon Mackenzie King, 1: 1874–1923 (London, 1958)

Dewey, A. G., *The Dominions and Diplomacy*, 2 vols (London, 1929)

Drummond, I., *British Economic Policy and the Empire, 1919–1939* (London, 1972)
   Imperial Economic Policy, 1917–1939: studies in expansion and protection (London 1974)

Eayrs, J., *In Defence of Canada, 1: From the Great War to the Great Depression* (Toronto, 1964)
   The Art of the Possible (Toronto, 1961)

Fiddes, G., *The Dominions and Colonial Offices* (London, 1926)

Forsey, E., *The Royal Power of Dissolution of Parliament in the Commonwealth* (Toronto, 1943)

Glazebrook, G. P., *A History of Canadian External Relations* (London, 1950)
   Canada at the Paris Peace Conference (Toronto, 1942)

Gollin, A., *Proconsul in Politics* (London, 1964)

Gordon, D. C., *The Dominion Partnership in Imperial Defense, 1870–1914* (Baltimore, 1965)

Graham, R., *Arthur Meighen, 1: The Door of Opportunity* (Toronto, 1960); II: *And Fortune Fled* (Toronto, 1963)
   (ed) *The King–Byng Affair, 1926: A Question of Responsible Government* (Toronto, 1967)

Hall, D., *Commonwealth* (London, 1971)

Hancock, W. K., *Smuts, 1: The Sanguine Years, 1870–1919* (Cambridge, 1962); II: *The Fields of Force, 1919–1950* (Cambridge, 1968)
   Survey of British Commonwealth Affairs, 1: Problems of Nationality, 1918–1936 (London, 1937); II: *Problems of Economic Policy*, pt 1 (London, 1940)

Hankey, Lord, *The Supreme Command*, 2 vols (London, 1961)
   The Supreme Control at the Paris Peace Conference (London, 1963)

Harkness, D., *The Restless Dominion: The Irish Free State and the British Commonwealth of Nations, 1921–1931* (London, 1969)

Hewins, W., *The Apologia of an Imperialist*, 2 vols (London, 1929)

Jenkins, R., *Asquith* (London, 1967)

Jones T., *Whitehall Diary*, I: *1916–1925* (London, 1969)

Kendle, J. W., *The Colonial and Imperial Conferences, 1887–1911* (London, 1967)

Keynes, J. M., *The Economic Consequences of the Peace* (London, 1920)

Lloyd George, D., *War Memoirs*, 2 vol ed (London, 1938)

Lloyd George, F., *The Years that are Past* (London, 1967)

Lyons, F. S. L., *Ireland Since the Famine* (London, 1971)

MacNutt, W., *The Atlantic Provinces* (Toronto, 1965)

Mansergh, P. N. S., *The Commonwealth Experience* (London, 1969)

    Survey of Commonwealth Affairs, I: *Problems of External Policy, 1931–1939* (London, 1952)

Marder, A., *From the Dreadnought to Scapa Flow*, I: *The Road to War, 1904–1914* (London, 1961)

Marston, F. S., *The Peace Conference of 1919: Organisation and Procedure* (London, 1944)

Massey, V., *What's Past is Prologue* (London, 1963)

Middlemas, K., and Barnes, J., *Baldwin, A Biography* (London, 1969)

Miller, J. D., *Richard Jebb and the Problem of Empire* (London, 1956)

    Britain and the Old Dominions (London, 1966)

Lord Milner, *The British Commonwealth* (London, 1919)

Neatby, H. B., *William Lyon Mackenzie King*, II: *1924–1932, The Lonely Heights* (London, 1963)

Nicolson, H., *Peacemaking 1919* (London, 1964)

    Curzon, the last phase (London, 1934)

Nimocks, W., *Milner's Young Men: The 'Kindergarten' in Edwardian Imperial Affairs* (London, 1970)

Nish, I., *Alliance in Decline* (London, 1972)

Northedge, F. S., *The Troubled Giant: Britain among the Great Powers, 1916–1939* (London, 1966)

Preston, R., *Canada and 'Imperial Defense'* (Toronto, 1967)

Lord Riddell, *Intimate Diary of the Peace Conference and After, 1918–1923* (London, 1933)

Roskill, S., *Hankey, Man of Secrets*, I: *1877–1918* (London, 1970); II: *1919–1926* (London, 1974)

    Naval Policy between the Wars, I: *The Period of Anglo-American Antagonism, 1919–1929* (London, 1968)

Skilling, H., *Canadian Representation Abroad* (Toronto, 1945)

Swettenham, J., *Allied Intervention in Russia, and the part played by Canada* (London, 1967)

Taylor, A. J. P., *English History, 1914–1945* (Oxford, 1965)

Toynbee, A., *The Conduct of British Empire Foreign Relations since the Peace Settlement* (London, 1928)

Tucker, G. N., *The Naval Service of Canada*, 1: *Origins and Early Years* (Ottawa, 1952)

Underhill, F., *The Image of Confederation* (Toronto, 1973)

Wade, M., *The French Canadians*, 2 vol ed (London, 1968)

Walder, D., *The Chanak Affair* (London, 1969)

White, T., *Kevin O'Higgins* (London, 1948)

Wilson, H. A., *The Imperial Policy of Sir Robert Borden* (Florida, 1966)

Winks, R. W., *Canadian–West Indian Union: A Forty-Year Minuet* (London, 1968)

Index